Birnbaum's

Walt Disney World®
Expert Advice from the Inside Source

THE OFFICIAL GUIDE

Jill Safro EDITOR

Deanna Caron MANAGING EDITOR

Todd Sebastian Williams ART DIRECTOR

Suzy Goytizolo ASSISTANT EDITOR

Alice Garrard CONTRIBUTING EDITOR

Alexandra Mayes Birnbaum CONSULTING EDITOR

Stephen Birnbaum FOUNDING EDITOR

HYPERION AND HEARST BUSINESS PUBLISHING, INC.

Table of

Getting Ready to Go

7

Here is all the practical information you need to organize a Walt Disney World visit, down to the smallest detail: when to go; how to get there; how to save money; plus hints for parents, travelers with disabilities, singles, and older visitors.

Transportation & Accommodations

39

Two big questions about Walt Disney World are where to stay and how to get around. Accommodations range from plush suites to modest campsites, with thousands of rooms, villas—even treehouses—in between. Our guide describes every Disney resort, along with some off-property options. And we explain the World's vast transportation system.

Magic Kingdom

85

The enchantment of Walt Disney World is most apparent in the wealth of attractions and amusements that fill this, the most famous entertainment zone of all. Our land-by-land guide describes all there is to see and do, where to shop, and how to avoid the crowds, plus plenty of other insider tips.

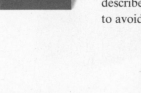

Epcot

115

A gleaming silver geosphere introduces Walt Disney World's wonderland of discovery—an ambitious exploration of the world of the future as well as the present. Future World and World Showcase offer every visitor the opportunity to be a global and cerebral voyager, without setting foot outside Florida. Here's how to make the most of this uniquely fascinating destination.

Disney-MGM Studios

147

Now's your chance to be part of Hollywood's golden years. Everything from the magic of animation to the excitement of daring stunts and special effects is waiting to be enjoyed. There are also opportunities to go behind the scenes and to create sound effects. We've developed strategies for seeing this Tinseltown, ensuring the most fun and the least time standing around.

Contents

Animal Kingdom

This recent addition to Disney's theme park lineup celebrates the circle of life and all the wonders of the animal world. Amid nature's soothing majesty, you'll experience a stirring African safari, dodge dastardly dinosaurs, and ride raging rapids. Our expanded coverage—which includes the park's newest land, Asia—guarantees a fun-filled trip to a place where humans are humbly reminded of their tenuous position in the food chain.

Everything Else in the World

Beyond the theme park boundaries lie countless acres full of just the sorts of wonders for which Walt Disney World is famous: state-of-the-art water parks; a nighttime entertainment, shopping, and dining district; and the Disney Institute among them. So if you want to ride down watery slides, dance the night away, shop at elegant boutiques, or "go to school" behind the scenes, this chapter will help you find your way.

Sports

Walt Disney World has more tennis courts and golf greens than most posh resorts, plus plenty of places for boating, biking, horseback riding, swimming, and fishing. The rest of the sporting bases are covered by Disney's Wide World of Sports complex, a multi-sport facility that aims to please athlete and spectator alike. Here's how to combine these options with the rest of the fun at Walt Disney World.

Good Meals, Great Times

Restaurants around the Walt Disney World property run the gamut from simple snack shops to bastions of haute cuisine. The choices are nearly endless, so we've organized them all into alphabetical, area-by-area, and meal-by-meal directories that let you know where each restaurant is located and what specialties it offers. We also tell you about the various dinner shows, the best family fare, where to dine with the Disney characters, and where to enjoy an after-dinner drink.

For Steve, who merely made all this possible

Other 1999 Birnbaum's Official Disney Guides

Disneyland
Walt Disney World For Kids, By Kids
Walt Disney World Without Kids

A WORD FROM THE EDITORS

For some of us, our first Walt Disney World experience dates back to 1971, the year this new "Disneyland in Florida" made its debut. At that time, the Magic Kingdom was the only theme park, and it could be explored easily in a few days. Early visitors will remember, too, that many attractions were still under construction. Nonetheless, for those who came, it was love at first sight, and we've returned again and again.

Never before has there been so much incentive to visit (and revisit) the memory-making capital of the world. Even those fortunate enough to have experienced Animal Kingdom in its premiere year have a whole new land to discover within its boundaries: Asia. We are both privileged and proud to provide readers with exclusive coverage of Asia, as

Todd Sebastian Williams (left), Mickey Mouse, Jill Safro, and Deanna Caron.

well as an expanded look at Disney's Animal Kingdom. The same sentiment applies to our insider coverage of the new entertainment extravaganzas at Downtown Disney, thrill rides like Rock 'n' Roller Coaster at the Disney-MGM Studios and Test Track at Epcot, and family favorites such as Buzz Lightyear's Space Ranger Spin at the Magic Kingdom.

When Steve Birnbaum launched this guide back in 1981, he made it clear what was expected of anyone who worked on it. The book would be meticulously revised each year, leaving no attraction untested, no snack or meal untasted, no hotel untried. Experiences like these, accumulated over the years, make this book the most authoritative guide to the World. Our expertise, however, was not achieved by being escorted through back doors of attractions or bypassing lines (although we would have thoroughly enjoyed that). Instead, we waited with all the other visitors in hopes of uncovering strategies that would allow readers to avoid the pitfalls many first-timers encounter. In one typical case, an editor waited more than an hour to take a backstage tour at the Studios. Standing in line with notebook and tape recorder in hand, she was asked by the man behind her if there was a quiz at the end. When she explained what she was doing, he expressed surprise to learn that she was waiting with the rest of the hordes. How better, she replied, to help people like you?

After more than a quarter of a century, the World and the number of visitors have expanded—and so has our knowledge of the most popular vacation destination on the planet. On some occasions we've encountered sweltering weather and swelling crowds, times when even the happiest of families or best of friends turn into archenemies for a day. At times the lines seemed endless and, in a triumph of bad planning, we managed to take in just a few attractions before dinnertime. Had we known then what we know now, we could have spared ourselves some trying experiences.

We've done our best to keep you from making the same mistakes. We realize that even the most meticulous vacation planner needs detailed, accurate, and objective information to prepare an intelligent itinerary. Anyone who takes the time to read even the outlines of the pages that follow will find an emerging pattern that fits his or her special needs and tastes; for those unwilling to exert even that much effort, we've compiled specific day-by-day itineraries for visits of varying length—in order to protect you from yourself.

This guidebook owes an enormous debt to the extraordinary people who manage and run Walt Disney World. Despite the designation "Official Guide," we want to stress that *the Walt Disney World staff members have exercised no veto power whatsoever over the contents of this book.* What they *have* done is open their files and explain operations to us in the most generous way, so that we could prepare comprehensive appraisals to help visitors understand the complex workings of a very complex enterprise.

We daresay there have been times when the Disney folks are less than delighted with some of our opinions, yet these statements all remain in the guide. We've even sprinkled "Birnbaum's Bests" throughout the book, highlighting *our* favorite attractions—the crowd-pleasers we believe stand head, shoulders, and ears above the rest.

You, the reader, benefit from the combination of our years of experience and independent voice that, together with our access to accurate, up-to-date inside information from the Disney staff, makes this guide unique. We like to think it's indispensable, but we'll let you be the judge of that a few hundred pages from now.

The fact remains that this guide would never have become as useful as it is without the extremely forthcoming cooperation of Walt Disney World personnel at every level. Both in the park and behind the scenes, they've been the source of the most critical factual data. We hope we're not omitting any names in specifically thanking Kim Carlson (Information Management); Robin Domigan (Resorts); Rick Sylvain (Media Relations); Gene Duncan (Photography); and Tim Lewis (Disney Publishing); Bo Boyd, Marty Sklar, Charlie Ridgway, Tina Rebstock, Jacqui Cintron, Karen Haynes, and Todd Crawford. To Linda Warren, Julie Woodward, Laura Simpson, Diane Hancock, Regina Maher, Kevin Banks, and Carter Schultz, who do so much to make our job easier (and often possible), more thanks for their extraordinary help.

We'd also like to thank our favorite off-site Disney expert, Wendy Lefkon, who edited these guides for many years and is still instrumental in their publication as executive editor at Hyperion. Hats off to Editorial Director Tom Passavant, for his discerning diplomacy and editorial expertise; Shari Hartford, for keeping our cast of characters on schedule; Laura Vitale, for her wondrously uncompromising sense of style; and Louise Collazo, for her copyediting finesse.

Of course, no list of acknowledgments would be complete without mentioning our founding editor, Steve Birnbaum, whose spirit, wisdom, and humor still infuse these pages, as well as Alexandra Mayes Birnbaum, who continues to be a guiding light—to say nothing of a careful reader of every word.

Finally, it's important to remember that every worthwhile travel guide is a living enterprise; the book you hold in your hands is our best effort at explaining how to enjoy Walt Disney World at this moment, but its text is in no way etched in stone. Walt Disney World is constantly changing and growing, and in each annual edition we refine and expand our material to serve your needs even better. For this year's edition, though, this must be the final word.

Have a great visit!

The Editors

Don't Forget to Write

No contribution is of greater value to us in preparing the next edition of this book than your comments on what we have written and on your own experiences at Walt Disney World. Please share your insights with us by writing to:

The Editors, Official Disney Guides
Birnbaum's Walt Disney World 1999
1790 Broadway, Sixth Floor
New York, NY 10019

Getting Ready to Go

The key to a fabulous vacation at Walt Disney World is advance planning. This remarkably varied complex is too vast and diverse to allow a spontaneous visit to be undertaken with much success—especially when you consider the rapid rate at which the World is expanding. That does not mean that even the most casual visitors can't have some significant fun, but they are bound to have regrets about things they missed because of time pressures or a simple lack of information. The main purpose of this guide is to eliminate that potential frustration.

What follows, then, is meant to provide a sensible scheme for planning a satisfying visit to Walt Disney World, one that will offer the most fun and the least amount of disappointment. But how do you know which of the countless activities will be the most enjoyable for you and your family? Do your homework—the best strategy is to make sure you have a clear idea of all that is available *before* you arrive in the Orlando area.

Unless otherwise noted, all phone numbers are in area code 407.

WHEN TO GO

When talk finally turns to the best time to make a trip to Walt Disney World, Christmas and Easter are often mentioned, as well as the weeks that make up the traditional summer vacation period—especially if there are children in the family. But there is also good reason to avoid these periods, namely the hordes they inevitably attract. And when Walt Disney World is crowded, it can be very crowded indeed. On the busiest days, visitors may wait as much as two hours to see some of the more popular attractions. That's at least twice as long as during less crowded times of the year.

Considering seasonal hours, the weather, and the crowd patterns described in the charts that follow, optimal times to visit Walt Disney World are usually mid-January through early February, late April through late May, and September through December (except Thanksgiving and Christmas weeks).

Note that during some of the less crowded times of the year—particularly during January

The period beween the end of Thanksgiving weekend and the week before Christmas is one of the least crowded and most festive times of the year. The World is teeming with holiday parties, parades, fireworks, and other special events.

and February—some attractions are typically closed for renovations. In addition, the water parks are often closed for refurbishment during the cooler months. Call 824-4321 or check the WDW Web site (*www.disneyworld.com*) for a current schedule, updated each season.

Late December is an especially festive time of year the world over, and Walt Disney World is no exception. All of the theme parks are decorated to the nines for the holiday season. The Magic Kingdom, Epcot, and the Disney-MGM Studios feature nightly tree-lighting ceremonies. Many other special events are held during this period, including Mickey's Very Merry Christmas Party in the Magic Kingdom (separate admission ticket required). The party brings a dusting of snow to Main Street from 8 P.M. to 1 A.M. for several days during the first three weeks of December. It also features holiday shows around the park, including Mickey's Very

DID YOU KNOW...

Each month, Walt Disney World donates nearly 300,000 pounds of unserved food to Central Florida food banks.

Merry Christmas Parade, plus a special finale of Fantasy in the Sky fireworks. Select performances from Mickey's Very Merry Christmas Party are also staged in the park during regular hours throughout the holiday season.

Epcot celebrates the season with Holidays Around the World, including the nightly Candlelight Processional, complete with 450-voice choir, 50-piece orchestra, and a reading of the story of Christmas by a celebrity narrator. Dinner packages are available for select World Showcase restaurants, and the night ends with a holiday version of the fireworks show. The Disney-MGM Studios features a display of about four million twinkling lights depicting holiday scenes and a 65-foot "wall of angels" that together illuminate Residential Street.

There are holiday decorations at WDW hotels, too, including a turn-of-the-century Christmas at the Grand Floridian, a seaside party at the Yacht and Beach Club, a Southwestern Christmas at the Contemporary, and a Cajun holiday at Dixie Landings.

One way to take advantage of the festivities during this time of year is to book a Magical Holidays package, offered from late November through late December. Available for two to ten nights, most packages include unlimited admission to the theme parks and Pleasure Island. For reservations, contact a travel agent, or call W-DISNEY (934-7639) or the Walt Disney Travel Company at 800-828-0228.

Keeping WDW Hours

Because operating hours fluctuate, we advise calling 824-4321 or visiting *www.disneyworld.com* for up-to-the-minute schedules. The automated system is updated every two to three months.

THEME PARKS: Hours of operation at all Disney theme parks vary seasonally. For more than a third of the year—in May, September, October, parts of November and December, and all of January—the Magic Kingdom is usually open from 9 A.M. to 7 P.M.; Epcot is open from 9 A.M. to 9 P.M. (Future World opens at 9 A.M., World Showcase at 11 A.M.); the Disney-MGM Studios is open from 9 A.M. until about an hour after dusk; and Animal Kingdom is open from 7 A.M. until about an hour after dusk.

The Magic Kingdom keeps later hours through the summer and other high-attendance periods. Epcot and the Disney-MGM Studios stay open till midnight during certain holiday periods (Thanksgiving, Christmas, and Easter). With the exception of Animal Kingdom, the parks stay open until 1 A.M. or 2 A.M. on New Year's Eve. The Disney-MGM Studios often stays open till midnight in the summer, too. On select days, WDW resort guests can enter the Magic Kingdom, Epcot, or the Disney-MGM Studios up to 1½ hours before the official opening time. Note that only some attractions in a given park open early. For details about early-entry days, see "Park Primer" in each theme park chapter (pages 88, 118, 150, and 166).

DOWNTOWN DISNEY MARKETPLACE: Shops are usually open from 9:30 A.M. until 11 P.M. daily. Restaurant hours vary.

DOWNTOWN DISNEY WEST SIDE: At the AMC Theatres cineplex, movies are shown beginning at about 1 P.M. Restaurants are generally open from about 11:30 A.M. to 2 A.M. Shops are open from 10:30 A.M. to 11 P.M.

PLEASURE ISLAND: Clubs on the island are open from about 7 P.M. to 2 A.M. daily; shops, from 11 A.M. to 2 A.M.; and restaurants, from about 11:30 A.M. to midnight.

WATER PARKS: Although hours vary, the water parks are generally open from about 10 A.M. to 5 P.M., with extended hours in effect during summer months.

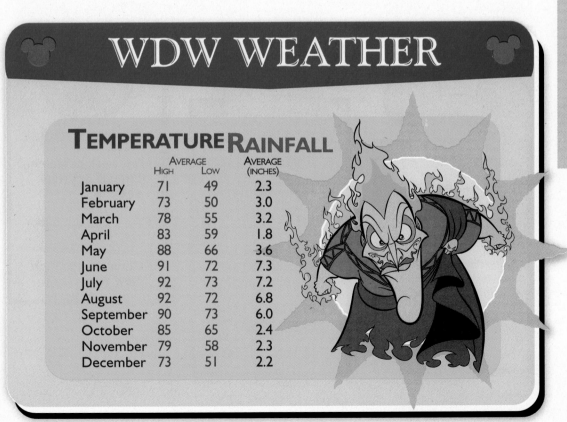

WDW WEATHER

TEMPERATURE RAINFALL

	Average High	Low	Average (inches)
January	71	49	2.3
February	73	50	3.0
March	78	55	3.2
April	83	59	1.8
May	88	66	3.6
June	91	72	7.3
July	92	73	7.2
August	92	72	6.8
September	90	73	6.0
October	85	65	2.4
November	79	58	2.3
December	73	51	2.2

Crowd Patterns

Day-to-Day Trends

Many visitors to Walt Disney World assume that weekends are the busiest days in the theme parks—and they generally are quite crowded. However, with the exception of certain holiday periods, each park tends to be the most crowded on its "early-opening" days: Monday, Thursday, and Saturday at the Magic Kingdom; Tuesday and Friday at Epcot; and Wednesday and Sunday at the Disney-MGM Studios. Given the relative novelty of Disney's newest theme park, Animal Kingdom, we expect Saturdays and Sundays to be among the busiest days at this park.

When the time comes to plot an itinerary, it's helpful to know about crowd patterns beyond the four theme parks as well. As a rule, Downtown Disney (Pleasure Island, Marketplace, and West Side) and Disney's water parks host their largest throngs on weekends. Of course, in these circles, a bigger crowd can often mean a better time.

Golfers should note that weekend tee times are typically in the highest demand, while Monday and Tuesday times are the easiest to come by.

Seasonal Shifts

The chart below indicates the density of crowds in the theme parks throughout the year. Though it's tough to generalize about a property as vast and ever-changing as Walt Disney World—special events and package deals can swell park attendance during a period typically marked by smaller crowds—the chart highlights historic trends.

Least crowded means that there may be lines but most attractions can be visited without much waiting, average attendance refers to times when there are lots of people around but lines are manageable, and most crowded reflects times when lines at popular attractions can mean a wait of as much as two hours.

Least Crowded

- 2nd week of January through 1st week of February

- Week after Labor Day until Thanksgiving

- Week after Thanksgiving through week before Christmas

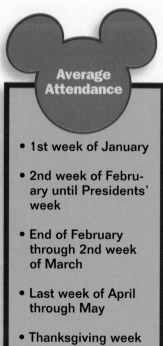

Average Attendance

- 1st week of January

- 2nd week of February until Presidents' week

- End of February through 2nd week of March

- Last week of April through May

- Thanksgiving week

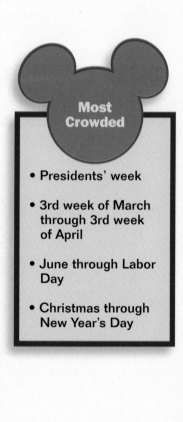

Most Crowded

- Presidents' week

- 3rd week of March through 3rd week of April

- June through Labor Day

- Christmas through New Year's Day

Holidays & Special Events

Special affairs are staged throughout the year, not only to mark holidays but also to celebrate other interests. The Magic Kingdom, Epcot, the Disney-MGM Studios, and Downtown Disney host many happenings, from sporting events to festivals geared toward jazz, gardens, technology, and even soap operas. The most popular are listed below. Schedules are subject to change; call 824-4321 or check out the WDW Web site (*www.disneyworld.com*) for specific dates and additional information about listed events.

JANUARY

Walt Disney World Marathon (January 11): Some 10,000 entrants run through several theme parks, Disney's Wide World of Sports complex, and other scenic areas of the World during this 26.2-mile race. Live bands, hot-air balloons, and Disney characters are on hand to inspire runners. There's also a 5K run for children. Special packages are available. Call 939-7810 for additional information.

Indy 200 (January 22–24): Indy race cars burn rubber in this annual event, held at the Walt Disney World Speedway, a one-mile track just south of the Magic Kingdom. Special packages are available.

FEBRUARY

Mardi Gras (February): Jazz bands, Creole food, and street performers toast New Orleans' biggest party at Pleasure Island. At Epcot, visit World Showcase to see how other countries celebrate Mardi Gras.

Black Heritage Celebration (February): Walt Disney World honors African American achievers during black history month.

MARCH

Epcot Science Jam (March): For three weeks, a series of special events highlight the latest inventions, discoveries, and new ways to have fun with science and technology.

Saint Patrick's Day (March 17): Everyone is Irish on Saint Patrick's Day—especially at Pleasure Ire-land. Don't forget to wear something green to celebrate the Emerald Isle.

APRIL–MAY

Easter (April 4): A nationally televised parade in the Magic Kingdom helps make this holiday celebration special. All of the Disney theme parks stay open late during the two weeks straddling the Easter holiday. This is an extremely busy time to visit.

Epcot International Flower and Garden Festival (April 16–May 30): Epcot is blooming with elaborate gardens (including more than 30 million blossoms) and topiary displays, behind-the-scenes tours, gardening workshops, and guest speakers. Learn from the experts how to create a beautiful garden at home.

JUNE

Black Music Month Celebration (June): Pleasure Island and *Vibe* magazine showcase gospel, rap, R & B, reggae, jazz, and more.

JULY

Fourth of July Celebration: Double-size fireworks over the Magic Kingdom, Epcot, and the Disney-MGM Studios make for a colorful night. This is a very busy time to visit.

SEPTEMBER

Disneyana Convention (September): A veritable heaven for collectors. Packages are necessary for full admission to the auction, seminars, workshops, and behind-the-scenes tours, and include accommodations. For more information, call 827-7600.

ABC Super Soap Weekend (September): A celebration of ABC daytime dramas is held at the Disney-MGM Studios. Guests meet more than 30 soap stars; collect autographs; compete in trivia contests; see the sets, props, and costumes from the shows; and even have a shot at acting in a scene with the stars. For more information, call 397-6808.

Night of Joy (September 11–12): Two nights of musical celebration highlight the best in contemporary Christian music during this special-ticket event.

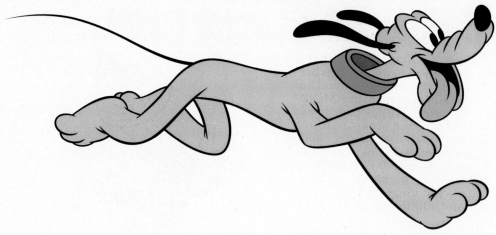

OCTOBER

Pleasure Island Jazz Fest (October): Great jazz from today and yesterday is performed for one weekend throughout the island.

Teddy Bear & Doll Convention (October): Collectors go to the Contemporary resort and Epcot to see world-renowned craftspeople's creations. Packages are required for full participation, and include accommodations, park tickets, seminars and workshops, an auction, a limited-edition private sale, parties, and an awards ceremony. For more information, call 827-7600.

National Car Rental Golf Classic (October 21–24): Top PGA Tour players compete alongside amateurs in this big tourney, played on the Palm and Magnolia. Special packages are available. For more information, call 824-2250.

Epcot International Food and Wine Festival (late October–November): World Showcase celebrates the flavors of a variety of countries (even those not represented around the lagoon) through tastings ($1 to $3 per sample), demonstrations, and wine and cooking seminars (special ticket needed for seminars).

Mickey's Not-So-Scary Halloween Party (October 28 and 30): Even the Magic Kingdom gets dressed up in festive Halloween decor. Special-ticket activities include a Halloween costume parade, appearances by Disney villians, trick-or-treating, plus fireworks.

NOVEMBER–DECEMBER

Festival of the Masters (November): This three-day fine arts show draws over 200 top artists to Downtown Disney.

Disney's Magical Holidays (December): Decorations and festivities abound in Walt Disney World's parks and resorts. The Magic Kingdom hosts Mickey's Very Merry Christmas Party on several nights during the first three weeks of December, complete with snow flurries on Main Street and hot cocoa.

Entertainment for the special-ticket party includes Mickey's Very Merry Christmas Parade and a holiday edition of Fantasy in the Sky fireworks; select performances are also staged during regular hours throughout the holiday season. Epcot's Holidays Around the World features a special fireworks spectacular on the World Showcase Lagoon, "The Lights of Winter," and a Candlelight Processional with choral concert. The Osborne Family Spectacle of Lights brightens the Disney-MGM Studios with about four million sparkling lights on Residential Street. A variety of packages include admission to special-ticket parties. For information on these events and the Magical Holidays packages, call the Walt Disney Travel Company at 800-828-0228.

New Year's Eve Celebration (December 31): There are extra-large fireworks displays over the Magic Kingdom, Epcot, and the Disney-MGM Studios. (The Magic Kingdom and Epcot are open until 2 A.M. and the Studios is open until 1 A.M. for the occasion.) Pleasure Island hosts a grand special-ticket bash. Many of the resorts, as well as the clubs at Downtown Disney West Side, also welcome the new year Disney-style.

A New Millennium

It's not often you get to ring in a new millennium—and Walt Disney World has big plans for the big event. Special shows and exhibits will engage guests in a 15-month celebration of the human spirit, focusing on everything from science and technology to kids and creativity. Epcot serves as millennium central for this property-wide celebration beginning on October 1, 1999, and continuing through January 1, 2001.

HOW TO GET THERE

By Car

While most visitors to the Orlando area fly in, some prefer to drive. If you opt for a road trip, pack lots of tapes and figure on logging 350 to 400 miles a day—a reasonable distance that won't wear you down so much that you can't enjoy your trip.

Contact state tourist boards about the availability of free maps; for a Florida map and guide, call 888-735-2872. Other sources for maps are the *Rand McNally Road Atlas* ($13.95) and the *AAA North American Road Atlas* ($12.95); both are sold in bookstores.

DID YOU KNOW...

It's perfectly legal to make a right turn at a red light on roads throughout the state of Florida.

Driving directions from most cities are also available on the Web. One site to try is *www.mapquest.com.*

Reputable national automobile clubs can offer help with breakdowns en route; emergency towing; insurance that covers personal injury, accidents, arrest, bail bond, and lawyers' fees for defense of contested traffic cases; and travel-planning services, including free maps and route mapping. Services vary from one club to the next, and membership fees range

From the Airport

By car: For the shortest route to Walt Disney World, take the North Exit to Route 528 (Beeline Expressway), going west toward Tampa. Pick up I-4 west, and follow it until you reach the appropriate WDW exit. The distance is 22 miles, the trip takes about half an hour, and the tolls add up to $1.25. Note that this route is heavily trafficked by locals. During traditional rush hour times, take the airport's South Exit to the Central Florida Greeneway (Route 417) to Route 536, which leads directly to Walt Disney World. The tolls total $2.

Shuttles: It's also possible, and easy, to get to WDW resorts from Orlando International Airport without a car. Mears Motor Shuttles offers vans about every 15 to 20 minutes around the clock, serving Disney resorts, the resorts on Hotel Plaza Boulevard, and other area hotels. The cost to most hotels is $14 one way, $25 round-trip per adult; $10 one way, $17 round-trip per child 4 through 11; free for children under 4. Fares to International Drive properties are $2 to $4 lower. Call 423-5566 for information.

widely, from $40 to $90 a year. Among the leading clubs are Allstate Motor Club (800-347-8880), American Automobile Association (800-564-6222), Amoco Motor Club (800-334-3300), Ford Auto Club (800-348-5220), and Gulf Motor Club (800-633-3224).

By Air

Each year, millions of visitors funnel through Orlando International Airport, where monorails transport passengers to and from the central terminal and a well-stocked Disney Store portends what's to come.

If there's a trick to unearthing the most economical fares, it's this: Shop around. Call a travel agent, and keep these tips in mind:

- Watch the newspapers for ads announcing short-term promotional fares.
- The more flexible you can be in your dates and duration of stay, the more money you're likely to save.
- Fly when most people don't: For vacation destinations, that usually means midweek.
- Take advantage of advance-purchase fares (lower rates that apply if a ticket is bought at least two to three weeks prior to departure).
- Keep in mind that the lowest airfares usually carry a penalty if you have to revise your flight schedule, and that certain discount fare tickets are nonrefundable.

- When you call to make a reservation, inquire about any applicable fare restrictions, including an obligatory Saturday night stayover.
- If a fare comes down after you've purchased a ticket, you can request a refund from the airline.
- Check out airline Web sites. Often they will e-mail you with information about special discounted fares.

By Train

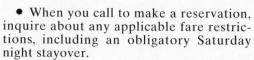

Amtrak serves the Orlando area twice daily from New York City, with various stops along the way. The trip takes about 22 hours and costs from $146 to $408 round-trip, coach. (Book early for lower fares; discounts are often available, so be sure to ask.) If you're staying at Walt Disney World, disembark in Kissimmee. It's closer and cab fares are cheaper. Rental cars are available by shuttle.

For reservations and information on these and other routes, call 800-USA-RAIL (800-872-7245), visit Amtrak's Web site at *www.amtrak.com*, or contact a travel agent.

By Bus

Relatively few vacationers travel to Walt Disney World by bus. But the bus can be economical, although the greater the distance involved, the more likely the lowest available airfare will be competitive.

Greyhound provides frequent direct service to Orlando and Kissimmee (the latter is closer to Walt Disney World). From either destination, you can take a taxi to your hotel, but first check to see if your hotel offers shuttle service.

For further information, contact Greyhound at 800-231-2222.

GETTING READY TO GO

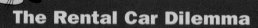

The Rental Car Dilemma

If you plan to spend all of your time on WDW turf, you can spare yourself the expense. Shuttle service from the airport to all area hotels is available around the clock, and taxis are in good supply. Within the World, an exhaustive (occasionally exhausting) network of transportation brings guests from point to point. Most area hotels offer their own bus service to and from Walt Disney World theme parks (inquire in advance about schedules and costs, if any). See "From the Airport" on the previous page for airport shuttle information and the *Transportation & Accommodations* chapter for details on WDW internal transportation.

However, for those planning to visit Orlando-area restaurants and any attractions outside Walt Disney World, a rental car is a must. Also, certain routes are more convenient by car. It's easiest to rent from one of the companies at the airport: Avis (800-331-1212), Budget (800-527-0700), Dollar (800-800-4000), or National (800-227-7368). Other rental agencies provide shuttles from the airport, so it may be worth the extra time if you get a good deal. For day trips, consider National InterRent at the Car Care Center (824-3470) or one of the rental agencies that have desks at the resorts on Hotel Plaza Boulevard.

PLANNING AHEAD
Logistics

Organizing a trip properly takes time, but most travelers find the increased enjoyment well worth the effort. The fact is, planning can become a pleasant sort of "armchair" exercise, and kids will enjoy their visit to Walt Disney World all the more if they, too, are involved in the process.

To aid in that effort, we immodestly recommend our guide *Birnbaum's Walt Disney World For Kids, By Kids* ($10.95), a comprehensive look at the World from a young person's perspective, written for kids ages 7 through 14. For adults traveling sans children, our *Birnbaum's Walt Disney World Without Kids* ($11.95) is the definitive source.

Information Sources

For information about Walt Disney World, call WDW Information at 824-4321. Lots of up-to-the-minute specifics, such as park hours, ticket prices, refurbishment schedules, and directions, are available through the automated system 24 hours a day. To speak with a representative, call weekdays 7 A.M. to 7 P.M. or weekends 7 A.M. to 8 P.M. For information by mail, write to Walt Disney World; Box 10000; Lake Buena Vista, FL 32830-1000. Internet users can tap into updates about the World, order tickets, obtain theme park hours and special events listings, and make WDW resort or package reservations by entering *www.disneyworld.com*.

For information and discounts on Orlando-area attractions, restaurants, and hotels, contact the Official Visitor Information Center; 8723 International Dr., Suite 101; Orlando, FL 32819; 363-5871 or 800-551-0181; *www.goflorida.com/Orlando*. One Web site worth checking out for Orlando happenings is *www.orlando.digitalcity.com*.

For details about other Central Florida attractions, contact Visit Florida; Box 1100; Tallahassee, FL 32302; 888-735-2872 (to request a free visitors guide and map) or 850-224-6360; *www.flausa.com*.

Disney/AAA Travel Center: This full-service visitors center, located at the intersection of I-75 and S.R. 200 in Ocala, Florida, about 90 miles north of Orlando, is equipped to help WDW-bound vacationers plan their time, book (or confirm) hotel reservations, purchase theme park tickets, and even make dining reservations. For departing guests who didn't buy enough Mouse ears, it also stocks character merchandise; 352-854-0770.

On-Site Resources: A variety of other information sources are available upon arrival. Those staying at WDW resorts should consider their hotel's Guest Services desk the primary resource. WDW resort guests can also turn their room TV to Channel 5 for a preview of attractions (a good orientation for first-time visitors). Fort Wilderness campers are advised to stop at the Pioneer Hall

What to Pack

While there is hardly a dress code at Walt Disney World, casual clothing is the rule, with few exceptions. Most notably, jackets are required for men at Victoria & Albert's restaurant in the Grand Floridian resort. More generally, T-shirts and shorts are acceptable during the day. For evening, slacks, jeans, or Bermuda shorts are appropriate. Bathing suits are a must, along with the appropriate attire for any sport you want to pursue.

Lightweight sweaters are necessary even in summer—to wear indoors when the air-conditioning gets frigid. From November through March, warmer clothing is a must for evening. Pack for weather extremes so you'll be comfy should it become unseasonably warm or cool. Always bring plenty of sunscreen, and don't forget the bug spray. If possible, pack lightweight rain gear and a compact umbrella. The most important item of all? Comfortable walking shoes.

Information and Ticket Window, call extension 2788, or touch 11 on a phone at any comfort station.

Guests at the resorts on Hotel Plaza Boulevard can access a tourist-information TV program of their own. Some other area hotels also show a version of the orientation, usually aiming to provide an overview of all Central Florida attractions.

For Day Visitors: All day visitors—that is, those staying off Disney property or living in the Orlando area—receive a useful handout at the Auto Plazas. When purchasing one-day admission to a given theme park, guests receive a guidemap to that park. Multi-day pass holders may receive all four park guides upon request. Extra guides are available at City Hall (in the Magic Kingdom) and at Guest Relations (in Epcot, the Disney-MGM Studios, and Animal Kingdom), as well as in many park shops and restaurants.

Package Pointers

The sheer number and diversity of packages offering vacations in Central Florida are enough to bewilder even the savviest traveler. Still, such plans are worth exploring. They offer the convenience of a vacation that's completely organized in advance, and that will generally cost less than the sum of the same transportation, accommodations, and admission elements purchased separately. Also, since most package providers purchase blocks of Disney rooms, they are an excellent source for securing a room on Disney property when the hotel of your choice is booked.

American Airlines Vacations (800-321-2121), Delta Vacations (800-872-7786), TWA Getaway Vacations (800-438-2929), US Airways Vacations (800-455-0123), American Express Travel (800-297-6898), and the Walt Disney Travel Company (800-828-0228) offer packages featuring WDW on-site hotels, as well as off-property accommodation. Most packages include the added attraction of low-cost air transportation. AAA members should inquire about AAA Disney Driveaway Vacations and other packages, which offer perks for drivers to the World. Check the travel section of your local newspaper, and with your travel agent, for other possibilities, such as Kingdom Vacations or Go Go Tours.

The Walt Disney Travel Company's offerings run from value to deluxe lodging, with airfare, theme park admission, or meals sometimes included. Certain packages allow you to add a meal plan or recreation options. Some WDW vacation plans are available year-round; others, such as Magical Holidays, Sunshine Getaway, and Fall Fantasy, are offered seasonally. Others are designed around a specific type of vacation—a golf getaway, a honeymoon—and include special elements, such as unlimited tee times or champagne upon arrival. The Disney Institute has a variety of such packages to choose from. Still others are tied to an annual WDW event, such as the Disneyana Convention, and may be required

DID YOU KNOW...

In all, Walt Disney World covers 47 square miles of property. That's twice the size of Manhattan!

for participation (see "Holidays & Special Events" in the *Getting Ready to Go* chapter). Finally, add-on escapes allow guests to combine a WDW vacation with a short cruise or a stay at the Disney resort at Vero Beach (see pages 74–75 and page 70 in the *Transportation & Accommodations* chapter for more information about these options).

The value of a package depends on your specific needs. Before considering your options, use this book to help determine which of the myriad accommodations, activities, and attractions at Walt Disney World most appeal to you. There's real value in some package elements, such as airport transfers and meal discounts. Several packages also include meals with the Disney characters, tennis lessons, golf greens fees, tennis court fees, boat rentals, and the like. Never choose a package that includes elements you don't want or won't have time for. While extras such as welcoming cocktails may sound appealing, their cash value is negligible. Also beware of any packages that tout as selling points certain services that are available to every Walt Disney World guest.

Cost-Cutting Tips

While there's no denying that a Walt Disney World vacation can be an expensive undertaking, it's quite possible to keep costs down. When budgeting for your trip, it's helpful to know that Walt Disney World prices are comparable to those in a large city. Here are our tips.

Lodging: When it comes to saving money on accommodations, timing is the key. While off-season dates vary, depending on the hotel, value season for most Disney resorts generally means January through early February and late August through late December.

Also consider how much time you will actually spend at your hotel, and don't pay for a place packed with perks you won't have time to enjoy.

Hotels often allow children to stay free in parents' rooms, but the cutoff age does vary. Budget chains—well represented in the Orlando area—are economical but usually offer few frills. One source of information is the *State by State Guide to Budget Motels*, by Loris G. Bree ($12.95 in bookstores or $15.95 from Marlor Press; 4304 Brigadoon Dr.; St. Paul, MN 55126; 800-669-4908).

When considering the cost-effectiveness of off-property lodging, factor in the time, money, and inconvenience of commuting to and from attractions. Realize, too, that the advantages of staying on-property (access to WDW transportation tops among them) also apply to those staying in the least expensive rooms in Disney's brood of hotels. The most important addresses for budget-watching Disney fans, the three All-Star resorts, offer the lowest rates on WDW property. Rooms at Caribbean Beach, Dixie Landings, Port Orleans, and Coronado Springs are slightly higher priced. Also, note that usually the only difference between the least and most expensive rooms in a hotel is the view. Consider how often you'll be looking out that window. See the *Transportation & Accommodations* chapter for details.

Food: Visit fancier dining establishments (if you've a yen) at lunchtime rather than at dinner; the same entrées often cost less then. Sometimes Epcot has an early-bird dinner deal, so it pays to ask. Many lounges at the Disney resorts offer short (often less expensive) menus. Carry sandwich fixings and have lunches alfresco whenever possible (keeping in mind that outside food is not welcome inside Disney parks). Look for lodging with kitchen facilities: The savings on food, at breakfast time, may be more than the extra accommodations expense. Refrigerators are available for $6 a day at many Disney resorts. A plastic mug can be purchased at most resorts, good for unlimited refills during your stay at the resort. The food court at Dixie Landings has an all-you-can-eat breakfast.

Transportation: Comparison shop for the best airfares and rental car fees. If you decide to fly, factor in the cost of getting to and from the airport. For help weighing the rental car options, see the box on page 14 in the "How to Get There" section in this chapter.

Discounts: Membership in the Magic Kingdom Club nets discounts on Disney vacation packages, including the Disney Cruise Line, and accommodations (based on limited availability); park admission; car rentals; select theme park restaurant meals; select merchandise at Downtown Disney Marketplace, Pleasure Island, and in The Disney Store and The Disney Catalog; and more. Just ask if they offer the discount before making a purchase. Many companies offer free membership in the club as an employee benefit. Otherwise, The Gold Card costs $65 for a two-year family membership ($50 for seniors 55 and over). Outside the United States it's $85. For information, call 800-893-4763. Allow at least two weeks to receive membership materials.

Annual passholders receive so many discounts on meals, dinner shows, tours, room rates, and more that it may be worth purchasing the pass for longer visits or if you plan more than one trip within a year. Call 560-PASS (560-7277) for specifics.

Certain discounts on resort rates and park tickets are also available to Florida residents, and other seasonal promotions occur. Call 824-4321 for up-to-the-minute details. Some off-property hotels offer discounts to seniors and AAA or AARP members as well. AAA also offers its members 10% off the price of some theme park passes. Discount chains, such as Filene's Basement and BJ's Wholesale Club, sell some WDW vacation packages at a reduced rate. Certain discounts are available to guests who charge a minimum of two nights in a WDW resort to their American Express card; for information, call 934-7639.

To receive a free copy of The Orlando Magicard, call 800-551-0181. Cardholders receive discounts at many Orlando-area hotels, restaurants, attractions, and shops, as well as on rental cars. Similar coupon books can be found at the airport and Walt Disney World's Auto Plazas.

All About Theme Park Tickets

The Disney organization defines a ticket as admission for one day only; admission media valid for longer periods are called passes. All passes are nontransferable. Prices and ticket options are subject to change. Call 824-4321 for current information.

Ticket Options

One-Day Ticket: Tickets are valid for admission to one park only—the Magic Kingdom, Epcot, the Disney-MGM Studios, or Animal Kingdom.

Four-Day Value Pass: This pass is valid for one day each at the Magic Kingdom, Epcot, the Disney-MGM Studios, and Animal Kingdom. It can't be used at more than one park on the same day. It includes use of WDW transportation. Days need not be used consecutively, and unused days never expire.

Five-Day Park Hopper Pass: This pass can be used at all four theme parks—the Magic Kingdom, Epcot, the Disney-MGM Studios, or Animal Kingdom—on the same day. It also includes use of WDW transportation. Days need not be used consecutively, and unused days never expire.

All-In-One Hopper Pass: One of the most comprehensive options, this pass can be used at all four theme parks on the same day. In addition, it allows admission to Blizzard Beach, Typhoon Lagoon, River Country, Disney's Wide World of Sports complex, Discovery Island, and Pleasure Island. Available for six or seven days, it also includes use of WDW transportation. Days need not be used consecutively, and unused days never expire.

Length of Stay Pass: WDW resort guests can buy a multi-day pass geared to the length of their visit. This pass offers unlimited admission to the theme parks, water parks, Disney's Wide World of Sports complex, Discovery Island, and Pleasure Island for the duration of a guest's stay.

E-Ride Nights

Imagine having the Magic Kingdom practically to yourself for an entire evening. It can happen if you're a WDW resort guest with a multi-day pass and ten dollars to spare. The "E-Ride" pass lets you stay in the park *after* it closes to enjoy the Magic Kingdom's best attractions time and time again. It's only available select nights throughout the year, so ask about it when you check in.

Theme Park Annual Pass: This pass offers unlimited admission to the theme parks for a year. It can be used in more than one park on the same day, and also includes use of the WDW transportation system.

Premium Annual Pass: This pass offers unlimited admission to the theme parks, water parks, Disney's Wide World of Sports complex, Discovery Island, and Pleasure Island for a year. It can be used in more than one park on the same day, and also includes use of the WDW transportation system. Passholders are eligible for many discounts.

Deciding Factors

Choosing the Right Ticket: Only have a couple of days? Pick which parks you'd like to visit and purchase day passes. Single-day tickets are valid for admission to one park only, while most multi-day passes can be used at all

DID YOU KNOW...

The phrase "E-ticket ride" is American slang for "the ultimate in thrills." It comes from the early days of Disney parks, back when tickets were used for each attraction. "A" tickets were for simple rides, "B's" the slightly more elaborate, all the way through "E's"—which were reserved for the most exciting rides of all.

parks on the same day. Will you have time to explore the rest of the World? The All-In-One Hopper Pass also allows admission to the water parks, Disney's Wide World of Sports complex, Discovery Island, and Pleasure Island for either six or seven days. If you plan to concentrate on the theme parks, buy a Five-Day Park Hopper Pass. If you don't have the time or inclination, forego park-hopping privileges and get a Four-Day Value Pass.

For the most freedom, Disney resort guests can purchase a Length of Stay Pass good nearly anywhere for the entire trip. But first compare prices with multi-day passes for the same time frame; passes for longer lengths of time are generally more cost-effective. Note that Length of Stay Passes can't be used on a future visit.

If you are planning a longer visit, or two trips within one year, consider the annual pass option. In addition to unlimited admission to the theme parks, you'll get discounts on everything from dinner shows to room rates.

Passes with Unused Days: Remaining days on any multi-day pass—with the exception of Length of Stay Passes—may be used during a future visit. Passes bought prior to the opening of Animal Kingdom must be upgraded for admission to the new park.

Upgrading: Most passes can be upgraded to include admission to Animal Kingdom. Check at Guest Relations at one of the four theme parks for details, or call 824-4321.

Purchasing Tickets and Passes

Admission media are sold at park entrances, WDW resorts, the resorts on Hotel Plaza Boulevard, Orlando International Airport, the Transportation and Ticket Center (TTC), and Downtown Disney Guest Services. Cash, traveler's checks, personal checks (with ID), American Express, Visa, MasterCard, and The Disney Credit Card are accepted. Not all passes are available at each location, so be sure to check. Call 824-4321 to confirm.

We recommend avoiding the lines by buying passes in advance from a travel agent or The Disney Store, or in one of the following ways.

Passes by Phone: Multi-day passes can be purchased by calling 824-4321. There is a $2 handling fee. Allow two to three weeks for delivery.

At the end of your visit, make a note of the number of unused days remaining on a multi-day pass. (Write it on the pass itself.)

Passes On-Line: Multi-day passes can be purchased through WDW's Web site (*www.disneyworld.com*). There is a $2 handling fee. Allow three weeks for delivery.

Passes by Mail: Allow three to four weeks for requests to be processed, and include a return address. Send a check or money order (for the exact amount plus $2 for handling), payable to Walt Disney World Company, to:

Walt Disney World
Box 10140
Lake Buena Vista, FL 32830-0030
Attention: Ticket Mail Order

ADMISSION PRICES

ONE-DAY TICKET
Adult $44.52
Child* $36.04

FOUR-DAY VALUE PASS
Adult $157.94
Child* $126.14

FIVE-DAY PARK HOPPER PASS
Adult $200.34
Child* $160.06

ALL-IN-ONE HOPPER PASS
Six Days
Adult $263.96
Child* $210.95

Seven Days
Adult $290.46
Child* $232.15

LENGTH OF STAY PASS

Length of Stay	Adult	Child*
2 days	$117.67	$94.36
3 days	$161.14	$129.34
4 days	$202.47	$162.20
5 days	$232.15	$185.52
6 days	$259.72	$207.77
7 days	$285.16	$227.91
8 days	$308.49	$247.01
9 days	$329.68	$263.96
10 days	$348.77	$278.81

THEME PARK ANNUAL PASS
Adult $316.94
Child* $269.24

Renewals
Adult $285.14
Child* $242.74

PREMIUM ANNUAL PASS
Adult $422.96
Child* $359.36

Renewals
Adult $380.57
Child* $323.32

Prices include sales tax and were correct at press time but will change during 1999.

*3 through 9 years of age; children under 3 free

At-a-Glance Reservations Guide

Walt Disney World vacations go more smoothly when details are planned early. Procrastinators may find no room at the inn, or no space left for a show that they wanted to see, particularly during busy seasons. Golf starting times, tennis courts, restaurant priority seating, and other affairs should also be reserved in advance. Be sure to inquire about cancellation policies; after a certain date you may be charged full price. (To avoid forfeiting your deposit, cancel resort reservations at least three days before scheduled arrival. Dinner shows and golf tee times must be canceled 48 hours in advance, or you will be charged full price.)

Accommodations: It's very important to book a room ahead of time to get your first choice. Stays during popular summer and holiday periods must be booked well in advance. Contact a travel agent, or call Walt Disney World's Central Reservations Operations at W-DISNEY (934-7639). The office is open weekdays from 7 A.M. to 10 P.M.; weekends from 7 A.M. to 8 P.M. Have pen and paper (and a credit card) handy when calling, to jot down dates and confirmation numbers. (Parties reserving ten or more rooms should call 828-3318.) For more information, see our "WDW Resort Primer" on page 45. Reservations can also be made through Disney's Web site (*www.disneyworld.com*).

Packages: For Walt Disney Travel Company package reservations, call 800-828-0228, or visit *www.disneyworld.com*. For more details, refer to "Package Pointers" on page 16.

Dining: Priority seating has replaced reservations at almost all WDW restaurants except for dinner shows (see page 245 of the *Good Meals, Great Times* chapter for details). Most dinner show reservations and restaurant priority seating arrangements are handled by one phone number: WDW-DINE (939-3463), open from 7 A.M. to 10 P.M. Monday through Friday; 7 A.M. to 8 P.M. Saturday, Sunday, and holidays.

Sports: Reservations for sporting activities are handled by WDW-PLAY (939-7529). It's wise to reserve your place as far in advance as possible. (See chart below.) For information on Disney's Wide World of Sports complex, turn to page 208.

Activity	Phone for reservations (area code 407)	Advisability of reservations	How far in advance can reservations be made?
SPORTS			
Golf starting times— all courses	WDW-GOLF (939-4653)	Necessary from January through April; suggested at other times	90 days for guests with golf packages; 60 days for guests at WDW resorts or resorts on Hotel Plaza Boulevard; 30 days for others
Golf lessons Palm and Magnolia courses	WDW-GOLF	Necessary	1 year
Tennis Contemporary Disney Institute Swan and Dolphin	WDW-PLAY (939-4653)	Suggested Suggested Suggested	90 days 90 days no limit
Tennis lessons Contemporary Disney Institute	WDW-PLAY	Necessary Necessary	90 days 90 days
Trail rides Fort Wilderness	WDW-PLAY	Necessary	30 days
Fishing trips BoardWalk Fort Wilderness Dixie Landings Downtown Disney Marketplace Yacht and Beach Club	WDW-PLAY	Necessary Necessary Necessary Necessary Necessary	60 days 60 days 60 days 60 days 60 days
Waterskiing	WDW-PLAY	Necessary	60 days

NOTE: ALL RESERVATIONS POLICIES WERE CORRECT AT PRESS TIME BUT ARE SUBJECT TO CHANGE

Priority Seating for...	Phone #	Advisability	How far in advance?	Which meals?
GOOD MEALS				
Polynesian resort	WDW-DINE		60 days	
'Ohana	(939-3463)	Suggested		B, D
Kona Cafe		Available		B, L, D
Grand Floridian resort	WDW-DINE		60 days	
Victoria & Albert's		Necessary		D
Narcoossee's		Suggested		L, D
Cítricos		Suggested		D
1900 Park Fare		Suggested		B, D
Grand Floridian Cafe		Available		B, L, D
Contemporary resort	WDW-DINE		60 days	
California Grill		Suggested		D
Concourse Steakhouse		Suggested		B, L, D
Chef Mickey's		Suggested		B, D
Wilderness Lodge	WDW-DINE		60 days	
Artist Point		Suggested		B, D
Whispering Canyon Cafe		Suggested		B, L, D
BoardWalk resort	WDW-DINE		60 days	
Flying Fish Cafe		Suggested		D
Spoodles		Suggested		B, L, D
Yacht and Beach Club resort	WDW-DINE		60 days	
Cape May Cafe		Suggested		B, D
Yachtsman Steakhouse		Suggested		D
Yacht Club Galley		Suggested		B, L, D
Caribbean Beach resort	WDW-DINE		60 days	
Captain's Tavern		Suggested		D
Dixie Landings resort	WDW-DINE		60 days	
Boatwright's Dining Hall		Suggested		B, D
Port Orleans resort	WDW-DINE		60 days	
Bonfamille's Cafe		Suggested		B, D
Coronado Springs resort	WDW-DINE		60 days	
Maya Grill		Suggested		B, D
Old Key West resort	WDW-DINE		60 days	
Olivia's Cafe		Suggested		B, L, D
Disney Institute	WDW-DINE		60 days	
Seasons Dining Room		Suggested		B, L, D
Dolphin resort	934-4889		60 days	
Harry's Safari Bar & Grill		Suggested		D*
Juan & Only's		Suggested		D
Swan resort	934-1609		60 days	
Garden Grove Cafe		Suggested		B, L, D
Palio		Suggested		D
Fulton's Crab House	934-2628	Suggested	30 days	B, D**
Portobello Yacht Club	934-8888	Suggested	60 days	L, D
Wolfgang Puck Cafe (Dining Room)	WDW-DINE	Suggested	60 days	D
In the theme parks	WDW-DINE	Suggested	60 days	B, L, D
GREAT TIMES				
Hoop-Dee-Doo Musical Revue Fort Wilderness	WDW-DINE	Necessary	2 years	D
Polynesian Luau Polynesian resort	WDW-DINE	Necessary	2 years	D
Mickey's Tropical Luau Polynesian resort	WDW-DINE	Necessary	2 years	D
WDW Character Meals (see page 246 for locations)	WDW-DINE	Suggested	60 days	B, L, D

* Also serves lunch. Priority seating not accepted.

** Serves Sunday brunch. Priority seating recommended.

First Things First

● Make hotel and transportation arrangements as far in advance as possible. Note that weekend flights into the Orlando area are quite popular, and many Disney hotels fill up at least six months in advance. Call W-DISNEY (934-7639) to book a room at a Disney hotel; your room confirmation should arrive within two weeks.

● Plan out a simple day-by-day schedule, deciding which theme park or area of Walt Disney World to visit for each day of your vacation. This will be helpful when making restaurant and recreation reservations. See page 23 for tips.

● Dinner show reservations can be made up to two years in advance. Consult page 245 for details and call WDW-DINE (939-3463) for reservations.

6 Months

Unless you purchased a travel package that includes theme park admission, it's time to order tickets. Refer to pages 18–19 for details and call 824-4321; your passes should arrive within four weeks.

3 Months

● Find out park hours for your stay, and add them to your day-by-day schedule. Closing times will be particularly helpful when making dining arrangements. Call 824-4321 or consult WDW's Web site (*www.disneyworld.com*).

● If you'd like to add a behind-the-scenes tour to your vacation, now is the time to make a reservation. See page 200 for details and call WDW-TOUR (939-8687).

● Some attractions may be closed for refurbishment during your visit. A new refurbishment schedule is released each season. Call 824-4321.

● Tennis lessons and courts may be reserved by calling WDW-PLAY (939-7529). Turn to page 204 for more information.

2 Months

● Choose some dining spots from among those listed in the *Good Meals, Great Times* chapter. Call WDW-DINE to make priority seating arrangements (see page 247 for details). Add each restaurant name, dining time, and priority seating number to your day-by-day schedule.

● If you will be staying at a WDW resort or a resort on Hotel Plaza Boulevard, you can book a tee time on one of WDW's golf courses now (see page 203 for details). Call WDW-GOLF (939-4653) for reservations. (Those not staying on WDW property can make reservations one month ahead.)

● Golf lessons can be booked up to a year in advance, but two months ahead is fine. See page 203 for details and call WDW-PLAY for reservations.

● Fishing excursions (refer to pages 206–207), and waterskiing sessions (page 206) can be booked by calling WDW-PLAY.

● If you have not purchased a Disney Institute package but would like to participate in one of the programs (see pages 198–199), call 800-282-9282 for reservations.

1 Month

● Trail ride reservations can be made up to 30 days in advance. Call WDW-PLAY.

2 Weeks

Airline tickets and travel package vouchers should have arrived in the mail by now. Contact your travel agent or the travel company if they have not.

1 Week

● Confirm all reservations and priority seating arrangements. Finalize your day-by-day schedule, including all confirmation numbers. Make one copy for your suitcase and one to carry with you in the parks.

● Keep an eye on Orlando-area weather and pack accordingly.

Step-by-Step Sample Schedules

It's no exaggeration to say that you could spend two weeks at Walt Disney World and still not have time to see everything that's worthwhile. The theme parks alone require every bit of four days, and that's not enough time to take in everything. Given the rate at which the World is expanding, there's even more reason to allow plenty of time to explore.

Planning Your Days: The schedules suggested here should help put you on the right track—and maybe even keep you there. The one-day schedules for each theme park allow you to hit many of the highlights (albeit at a somewhat harried pace). In addition, consider following the two-day schedules for the Magic Kingdom and Epcot, which require more time to cover fully. Consider mixing and matching

Free guidemaps are available at each park entrance, as well as at many shops and all resorts. Keep them with you at all times!

the days to suit your schedule or to correspond with the parks' least crowded days (see "Crowd Patterns" in this chapter for tips).

On each day, the idea is to make a quick tour of the park, visiting major attractions during the least crowded hours of the early morning, then repeating the circuit again later in the day. Deviations from the programs we describe are best based on our "Hot Tips" (pages 114, 146, 162, and 178, and throughout the book) and your own preferences.

Note that these schedules are for periods when extended park hours are in effect. However, you may be able to cover the same area during other seasons, when smaller crowds generally mean shorter lines.

Get There Early: It's crucial to begin days in the theme parks promptly at park opening—or earlier, since the gates often open a half hour or more before the officially posted time. Arrive about 45 minutes before park opening for best results. If you don't arrive at opening time, skip the first step of that day's schedule, since lines for the most popular attractions build up quickly. You can do anything you missed later in the day.

WDW resort guests might consider taking advantage of early admission (up to 1½ hours before the park opens to the public) to get a crack at selected attractions in the designated park. When the remainder of the park opens, begin following these schedules. (Keep in mind that others are apt to have the same idea, so if you have a park hopper pass, spend the rest of the day at a different park.) See "Park Primer" at the beginning of each theme park chapter (pages 88, 118, 150, and 166) for details about early-entry days.

As soon as you get to the park, pick up a guidemap and consult it for showtimes. Also, make any last-minute priority seating arrangements at Guest Relations.

Arrival Day: Check in as early as possible. If you arrive before check-in time, you can usually stow your bags. WDW resort guests should make last-minute priority seating arrangements at Guest Services. Then spend time by the pool, have a leisurely dinner, and pop over to Downtown Disney or BoardWalk in the evening. If the parks are open late and you have a multi-day pass, you may prefer to head straight to one of the theme parks.

Saving a Rainy Day

Florida rain showers come and go with such regularity that you could set your watch by them (*especially* during summer months). They're usually brief, though torrential. Of course, there are times that gray clouds linger longer. Here are some ways to make the most of a soggy day:

- Head for DisneyQuest, a huge interactive play zone at Downtown Disney. It'll keep the whole family entertained (and dry) for hours.
- See a movie on one of AMC Theatres' 24 screens at Downtown Disney.
- Call Disney's Wide World of Sports complex to find out if you can catch an indoor event (363-6600 for information).
- Don your raingear (ponchos are sold throughout Walt Disney World for about $5 each) and go to Epcot. The pavilions in Future World house a bounty of sheltered diversions.

One-Day Schedules

MAGIC KINGDOM

- If you'd like a table-service meal and you haven't made advance plans, make priority seating arrangements for an early dinner. Try a character meal at Crystal Palace.
- Move rapidly from one attraction to the next—first to Space Mountain, Buzz Lightyear's Space Ranger Spin, and Alien Encounter, then to Splash Mountain, Big Thunder Mountain, The Haunted Mansion, Pirates of the Caribbean, and the Jungle Cruise.
- If you are traveling with young children, your best bet is to begin by taking the Walt Disney World Railroad directly to Mickey's Toontown Fair and then visiting the Fantasyland attractions.

Hot Tip

Fantasyland and Mickey's Toontown Fair tend to be the least crowded in the late evening hours.

- Plan on lunching at around 11 A.M. to avoid mealtime lines (try one of the fast-food spots wherever you happen to be at the time). After visiting the most popular attractions, see The Enchanted Tiki Room—Under New Management, Tom Sawyer Island, and the Country Bear Jamboree before or after lunch, as time allows.
- Make a second trip around the park, stopping at The Timekeeper, Legend of the Lion King, It's a Small World, Peter Pan's Flight, The Hall of Presidents, the shops and entertainment en route, and anything else that catches your eye.
- Eat an early dinner at your chosen dining spot. It's also easy to take the monorail to the Contemporary, Polynesian, or Grand Floridian resorts, each of which offers a variety of dining options (see the *Good Meals, Great Times* chapter for recommendations, and be sure to make priority seating arrangements in advance).
- During busy seasons, when many Walt Disney World attractions are open late, we recommend spending the time after dinner at the Magic Kingdom, where fireworks and the late installment of SpectroMagic combine to make an evening especially memorable. This is also a great time to visit favorite attractions once again, since lines are usually shorter during the parades and before closing.
- Another option is to eat at Planet Hollywood or another Downtown Disney restaurant. Spend the rest of the evening exploring the clubs and shopping at Downtown Disney. Or head to the BoardWalk resort for dinner and a nostalgic walk on the boards.

EPCOT

- If you haven't made advance plans, go immediately to Guest Relations to arrange for dinner priority seating around 7:30 P.M. at one of the international restaurants in World Showcase.
- Test Track (expected to open by early 1999) is likely to be an extremely popular attraction, so stop there first, before the lines build up. Next, go to Honey, I Shrunk the Audience, at Journey into Imagination. Then see as much as you can of The Land. As soon as World Showcase opens at 11 A.M., head there and see *O Canada!* in the Canada pavilion and *Impressions de France* in the France pavilion.
- Pausing to grab a bite at one of the international food spots when hunger calls, travel from country to country, making sure to catch the show at The American Adventure (stop by for showtimes) and the boat ride in Norway. Check out the street entertainment and any shops that catch your eye.
- Try to return to Future World by mid-to-late afternoon. Explore Wonders of Life first. Then see Universe of Energy and Spaceship Earth. Spend some time at Innoventions before heading back to World Showcase for dinner.

• Keep an eye on the clock so that you can secure a good spot around the World Showcase Lagoon to watch the evening's spectacular fireworks show. (The area between Italy and The American Adventure is a prime viewing location.)

DISNEY-MGM STUDIOS

• Some attractions open later in the morning; consult a guidemap for exact times. Also, many shows here run on a schedule, so check the guidemap for times throughout the day. Note that this park is not the easiest to navigate. You'll need the map to orient yourself in the region beyond the Chinese Theater.

• If you'd like to try one of the table-service restaurants for lunch or dinner, and you haven't made advance plans, stop at the corner of Hollywood and Sunset boulevards or at the eatery to arrange for priority seating. Try the 50's Prime Time Cafe for some old-time TV nostalgia or the Sci-Fi Dine-In Theater for a meal that's "out of this world."

• If you're ready for a 13-story drop (or two), head to the Tower of Terror. Then try to see an early showing of Voyage of The Little Mermaid. Afterward, head for Muppet*Vision 3-D and Star Tours, since these attractions are very crowded later in the day.

• If small children are along, spend some time at the Honey, I Shrunk the Kids Movie Set Adventure. Take slightly older kids to see the new show Doug Rocks!

• Plan on grabbing a quick lunch at one of the fast-food eateries around 11 A.M. to avoid mealtime crowds.

• Slot in times to see Indiana Jones Epic Stunt Spectacular and the ABC Sound Studio (be sure to volunteer to participate). Be aware that the Mulan Parade passes through this area each afternoon. If you're not watching the parade, it's a good time to see The Magic of Disney Animation and The Great Movie Ride.

• Browse through the shops along Hollywood and Sunset boulevards, taking time to notice all the Studios' interesting details.

• Plan to catch the last showing of Beauty and the Beast Live on Stage (it's particularly enjoyable at night).

• At about 5 P.M., head for the Disney-MGM Studios Backlot Tour and Backstage Pass to 101 Dalmatians. Also see The Making of... for a behind-the-scenes perspective on the latest Disney release.

• After a leisurely dinner at your chosen spot, see any attractions you may have missed on previous circuits.

• Cap off the day with Fantasmic!—the Studios' new nighttime spectacular, featuring fireworks, Disney characters, and special effects galore. It's a must-see.

DISNEY'S ANIMAL KINGDOM

• If you haven't made previous arrangements and you'd like a table-service meal, try to secure priority seating for an early dinner at Rainforest Cafe. As the park's only full-service restaurant, expect it to be quite busy. (Because priority seating availability is limited, we suggest trying to make arrangements long before leaving home.)

• Pass quickly through The Oasis (the left path offers the fewest diversions), and walk straight ahead for the bridge to Safari Village. Your goal is to see two of the most thrilling (and popular) rides in Animal Kingdom early in the morning.

• As you approach The Tree of Life, gawk if you must, but don't stop. Instead, head directly to DinoLand U.S.A. for a thrilling ride on Countdown to Extinction. (If you don't arrive at park opening, it's best to skip this attraction until later in the day.)

• An alternative plan for those traveling with small children is to wander through The Oasis and get to know the animals there before moving on to the bigger animals. Then spend some time in Camp Minnie-Mickey, where all the animal character favorites are in residence. The stars from *The Lion King* put on a very popular show known as the Festival of the Lion King (check your guidemap and see the first performance if possible) and Pocahontas and her small animal friends can be found at Grandmother Willow's Grove.

• Next it's on to Africa and the Kilimanjaro Safaris ride, since the animals are most active in the early mornings.

• Spend time on the Gorilla Falls Exploration Trail before breaking for an early lunch (we recommend getting a quick bite at a fast-food spot in Safari Village or Africa's Harambe).

• When afternoon crowds descend, hop on the Wildlife Express to Conservation Station—and spend time exploring all the interactive exhibits when you arrive. Kids will particularly enjoy the Affection Section, where they can actually touch the animals.

- Take a relaxing ride on the Discovery River Boats that travel around Safari Village. One dock is in Safari Village near DinoLand U.S.A. and the second is across the river, near Asia; trips are one-way only. Wherever you get on, expect to find a few surprises lurking in the river.

- *Now* see the 3-D movie It's Tough to be a Bug! in The Tree of Life. Also explore the crisscrossing pathways of The Tree of Life Garden while you're here. Take time to notice the animal carvings on the tree and on all the shops of Safari Village; the detail throughout the land is impressive.

- Head back to DinoLand U.S.A. for a brief walk on the Cretaceous Trail. While you're here, slot in a time to see Journey into Jungle Book at the Theater in the Wild (check a guidemap for schedules). Kids will enjoy the huge sandbox and playground known as The Boneyard. Don't miss Chester and Hester's Dinosaur Treasures—the shop that's themed as a roadside souvenir stand.

- Spend the rest of the day exploring Asia, the newest land in Animal Kingdom (which was scheduled to open in stages, beginning in December 1998). After a hike through the rain forest on the Maharajah Jungle Trek, brave Tiger Rapids Run (opening in spring 1999).

- In the time before dinner, swing by Camp Minnie-Mickey (if you haven't done so already) to see the Festival of the Lion King (check a guidemap for schedules and get there early). Then wander about The Oasis.

- Since there are no fireworks (the animals must get their beauty rest), we suggest eating dinner at Rainforest Cafe. (Try to make priority seating arrangements in advance.) Consider it dining as entertainment, since thunderstorms, waterfalls, and exotic fish compete with the imaginative fare for your attention. If you have other plans, at least stop in for a peek.

Two-Day Schedules
DAY 1 MAGIC KINGDOM

- Have breakfast at one of the restaurants on Main Street that begin serving early and be at the Central Plaza end of Main Street at the park's official opening time. Then begin circumnavigating the park, taking in just the major attractions described for the first morning of a one-day visit.

- At about noon, consider leaving the park to go to Typhoon Lagoon, Blizzard Beach, or River Country. Have lunch and enjoy the water park's various swimming areas, water slides, and recreational activities. Golfers may want to reserve ahead to sample one of the World's first-rate golf courses instead.

- Return to the Magic Kingdom at about 5 P.M. and grab a quick dinner. Give your stomach time to digest before taking another ride on Space Mountain and Splash Mountain. By 8 P.M. head for Main Street to stake a claim to a section of curb for the 9 P.M. showing of the SpectroMagic parade. Watch the Fantasy in the Sky fireworks after the parade.

DAY 2 MAGIC KINGDOM

- Try one of the character breakfasts (described in *Good Meals, Great Times*).

- At the Magic Kingdom, spend the rest of the day following our guidelines for the afternoon of a one-day visit, taking time for any other attractions that catch your eye.

- If you'd like to see the afternoon parade, find a good spot on Main Street no later than 2:30 P.M. If you would like to participate, get there at least 45 minutes before the 3 P.M. start; volunteers are chosen randomly from along the parade route. If you don't want to see the parade, now is a good time to hit the more popular attractions or anything in Fantasyland.

- Stop for dinner when hunger strikes. If you have reservations, an alternative plan is to leave the Magic Kingdom at about 4 P.M. for the Hoop-Dee-Doo Musical Revue at Fort Wilderness. (Be sure to call to make 5 P.M. reservations long before leaving home, since they can be very hard to come by.)
- In the evening (if you have the energy), go to Pleasure Island for some dancing, comedy, or music. Or, if the Magic Kingdom is open late, return for another round of your favorites in the cooler evening hours. If tired feet prohibit such activity, see a movie in the cinema at Downtown Disney West Side.

DAY 1 EPCOT

- First ride Test Track (expected to open by early 1999). See Honey, I Shrunk the Audience, at Journey into Imagination, next.
- If you haven't had breakfast, grab a quick bite at the Sunshine Season Food Fair in The Land pavilion. Then spend as much time at The Land as possible before 11 A.M.
- Head for World Showcase when it opens (at 11 A.M.), and see the movies in Canada and France. Backtrack and explore France, the United Kingdom, and Canada. Perhaps have lunch at Le Cellier Steakhouse.
- Then return to Future World, where you'll spend the rest of the day. Check the Tip Board (which lets you know the waiting times for popular attractions) in Innoventions Plaza before proceeding to The Living Seas, Universe of Energy, Wonders of Life, and any other attractions you have not yet experienced.
- See Spaceship Earth late in the day. Spend the evening hours exploring Innoventions. Stop for dinner when hunger calls.
- Plan to be around World Showcase Lagoon for the fireworks show.

DAY 2 EPCOT

- If you were unable to make advance plans, go directly to Guest Relations to make priority seating arrangements for lunch and dinner in World Showcase. Secure a 1:30 P.M. seating for lunch and an 8:30 P.M. seating for dinner. (Refer to the *Good Meals, Great Times* chapter for additional guidance and our dining suggestions.)
- That done, take in any major attractions in Future World that you missed on your first day. Spend the remaining time before 11 A.M. at Innoventions.
- Next, head for World Showcase as close to its 11 A.M. opening time as possible. Start your route around the promenade with Mexico, making sure to catch the boat ride in Norway and the movie in China before heading to your lunch spot.
- Slot in a time to see the show at The American Adventure pavilion. Even if you hate shopping, browse through Germany's collectibles and toy shops, and Morocco's brass and leather bazaars. Check your guidemap for the best times to look in on the entertainers who perform daily along World Showcase Promenade.
- Stop at one of the many snack stands for a late-afternoon international treat. The hours between 6 P.M. and your scheduled dinner time should be spent seeing any World Showcase attractions that were missed on your previous circuits.
- Remember to allot enough time to walk to your dining spot. Skip dessert at the restaurant and instead head for the Boulangerie Pâtisserie in the France pavilion.
- If you couldn't get priority seating in the Epcot restaurant of your choice, or you need a change of pace, head for Downtown Disney or the BoardWalk, where there are plenty of restaurants from which to choose (see *Good Meals, Great Times*).

Making the Most of Longer Visits

A longer stay allows the chance to sample some of the World's myriad of other offerings. Spend another day in the one park you most enjoyed. Lounge by the pool, play tennis or golf, or bike. Go shopping at the Downtown Disney Marketplace. Cool off at one of Disney's innovative water parks. Have lunch at a WDW resort and try a special dinner at Victoria & Albert's at the Grand Floridian, or at Pleasure Island's Portobello Yacht Club. Check out the clubs at Pleasure Island or Downtown Disney West Side, or spend the evening at the Board-Walk. Take golf or tennis lessons. Go fishing, waterskiing, or horseback riding. Visit the spa at the Disney Institute or the Grand Floridian resort. Participate in a behind-the-scenes program. Play miniature golf at Fantasia Gardens. See a game at Disney's Wide World of Sports complex. Enroll for a stay (or a day) at the Disney Institute; check out the Sports & Fitness Center. For more ideas, see our *Sports, Everything Else in the World*, and *Good Meals, Great Times* chapters.

CUSTOMIZED TRAVEL TIPS
Traveling with Children

Tell youngsters that a Walt Disney World vacation is in the works and the response is apt to be overwhelming. Our guide, *Birnbaum's Walt Disney World For Kids, By Kids* ($10.95), written by and for children ages 7 through 14, can be a useful resource for getting them involved in the planning from the outset. Filled with information about the World from a kid's perspective, it can be used as a reference before and during the trip, and as a souvenir after.

Walt Disney World ranks among the easiest spots on earth for families with children. Older kids don't need to be driven around, and the general supervision is such that kids are hard pressed to get into trouble. Keep in mind, however, that kids under seven must be accompanied by an adult to enter the theme parks; kids under ten must be accompanied at the water parks. With teens, it's enough to establish a meeting place and time inside the Magic Kingdom, Epcot, the Studios, or Animal Kingdom. Remember that many spots have more than one entrance, so be specific, and don't choose a crowded area (such as in front of Cinderella Castle).

Theme Park Favorites: Although kids are usually enchanted by all of Walt Disney World, some attractions hold their interest more than others. If you're traveling with very young children, your best bet is the Magic Kingdom. Visit Mickey's Toontown Fair first and then Fantasyland, keeping in mind that some attractions frighten kids who are afraid of the dark. For older kids, thrill rides get the highest rating. Don't miss Space Mountain, Alien Encounter, Splash Mountain, and Big Thunder Mountain Railroad in the Magic Kingdom; Epcot's Body Wars and Test Track; Star Tours and Tower of Terror at the Disney-MGM Studios; and Countdown to Extinction at Animal Kingdom.

Other favorites include The Haunted Mansion, Legend of the Lion King, Pirates of the Caribbean, and Peter Pan's Flight in the Magic Kingdom; Wonders of Life, Journey into Imagination, Innoventions, and Norway in Epcot; and Muppet*Vision 3-D, Star Tours, and the Voyage of The Little Mermaid in the Studios. In Animal Kingdom, It's Tough to be a Bug! and Camp Minnie-Mickey are surefire kid pleasers, as are the thrilling Kilimanjaro Safaris and Tiger Rapids Run attractions.

Restaurant Picks: Fast-food, buffet, and food court meals win with most kids, but there are a few specifics in the theme parks. In the Magic Kingdom, Pinocchio Village Haus in Fantasyland and Crystal Palace on Main Street are favorable spots for lunch. Aunt Polly's on Tom Sawyer Island is a good bet for a snack; while adults sip lemonade, the kids can explore every nook and cranny on the island. At Epcot, kids prefer Sunshine Season Food Fair in The Land and Liberty Inn at The American Adventure. Sci-Fi Dine-In Theater and 50's Prime Time Cafe at the Studios are good choices as well. (Always ask to see the kids' menu at full-service restaurants.) At

Parental Perk

Families with small children should know about the "kid switch" policy at the theme parks. At attractions with age or height restrictions, a parent who waits with a young child while the other parent rides the attraction can go right on when the first parent comes off. (Be sure to ask the attendant.)

Animal Kingdom, Restaurantosaurus is a safe bet for kids. Character meals are hits with kids of all ages (see page 246 in *Good Meals, Great Times* for details).

Resort Fun: All Walt Disney World resorts have at least a small room full of video games; the arcades at the Contemporary and All-Star resorts are positively vast. Most of the hotels have playgrounds; the ones located at the Polynesian, Dixie Landings, Caribbean Beach, and All-Star resorts get high marks from children. The best pools for kids are at the Yacht and Beach Club, Port Orleans, Contemporary, Caribbean Beach, Coronado Springs, and BoardWalk.

Child Care: The Polynesian, Grand Floridian, Contemporary, Wilderness Lodge, Yacht and Beach Club, BoardWalk, Swan, and Dolphin have child care facilities. In-room child care can be summoned to all WDW resort locations; contact the Guest Services desk. There is also a center known as KinderCare, which accepts kids ages one to four. For details and availability, phone 827-5444.

Strollers: Available for rent for $5 (plus a $1 refundable deposit) at stroller and wheelchair rental shops at the following locations: on the east side of Main Street at the entrance to the Magic Kingdom, on the east side of the Entrance Plaza and at the International Gateway at Epcot, Oscar's Super Service at the Disney-MGM Studios, and Garden Gate Gifts near The Oasis at Animal Kingdom. You'll need to present the receipt when returning the stroller to get a Disney Dollar back.

Keep in mind that strollers are not permitted inside the attractions (they can be parked near each attraction entrance). If the stroller disappears while you're in an attraction, a replacement may be obtained at Merchant of Venus in Tomorrowland, the Frontier Trading Post in Frontierland, Tinker Bell's Treasures in Fantasyland, the World Traveler shop at Epcot's International Gateway and the Germany pavilion in World Showcase, Oscar's at the Disney-MGM Studios, and Garden Gate Gifts in Animal Kingdom. Guests have to pay only once a day for a stroller. If you rent one in the morning and plan to spend the afternoon at another park, just present your receipt for a stroller there.

Baby Care Centers: Located in each of the theme parks, these centers are helpful to parents with young children. There are rooms with rocking chairs and love seats for nursing mothers, and cheery feeding rooms. Baby centers have facilities for changing infants, preparing formula, and warming bottles. Disposable diapers, bottles, formula, pacifiers, juices, and baby food are among the supplies for sale. The decor is soothing and the atmosphere is such that it seems a million miles away from the parks. Changing areas are available in most women's and some men's restrooms as well.

Lost Children: The security forces inside Disney theme parks are far more serious than the happy appearance of things indicates. This is a welcome thought on those rare instances when a child suddenly disappears or fails to show up on schedule. If this happens, check the lost children's logbooks at the Baby Care Center or City Hall in the Magic Kingdom; at Guest Relations or the Baby Care Center (behind the Odyssey Center) in Epcot; at Guest Relations at the Disney-MGM Studios; or at Guest Relations, just inside the park entrance, in Animal Kingdom. All Disney employees know what to do if a lost child starts to call for his

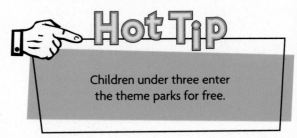

Children under three enter the theme parks for free.

or her parents. There are no paging systems in the parks, but in serious emergencies an all-points bulletin can be put out among employees. The Guest Relations staff at the entrances to all theme parks can also assist.

Disney has special name tags for very young children. Guests may pick them up at the Magic Kingdom's City Hall or Baby Care Center, Epcot's Guest Relations or Baby Care Center, or Guest Relations in the Disney-MGM Studios or Disney's Animal Kingdom.

Traveling Without Children

Walt Disney World has become a popular destination for adults without children, appealing to singles, young couples, and empty nesters alike. Disney has responded to the demand with an expanded entertainment complex and sophisticated dining for grown-ups without kids in tow.

- Consider perusing *Birnbaum's Walt Disney World Without Kids* ($11.95), our adult-oriented companion guide to this book.
- Crowds can be overwhelming during traditional school break times. Schedule your visits for off-peak seasons.

Older Travelers

Walt Disney World may be a cinch for a five-year-old to maneuver, but it can sometimes be overwhelming for older travelers. The theme parks can be disorienting because of the crisscrossing pathways. And the heat, particularly in summer, can be hard to take. But with the proper planning and precautions, it's just as delightful for older visitors as for kids.

- Try to eat early or late to avoid the mealtime crowds. In the Magic Kingdom, select restaurants such as Cinderella's Royal Table in Cinderella Castle. Or take the monorail to the peaceful Polynesian, Contemporary, or Grand Floridian resorts, where pleasant dining options abound (check ahead to find out which restaurants serve lunch). In Epcot, the Coral Reef restaurant and Le Cellier Steakhouse are especially restful spots. At the Disney-MGM Studios, the Hollywood Brown Derby offers a relaxing sit-down meal.

Lost Adults

Occasionally, traveling companions get separated in the crush of the crowds, or someone may fail to show up at a meeting spot. When this happens, it's good to know that messages can be left for fellow travelers at Guest Relations in any of the four theme parks.

- The Florida sun tends to be brutal year-round—always wear sunscreen.
- Don't underestimate distances at Epcot or Animal Kingdom; you may need to walk more than three miles in a day. If that's daunting, treat yourself to a wheelchair. (Epcot's *FriendShip* boats on the lagoon can also ease the burden on weary feet.)
- Pace yourself. It's smart to head back to your hotel for a swim or a nap in the afternoon and then return to the parks later on. The hotels connected by monorail are particularly convenient for this.
- Many Orlando-area hotels and attractions offer discounts to seniors and AARP members. Contact the Official Visitor Information Center (363-5872) for details.

Young Singles

While it's not exactly a happening singles scene, Walt Disney World is a lot of fun to visit with friends.

- Downtown Disney's clubs and restaurants can prove to be fertile meeting places. The BoardWalk is another lively destination. Sports fans find the ESPN Club most inviting.
- The lounges at Walt Disney World hotels are relaxed and welcoming. The same atmosphere prevails at the Catwalk Bar at the Disney-MGM Studios, and at the Rose & Crown Pub (in the United Kingdom pavilion) and the Matsu No Ma lounge (Japan) in Epcot's World Showcase.

Solo Travelers

Those who travel alone for the freedom and fun of it can have as memorable a time here as they would anywhere else.

- Solo travelers on the lookout for company might sign up for a behind-the-scenes tour. The Disney Institute is also a good place to meet folks with similar interests.
- The Biergarten in World Showcase's Germany pavilion and the Teppanyaki Dining Rooms in Japan's Mitsukoshi restaurant are especially convivial, as parties are seated together at large tables. Many of the finer restaurants now have counters to sit at—perfect for lone diners.
- Need a tennis partner? Check out the player matching program at Disney's Racquet Club (824-3578).
- **A Note for Budget Watchers:** Rates at all WDW resorts, the resorts on Hotel Plaza Boulevard, and most other area accommodations are the same whether one or two persons occupy a room. The Disney Institute, however, does offer single rates on packages.

Travelers with Disabilities

Walt Disney World gets high marks from travelers with disabilities because of the attention paid to special needs. Below is an overview of the services provided.

GETTING AROUND: Special parking is available for guests at all four theme parks; ask for directions at the Auto Plazas upon entering. From the Transportation and Ticket Center (TTC), the Magic Kingdom is accessible by ferry or by monorail (for those using wheelchairs, the former is preferable, since the monorail ramp has a steep slant). Note that all WDW monorail stations are accessible to wheelchairs except at the Contemporary resort. Valet parking is available at Downtown Disney and is free to guests with disabilities.

Wheelchairs: Wheelchairs can be rented in all theme parks; they cost $5 per day, with a $1 refundable deposit. In the Magic Kingdom, wheelchairs are available at the Stroller and Wheelchair Rental on the right side of the souvenir area, just inside the turnstiles. Epcot's rental area is just inside the turnstiles on the left. Oscar's Super Service rents wheelchairs at the Disney-MGM Studios. At Animal Kingdom, wheelchair rental is available at Garden Gate Gifts near The Oasis.

Electric Convenience Vehicles (ECVs) are available for rent in every park. They cost $30 plus a $10 refundable deposit, per park per day. They usually sell out early.

There are designated areas for guests in wheelchairs to view the fireworks at Epcot, and to view the parades in the Magic Kingdom and the Disney-MGM Studios. Check a park guidemap for locations.

Accessibility: It's easy to get around the theme parks by wheelchair. Most attractions are accessible to guests who can be lifted from chairs with assistance from a member of their party, and many can accommodate guests who must remain in wheelchairs at all times. Consult the *Guidebook for Guests with Disabilities* (see box) for details about attraction access, or check with the ride host or hostess. At the water parks, life jackets are available for travelers with disabilities.

All WDW hotels have accommodations for guests with disabilities, including roll-in showers. For assistance in selecting one that best fits your requirements, ask for the Special Requests Department when you call Central Reservations (934-7639).

RESOURCES: Guests with visual disabilities can rent a tape recorder and a cassette that describes each theme park, as well as a Braille guidebook. Each requires a $25 refundable deposit. Service animals are permitted in all the parks.

Guests who use Text Typewriters (TTYs) can call 827-5141 for WDW information. TTYs are available free of charge at City Hall in the Magic Kingdom; Guest Relations in Epcot, the Disney-MGM Studios, and Animal Kingdom; and Guest Services at Downtown Disney and at all resorts. Sign language interpretation is available for select shows. Call at least two weeks in advance to make arrangements.

Listening devices that amplify attraction sound tracks are available at City Hall in the Magic Kingdom and at Guest Relations in Epcot, Animal Kingdom, and the Disney-MGM Studios. A $25 refundable deposit is required. Sites with assistive listening systems are listed on park guidemaps.

Be sure to inquire about the availability of reflective and video captioning devices. The former project show dialogue onto panels positioned in front of a guest; the latter activate captioning on video monitors. The park guidemaps indicate at which attractions these devices can be used. Also, written scripts are available at Guest Relations and at each show and attraction for use by guests with hearing disabilities. Contact a park employee for assistance.

Tours: The following organization and travel agencies are experienced at booking trips for travelers with disabilities:

- The Society for the Advancement of Travel for the Handicapped (347 Fifth Ave., Suite 610; New York, NY 10016; 212-447-7284). Send a check or money order for $5 to receive a listing and other information; membership costs $45; $30 for seniors 62 and older and for students.

- Flying Wheels Travel (143 W. Bridge St.; Owatonna, MN 55060; 800-535-6790)

- Directions Unlimited (720 N. Bedford Rd.; Bedford Hills, NY 10507; 800-533-5343)

GETTING READY TO GO

Theme Park Resource

The *Guidebook for Guests with Disabilities* provides details on the accessibility and services available in all WDW theme parks. It's available at wheelchair rental locations, Guest Relations, and ticket booths. To receive this information in advance, visit WDW's Web site (*www.disneyworld.com*) or write to Walt Disney World Guest Communications; Box 10000; Lake Buena Vista, FL 32830.

WDW Weddings & Honeymoons

Walt Disney World is the most popular honeymoon destination in the country. The resorts offer some romantic stretches of white-sand beaches for evening strolls, fine restaurants for candlelight dinners, and a host of activities to rival almost any Caribbean or Hawaiian destination. Add to that the fantasy of the Magic Kingdom, the wonder of Epcot, the glamour of the Disney-MGM Studios, and the majesty of Animal Kingdom, plus Downtown Disney and BoardWalk nightlife, and water park thrills, and it's not very hard to see why Walt Disney World is number one with newlyweds. Because honeymooners have been flocking to the WDW resorts for many years, a variety of packages cater specifically to newly married couples. For information, call 827-7200. (You don't have to buy a package to get special treatment; just let the staff know you're on your honeymoon.)

For years, the folks at Walt Disney World received hundreds of requests from couples who wanted to marry at a Walt Disney World theme park. Today, couples can tie the knot in evening ceremonies at many of them during seasons when the parks close early. (The area in front of Cinderella Castle is one of WDW's wedding hot spots.) The Yacht and Beach Club, BoardWalk, Polynesian, Wilderness Lodge, and Contemporary resorts also host their share of weddings, with The Villas at the Disney Institute providing a more rustic option.

The Wedding Pavilion near the Grand Floridian offers a Victorian-style indoor setting with a prime view of Cinderella Castle. A combination of stained glass, sage green and soft pink florals, and benches with heart-shaped cutouts (seating around 250) creates the romantic ambience. Couples can fill their wedding albums with photos taken at Picture Point, under a trellis of climbing white roses, with the faraway castle prominently in the background. Private ceremonies can also be performed at this scenic spot.

Weddings range from elegant affairs, without a hint of Disneyana, to ceremonies in which the bride and groom arrive in Cinderella's coach and Mickey and Minnie are among the guests. At Franck's Bridal Studio, WDW coordinators work with couples to customize each wedding. Unique merchandise is available for purchase. Among the services offered are cakes, invitations, photography, hairstyling, flower arranging, and musical entertainment. Specialists can help arrange accommodations, rehearsal dinners, bachelor parties, and more. For information about a WDW wedding, call 828-3400; for honeymoon packages, call 827-7200.

FINGERTIP REFERENCE GUIDE

BARBERS AND SALONS

The most amusing place to get a haircut is the old-fashioned Magic Kingdom's Harmony Barber Shop. It's tucked away at the end of the cobblestone cul-de-sac just off the west side of Main Street.

Haircuts, coloring, manicures, and other services are available at the following resorts: the salon in the Contemporary (824-3411), the Periwig Salon at the Yacht and Beach Club (934-3260), Ivy Trellis at the Grand Floridian (824-3000, ext. 2581), the Niki Bryan shop at the Swan and Dolphin (934-4250), and the Casa de Belleza at Coronado Springs (939-3965).

BUSINESS SERVICES

Disney provides a range of services for those who simply must mix business with pleasure. Photocopiers, fax machines (also found at Guest Relations in the theme parks), pocket pagers, and FedEx materials are available at Guest Services at any Walt Disney World resort. In addition, the Contemporary, Grand Floridian, Yacht and Beach Club, Disney Institute, and Coronado Springs each provide secretarial services, computers, printers, and Internet access for a fee. The Web can be surfed without charge at Contemporary Grounds in the Contemporary resort, and at Innoventions in Epcot. A Vista-United videoconferencing center (827-2000) is located near Downtown Disney.

CAMERA NEEDS

Photo spots around the theme parks can help you capture the best shots. To photograph fireworks, your camera must have a manually adjustable shutter speed and aperture. Use color negative film (ASA 400). Set the aperture at f/8 and the shutter speed at B. Hold the lens open for three to five seconds at each burst; cover between explosions.

Flash photography is not permitted inside any WDW attractions. Film and disposable cameras are available at many shops around Walt Disney World. The best selection can be found at the camera shops in each park. Also, when capturing moments with Disney characters on videotape, refrain from using camera lights. (The lights are too bright for the characters' sensitive eyes.)

Minor Repairs: If your camera isn't working, take it to the Kodak Camera Center on Main Street in the Magic Kingdom; the Camera Center near Spaceship Earth, Cameras and Film at Journey into Imagination, or World Traveler at International Gateway in Epcot; The Darkroom on Hollywood Boulevard in the Disney-MGM Studios; or Garden Gate Gifts near The Oasis in Animal Kingdom.

Film Processing: Two-hour processing is available at the Magic Kingdom, Epcot, the Disney-MGM Studios, and Animal Kingdom, WDW resorts, and Downtown Disney wherever a Photo Express sign is displayed. Film is processed on-site.

CAR CARE

Several Exxon gas stations with convenience stores are on the property, all of which are open 24 hours a day. One is on Buena Vista Drive across from Pleasure Island; another is on Floridian Way near the Magic Kingdom Auto Plaza. The third, near the BoardWalk resort on Buena Vista Drive, also has a car wash.

Breakdowns sometimes occur, but they don't spell disaster. All WDW roads are patrolled constantly by security vehicles equipped with radios that can be used to call for help. If you need a tow, contact security (824-4777). If your car needs servicing but does not need to be towed, call the AAA Car Care Center (824-0976). Located in the Magic Kingdom Auto Plaza, the AAA Car Care Center offers full mechanical services and free towing on-property, Monday through Saturday. For off-property car care needs, rely on Riker's Wreckers (352-0842 for towing; 828-0362 for repairs), or AAA (if you're a member).

DRINKING LAWS

In Florida, the legal drinking age is 21. There are many bars and lounges all over Walt Disney World; minors are permitted to accompany their parents but are prohibited from sitting or standing at the bar. No alcohol is served in the Magic Kingdom, but alcoholic beverages are sold at restaurants and bars in Epcot, the Disney-MGM Studios, Animal Kingdom, and Downtown Disney.

Alcoholic beverages are sold in at least one shop at most WDW resorts. Liquor may be purchased from room service at the Polynesian, Contemporary, Grand Floridian, Yacht and Beach Club, BoardWalk, Swan, and Dolphin resorts; beer and wine are usually available for delivery at other resorts.

LOCKERS

Attended lockers can be found in the following theme park locations: underneath Main Street Railroad Station in the Magic Kingdom, on the west side of Spaceship Earth in Epcot, next to Oscar's Super Service near the main entrance at the Disney-MGM Studios, and just inside the entrance and to the left and right at Animal Kingdom. Lockers are also available at the Transportation and Ticket Center (TTC). Items too big to fit can be checked with the locker attendant at the Magic Kingdom, at package pickup in Epcot, and at Guest Relations at the Disney-MGM Studios and Animal Kingdom. Cost is $5 per day (plus a $1 deposit) for unlimited use. Be sure to save your rental receipt; it can be used again that day for a locker in any of the four theme parks.

LOST & FOUND

The extensive indexing system maintained by Walt Disney World's Lost and Found department is impressive, especially when a prized possession turns up missing, whether it's false teeth or a camera. (Both have been lost in the past; the dentures were never claimed.)

If you lose (or find) something, report it at any one of these Lost and Found locations: the Ticket and Transportation Center (TTC), City Hall in the Magic Kingdom, the Gift Stop in the entrance plaza at Epcot, Oscar's Super Service just inside the Disney-MGM Studios, Guest Relations near the Animal Kingdom entrance, or Guest Services at any WDW resort. At Fort Wilderness, dial 7-2726 from a comfort station telephone; from outside the campground, phone 824-2726; and from Downtown Disney, phone 828-3058.

Items lost in one of the theme parks can be claimed on the day of the loss at the park's Lost and Found, and thereafter at the main Lost and Found station at the TTC. To report lost items after your visit, call 824-4245. Hats, strollers, and sunglasses are kept one month; everything else is kept three months.

MAIL

Postage stamps can be purchased at all WDW resorts; at City Hall in the Magic Kingdom; at most shops near the lockers in Epcot, the Disney-MGM Studios, and Animal Kingdom; and at Guest Services in the Downtown Disney Marketplace.

The old-fashioned mailboxes in the theme parks are not official U.S. post boxes, but letters can be mailed from them. Postmarks read "Lake Buena Vista," not "Walt Disney World."

A post office at the Shoppes at Lake Buena Vista shopping center (opposite Summerfield Suites) is open from 9 A.M. to 4 P.M. weekdays and 9 A.M. to noon on Saturday (238-0223). In Orlando, there's a post office at 10450 Turkey Lake Road (351-9037), near the Official Visitor Information Center.

Mail may be addressed to guests care of their hotel; the address for all WDW resorts is Walt Disney World; Box 10000; Lake Buena Vista, FL 32830.

MEDICAL MATTERS

For travelers with chronic health problems, it's a good idea to carry copies of all prescriptions and to get names of local doctors from hometown physicians. However, Walt Disney World is equipped to deal with many types of medical emergencies. In the Magic Kingdom, next to the Crystal Palace, there's a First Aid Center staffed by a registered nurse; there is another at Epcot in the Odyssey Center complex. At the Disney-MGM Studios, the First Aid Center is in the Guest Relations building at the main entrance, accessible from both inside and outside the park. The Animal Kingdom First Aid Center is in Safari Village near the back side of Creature Comforts.

Walt Disney World resort guests and those staying at other area hotels have access to services providing nonemergency medical care. HouseMed can have medications delivered (239-1195 or 396-1195). The service also operates a walk-in medical treatment center, just east of I-4 on U.S. 192; open 8 A.M. to 8 P.M. daily. Centra Care Walk-In Medical Care has two locations (call 239-6463 for either): One, at 12500 South Apopka-Vineland Road, is open 8 A.M. to midnight weekdays, 8 A.M. to 8 P.M. weekends; the other, at 12139 South Apopka-Vineland Road, is open 9 A.M. to 5 P.M. weekdays. Courtesy transportation is available from most area hotels to all three clinics.

Waits in a walk-in clinic can be up to three hours on a busy day. For those who don't feel up to that prospect, Centra Care offers 24-hour in-room visits by doctors (238-2000), as does HouseMed (239-1195 or 396-1195).

The most common malady? Simple sunburn. So be prepared: Wear a hat, and slather on sufficient sunblock or sunscreen, especially during the spring and summer.

For emergencies dial 911 or call nearby Sandlake Hospital (351-8550).

For Diabetics: Walt Disney World resorts provide refrigeration services for insulin. All villa accommodations have their own refrigerators, and small refrigerators are available at other resorts for $6 a night.

Prescriptions: For a referral to the closest pharmacy or to have medications delivered, call HouseMed (239-1195 or 396-1195).

MONEY

Cash, traveler's checks, personal checks, American Express, MasterCard, Visa, and The Disney Credit Card are accepted as payment for most charges at Walt Disney World. Checks must bear your name and address, be drawn on a U.S. bank, and be accompanied by proper identification—a valid driver's license and a major credit card. Note that some snack stands accept only cash.

A Disney resort guest perk: Leave a credit card imprint at check-in and the hotel IDs may be used to cover purchases in shops, lounge and restaurant charges, and recreational fees incurred inside Walt Disney World. These cards are not valid for charges made past check-out time.

ATMs: Automated Teller Machines are scattered throughout Walt Disney World. Theme park locations include the Magic Kingdom (under the train station on Main Street, U.S.A., in Adventureland near The Enchanted Tiki Room, and in the Tomorrowland arcade), Epcot (near the main entrance, on the pathway between Future World and World Showcase, and in Germany), the Disney-MGM Studios (at the entrance), and Animal Kingdom (at the entrance), plus the TTC. All WDW resorts have ATMs in the lobby; the Fort Wilderness ATM is outside Pioneer Hall. Three can be found in Downtown Disney: near the Rock 'n' Roll Beach Club at Pleasure Island, next to Cap'n Jack's Oyster Bar in the Marketplace, and next to Forty Thirst Street at Downtown Disney West Side. Most bank cards and credit cards are accepted; there is a $2 fee for use.

Banking: SunTrust, located across from the Downtown Disney Marketplace, offers a variety of services. Guests can get cash advances on MasterCard and Visa credit cards, receive incoming wire transfers (for a $30 fee), and cash, replace, or purchase American Express traveler's checks.

SunTrust is open from 9 A.M. to 4 P.M. weekdays (until 6 P.M. Thursdays); drive-in teller windows are open from 8 A.M. to 6 P.M. weekdays (237-4786 or 828-6106).

Disney Dollars: Money bearing Mickey's, Goofy's, or Minnie's image is available at City Hall (Magic Kingdom) and Guest Relations (Epcot, the Disney-MGM Studios, and Animal Kingdom) in $1, $5, and $10 denominations. It is accepted as cash throughout Walt Disney World.

Traveler's Checks: Even the most careful of vacationers occasionally loses a wallet, and traveler's checks can take the sting out of that loss. Look for promotions by banks at home in the months preceding a vacation to see if one of the major brands—American Express, MasterCard, Visa, Citicorp, and Bank of America—is available free. Stash the receipt bearing the check numbers in a place separate from the checks themselves, along with a piece of identification such as a duplicate driver's license or a spare credit card to speed the refund process should your checks get lost.

To purchase, cash, or replace American Express traveler's checks, go to the SunTrust bank near Downtown Disney (a referral number is required for check replacement; call 800-221-7282) or one of the American Express travel offices (in Epcot or the Contemporary resort). AAA members can visit the AAA Travel Center in the Magic Kingdom for traveler's check assistance.

Foreign Currency Exchange: Up to $500 per person in foreign currency may be exchanged daily at Guest Relations in the theme parks, at the Guest Services desk at WDW resorts, or at the SunTrust across from Downtown Disney Marketplace.

PETS

No pets (other than service dogs) are allowed in the Magic Kingdom, Epcot, the Disney-MGM Studios, Animal Kingdom, or the WDW resorts, except at certain campsites at Fort Wilderness (request a pet site for $3 extra per day). Travelers who bring pets along can lodge them in one of the five air-conditioned Pet Care Kennels: near the Transportation and Ticket Center (TTC), to the left of the Epcot Entrance Plaza, at the entrance to the Disney-MGM Studios, at the Animal Kingdom entrance, and at the Fort Wilderness campground entrance, next to a huge field where pet owners can take their animals out for a run. During busy seasons, it is best to arrive before the 9 A.M. morning rush hour. Note that the kennels close one hour after the theme parks close.

Animals such as bears, cougars, and ocelots have all been accommodated by the kennels, and exotic pets may be accepted—if a bit reluctantly. However, owners themselves must put the more unusual animals into the kennels' cages, and rabbits, birds, turtles, hamsters, nonpoisonous snakes, and other animals unsuited (because of their size) to cat- and dog-size cages must have their own escape-proof accommodations.

Guests may board their pets overnight in any Walt Disney World kennel. Cost is $11, including Friskies dry food (WDW resort guests pay $9 per night to leave pets overnight); a day stay is $6, with one feeding. Guests who board pets overnight are encouraged to stop by to walk them at least twice a day, as the animals are not otherwise let out of their cages. Pets will be fed special food, if provided. For more information, call 824-6568. Reservations are not accepted.

Be sure to bring along your pet's certificate of vaccinations, since Florida law requires proof of immunization for animals involved in biting incidents. And never leave pets in your car. It is extremely dangerous for the animal and is against the law in the state of Florida.

Outside Walt Disney World: A number of hotels in the Orlando area permit pets to stay with guests. Contact the Orlando/Orange County Convention & Visitors Bureau (363-5871 or 800-551-0181).

POCKET PAGERS

Two types of devices are available to signal a telephone call or message. They can be rented at nearly all WDW hotels; inquire at the front desk.

RELIGIOUS SERVICES

A number of services are held at Walt Disney World and in the surrounding area. For more information on nearby Catholic and Protestant services, call the Christian Service Center at 425-2523.

Protestant: 9 A.M. on Sunday at Luau Cove at the Polynesian resort.

Muslim: Muslim services are held at Jama Masijid; 11543 Ruby Lake Rd. Call 238-2700 for information.

Catholic: 8 A.M. and 10:15 A.M. on Sunday at Luau Cove at the Polynesian resort. For more information, check with Guest Services at any WDW hotel or call 824-4321. The closest Catholic church off the property is Mary, Queen of the Universe Shrine, 2½ miles north of Lake Buena Vista on the I-4 service road. This enormous church seats 3,000 people and has beautiful gardens and fountains. Call 239-6600 for mass times.

Jewish: Reform services are held at the Congregation of Liberal Judaism (928 Malone Dr., Orlando; 645-0444), near Winter Park about 20 miles from WDW. Conservative services are held at Temple Ohalei Rivka, also known as the Southwest Orlando Jewish Congregation (11200 Apopka-Vineland Road; 239-5444), about three miles from Downtown Disney.

SHOPPING FOR NECESSITIES

Almost any everyday item can be purchased right on the property. At least one shop in every WDW resort stocks toiletries. In addition, a number of over-the-counter health aids, plus many other useful items, can be purchased at the Emporium on Main Street in the Magic Kingdom; they're kept behind the counter, so ask for what you want. Aspirin and sunscreen are also available at Island Supply in Adventureland, and Mickey's Star Traders in Tomorrowland. In Epcot, sundries are sold in at least one shop in each World Showcase pavilion and at all Future World stores. At the Disney-MGM Studios, stop by the Crossroads of the World and Movieland Memorabilia shops. At Animal Kingdom, you can pick up bare necessities at Island Mercantile.

Reading Matter: Newspapers, magazines, best-sellers, and paperbacks are available at all WDW resorts. At least one shop carries the daily papers from Orlando and Miami, *The Wall Street Journal*, and, on Sunday, *The New York Times* and *The Chicago Tribune*. By far, 2R's Reading and Riting at the Downtown Disney Marketplace is the best source for books. Another possibility is the Emporium in the Magic Kingdom, which carries children's books. In World Showcase, the United Kingdom's The Toy Soldier and Germany's Der Bücherwurm also stock kid's books. Books related to themes of Epcot's Future World pavilions are sold at Centorium. At the Disney-MGM Studios, adult and children's books are sold at Legends of Hollywood; Animation Gallery stocks books about animation; and Buy the Book has a far-reaching selection. White's, at Crossroads of Lake Buena Vista and in Celebration, is a source for books on Central Florida.

SMOKING

Disney is committed to providing guests with a smoke-free environment. All buildings and attraction waiting areas are designated no-smoking areas. All WDW–owned

restaurants are included, with the exception of outdoor seating areas. However, most clubs (except Adventurers Club and Comedy Warehouse at Pleasure Island), as well as many of the Walt Disney World resort lounges, allow smoking in certain areas.

TELEPHONE NUMBERS

The folks at home can reach Walt Disney World resort guests at the following phone numbers (all are in area code 407):

All-Star Movies:	939-7000
All-Star Music:	939-6000
All-Star Sports:	939-5000
Beach Club:	934-8000
BoardWalk Inn:	939-5100
BoardWalk Villas:	939-6200
Caribbean Beach:	934-3400
Contemporary:	824-1000
Coronado Springs:	939-1000
Dixie Landings:	934-6000
Dolphin:	934-4000
Fort Wilderness:	824-2900
Grand Floridian:	824-3000
Old Key West:	827-7700
Polynesian:	824-2000
Port Orleans:	934-5000
Swan:	934-3000
Villas at the Disney Institute:	827-1100
Wilderness Lodge:	824-3200
Yacht Club:	934-7000

TIPPING

Walt Disney World is not a place where bellmen stick out their hands before they even put down your luggage. Instead, they seem genuinely glad to help. Oddly enough, this pleasant attitude seems to discourage tipping at the same time it arouses sentiments that make most travelers reach for their wallets.

Tips are no less valued at WDW resorts than at any other hotel—$1 per bag is appropriate for lugging luggage; $1 to $2 per night for housekeeping service. Gratuities of 15% to 18% are customary at full-service restaurants. (As always, if service is exceptional, gratuities should be adjusted accordingly.)

Gratuity is included in the room service bill at WDW resorts and some off-property hotels. Check before you tip twice. Gratuities are not required in fast-food restaurants. Give cab drivers a 15% tip. Baggage handlers at the train station and airport expect about $1 per bag. In salons, it's customary to leave a tip of about 15% of the total bill.

WEATHER

Call Walt Disney World Weather Information (824-4104), or check The Weather Channel Web site (*www.weather.com*).

Magical Milestones

Even frequent visitors have trouble keeping up with all the changes at Walt Disney World. The time line below will help you determine which major attractions have opened since your last visit.

GETTING READY TO GO

1971—Magic Kingdom; Polynesian; Contemporary; Fort Wilderness

1972—Carousel of Progress and If You Had Wings (now Buzz Lightyear's Space Ranger Spin)

1973—Pirates of the Caribbean, Tom Sawyer Island; Golf Resort (now Shades of Green)

1974—Star Jets (now Astro Orbiter); Treasure Island (now Discovery Island)

1975—Space Mountain and WEDway People-Mover (now Tomorrowland Transit Authority)

1976—River Country

1977—Main Street Electrical Parade (now SpectroMagic)

1980—Big Thunder Mountain Railroad

1982—Epcot

1983—Journey into Imagination and Horizons

1984—Morocco pavilion

1986—Captain EO (now Honey, I Shrunk the Audience) and The Living Seas

1988—Wonders of Life, Norway, and IllumiNations; Mickey's Birthdayland; Grand Floridian and Caribbean Beach

1989—The Disney-MGM Studios; Mickey's Starland (replaced Mickey's Birthdayland); Body Wars and Cranium Command; Typhoon Lagoon; Pleasure Island

1990—Star Tours and Honey, I Shrunk the Audience Movie Set Adventure; Yacht and Beach Club; Swan and Dolphin

1991—SpectroMagic (replaced the Main Street Electrical Parade); Jim Henson's Muppet*Vision 3-D; Port Orleans

1992—Splash Mountain; Voyage of The Little Mermaid; Disney's Old Key West and Dixie Landings

1993—New productions of The Hall of Presidents and Carousel of Progress; new production of The American Adventure

1994—Legend of the Lion King and The Timekeeper opened (20,000 Leagues Under the Sea closed); Innoventions (replaced Communicore), Honey, I Shrunk the Audience (replaced Captain EO), Food Rocks (replaced Kitchen Kabaret), and The Circle of Life; The Twilight Zone Tower of Terror; Blizzard Beach; All-Star Sports and Music; Wilderness Lodge

1995—Alien Encounter; Wedding Pavilion

1996—Mickey's Toontown Fair (replaced Starland); Ellen's Energy Adventure; Backstage Pass to 101 Dalmatians and Disney's The Hunchback of Notre Dame—A Musical Adventure; Disney Institute; Fantasia Gardens Miniature Golf; Celebration; BoardWalk

1997—Disney's Wide World of Sports complex; Coronado Springs; Downtown Disney West Side

1998—Disney's Animal Kingdom; Buzz Lightyear's Space Ranger Spin and The Enchanted Tiki Birds—Under New Management; Disney Cruise Line, DisneyQuest

WHAT'S NEW?

To spotlight recent openings, some listings are marked with our special stamp, shown here. Look for it throughout the book. Here are a few highlights:

- **All-Star Movies resort** (page 71)
- **Buzz Lightyear's Space Ranger Spin** (page 105)
- **Test Track** (page 127)
- **Rock 'n' Roller Coaster** (page 152)
- **Fantasmic!** (page 161)
- **Asia** (page 172)
- **Cirque du Soleil** (page 185)
- **DisneyQuest** (page 185)

Transportation & Accommodations

The popularity of Walt Disney World has made the region around Orlando one of the world's major tourism and commercial centers, and transportation facilities from a state-of-the-art airport to an efficient network of highways bring visitors to the area by the millions.

There's no doubt that getting to and around the Walt Disney World region can be very confusing. The only more perplexing dilemma may be choosing the best accommodations for your family from among the huge assortment of hotels and motels.

The accommodations operated by Walt Disney World itself range from futuristic high-rise towers to treehouses buried deep in piney woods. In between are resorts that evoke striking images of the South Pacific, old Florida, the Pacific Northwest, the Caribbean, New England, early Atlantic City, Louisiana, Mexico, and the sports, movie, and music worlds, plus efficient trailer-type facilities and cabins in a sprawling, beautifully maintained campground. And that list doesn't include the many villas that provide extraordinary space and luxury, or the studios and homes with one, two, and three bedrooms that can be purchased through a special vacation-ownership system. What follows should help travelers sort out all the lodging options on Walt Disney World property, as well as shed light on the broad range of possibilities that exist outside the WDW gates.

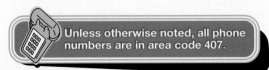

Unless otherwise noted, all phone numbers are in area code 407.

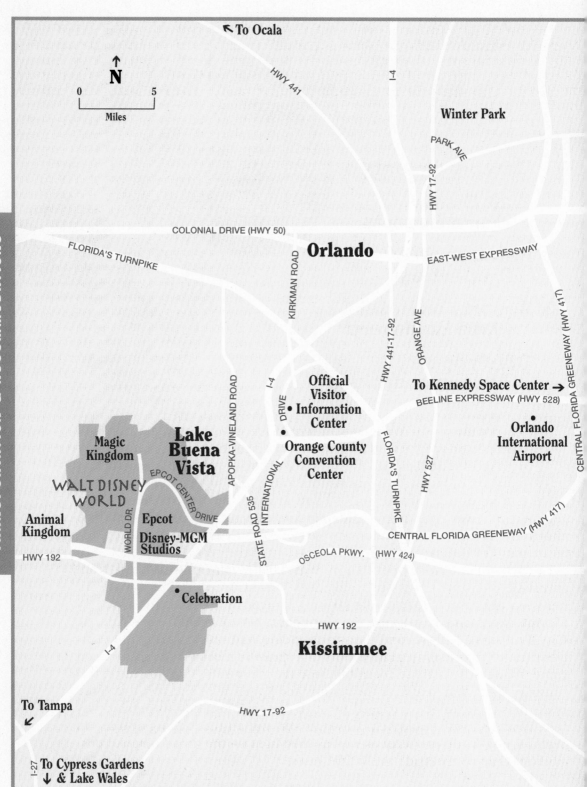

To Ocala

N
0   5
Miles

HWY 441

I-4

Winter Park

PARK AVE

HWY 17-92

COLONIAL DRIVE (HWY 50)

FLORIDA'S TURNPIKE

Orlando

EAST-WEST EXPRESSWAY

KIRKMAN ROAD

HWY 441-17-92

ORANGE AVE

To Kennedy Space Center →

CENTRAL FLORIDA GREENEWAY (HWY 417)

BEELINE EXPRESSWAY (HWY 528)

APOPKA-VINELAND ROAD

I-4

DRIVE

Official
Visitor
• Information
Center

Magic
Kingdom

Lake
Buena
Vista

WALT DISNEY
WORLD

EPCOT CENTER DRIVE

• Orange County
Convention
Center

Orlando
International
Airport

FLORIDA'S TURNPIKE

HWY 527

Animal
Kingdom

WORLD DR.

Epcot
Disney-MGM
Studios

STATE ROAD 535

STATE INTERNATIONAL

CENTRAL FLORIDA GREENEWAY (HWY 417)

HWY 192

OSCEOLA PKWY.   (HWY 424)

• Celebration

HWY 192

Kissimmee

To Tampa
↙

HWY 17-92

I-27 To Cypress Gardens
↓   & Lake Wales

40

GETTING ORIENTED

Orlando, the Central Florida city of more than one million residents, is the municipality with which Walt Disney World is most closely associated. Walt Disney World, however, is in a far smaller community called Lake Buena Vista, 15 miles from Orlando's business center. A number of hotels and restaurants are located in Lake Buena Vista, though there are many more in Orlando.

ORLANDO-AREA HIGHWAYS: The most important Orlando traffic artery is I-4, which runs diagonally through the area from southwest to northeast, cutting through the southern half of Walt Disney World. It then angles on toward Orlando and Winter Park, ending near Daytona Beach at I-95, which runs north and south along the coast.

All the city's other important highways intersect I-4, and each has a name as well as a number. From south to north, they include U.S. 192 (a.k.a. Irlo Bronson Memorial Highway), which takes an east–west course that crosses the WDW entrance road and leads into downtown Kissimmee on the east; S.R. 528 (a.k.a. the Beeline Expressway), which shoots eastward from I-4; S.R. 435 (a.k.a. Kirkman Road) which runs north and south and intersects International Drive, where many motels catering to WDW visitors are located; U.S. 17-92-441 (a.k.a. the Orange Blossom Trail), which runs due north and south, paralleling Kirkman Road on the east; and S.R. 50 (a.k.a. Colonial Drive), which runs due east and west.

WALT DISNEY WORLD EXITS: The 47-square-mile tract that is Walt Disney World is roughly rectangular. I-4 runs through its southern half from southwest to northeast. The major WDW destinations are most efficiently reached by taking the I-4 exits suggested below; off the highway, clear signage makes it easy for visitors to get anywhere in the World. Keep in mind that special events will often require rerouting of traffic patterns, so it's best to follow signs as directed.

- **Exit 27**, marked "S.R. 535/Lake Buena Vista," is the route taken to the resorts on Hotel Plaza Boulevard and the Crossroads of Lake Buena Vista shopping center.
- **Exit 26B**, marked "Epcot/Downtown Disney" leads to Epcot, Typhoon Lagoon, Downtown Disney, Lake Buena Vista golf course, the Disney Institute, Bonnet Creek Golf Club, and the BoardWalk, Caribbean Beach, Swan, Dolphin, Yacht and Beach Club, Port Orleans, Dixie Landings, and Old Key West resorts. It is also a good alternate route to the Disney-MGM Studios.

- **Exit 25**, marked "192/Magic Kingdom," leads to the Magic Kingdom, Disney-MGM Studios, Animal Kingdom, Blizzard Beach, Fort Wilderness, River Country, Palm and Magnolia golf courses, Disney's Wide World of Sports complex, and the All-Star Music, All-Star Sports, All-Star Movies (opening in early 1999), Coronado Springs, Contemporary, Polynesian, Grand Floridian, and Wilderness Lodge resorts.

WDW TRANSPORTATION: The internal transportation system at Walt Disney World is quite extensive, with boats, buses, and the famed monorail all doing their part to shuttle guests around property. The system is always being revised to serve the ever-increasing number of attractions and accommodations. Visitors staying at WDW hotels should receive a detailed brochure about transportation options upon checking in. (If you don't, just ask.) For information about WDW transportation, call 824-4321.

The system's central hub is called the Transportation and Ticket Center (TTC), located near the Magic Kingdom. Monorail, bus, and ferry service connect the TTC to points throughout the World. Day visitors must park here before taking a monorail or ferry to the Magic Kingdom. (Most Disney resort guests can bypass the TTC via direct buses.)

Walt Disney World's monorail train runs along a circular route near the Magic Kingdom, stopping at the TTC, Polynesian, Grand Floridian, Contemporary, and Magic Kingdom. It can take up to 20 minutes to complete an entire loop. A separate extension of the monorail system connects the TTC to Epcot. Monorails run from 7 A.M. until about two hours after park closing.

Bus service is the cornerstone of the Walt Disney World transportation system. It is efficient, if occasionally confusing. With a few exceptions, buses circulate every 15 to 20 minutes, from one hour prior to park opening until about one hour after closing; bus stops are clearly marked. Travel times vary, depending on the route.

Although Disney resort guests receive complimentary transportation to all sites on-property, that transportation is not always direct. Build in extra time for travel, especially if you have made priority seating arrangements at a restaurant. Also, know that traveling between resorts is often time-consuming, requiring at least one transfer.

From several Walt Disney World locales, water launches usher guests to the Magic Kingdom, Epcot, the Disney-MGM Studios, Downtown Disney, or between resorts. Boats generally depart every 20 to 30 minutes.

TRANSPORTATION ID REQUIREMENTS: Guests wishing to use the Walt Disney World transportation system may be asked to present proof of their riding privileges. Accepted IDs afford different degrees of access. WDW resort ID cards, Four-Day Value Passes, Five-Day Park Hopper Passes, All-In-One Hopper Passes, Length of Stay Passes, and Annual Passes allow guests unlimited use of any WDW buses, monorails, and boats. Valid one-day theme park tickets permit guests to use all monorails and the ferries running between the TTC and the Magic Kingdom, but do not allow use of WDW buses.

TAXI SERVICE: Cabs are available for about $1.50 per mile. Stick with the yellow cabs, and avoid using independent "gypsy" cabs whenever possible. Disney employees can direct you to authorized taxis.

DID YOU KNOW...

The Walt Disney World monorail system—a 14.7-mile highway in the sky—has carried more than a billion passengers since 1971.

ACCOMMODATIONS

When it comes to securing accommodations for a Walt Disney World vacation, there are two major categories to consider: those on Walt Disney World property and those off-property, or outside Disney boundaries. Both offer a wide selection of rooms, usually with two standard double beds, a television set, and a private bathroom. The biggest differences among accommodations, on- and off-property, seem to be in the dimensions of the rooms and bathrooms, attention to decor, level of service, variety of dining options, recreational facilities, landscaping, location, and, of course, cost.

The Disney Touch: Although rates are generally higher at WDW addresses than at many others in the area, there are Disney accommodations starting as low as $74 per night. We highly recommend staying on WDW property. Why? For starters, Disney resorts offer guests early admission to the Magic Kingdom, Epcot, and the Disney-MGM Studios on designated days; use of the WDW transportation system; the convenience of charging nearly every purchase to your hotel bill; rooms equipped with The Disney Channel, ESPN, and a closed-circuit TV station announcing WDW events; free delivery of packages back to the resort; and excellent access to Guest Services personnel. Guests can also reserve tee-off times on the golf courses up to 60 days in advance.

In addition to the aforementioned perks, there is another important, if less tangible factor to consider: atmosphere. At the end (or in the middle) of a day, when you leave the parks behind, you take the "magic" with you: Every Disney resort offers a full battery of whimsical diversions and a never-ending supply of festive ambience. And the transportation system is easily accessible and usually efficient. Be wary of anyone who encourages you to stay elsewhere for reasons other than a major difference in price.

Within the "on-property" Walt Disney World Resorts category, there are two subcategories: resorts that are owned and operated by Disney and those that are not. The resorts that fall into the latter category include the Swan and Dolphin and those on Hotel Plaza Boulevard. While each of these resorts shares the perk of overall convenience and is held to similar standards of excellence, some guest privileges do vary. For information about specific guest privileges, call the resort directly. (Telephone numbers are provided within each resort's entry in this chapter. Unless otherwise listed, all numbers are in area code 407.)

Weigh the Options: If you plan to stay outside the World, select accommodations based on your budget, location (proximity to Walt Disney World and other area attractions), and the availability and cost of transportation to and from Walt Disney World as well as restaurants and other amenities.

Several off-property options are described in the latter part of this chapter. Those closest to Walt Disney World are located on or just off S.R. 535 in Lake Buena Vista. Others are a few miles away in Kissimmee, along U.S. 192 (which runs east and west) intersecting the WDW entrance road; still others line International Drive (off S.R. 435 at the Orlando city limits), ten miles from the WDW theme park gates. The I-Drive area represents the most extensive array of accommodations, restaurants, and other attractions. Its proximity to still more of the same in Orlando, just a few miles north, constitutes an additional lure.

If you're traveling with children, remember to check the cutoff age at which children accompanying adults and staying in the same room will be billed as extra adults. (At Walt Disney World resorts, guests age 17 and older are considered adults.) Those with large families should note that the Disney villa-type accommodations, which may seem more expensive at first, could prove less costly in the long run—by eliminating the necessity of an additional room and by providing cooking facilities that can mean big savings on meals.

WALT DISNEY WORLD RESORTS

With the addition of moderately priced resorts, such as Dixie Landings, Port Orleans, and the even more economical All-Star resorts, we find it difficult to recommend staying off Disney property. Many visitors to Walt Disney World seem to agree, since the more than 25,000 rooms on-property tend to book well in advance.

In general, rooms at the Contemporary, Polynesian, Grand Floridian, Yacht and Beach Club, BoardWalk Inn, and the Swan and Dolphin are large and can accommodate up to five guests in a room. Rooms at the Wilderness Lodge, Caribbean Beach, Port Orleans, Dixie Landings, Coronado Springs, and all three All-Star resorts accommodate up to four people. Many rooms have patios or balconies. Even rooms without dramatic views often have pleasant vistas, if only across gardens (and the occasional parking lot). All resorts offer adjoining rooms, nonsmoking rooms, and rooms equipped for guests with disabilities.

The Villas at the Disney Institute, which can accommodate larger groups, makes good sense for families, especially those who want to cook some meals "at home." The vacation villas at Old Key West and BoardWalk are also popular with families. At Fort Wilderness there are campsites and fully equipped Wilderness Homes and Cabins set on 700 acres of peaceful woods.

All WDW resorts offer laundry facilities and dry-cleaning services, and rooms feature clock radios, safes, and voice-mail messaging. Hair dryers, irons (with boards), and coffeemakers may be requested. Some resorts have a limited number of microwave ovens available. It's helpful to think of resorts on the Walt Disney World grounds in terms of their location. Therefore, the WDW properties described in this chapter are divided into the following sections: Magic Kingdom, Epcot, Animal Kingdom, and Downtown Disney areas, as well as the Disney Cruise Line and the resorts on Hotel Plaza Boulevard. Note that restaurants mentioned in this chapter are described at length in the *Good Meals, Great Times* chapter.

WDW Resort Primer

The Walt Disney World hotels and villas have some important operating procedures that first-time guests don't always take seriously—much to their later dismay.

Deposit Requirements: Deposits equal to one night's lodging (or campsite rental) are required within 21 days of the time that a reservation is made. Personal checks, traveler's checks, cashier's checks, and money orders are acceptable forms of payment. To have deposit charges billed to an American Express, Visa, MasterCard, or The Disney Credit Card account, you'll need to provide the reservation agent with your credit card number and its expiration date. *Deposits will be fully refunded only if your reservation is canceled at least 72 hours before your scheduled arrival.*

Note: Reservations are automatically canceled if deposits are not received by the 21-day deadline. (Reservations booked less than 30 days prior to arrival will receive special instructions for deposits.)

Check-In and Check-Out Times: The early check-out time (11 A.M. at all WDW lodging places) and the late check-in times (1 P.M. at the campsites, 3 P.M. in most hotels, 4 P.M. at the Villas at the Disney Institute, BoardWalk Villas, All-Star resorts, and Old Key West) often come as a surprise. They need not be an inconvenience, however. When checking in, guests should preregister, purchase passes, and head for the parks. Luggage can be stored at the resorts for free.

Payment Methods: Hotel bills may be paid with credit cards (American Express, Visa, MasterCard, or The Disney Credit Card), traveler's checks, cash, or personal checks. Checks must bear the guest's name and address, be drawn on a U.S. bank, and be accompanied by proper ID (a valid driver's license or a government-issued passport).

Additional Per-Person Charges: Certain charges apply when more than two adults (over 17 years of age) occupy a standard room. The fee is $5 per extra adult per day at Fort Wilderness homes and cabins; $2 per extra adult per day at Fort Wilderness campsites; $10 per extra adult per day at the All-Star resorts; $15 per extra adult per day at Caribbean Beach, Port Orleans, Dixie Landings, and Coronado Springs; and $25 per extra adult per day at all other WDW resorts and at the Swan and Dolphin. Note that in some resorts, an additional bed may be required to sleep an extra adult. If so, the cost for the bed is generally $15.

WDW ID Cards: Issued on arrival at WDW-owned resorts, these cards are among resort guests' most valuable possessions while in Walt Disney World. They entitle you to:

- Theme park admission if you've purchased a Length of Stay Pass.
- Unlimited transportation by bus, monorail, and watercraft.
- Use of many of the roadways within Walt Disney World.
- Charge privileges: If you've left a credit card imprint with your hotel, ID cards may be used (up to certain account limits) to cover purchases in shops, lounges, full-service restaurants, fast-food spots, and some snack carts, as well as recreational fees incurred anywhere in the World.

Note: ID cards are valid for use of transportation facilities through the end of the last day of your stay but are not valid for charging past check-out time. Swan and Dolphin guests may not use their IDs to charge meals at restaurants outside the two hotels or have purchases delivered to their rooms. Other restrictions may apply. Read the information on the cards carefully when checking in.

Rates at Walt Disney World Properties

TRANSPORTATION & ACCOMMODATIONS

	CHARGE FOR SINGLE OR DOUBLE OCCUPANCY		
	Value	Regular	Peak
DELUXE			
BoardWalk Inn			
Rooms (5)	$254–$325	$274–$355	$304–$385
Rooms–Concierge (4)	$395–$465	$425–$495	$455–$530
Suites (6)		Call 934-7639 for prices	
Contemporary			
Rooms–Garden Buildings (5)	$214–$275	$234–$295	$264–$325
Rooms–Tower (5)	$300–$350	$330–$380	$360–$410
Suites (7 to 12)		Call 934-7639 for prices	
Grand Floridian			
Rooms (5)	$299–$370	$319–$390	$349–$420
Rooms–Concierge (5)	$510–$525	$435–$555	$465–$590
Suites (4 to 10)		Call 934-7639 for prices	
Polynesian			
Rooms (5)	$274–$345	$294–$370	$324–$395
Rooms–Concierge (5)	$345–$425	$370–$455	$395–$485
Suites (4 to 6)		Call 934-7639 for prices	
Swan and Dolphin			
Rooms (5)	$275–$330	not applicable	$310–$395
Rooms–Club Level (5)	$405	not applicable	$430
Suites (5 to 10)	$550–$2,600	not applicable	$640–$2,600
Wilderness Lodge			
Rooms (4)	$180–$304	$200–$329	$230–$359
Suites (4 to 6)		Call 934-7639 for prices	
Yacht and Beach Club			
Rooms (5)	$264–$310	$284–$340	$314–$370
Rooms–Concierge* (5)	$395–$430	$425–$460	$455–$490
Suites (5 to 10)		Call 934-7639 for prices	
*Yacht Club only			
HOME AWAY FROM HOME			
Disney's BoardWalk Villas Resort			
Studios (4)	$254–$264	$274–$284	$304–$314
1-BR Villas (4)	$315–$355	$345–$385	$375–$415
2-BR Villas (8)	$440–$480	$555–$595	$679–$729
Grand Villas (12)	$1,150	$1,250	$1,350
Disney's Old Key West Resort			
Studios (4)	$229	$244	$274
1-BR Vacation Home (4)	$305	$325	$355
2-BR Vacation Home (8)	$420	$450	$480
3-BR Grand Villas (12)	$850	$890	$940
Fort Wilderness			
Homes (4 to 6)	$179	$199	$214
Cabins (6)	$204	$229	$249

	CHARGE FOR SINGLE OR DOUBLE OCCUPANCY		
	Value	**Regular**	**Peak**
HOME AWAY FROM HOME			
The Villas at the Disney Institute			
Bungalows (4)	$204	$229	$249
1-BR Townhouses (4)	$245	$265	$280
2-BR Townhouses (6)	$335	$360	$380
Treehouse Villas (6)	$365	$385	$399
Fairway Villas (6 to 8)	$395	$430	$450
Grand Vista Homes (6 to 8)	$1,025–$1,200	$1,025–$1,200	$1,050–$1,250
MODERATE			
Caribbean Beach			
Rooms (4)	$119–$139	$134–$154	$149–$169
Coronado Springs			
Rooms (4)	$119–$139	$134–$154	$149–$169
Suites (4 to 6)		Call 934-7639 for prices	
Dixie Landings			
Rooms (4)	$119–$139	$134–$154	$149–$169
Port Orleans			
Rooms (4)	$119–$139	$134–$154	$149–$169
VALUE			
All-Star Movies, All-Star Music, and All-Star Sports			
Rooms (4)	$74	$89	$94
CAMPGROUND			
Fort Wilderness Campsites			
Sites w/partial hookup (10)	$35	$45	$51
Sites w/full hookup (10)	$39	$55	$61
Preferred Sites (10)	$49	$60	$66

Check-in time: 3 P.M. except at The Villas at the Disney Institute, BoardWalk Villas, All-Star resorts, and Old Key West, where check-in is at 4 P.M. and at Fort Wilderness, where it's 1 P.M. **Check-out time:** 11 A.M. for Fort Wilderness and all hotels.

Value rates apply: January 1, 1999, through February 11, 1999, and August 29, 1999, through December 25, 1999, for all Value and Moderate resorts, and Wilderness Lodge; January 5–15 and May 16 through December 19 for Swan and Dolphin; and January 1, 1999, through February 11, 1999, and July 5, 1999, through December 25, 1999, for all other WDW properties. **Regular rates apply:** April 25, 1999, through August 28, 1999, for all Value and Moderate resorts, and Wilderness Lodge; and April 25, 1999, through July 4, 1999, for all other WDW properties (except Swan and Dolphin). **Peak rates apply:** February 12, 1999, through April 24, 1999, for all WDW properties; and January 16 through May 15 and December 20–31 for Swan and Dolphin. **Holiday rates apply:** December 26, 1999, through December 31, 1999. (Rates are higher during this period—call for information.) These designations in no way reflect park attendance.

Room capacity: Numbers in parentheses reflect maximum occupancy based on existing beds. A trundle bed (which sleeps one) can be rented at select properties for $15 a day. Cribs can be requested for free in most resorts.

Note: The prices provided here were correct at press time, but rates do change, so be sure to double-check with the hotels before setting your final budget.

CALL W-DISNEY (934-7639) FOR RESERVATIONS

TRANSPORTATION & ACCOMMODATIONS

Disney Rates the Resorts

The Walt Disney World rating system helps you choose the hotel, villa, or campsite that best suits your needs. Here's a breakdown of the core amenities, range of room rates, and resorts in each category. For specific pricing, see the chart on pages 46 and 47.

Deluxe ($180 to $485)
- Full-service restaurants, room service
- Bellman luggage service, valet parking
- Swimming pools, beach access
- On-site recreation, such as boat rental
- Most rooms sleep five
- On-site child care programs
- Monorail, boat, or bus transportation to all theme parks

Resorts
- BoardWalk Inn (page 63)
- Contemporary (page 49)
- Grand Floridian Resort and Spa (page 52)
- Polynesian (page 50)
- Swan and Dolphin (page 60)
- Wilderness Lodge (page 54)
- Yacht and Beach Club (page 59)

Home Away From Home ($179 to $1,350)
- Kitchen facilities, pizza delivery
- Luggage service
- Swimming pools
- On-site recreation, such as boat rental
- Front-door parking for your vehicle
- Flexible room arrangements accommodating 4 to 12 guests
- Full-service restaurants
- Bus or boat transportation to theme parks

Resorts
- Disney's BoardWalk Villas Resort (page 63)
- Disney's Old Key West Resort (page 69)
- Fort Wilderness Homes and Fort Wilderness Cabins (page 55)
- The Villas at the Disney Institute (page 67)

Moderate ($119 to $169)
- Full-service restaurants, food courts, limited room service
- Bellman luggage service
- Swimming pools with slides
- On-site recreation, such as bike and boat rental
- Rooms sleep four
- Bus transportation to all theme parks

Resorts
- Caribbean Beach (page 57)
- Coronado Springs (page 73)
- Dixie Landings (page 66)
- Port Orleans (page 65)

Value ($74 to $94)
- Food courts, pizza delivery
- Hourly luggage service
- Swimming pools
- Bus transportation to all theme parks

Resorts
- All-Star Movies (page 71)
- All-Star Music (page 71)
- All-Star Sports (page 71)

Campground ($35 to $66)
- Received perfect ratings from *Trailer Life* magazine and from Woodall's
- Bus transportation to all theme parks

- Fort Wilderness Campground (page 55)

Magic Kingdom Area

Contemporary

Watching the monorail trains disappear into this hotel's enormous 15-story A-frame tower never fails to amaze first-timers. The sleek trains look like long spaceships docking as they slide inside. (Note that guests with non-collapsible strollers or those who use wheelchairs cannot enter the monorail here.)

Passengers, for their part, are impressed by the cavernous lobby, with its tiers of balconies and, at its center, the soaring 90-foot-high, floor-to-ceiling tile mural depicting Native American children, stylized flowers, birds, and other scenes from the Southwest. (Look carefully and you may be able to spot the five-legged goat.)

This imposing structure has 1,041 rooms in its tower and the garden buildings that flank it on either side. There are six shops, three restaurants, three snack bars, two lounges, a marina, a beach, a health club, and more. The pool area incorporates two whirlpools, a water slide, and water jets. The lively Food and Fun Center—a vast area with an arcade and snack bar—is open 24 hours a day. The large convention center offers access to business services. Perhaps the resort's most notable feature is its 15th-floor observation deck. From here guests can enjoy a spectacular bird's-eye view of the Magic Kingdom.

A concierge package is available for guests who stay in the hotel's 14th-floor suites. Amenities include express check-in and check-out, complimentary continental breakfast, hors d'oeuvres and refreshments at night, and nightly turndown service. The 12th Floor Tower Club also provides guests with special concierge privileges. To contact the Contemporary resort, call 824-1000.

ROOMS: Bold colors drive the otherwise uninspired decor of rooms evenly apportioned among the tower and two garden buildings. Rooms in the tower boast private balconies and views of Bay Lake or the Magic Kingdom. Most rooms can accommodate five guests (plus one child under three). Typical units have a day bed and two queen-size beds; some rooms have a king-size bed and a daybed. Connecting rooms may be requested. Bathrooms in the Contemporary resort are spacious and well laid out. A variety of suites, consisting of a living room and one or two bedrooms, can accommodate 7 to 12 people.

WHERE TO EAT: In addition to the many restaurants and snack spots, 24-hour room service provides a wide range of offerings.

California Grill: On the 15th floor. The specialty is California fare, including pizza baked in wood-burning ovens, grilled meats, seafood, and market vegetables. An added treat: the spectacular view of the Magic Kingdom fireworks and sensational sunsets.

Chef Mickey's: Located on the fourth-floor concourse. Mickey and his friends host daily buffets. Breakfast features Mickey Mouse pancakes as well as more traditional items. Dinner offers two carved meats, prime rib, nightly specials, peel-and-eat shrimp, and a variety of entrées, plus a sundae and dessert bar.

Concourse Steakhouse: On the fourth-floor concourse. A full breakfast; burgers, salads, and sandwiches for lunch; steaks, seafood, and pasta for dinner.

Food and Fun Center: On the first floor. Serves light fare 24 hours a day.

WHERE TO DRINK: The Magic Kingdom's no-alcohol policy doesn't trickle over to its nearest neighbor.

California Grill Lounge: On the resort's 15th floor, adjoining the California Grill. Prime views provide a dramatic backdrop for sipping California wines and other drinks, and nibbling on appetizers.

Contemporary Grounds: A lobby coffee bar, near the escalators. Serves cappuccino, espresso, lattes, and other gourmet coffees, as well as biscotti. Free WebTV keeps guests connected to the outside world.

Outer Rim: On the fourth-floor concourse, overlooking Bay Lake. Serves appetizers, cocktails, and specialty drinks.

Sand Bar: This poolside spot offers drinks, fruit plates, and light snacks from the grill.

WHAT TO DO: Volleyball nets are set up on the beach and a basketball court is nearby. Waterskiing and fishing excursions may be arranged (see *Sports* for details).

Boating: Sailboats (including Sunfish and Hobie Waves), canopy boats, Water Mouse boats, and jet boats are available for rent at the marina, near the pool.

Children's Program: The Mouseketeer Clubhouse is open from 4:30 P.M. to midnight for kids ages 4 through 12 (four-hour maximum stay). Cost is $5 per hour per child. Reservations are necessary; call 824-1000, ext. 3897.

Health Club: The Contemporary Fitness Center has modern Nautilus equipment, stair climbers, bicycles, a sauna, lockers, and massage (by appointment).

Salon: Contemporary Resort Salon on the third floor of the tower provides haircuts, facials, manicures, and other services.

Shopping: The fourth-floor concourse is home to several first-class shops. Fantasia sells Disney character merchandise, including plush animals and clothing, for both children and adults. Contemporary Woman offers quality women's clothing (and plenty of bathing suits) in all price ranges, and the adjoining Contemporary Man stocks casual clothes and resortwear. The adjacent Kingdom Jewels Ltd. specializes in jewelry, including Disney character jewelry. Bayview Gifts carries souvenirs and fresh flowers. Concourse Sundries & Spirits has newspapers, magazines, books, snacks, and liquor—just what's needed for a cocktail party on the terrace.

Swimming: In addition to a round quiet pool that is practically on top of Bay Lake, the free-form pool features a 17-foot-high curving slide. Two large whirlpools have been added, one on a peninsula protruding into the pool. Water jets shoot unexpectedly while smaller fountains spout randomly, delighting older and younger kids alike.

Tennis: Disney's Racquet Club, Walt Disney World's premier tennis center, is located near the north wing. It features six state-of-the-art hydrogrid clay courts. Private lessons are available (see *Sports* for details). The shop here has tennis equipment, fashions, and shoes. Racquet restringing is also available.

Video Arcade: On the first floor, the Food and Fun Center boasts everything from Skee-Ball to air hockey, and all the favorites of the pinball-and-electronic-games-playing set. It's one of the best gamerooms at WDW.

TRANSPORTATION: The resort is connected to the TTC and the Magic Kingdom by monorail. Board just above the fourth-floor concourse, inside the atrium area of the tower. From the TTC, Epcot can be reached via monorail, and Typhoon Lagoon and Downtown Disney can be reached by bus. Buses go to the Disney-MGM Studios, Animal Kingdom, and Blizzard Beach. Watercraft travel from the marina to Fort Wilderness, Wilderness Lodge, and River Country.

Polynesian

The Polynesian resort is as close an approximation of the real thing as Walt Disney World's designers could create. The vegetation is lush, and the architecture summons the tropics.

The mood is set by a three-story garden that occupies most of the lobby. Water cascades over craggy volcanic rocks, while coconut palms tower over about 75 different species of tropical and subtropical plants.

The structure that contains this mass of greenery, the Great Ceremonial House, is the central building in the Polynesian complex. The front desk, shops, and most of the restaurants are located here. Flanking the Great Ceremonial House on either side are 11 two- and three-story village longhouses named for various Pacific islands. These structures house the resort's 853 rooms. The monorail stops at

DID YOU KNOW...

The white sand on the beaches near the Polynesian and Grand Floridian and along the Seven Seas Lagoon actually came from the bottom of Bay Lake, the Disney-made lake behind the Contemporary resort.

this hotel, making it an especially convenient place to stay; in fact, it's just a few minutes' ride to the Magic Kingdom.

The Polynesian's concierge service offers such amenities as express check-in and check-out, continental breakfast, cookies and soft drinks every afternoon, hors d'oeuvres and desserts every evening, and access to a lounge with a prime fireworks view. Concierge rooms and suites are located in the Tonga and Bali Hai buildings. The telephone number for the Polynesian resort is 824-2000.

ROOMS: Many rooms, which were completely refurbished in 1998, have balconies, and most have a view of the gardens, Seven Seas Lagoon, or one of the resort's swimming pools; rooms in the Oahu, Moorea, and Pago Pago buildings are the largest. Most rooms have two queen-size beds and a daybed, and can accommodate five guests (plus a child under age three). Connecting or adjoining rooms may be requested. The resort's suites—located exclusively in the Bali Hai building—can accommodate four to six guests. Some have a king-size bed in the bedroom and one queen-size bed in the parlor.

WHERE TO EAT: A variety of specialties are available from room service between 6:30 A.M. and midnight. Also, some interesting eating spots are located here.

Captain Cook's Snack Company: On the lobby level of the Great Ceremonial House. This is a good spot for continental breakfast. Snacks are available 24 hours a day.

Kona Cafe: On the second floor of the Great Ceremonial House. This new family restaurant serves lunch and dinner with a decidedly Asian flair, while the breakfast menu is filled with more traditional American selections. An expansive coffee bar provides the perfect capper to any meal.

'Ohana: On the second floor of the Great Ceremonial House. 'Ohana serves family-style dinners roasted in the World's largest fire pit. Minnie hosts a character breakfast every morning.

WHERE TO DRINK: The Polynesian theme has inspired a whole raft of deceptively potent potables. As might be expected, both the drink offerings and the settings in which they are served are as tropical as they come.

Barefoot Bar: Adjoining the Swimming Pool Lagoon, and open seasonally.

Tambu: There's a tropical air about this lounge adjoining 'Ohana. The bar serves appetizers and exotic specialty drinks.

WHAT TO DO: A wide range of activities are available at the Polynesian resort, including a scenic jogging path. Waterskiing and fishing excursions can also be arranged (see *Sports* for details).

Boating: Several types of sailboats (including catamarans), speedy little Water Mouse boats, canopy boats, and pontoon boats are available for rent at the marina.

Children's Program: The Never Land Club is a supervised evening activity program for children ages 4 through 12. The program operates between 5 P.M. and midnight, with a kids' buffet from 6 P.M. to 8 P.M. The cost is $8 per hour. Reservations are necessary; call 939-3463.

Playground: The playground near the Swimming Pool Lagoon features apparatuses for climbing, swinging, and sliding.

Shopping: News from Civilization, on the first floor of the Great Ceremonial House, is the locale for hotel and Polynesian items, as well as newspapers, magazines, film, sun care products, and gifts. Robinson Crusoe, Esq. sells casual sportswear and swimwear for men; the Polynesian Princess stocks brightly colored resort fashions, bathing suits, and accessories for women. Upstairs, Trader Jack's sells a variety of

51

Disney souvenirs, toys, fashions, and other items; the Grog Hut has food, liquor, wine, beer, soft drinks, and other fixings for an impromptu party.

Swimming: There are two main pools here: the elliptical East Pool, in the shadow of the Oahu, Tonga, Hawaii, Bora Bora, and Moorea buildings, and the larger free-form Swimming Pool Lagoon, found closer to the marina and main beach. The latter is framed by a large cluster of boulders that forms a water slide much beloved by youngsters; to get to the ladder they must duck underneath a waterfall. Toddlers have their own shallow wading pool. The pools feature underwater music.

Video Arcade: Moana Mickey's Arcade has a large assortment of video games. It is located on the eastern edge of the property near the Oahu guest building.

TRANSPORTATION: The resort is on the monorail line to the Magic Kingdom and the TTC; the platform is on the second floor of the Great Ceremonial House. From the TTC, Epcot is accessible by another monorail, and Typhoon Lagoon and Downtown Disney can be reached by bus. Buses go to the Disney-MGM Studios, Animal Kingdom, and Blizzard Beach. Launches leave from the Polynesian dock for the Magic Kingdom and the Grand Floridian.

Shades of Green

This 228-room resort (formerly the Disney Inn) is situated near the Grand Floridian but is not linked with the monorail system. It is a recreational retreat for active and retired military personnel and their families, members of the reserves and the National Guard, and Department of Defense employees.

The resort features two tennis courts, two pools, a small health club, restaurant, bar and lounge, gift shop, arcade, laundry facilities, and free transportation around WDW.

Room rates are based on military or civilian grade. Discounted Length of Stay Passes are also available. The property's three golf courses—the Palm, the Magnolia, and Oak Trail—are open to all WDW guests (see *Sports* for details). All other activities are for hotel guests and their families only. The telephone number for Shades of Green is 824-3400. For reservations, call 824-3600.

Grand Floridian Resort & Spa

At the turn of the century, Standard Oil magnate Henry M. Flagler saw the realization of his dream: The railroad he had built to "civilize" Florida had spawned along its right-of-way an empire of grand hotels, lavish estates, prominent families, and opulent lifestyles. High society blossomed in winter, as the likes of John D. Rockefeller and Teddy Roosevelt checked into the Royal

Poinciana in Palm Beach, enjoying the sea breezes from the oceanside suites.

The hotel later burned to the ground, and Florida's golden era faded with the Depression. But nearly a century after Flagler first made Florida a fashionable resort destination, Walt Disney World opened a grand hotel—a 900-room Victorian structure with gabled roofs and carved moldings—on 40 acres of Seven Seas Lagoon shorefront, between the Magic Kingdom and the Polynesian resort.

Like its late-19th-century predecessors, the Grand Floridian resort boasts abundant verandas, ceiling fans, intricate latticework and balustrades, turrets, towers, and red-shingle roofs. And yet, it offers all the advantages of 20th-century living—including monorail service. With five restaurants, two lounges, five shops, and an arcade, plus a child care facility, convention center, swimming pool, marina, and full-service health club and spa, the Grand Floridian is not only a grand hotel but a complete resort.

The main building houses the Grand Lobby, a palatial space soaring five stories to a ceiling of stained-glass domes and glittering chandeliers. Palms and an aviary decorate the sitting area; an open-cage elevator carries guests to the shops and restaurants on the second floor. The turn-of-the-century theme is everywhere, from the costumes worn by the employees to the shop displays, restaurants, and room decor. The telephone number for the Grand Floridian resort is 824-3000.

ROOMS: The rooms are decorated as they might have been a century ago—in soft colors, with printed wall coverings, marble-topped sinks, ceiling fans, and Victorian woodwork. Amenities include hair dryers, bathrobes, minibars, nightly turndown service, and daily newspaper delivery.

The main building houses concierge rooms and suites; lodge buildings, each four and five stories high, contain standard rooms, slightly smaller "attic" chambers, and suites. Most rooms measure about 400 square feet and include two queen-size

DID YOU KNOW...

Movie buffs may find the Grand Floridian strangely familiar. Its design is based, in part, on that of the Del Coronado Hotel in California. Scenes from the classic film *Some Like It Hot* were shot there.

beds, plus a daybed, to accommodate five people. Many rooms have terraces. Suites include a parlor, plus one, two, or three bedrooms; there are king-size or queen-size beds in the bedrooms. Most of the 15 honeymoon rooms, located on the second, third, fourth, and fifth floors, enjoy wonderful views. In the main building, access to

the upper three concierge-suite levels is restricted by private elevator.

On the third floor, the concierge desks offer such services as reservations and information. The fourth floor features a quiet seating area where continental breakfast and evening refreshments are served. Concierge service is also available in lodge building 6.

WHERE TO EAT: Most of the restaurants and lounges are located on the first two floors of the main building. Room service offers a wide assortment of items 24 hours a day.

Cítricos: On the Alcazar Level (second floor). The largest of the hotel's restaurants is also the newest. It features market-fresh Mediterranean fare with Floridian influences that changes with the seasons. Open for dinner. Some seating affords excellent views of the nightly fireworks presentation at the Magic Kingdom.

Gasparilla Grill & Games: This 24-hour snack bar on the first floor offers light items for all-day dining and snacking, plus a selection of video games.

Grand Floridian Cafe: Located on the first floor. Its peaches-and-cream color scheme and veranda-like feel make this the best place to get a quick, sit-down breakfast. Lunch and dinner are also available.

Narcoossee's: This casual restaurant and bar has a romantic shoreline location overlooking the Seven Seas Lagoon. The ever-changing menu includes such staples as roast lamb chops and Florida seafood. The partially open kitchen is the focal point of the restaurant. Guests can sip wine and cocktails on the veranda.

1900 Park Fare: A buffet restaurant on the Windsor Level (first floor), decorated with carousel horses, plants, and Big Bertha—the carnival organ. Breakfast and dinner with the characters are served daily.

Victoria & Albert's: On the second floor. Walt Disney World's finest dining establishment, it is named after the former queen and prince consort of England. Elegant meals are served to no more than 60 guests; service is impeccable. Jackets are required for men and priority seating is a must.

WHERE TO DRINK: Guests will find the refined lounges here to be nice escapes. Cocktail service is provided in the lobby from 4 P.M to 11 P.M. daily. Cítricos and Narcoosee's both have lounges.

Garden View: This pleasant spot on the first floor offers a view of the hotel's lush, landscaped garden and pool area. Afternoon tea is served.

Mizner's: Named after the eccentric, wildly prolific architect who defined much of the flavor of Palm Beach County, this bar is on the second floor.

St. John's Pool Bar: The place for pool and beachside refreshments, this spot features a variety of snacks and beverages.

WHAT TO DO: The Grand Floridian offers all the recreational facilities of a typical beachside resort—and much more. Waterskiing and fishing excursions can be arranged (see the *Sports* chapter for details). Volleyball equipment is available.

Boating: Sailboats (including catamarans), canopy boats, and Water Mouse boats are available for rent at Captain's Shipyard Marina. The *Grand 1* yacht (complete with a captain and first mate) can be rented for $275 an hour.

Children's Program: The Mouseketeer Club is a supervised program for kids ages 4 through 12. It's open from 4:30 P.M. to midnight; the cost is $5 per hour for each child. There is a four-hour maximum. Reservations are required; phone 824-2985.

Health Club: The health club boasts state-of-the-art exercise equipment, plus men's and women's saunas, whirlpools, and steamrooms.

Playground: Adjacent to the Mouseketeer Clubhouse, the play area includes swings and a climbing apparatus.

Salon: The Ivy Trellis salon offers a full line of hair care services.

Shopping: On the first floor (Windsor Level) of the main building is Summer Lace, a women's apparel shop, and Sandy Cove, where guests may purchase gifts and sundries. One floor up at the Alcazar Level is the M. Mouse Mercantile character shop, a Bally leather-goods store, and Commander Porter's, a men's shop.

Spa: The spa offers 16 treatment rooms for massage, herbal wraps, and aromatherapy. Some spa programs are available for children.

Swimming: In addition to the swimming pool just outside the main building, the hotel has a whirlpool and its own white-sand beach along Seven Seas Lagoon.

Tennis: There are two clay courts for play. Reservations are suggested; call WDW-PLAY (939-5729).

Video Arcade: Gasparilla Grill & Games is located on the first floor of the main building.

TRANSPORTATION: The Grand Floridian is connected to the TTC and the Magic Kingdom by monorail. The platform is located outside the hotel under an awning on the second floor. From the TTC, Epcot is accessible by another monorail, and Typhoon Lagoon and Downtown Disney can be reached by bus. Buses go to the Disney-MGM Studios, Animal Kingdom, and Blizzard Beach. Launches leave from Tocoi Landing for the Magic Kingdom and the Polynesian.

Wilderness Lodge

This resort recalls both the spirit of the early American West and the feeling of the National Park Service lodges built during the early 1900s. These grand structures architecturally unified the elements of the unspoiled wilderness parks, kept harmony with nature, and incorporated the culture of Native Americans. The Wilderness Lodge artfully recaptures this rustic charm.

The resort is located between the Contemporary and Fort Wilderness on Bay Lake. The lobby is in an eight-story, log-structured building. Massive bundled log columns support a series of trusses, while two Pacific Northwest

totem poles soar 55 feet into the air. Four levels of corridors surround the lobby, providing access to guestrooms, sitting nooks, and terraces. Note that the resort is not accessible by monorail. The telephone number for the Wilderness Lodge is 824-3200.

ROOMS: The 728 guestrooms are located in a U-shaped building. Most rooms have two queen-size beds, a table and chairs, and a balcony. Some have a queen-size bed and a bunk bed. The bathrooms have separate vanity areas with double sinks. The wallpaper has a Native American–motif border, and the colorful bedspreads and plaid curtains add to the decor. Images of wildlife complete the theme.

WHERE TO EAT: The Northwest theme is carried out with flair in the hotel's eateries. Room service is available from 7 A.M. to 11 A.M.; dinner selections are available from 4 P.M. to midnight.

Artist Point: Decorated with art representing painters who first chronicled the Northwest landscape, this fine dining spot features salmon, game, steaks, seafood, and wines from the Pacific Northwest. Winnie the Pooh and friends host breakfast daily.

Lobby Coffee Bar: Continental breakfast is served, and evenings bring coffee and hot chocolate to this seasonal fireside spot.

Roaring Fork: Fast food is available here, next to the hotel's arcade.

Whispering Canyon Cafe: A casual, family-style restaurant with all-day dining.

WHERE TO DRINK: Two spots are available for a relaxing break.

Territory: This lounge honors the survey parties who led the move westward. In addition to a light lunch, specialty drinks, microbrewed beer, and espresso are served.

Trout Pass: The poolside bar features a variety of specialty drinks and snacks.

WHAT TO DO: A resort unto itself, it offers a plethora of activities. Teton Boat & Bike Rental is located in the Colonel's Cabin by the lake. Volleyball equipment is available. Waterskiing and fishing excursions on Bay Lake may also be arranged (see *Sports* for details). Or consider taking one of the two daily guided tours of the lodge.

Biking: Bicycles can be rented for a ride around the resort. A three-quarter-mile path leads to Fort Wilderness and River Country.

Boating: A variety of watercraft, including Water Mouse boats, canopy boats, sailboats, and pontoon boats, can be rented for a trip around Bay Lake.

Children's Program: The Cubs Den is a supervised dining and entertainment club for kids ages 4 through 12. Supervised activities, including Disney movies and western-themed arts and crafts, occupy kids from 5 P.M. to midnight. Cost is $7 per hour per child, including dinner. Call 939-3463 for reservations, which are required.

Playground: The playground is near the Teton Boat & Bike Rental.

Shopping: Wilderness Lodge Mercantile stocks necessities and sundries as well as a line of clothing with the Wilderness Lodge logo. A selection of Disney character merchandise is also featured.

Swimming: The pool looks as if it were carved from the rockscape. A beach, a kiddie pool, two whirlpools, and a geyser complete the design. Fire Rock Geyser erupts on the hour from early morning until 10 P.M.

Video Arcade: The Roaring Fork Arcade features about 30 games to keep kids occupied.

TRANSPORTATION: Boats go to the Magic Kingdom, Contemporary, and Fort Wilderness. Buses go to Epcot, the Disney-MGM Studios, Animal Kingdom, Blizzard Beach, and the TTC. From the TTC, transfer to buses for Typhoon Lagoon and Downtown Disney. It's possible to ride a bike to Fort Wilderness and River Country.

Fort Wilderness Resort & Campground

The very existence of this canal-crossed expanse—with more than 700 acres of cypress and pine—always surprises visitors who come to Walt Disney World expecting to find nothing more than theme parks.

Tucked among the campsites are 408 air-conditioned Wilderness Cabins and Homes available for rent, complete with daily maid service. The cost is comparable to that of some of the more expensive rooms at Disney hotels. The telephone number for the Fort Wilderness resort is 934-7639.

CAMPSITES: Fort Wilderness has 784 traditional sites. They feature electricity hookups (30/50–amp), water, sanitary disposal, and cable television. Partial-hookup campsites supply electricity and water hookups only. All campsites are bordered by wilderness and feature a paved driveway pad, picnic table, and charcoal grill. Most loops have at least one air-conditioned comfort station equipped with restrooms, private showers, an ice machine, phones, and a laundry room. A site allows for occupancy by up to ten. Each site has room

Hot Tip

Nonsmoking rooms and rooms equipped for guests with disabilities are available at all Walt Disney World resorts.

for one car (in addition to the camping vehicle). Other cars can be parked in the main lot.

The various campground areas are designated by numbers. The 100–500 loops are closest to the beach, the Settlement Trading Post, and Pioneer Hall. The 1500–2000 loops are farthest away from the beach and many other Fort Wilderness activities, but they are quieter and more private. Pets are welcome at certain campsites for a nightly charge of $3.

WILDERNESS CABINS: These woodland dwellings offer a rustic vacation escape. The interiors of the cozy six-person log-cabin-like buildings are decorated with wilderness accents. Each of the 249 cabins is shaded by a pine canopy. Cabins include two TVs, a VCR, full bath, hair dryer, iron, a large deck, picnic table, and charcoal grill.

WILDERNESS HOMES: The 159 Wilderness Homes here provide all the advantages of villa accommodations—with woodsy surroundings to boot. There are two types of homes. One model sleeps four adults and two children; it has a bedroom with a double bed, a bunk bed, plus a separate vanity area and a spacious living room with a pull-down double bed and a ceiling fan. Other trailers sleep four, with a double bed in the bedroom and a pull-down double bed in the living room. Both types come with a complete bathroom, TV, picnic table, and charcoal grill.

Note: No extra camping equipment is permitted on the site; all guests must be accommodated in a Wilderness Home or Cabin. (For complete price information, see pages 46–47.)

WHERE TO EAT: There are a couple of options, but most people cook here. Groceries and supplies are available at the Meadow Trading Post and the Settlement Trading Post (8 A.M. to 10 P.M. in winter, to 11 P.M. in summer). Gooding's supermarket is located at the Crossroads of Lake Buena Vista.

Trail's End Buffeteria: A log-walled, cafeteria inside Pioneer Hall, where home-style fare is served for breakfast, lunch, and dinner. Pizza is an option from 9:30 P.M. to 11 P.M. nightly. Beer and wine are available.

WHERE TO DRINK: Cocktails are served at **Crockett's Tavern** in Pioneer Hall.

FAMILY ENTERTAINMENT AFTER DARK: The Hoop-Dee-Doo Musical Revue is presented three times nightly. We recommend making reservations well in advance by calling WDW-DINE (939-3463). There's also a nightly campfire program held near the Meadow Trading Post. (For details, see *Everything Else in the World* and *Good Meals, Great Times*.)

WHAT TO DO: More activities are available at Fort Wilderness than at almost any other area in the World. There are pools, tennis courts, bikes to rent, trails to hike, horses to ride, even a museum to visit. There are two arcades, too: Davy Crockett's Arcade in Pioneer Hall and Daniel Boone's at the Meadow Trading Post.

All Fort Wilderness activities are described in detail in the *Everything Else in the World* and *Sports* chapters.

TRANSPORTATION: Buses circulating at 20-minute intervals provide transportation within the campground, while buses and watercraft connect Fort Wilderness to the rest of the World. The Magic Kingdom, the Contemporary, and the Wilderness Lodge are most efficiently reached via watercraft that depart regularly from the marina. Buses make the trip from the Settlement Depot to Blizzard Beach. To get to other WDW points, take a bus from the Fort Wilderness visitor parking lot to the TTC. Here, change to a monorail for Epcot or take another bus for the Disney-MGM Studios, Animal Kingdom, Typhoon Lagoon, and Downtown Disney.

Electric golf carts and bikes can be rented at the Bike Barn as alternative means of getting around within the campground. Call 824-2742 for reservations.

Epcot Area

Caribbean Beach

This colorful hotel is set on 200 acres southeast of Epcot and near the Disney-MGM Studios. It is composed of five brightly colored "villages" surrounding a 45-acre lake called Barefoot Bay. Each village is identified with a different Caribbean island—Martinique, Barbados, Trinidad, Aruba, and Jamaica—and features pastel walls, white railings, and vividly colored metal roofs. There are 2,112 rooms in all, making Caribbean Beach one of the largest hotels in the United States.

The villages consist of a cluster of two-story buildings, a swimming pool, a guest laundry, and a lakefront stretch of white-sand beach. Guests check in at the Custom House, a reception building that immediately projects the feeling of a tropical resort. Decor, furnishings, and staff costumes all reflect the Caribbean theme. Old Port Royale, a complex located near the center of the property, evokes images of an island market. Stone walls, pirates' cannons, and tropical birds and flowers add to the atmosphere. The area houses the resort's food court, restaurant and lounge, an arcade, and two shops.

The port opens onto a lakeside recreation area that includes a pool with waterfalls and a slide; the main beach; the Barefoot Bay Boat Yard and Bike Works, where boats and bicycles may be rented; a 1.4-mile promenade around the lake that's perfect for biking, walking, or jogging; and Parrot Cay Island, an area in the middle of Barefoot Bay. It should come as no surprise that children love it here. The telephone number for the Caribbean Beach resort is 934-3400.

ROOMS: Rooms are located in two-story buildings in each island village. A typical 340-square-foot room has two double beds and can sleep up to four. The rooms here are a bit larger than standard rooms at Disney's other moderately priced resorts, and the bathrooms are amply sized. Rooms are decorated in tones softer than the colors found on the exterior. Each room has a minibar and coffeemaker. A note for the budget-conscious: All rooms here are identical in terms of size and comfort, and the only difference between the most and least expensive is the view.

WHERE TO EAT: A full-service eatery called Captain's Tavern and a food court are located in Old Port Royale. Limited room service (pizza, chicken in a basket, and sandwiches) is available from 4 P.M. to midnight.

Bridgetown Broiler: Spit-roasted chicken and home-style meals are menu highlights.

Captain's Tavern: The menu at Old Port Royale restaurant includes prime rib, baked chicken, and a catch of the day. Tropical drinks, wine, beer, and cocktails are served.

Cinnamon Bay Bakery: Freshly baked rolls, croissants, and pastries are available in addition to ice cream and other treats.

Kingston Pasta Shop: A variety of pasta dishes is served.

Montego's Deli: Soups, salads, and cold sandwiches are offered.

Port Royale Hamburger Shop: Hot sandwiches and burgers are on the menu.

Royale Pizza Shop: Very good pizza is available by the slice or the pie, along with a variety of hot and cold pasta dishes.

WHERE TO DRINK: The tropical Caribbean theme is carried out in the specialty drinks found at **Banana Cabana**. Light snacks are also available at this poolside spot.

WHAT TO DO: There are many recreational opportunities. The 1.4-mile promenade around the lake is perfect for walking, biking, or a morning jog.

Biking: Bikes can be rented at the Barefoot Bay Boat Yard and Bike Works.

Boating: Sailboats, Water Mouse boats, canopy boats, canoes, and pedal boats are available for rent at the Barefoot Bay Boat Yard and Bike Works for use on the resort's scenic 45-acre lake.

Playgrounds: Playgrounds are located on Parrot Cay Island, as well as on the Barbados, Jamaica, and Trinidad beaches.

Shopping: At Old Port Royale, there's the Calypso Straw Market, which carries items with the Caribbean Beach resort logo and a variety of island-themed goods. Calypso Trading Post stocks a large selection of character merchandise and sundries.

Swimming: Each village has its own pool, and the main pool has a waterfall and a slide in a Caribbean-themed setting, conjuring up images of pirates and their swashbuckling adventures on the high seas.

Video Arcade: Goombay Games at Old Port Royale offers a selection of games.

TRANSPORTATION: Buses go to the Magic Kingdom, Epcot, the Disney-MGM Studios, Animal Kingdom, and Blizzard Beach. Other bus routes lead to Downtown Disney and Typhoon Lagoon.

Meetings & Conventions

Convention centers at Walt Disney World range in size from 20,000 to over 200,000 square feet. The Dolphin's center, featuring an exhibit hall and an executive boardroom, is the largest; the Swan provides additional space. The Contemporary has three ballrooms and a spacious pre-function area with lots of natural light. The convention center at the Yacht and Beach Club is reminiscent of a grand turn-of-the-century New England town meeting hall. The Grand Floridian has a lavish center with silk brocade walls. The BoardWalk offers a smaller conference area with a lakeside gazebo for outdoor events. And Coronado Springs, the first moderately priced Disney resort to offer convention facilities, boasts the largest hotel ballroom in the United States.

Among the unique services available to Disney conventioneers is the use of Disney characters and performers for events. Special events can even be held in the parks. Resort business centers have clerical staffs and computers, in addition to faxing and photocopying equipment. (These services are available to all resort guests.)

Those interested in scheduling a convention should call 828-3200 for reservations or information. Organizers are advised to book their events six months in advance, especially for large groups. Keep in mind that the busiest times are January, May, September, and October.

Yacht & Beach Club

The New England seaside exists at Walt Disney World in the form of the Yacht and Beach Club. Situated just west of Epcot, the hotels, designed by noted architect Robert A. M. Stern, are set around a 25-acre lake. The adjacent properties share most facilities—including a convention center offering access to business services—and transportation options.

The Yacht Club's design evokes images of the New England seashore hotels of the 1880s. Guests enter the five-story oyster-gray clapboard building along a wooden-planked bridge. Hardwood floors, millwork, and brass enhance the nautical theme. A lighthouse on the pier serves as a beacon to welcome guests back to the hotel from WDW attractions. To reach the Yacht Club by telephone, call 934-7000.

Distance from the ocean is irrelevant at the sand- and surf-focused Beach Club resort, approached along an entrance drive flanked by oak trees. A patterned walkway leads past a croquet court to beachside cabanas on the white-sand shore. Guests are met by hosts and hostesses dressed in colorful beach resort costumes of the 1870s. The telephone number for the Beach Club resort is 934-8000.

ROOMS: The rooms at the Yacht Club are spacious and decorated in a nautical motif. The Beach Club's rooms are also spacious and, naturally, reflect a beach motif. In each room the furniture is white, and the headboard design on the one king-size bed or two queen-size beds incorporates small ship's wheels. Some rooms have daybeds. Most of the suites have a king-size bed as well as two sleeper sofas. In the large bathrooms there is a separate vanity with double sinks and silver mirrors trimmed with brass. Each room has a ceiling fan, iron with board, hair dryer, newspaper delivery, minibar, wall-mounted

makeup mirror, table (complete with checkerboard top), and two chairs. Chess and checkers sets can be provided. Concierge rooms are available.

WHERE TO EAT: The themes of yachting and the sea play an important role in the restaurants that are found at their respective resorts. A wide variety of menu items are available from room service 24 hours a day.

Beaches & Cream Soda Shop: A classic American soda fountain where shakes, malts, and sundaes are the prime lures. The other specialty is the Fenway Park Burger, served as a single, double, triple, or home run. (The shop is located between the two resorts.)

Cape May Cafe: An indoor clambake is held here at the Beach Club each night. The varied buffet features several types of clams and mussels, plus pasta and chicken. Lobster is available for an extra charge. A character breakfast is presented daily.

Hurricane Hanna's Grill: Burgers, hot dogs, sausages, and other snacks are served at this spot on the shores of Stormalong Bay. A full bar is also located here, and poolside beverage service is available.

Yacht Club Galley: The buffet breakfast is bountiful. Breakfast, lunch, and dinner are available from an à la carte menu.

Yachtsman Steakhouse: Select cuts of aged beef are the specialty of the house. Fresh seafood and poultry are also offered.

WHERE TO DRINK: The lounges in both resorts offer a variety of specialty drinks in relaxing seaside settings.

Ale and Compass: This Yacht Club lobby lounge, featuring specialty coffees and drinks, provides a nice respite after a long day.

Crew's Cup: The place to try a wide assortment of beers shipped in from the world's seaports before dining at Yachtsman Steakhouse next door.

Martha's Vineyard: This lounge at the Beach Club offers selections from American and international vineyards, served in sample sizes and by the glass or bottle.

Rip Tide: The Beach Club lobby lounge features a variety of California wines, wine coolers, and frosty concoctions.

WHAT TO DO: There is enough to do here to fill an entire vacation. A sand volleyball court and a croquet court may be found on the Beach Club side of the property. Equipment for both pursuits is available at no cost at the Ship Shape health club. The Fantasia Gardens Miniature Golf complex is close at hand, and guided two-hour fishing excursions can be arranged (see *Sports* for details). Free 45-minute garden tours are available throughout the week. And last, but not least, the BoardWalk entertainment district is just a short trip around the lake.

Boating: Pedal boats, Hydro Bikes, canopy boats, and Water Mouse boats are available for rent at the Bayside Marina.

Children's Program: The Sandcastle Club, for children 4 through 12, is available from 4:30 P.M. to midnight. Cost is $5 per hour for each child. Reservations are required; call 939-3463. Toys, videos, games, and computers are on hand to keep children entertained. Milk and snacks are also served.

Health Club: The Ship Shape health club features Nautilus and cardiovascular machines, sauna, whirlpool, steamroom, and massage (by appointment). The health club is open to all WDW resort guests over the age of 13.

Playground: A small play area with a slide and climbing apparatus is located by the pool.

Salon: The Periwig salon for men and women is located in the central area.

Shopping: At the Yacht Club, Fittings & Fairings Clothes and Notions is an all-purpose shop offering nautical fashions, character merchandise, and sundries. At the Beach Club, Atlantic Wear and Wardrobe Emporium features a similar selection of goods (albeit with a beach theme).

Swimming: Between the marina and the beach is the centerpiece of the dual resort — Stormalong Bay, a three-acre pool that's really a mini water park. There is a lagoon expressly for relaxed bathing, and another "active" lagoon with currents, jets, and sand-bottomed areas. Several whirlpools are scattered throughout the area. Adjacent to the main pool is a shipwreck, where guests can enjoy a variety of unique water slides. An unguarded quiet pool and whirlpool can be found at the far end of each hotel.

Tennis: There are two lighted tennis courts on the Beach Club side of the property. Rental equipment is available at the Ship Shape health club.

Video Arcade: Lafferty Place Arcade, located in the central area, has about 60 video games and pinball machines.

TRANSPORTATION: Guests ride boats or walk to the nearby Epcot entrance (beside the France pavilion). Watercraft go to the Disney-MGM Studios. Buses go to the Magic Kingdom, Animal Kingdom, Downtown Disney, Typhoon Lagoon, and Blizzard Beach.

Swan & Dolphin

These massive sister resorts, situated on the shores of Crescent Lake, can easily be distinguished by the 46-foot swan and 56-foot dolphin statues that top them. The waterfalls, lush rows of palm trees, and beachfront location all reflect the tropical Florida landscape that was their inspiration. Both hotels were designed by noted architect Michael Graves as prime examples of "entertainment architecture." The rolling turquoise waves on the colored facade of the Swan's 12-story main building and two 7-story wings are clearly evidence of this design, as is the Dolphin's exterior mural, which features a playful banana-leaf pattern. The soaring 27-story triangular tower at the center of the Dolphin, once honored by *Progressive Architecture* magazine, is flanked by four 9-story guestroom wings.

The resorts share extensive convention facilities, many recreational options, and a host of restaurants. The Swan and Dolphin are operated by Westin and ITT Sheraton, respectively, but are treated as Walt Disney World resorts; guests here enjoy most WDW resort benefits. The phone number for the Swan is 934-3000; for the Dolphin it's 934-4000. Reservations can be made by calling 800-227-1500 or by visiting the Swan and Dolphin Web site at *www.swandolphin.com*.

ROOMS: The corridors outside the Swan guestrooms feature patterned carpets and murals on the walls that extend the wave theme from its exterior design. Inside, the rooms are decorated in shades of coral and

turquoise, and they feature such whimsical touches as lamps in the shape of birds and pineapples painted on the dressers. Each has one king-size or two queen-size beds; safes and minibars are among the amenities. There are 45 concierge rooms on the 11th and 12th floors, and 64 suites.

The 1,509 rooms at the Dolphin, including 136 suites, are decorated in a lighthearted fashion, with lamps in the shape of palm trees and colorful bedspreads and curtains. All feature two double beds or a king-size bed, as well as minibars, vanity dressing areas, irons and ironing boards, and coffee-makers. Concierge rooms are located in the main building. There are rooms equipped for guests with disabilities, and nonsmoking rooms are available at both resorts.

WHERE TO EAT: In addition to many restaurant choices, 24-hour room service provides an extensive all-day dining menu.

Cabana Bar & Grill: This full-service pool-side spot near the Dolphin serves burgers, sandwiches, yogurt, and fruit. The full bar serves specialty drinks.

Coral Cafe: Buffets, as well as à la carte selections, are served during breakfast, lunch, and dinner in a casual setting at the Dolphin.

Dolphin Fountain: Homemade ice cream is the specialty here. Huge sundaes, shakes, malts, and burgers are also offered.

Garden Grove Cafe: This Swan eatery features a greenhouse atmosphere, and serves breakfast and lunch daily. At dinner, the restaurant transforms into Gulliver's Grill. The theme is played out with exaggerated serving utensils, and steak and seafood entrées with imaginative names like Blushklooshen (red snapper). A buffet breakfast with the characters is held on Saturday, while a character dinner takes place four nights a week.

Harry's Safari Bar & Grille: This festive Dolphin eatery features grilled beef, poultry, and seafood; a character brunch takes place on Sundays.

Juan & Only's: Authentic Mexican food is served at this Dolphin hot spot. The atmosphere is festive, filled with warm hues and rich fabrics of old Mexico.

Palio: A pleasant Italian bistro, located at the Swan, featuring veal specialties, home-made pasta, and brick-oven pizza. There are tasty daily specials and live entertainment.

Splash Grill: A poolside cafe near the Swan serving breakfast, lunch, dinner, and snacks. A full-service bar is also located here.

Tubbi's: A cafeteria with a little flair. The checkerboard design makes this a pleasant place for a quick meal at the Dolphin resort. The 24-hour convenience store here sells snacks and sundries.

WHERE TO DRINK: Between the two resorts, it's easy to find a nice spot for a cocktail.

Copa Banana: The tabletops are shaped like slices of fruit, and the tropical atmosphere makes this a lively place for a drink. Deejay music, a dance floor, karaoke, and eight large-screen televisions provide the entertainment at this Dolphin fun spot.

Harry's Safari Bar: Pull up a stool and enjoy the junglelike atmosphere and frosty drinks. Located at the Dolphin.

Lobby Court: This spot at the Swan offers a respite from the hubbub. Enjoy gourmet coffees with fresh pastries in the morning and wine and specialty drinks at night in a European-style bistro setting.

Kimonos: The Asian decor helps make this Swan lounge an inviting place for sake, sushi, and other Japanese specialties.

Only's Bar & Jail: Patrons at the companion lounge to the Dolphin's Juan & Only's restaurant can enjoy the warm atmosphere here while sampling margaritas, sangria, rare tequilas, and beers from Mexico.

WHAT TO DO: The Swan and Dolphin share a multitude of recreation options. Volleyball nets and hammocks are set up on the beach. The Fantasia Gardens Miniature Golf complex and BoardWalk are nearby.

Special Room Requests

Central Reservations accepts requests for rooms with particular views or in certain locations. Agents will do their best to accommodate such requests but cannot guarantee they will be able to fulfill every wish. Call W-DISNEY (934-7639).

Boating: Pedal boats and Hydro Bikes are available for rent on the white-sand beach between the Swan and Dolphin.

Children's Program: Camp Dolphin, open to children 4 through 12, offers supervised activities from 1:30 P.M. to 4 P.M. The cost is $12 per child per hour. The Dinner Club (within Camp Dolphin) is open from 6 P.M. to 11 P.M. It costs $45 for the first child, $30 for a second child, and $20 for each additional child.

Health Clubs: A branch of Body By Jake (run by the famous fitness guru Jake Steinfeld) is near the pool area at the Dolphin.

State-of-the-art equipment is available, as are personal trainers. There are aerobics classes (including water aerobics), a sauna, steam room, large whirlpool, and massage therapists. There's also a smaller health club with basic exercise equipment near Splash Grill.

Playground: A play area with a slide, swings, wooden chain bridge, sandbox, and several jungle gyms is located next to the grotto pool.

Salon: The Niki Bryan shop at the Dolphin provides a full line of services, including haircuts, manicures, and pedicures.

Shopping: Disney Cabanas, located in the lobby of the Swan, features men's and women's fashions, character merchandise, and sundries. Four specialty shops are located at the Dolphin. A large selection of Cartier and other brand-name watches can be found at Brittany Jewels. Indulgences allows chocolate lovers the chance to sample some tasty concoctions. Statements of Fashion offers resortwear for men and women. Daisy's Garden is the place to find character goods at the Dolphin.

Swimming: A large rectangular pool near the Dolphin is perfect for swimming laps, a themed grotto pool with a slide lies between the Swan and Dolphin, a small rectangular pool is situated near the Swan, and several whirlpools are scattered around the area.

Tennis: Four hard-surface tennis courts are located behind the pool area closest to the Dolphin. They are lighted for night play and are open 24 hours a day.

Video Arcades: A room full of video games is located near Tubbi's. Another can be found adjacent to the pool.

TRANSPORTATION: Guests ride boats or walk to Epcot's entrance near the France pavilion. Boats make the trip over to the Disney-MGM Studios. Buses go to the Magic Kingdom, Animal Kingdom, Downtown Disney, Typhoon Lagoon, and Blizzard Beach.

BoardWalk Inn & Villas

The enchantment of a bygone era is recaptured in the BoardWalk. The resort combines a waterside entertainment complex with deluxe hotel accommodations and vacation villas. Dining, recreation, shopping, and entertainment venues line the boardwalk, and twinkling lights trim the buildings. The ambience continues throughout, with intricately detailed architecture featuring sherbet-colored facades, flagged turrets, and striped awnings, all reminiscent of the turn of the century. The BoardWalk resort is adjacent to Epcot's International Gateway and connected via walkway. The telephone number for BoardWalk is 939-5100.

ROOMS: Accommodations here evoke the charm of early eastern seaboard inns. All have private balconies or patios. The Board-Walk Inn has 378 deluxe hotel rooms decorated with cherry-wood furniture, boardwalk postcard–print curtains, and light green accents. Guestrooms at the Inn sleep up to five and feature two queen-size beds (or one king-size bed) and a child's daybed. Romantic two-story garden suites each have a private

garden enclosed by a white picket fence. They sleep four and feature a living room on the first floor and a king-size bed in the bedroom loft. The Inn also has concierge suites.

The 517 vacation villas are collectively called Disney's BoardWalk Villas Resort. These are Disney Vacation Club villas, available when not occupied by members. Each studio features a queen-size bed and double sleeper sofa, plus a wet bar with microwave, coffeemaker, and small refrigerator. Larger (one-, two-, and three-bedroom) villas sleep 4 to 12 people, and feature dining rooms, fully equipped kitchens, laundry facilities, master baths with whirlpool tubs, and VCRs. They also include king-size beds in the master bedroom, living rooms with queen sleeper sofas, and two queen-size beds (or one plus a double sleeper sofa) in any additional bedrooms. Rooms at both the Inn and Villas include an iron (with board), a hair dryer, and free newspaper delivery.

WHERE TO EAT: By virtue of its entertainment district status (see page 187 of the *Everything Else in the World* chapter), this resort has a wealth of dining and snacking options. A variety of vendors along the boardwalk tempt with hot dogs, crêpes on a stick, gourmet coffee, and more. For those looking to eat in, 24-hour room service is available.

Big River Grille & Brewing Works: This working brewpub features a full menu, complemented by fresh specialty ales. View the on-site brewmaster through floor-to-ceiling glass walls.

BoardWalk Bakery: A popular stop that offers baked goods, ice cream, espresso, and cappuccino. Huge display windows allow passersby to watch bakers at work. Bun rises are held here every morning.

ESPN Club: A serious sports bar for serious sports fans, it provides interactive sports video entertainment and all-day dining.

Flying Fish Cafe: This restaurant has a show kitchen, and its dinner menu emphasizes seafood, steak, and fresh seasonal items.

Seashore Sweets': An old-fashioned sweetshop serves candies, saltwater taffy, ice cream, frozen yogurt, and specialty coffees.

Spoodles: Mediterranean cuisine is the focus of this establishment geared toward families; the appetizers are meant for sharing.

WHERE TO DRINK: Guests of this resort have a multitude of options right in their backyard, with the BoardWalk's clubs and lounges on hand.

Atlantic Dance: Dance, twist, and shout to classic tunes at this waterfront dance club. Live bands perform on select nights; DJs take care of business on others. You must be 21 to enter.

Belle Vue Room: Listen to old-time tunes on antique radios and play board games in this cocktail lounge near the lobby. Appetizers are served.

Jellyrolls: Dueling pianos provide live entertainment in a casual warehouse atmosphere. Popcorn is served. The cover charge is between $3 and $5 on weekends.

Leaping Horse Libations: The carousel-themed pool bar at Luna Park serves a variety of cocktails, as well as tuna sandwiches, salads, hot dogs, fruit, and ice cream.

WHAT TO DO: The three-quarter-mile pathway encircling Crescent Lake (en route to Epcot) provides a ready venue for walkers and joggers. BoardWalk guests may rent boats from a neighboring resort's marina. The Fantasia Gardens Miniature Golf complex is nearby. At the resort itself, Ferris W. Eahlers Community Hall rents out equipment for just about any recreational pursuit imaginable, including croquet, shuffleboard, table tennis, pole fishing, badminton—even books and videos. Fishing excursions can be arranged.

Biking: Community Hall offers a variety of bicycles for rental. In addition, surreys (canopied quadracycles for four) can be rented along the boardwalk.

Children's Program: The Harbour Club provides supervised activities for children ages 4 through 12 from 4 P.M. to midnight. Cost is $5 per child per hour; dinner is available for an additional charge. Call 939-3463 for necessary reservations.

Health Club: Muscles & Bustles health club offers steam rooms, tanning, Nautilus machines, and circuit-training equipment, as well as massages (by appointment).

Midway Games: This area on the Board-Walk's Wildwood Landing features games of luck and skill similar to those found along traditional boardwalks.

Playground: An amusement park–themed play area offers kids a pool to clown around in and other fun activities.

Rolling Chair Ride: A trip along the boardwalk in a special rolling cart is available for a fee.

Shopping: Dundy's Sundries in the lobby is the source for film and basic necessities. Character Carnival on the boardwalk features children's apparel as well as a large selection of Disney character merchandise. Screen Door General Store stocks groceries, dry goods, snacks, and beverages. Thimbles & Threads, located on the boardwalk, carries resortwear, swimwear, and accessories for men and women. Wyland Galleries features marine and environmental art and collectibles (stop in for a peek even if you don't plan to make a purchase).

Swimming: The BoardWalk's swimming area, Luna Park, features a large pool with a 200-foot water slide, "Keister Coaster," patterned after a wooden roller coaster. A family of elephants is found posed throughout the area; their trunks act as a shower for adults on the pool deck or children in the wading pool. The resort's two quiet pools are heated: One is located within the Inn's courtyard; the other, adjacent to Community Hall in the Villas area. There are three whirlpools, one in each pool area.

Tennis: Two lighted soft-surface tennis courts are available for play.

Video Arcades: Side Show Games Arcade has poolside video games, and a sports-themed arcade called The Yard Arcade entertains at the ESPN Club.

TRANSPORTATION: Guests get to Epcot via boats or walkways, and to the Disney-MGM Studios by boats. Buses go to the Magic Kingdom, Animal Kingdom, Typhoon Lagoon, Blizzard Beach, and Downtown Disney.

A Room with a View

There's a lot to be said for throwing back the curtains and taking in a breathtaking view, provided you have the time to really appreciate it and that your view is on a par with your price range. The following is a breakdown of all the different "views" you have to select from at the various Walt Disney World resorts. Refer to it before booking accommodations—it will help you determine the best view for your budget. Although the categories vary, depending on the resort type, the "standard view" is always the lowest rate available. Call W-DISNEY (934-7639) for current rate information.

- **Value Resorts:**
  Standard View = Parking lot, pool, garden, and everything else

- **Moderate Resorts:**
  Standard View = Parking lot or landscaping
  Water View = Pool, marina, lake, river

- **Deluxe Resorts:**
  Standard View = Parking lot
  Garden View = Landscaping
  Water View = Pool, lake, or other water
  Lagoon = Seven Seas Lagoon

Downtown Disney Area

Port Orleans

This 1,008-room resort invites comparisons to the historic French Quarter of New Orleans. Starting at the entrance gate, with its wrought-iron portal and overgrown landscape, the appeal of the Delta City surrounds arriving guests. The entry drive leads to the heart of the city, which is Port Orleans Square. The central building, The Mint, was based on an original turn-of-the-century mint where farmers would go to trade their harvest for "dixes." A dix was a ten-dollar bill, and when the farmers said they were going to get their dixes, they probably didn't know they had coined a phrase. The Mint houses the hotel's check-in facilities, a shop, food court, arcade, and restaurant. It has a vaulted ceiling, and the check-in desks are designed as old-fashioned bank-teller windows. The mural behind the check-in counter, featuring a Mardi Gras street scene, was painted by an artist in three parts; each piece was shipped here separately. The musical notes in the mural are the notes to "When the Saints Go Marching In." The telephone number for Port Orleans is 934-5000.

ROOMS: The guestrooms are located in seven three-story buildings (with elevators). Each room has two double beds; some king-size beds are available. The rooms are a bit smaller than the standard rooms at the more expensive Disney hotels, but they are comfortable for a family of four. The photographs on the walls were donated by Disney employees, and the captions explain their history.

The buildings are painted cream, pink, blue, purple, and yellow, and feature wrought-iron railings of varying designs. About half of the rooms have doors that connect to a neighboring room. Connecting rooms can be requested but can't be guaranteed. The rates are based on the room's view. The least expensive rooms overlook gardens or parking areas and the most expensive rooms offer water views.

WHERE TO EAT: Options here include one restaurant with table service and a food court with counter-service stands. Also, the Sassagoula Pizza Express delivers pizza, chicken wings, and ice cream from 4 P.M. to midnight.

Bonfamille's Cafe: The name of this table-service eatery comes from the Disney movie *The Aristocats*. Steaks, seafood, and Creole cooking highlight the dinner menu. Breakfast is also served.

Sassagoula Floatworks & Food Factory: This food court has a 300-seat dining area. A variety of specialty foods are available, including gumbo, spit-roasted chicken with red beans and rice, fresh beignets, and other traditional Creole dishes. Burgers, pizza, ice cream, and baked goods are also served.

WHERE TO DRINK: The New Orleans theme is carried through in the hotel's watering holes.

Mardi Grogs: The poolside bar serves specialty drinks, popcorn, hot dogs, and ice cream during pool hours.

Scat Cat's Club: A traditional bar featuring nightly entertainment and a light menu of hors d'oeuvres.

WHAT TO DO: A special pool is the highlight of the recreational opportunities here.

Biking: Bicycles are available for rent at Port Orleans Landing.

Boating: Pedal boats, canoes, rowboats, canopy boats, and pontoon boats are available for rent at Port Orleans Landing.

Playground: A small play area with slides is located across from the food court.

Shopping: Jackson Square Gifts & Desires, located at Port Orleans Square, features Disney character merchandise, clothing bearing the Port Orleans logo, and sundries.

Swimming: Doubloon Lagoon is a pool built around a sea serpent that, as the legend goes, is still lingering underground. Its tail can be seen jutting up in spots along walkways, and the water slide is actually the serpent's tongue. The shower at the pool has an alligator's head, and there is a large clamshell where an alligator band serves as the centerpiece of a fountain. A whirlpool is located nearby. Port Orleans guests may also swim at Dixie Landings' Ol' Man Island.

Video Arcade: South Quarter Games is located at Port Orleans Square. It features state-of-the-art video and arcade games.

TRANSPORTATION: Buses go to the Magic Kingdom, TTC, Epcot, Animal Kingdom, the Disney-MGM Studios, Typhoon Lagoon, Blizzard Beach, and Downtown Disney. The Sassagoula River Cruise makes the trip to Dixie Landings and Downtown Disney.

Dixie Landings

The city feel of Port Orleans gives way to the rural South upriver at Dixie Landings. The resort is divided into "parishes." Closest to the "city," guestrooms are found in Mansion homes; farther upriver are the Bayou rooms, with a more rustic feel. The guest registration area is located in a building designed to resemble a steamship. When guests check in, they are booking passage on the steamboat. The food court, restaurant, lounge, and Fulton's General Store are all located in the same building. The telephone number for Dixie Landings is 934-6000.

ROOMS: The 2,048 Mansion and Bayou guestrooms are of the same size, and each room features two double beds (some king-size beds are available); 963 of the Bayou rooms have trundle beds (designed to sleep one child) as well. There is an additional fee of $15 per night for a trundle bed. The Magnolia Bend Mansion rooms, appointed with tapestries and cherry furniture, are situated in sprawling, elegant manor homes with stately columns and grand staircases. The Alligator Bayou rooms are in rustic, weathered-wood tin-roofed buildings that are tucked among trees and bushes native to the area. These rooms surround Ol' Man Island, a 3½-acre recreational area with a pool, playground, and old-fashioned fishing hole. Decorative touches in the rooms include wood and tin armoires and pedestal sinks with brass fittings. The beds have hickory bedposts. The rooms are a bit smaller than the standard rooms at the more expensive Disney hotels, but they are comfortable for a family of four.

WHERE TO EAT: In addition to a table-service restaurant and themed food court, the hotel offers limited room service via Sassagoula Pizza Express, which delivers from 4 P.M. until midnight.

Boatwright's Dining Hall: This 200-seat table-service eatery, next to Colonel's Cotton Mill, serves Cajun specialties and traditional American specialties for dinner. The restaurant is modeled after a boatmaking warehouse. Breakfast is also served.

Colonel's Cotton Mill: The hotel's food court resembles an old-fashioned cotton mill with a 30-foot working waterwheel that powers a real cotton press inside.

The five counter-service stands here offer all sorts of choices. Basic selections are available for breakfast. Acadian Pizza 'n' Pasta has pasta dishes, fresh pizza, and calzones. Bleu Bayou Burgers and Chicken offers fried and grilled chicken and an assortment of burgers. Cajun Broiler serves spit-roasted chicken and barbecued ribs. Riverside Market and Deli is a convenience store that stocks snack foods, soda, salads, sandwiches, beer, and wine. Southern Trace Bakery specializes in pastries, freshly baked pies, and sticky buns. Soft drinks can be refilled at no extra charge on a meal-by-meal basis.

WHERE TO DRINK: Two lounges possess a certain degree of charm.

Cotton Co-Op: Situated in a room designed as a cotton exchange, this lounge features specialty drinks, some light hors d'oeuvres, and live entertainment.

Muddy Rivers: The poolside bar serves specialty and traditional drinks plus hot dogs, popcorn, and ice cream during pool hours.

WHAT TO DO: Many of the resort activities are at Ol' Man Island, a 3½-acre recreation center featuring a pool, whirlpool, wading pool, playground, and fishing hole stocked with a variety of fish for catch and release.

Biking: Bicycles of all types can be rented at the Dixie Levee.

Boating: Pedal boats, canoes, rowboats, canopy boats, and pontoon boats are available for rent at the Dixie Levee.

Fishing: Two-hour guided fishing excursions are available, and guests may fish on their own at the Ol' Fishin' Hole.

Playground: An elaborate play area is located on Ol' Man Island next to the pool.

Shopping: Fulton's General Store in the Dixie Landings building stocks Disney character merchandise, clothing with the Dixie Landings logo, and sundries.

Swimming: In addition to the themed pool and children's wading pool at Ol' Man Island, there are five pools set among the parishes of the resort. Dixie Landings guests may also swim at Port Orleans' Doubloon Lagoon next door.

Video Arcade: The Medicine Show Arcade, located in the Dixie Landings building, features a small selection of games.

TRANSPORTATION: Buses go to the Magic Kingdom, Epcot, the Disney-MGM Studios, Animal Kingdom, Typhoon Lagoon, Blizzard Beach, and Downtown Disney. Port Orleans and Downtown Disney can also be reached aboard the Sassagoula River Cruise.

The Villas at the Disney Institute

The area near the Downtown Disney Marketplace and the Lake Buena Vista golf course is dotted with villa-type accommodations, many fitted out with fully equipped kitchens and other extras and amenities. Some may cost more than individual guestrooms at the conventional Disney hotels, but they accommodate more people as well. For families of more than five (who might otherwise need an extra hotel room), this is the most economical way to stay on-property. Smaller families can often break even by cooking some of their own meals (especially breakfast) in their villa.

The resort serves as headquarters for the Disney Institute (see the *Everything Else in the World* chapter for details). Guests participating in the Disney Institute's enrichment programs are housed in the Bungalows and Townhouses. Recreational facilities are available to all guests when not in use for programming (additional charges apply for use of the Sports & Fitness Center and The Spa at the Disney Institute).

The villas are exceptionally spacious, quiet, and secluded—albeit decorated on the dull side, at least as Disney accommodations go. The resort's pace is relaxed and the atmosphere is low-key (except at the Townhouses near Pleasure Island, which can be lively until

late in the evening). The Villas are conveniently located with respect to the Disney-MGM Studios, Epcot, Animal Kingdom, Downtown Disney, and Typhoon Lagoon. Note that Downtown Disney is within walking distance. The telephone number for The Villas at the Disney Institute is 827-1100.

TYPES OF ACCOMMODATIONS: There are five major types of villas. All have either full kitchens or wet bars with small refrigerators. Check-in and check-out for all guests take place at the Welcome Center near the Bungalows and the Fairway Villas. Note that only the Fairway Villas can accommodate guests with disabilities.

One-Bedroom Bungalows: The 316 Bungalows are slightly northeast of the Townhouses. The smallest one-bedroom units are roughly L-shaped, with a sitting area (equipped with a daybed, wet bar, refrigerator, microwave, and coffeemaker) that's pleasantly removed from the sleeping area, with its two queen-size beds. The layout provides families with a bit more privacy and space than they would get in the standard rooms at the WDW hotels. (The single disadvantage for families: small bathrooms.) All have a balcony or a patio.

One- and Two-Bedroom Townhouses: These accommodations are about a five-minute walk from Downtown Disney. They are simple in feeling and decor; living rooms have cathedral ceilings.

A one-bedroom unit can accommodate up to four; there's a queen-size bed in the loft bedroom and a queen-size sleeper sofa in the living room. A two-bedroom unit, which can accommodate six, features a queen-size bed in the master bedroom, two twin-size beds in the loft bedroom, and a queen-size sleeper sofa in the living room.

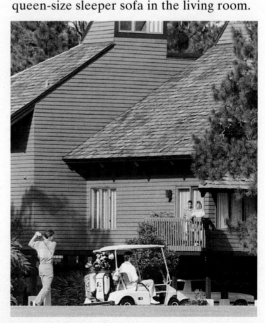

Fairway Villas: These cedar-sided, slant-roofed units, located near the first, second, eighth, and ninth fairways of the Lake Buena Vista golf course, are among the World's most spacious and attractive accommodations, with cathedral ceilings, rough-hewn walls, large windows, contemporary-styled furniture, and an overall feeling that there's a lot of elbow room. There is a queen-size bed in one bedroom, two double beds in the other, and either a pull-out bed or a double sleeper sofa in the living room. Each villa can sleep eight, plus there's room for a crib.

Treehouse Villas: Guests who lodge in one of these octagonal houses-on-stilts, scattered along a barbell-shaped roadway, go to sleep to a cacophony of crickets and wake up to a chorus of birds. You're literally in the woods, alongside some of the winding WDW canals, and you feel a million miles from the rest of the World. Upstairs are the small (but modern) kitchen, the living room (where the television set is located), two bedrooms (each with a queen-size bed), and two bathrooms; the entire floor is surrounded by a deck. Downstairs, there's a bedroom with a double bed and television, and a utility room equipped with a washer and dryer. The roadways—shady, flat, and generally untrafficked—are great for jogging.

Grand Vista Homes: Four ultraluxurious homes—each with two or three bedrooms and a fully equipped kitchen—are available for rent. Each features a master bedroom with a king-size bed, and most of the other bedrooms have two queen-size beds (some have two twins). Bed turndown service and daily newspaper delivery are provided, refrigerators are stocked with staples, and furnishings are all first-class. Use of golf carts and bicycles is included in the price. (For complete price information, see the chart "Rates at Walt Disney World Properties" starting on page 46.)

WHERE TO EAT: The **Seasons Dining Room** offers an ever-changing menu of fresh seasonal items. There's also **Reflections Gourmet Coffee & Pastries** for lunch, as well as many other options at nearby Downtown Disney and the resorts on Hotel Plaza Boulevard. (See *Good Meals, Great Times*.)

Groceries: In these parts, in-room grocery delivery is available and many guests cook their own meals. Dabblers, located in the Welcome Center, has a limited selection of groceries. The Gourmet Pantry at the Downtown Disney Marketplace stocks staples of all sorts. Purchases can be delivered to your villa; if you won't be there to receive them, arrangements may be made for the delivery person to be let in so that perishables can be

stashed in the refrigerator. It's also possible to order by phone; call 827-4147 for Disney Institute grocery delivery, or 828-3886 for the Gourmet Pantry. A Gooding's supermarket is located at the Crossroads of Lake Buena Vista shopping center nearby.

WHERE TO DRINK: Head for **Seasons Terrace**, located behind the Seasons Dining Room, or **Seasons Lounge**, in the lobby. At the Downtown Disney Marketplace, nearby, you'll find Cap'n Jack's Oyster Bar, or try the clubs at Pleasure Island or the West Side (for details, see *Everything Else in the World*).

WHAT TO DO: In addition to boating, pole fishing, and shopping at the Downtown Disney Marketplace (discussed in more detail in *Sports* and *Everything Else in the World*), you can also enjoy a variety of activities around the villas themselves. Two sand volleyball courts are situated among the villas.

Biking: The rustic pathways and meandering roads around the villas can make for an enjoyable hour of pedaling. Bicycles are rented at Recreation Rental Center.

Boating: Canoes are available by the hour or day at the Recreation Rental Center.

Golf: Fairways of the Lake Buena Vista course based here nudge right up to the Fairway and Treehouse villas. Practice greens and a driving range are available, along with top-quality rental clubs and shoes. (For fees and starting information, see the *Sports* chapter.)

Health Club: The large Sports & Fitness Center features a gymnasium, and Cybex equipment (complimentary to guests participating in programs; available to any WDW resort guest for a fee). A full-service spa is within the center (use of facilities included with purchase of treatments).

Playground: A play area is located near the Fairway Villas.

Shopping: Dabblers in the Welcome Center offers a mix of merchandise related to Disney Institute programs, as well as groceries, sundries, and more traditional Disney merchandise.

Swimming: There are six pools and several whirlpools dotted about the grounds.

Tennis: The four lighted clay courts are sometimes given over to Disney Institute programs but can be booked by any guest (with a fitness center pass) at other times.

TRANSPORTATION: Buses go to the Magic Kingdom, Epcot, the Disney-MGM Studios, Animal Kingdom, Blizzard Beach, Typhoon Lagoon, and Downtown Disney. They circulate through the villa areas, making pickups at bus stops located along the roadways.

Another option: transport to the Downtown Disney Marketplace via an electric golf cart or bike. Both are rented at the Recreation Rental Center.

Disney's Old Key West Resort

Escape to the spirit of the Florida Keys. Disney's Old Key West Resort is the flagship Disney Vacation Club property (see the box on the next page for details), but villas not occupied by members are available for nightly rental. It has the laid-back feel of a resort community and all the amenities that go with resort life. Conch Flats Community Hall provides a wide range of activities, from board games and movie rentals to basketball and table tennis, plus an activities director to schedule events. The homey accommodations have lots of space and the convenience of kitchen facilities, making the resort especially comfortable for longer stays. The villas are designed in a Key West theme, with soothing color schemes of seafoam green and mauve. The telephone number for Disney's Old Key West Resort is 827-7700.

VILLAS: There are studios and villas with one, two, and three bedrooms. A studio consists of a large bedroom with two queen-size beds, a table and chairs, and a kitchenette with a refrigerator, coffeemaker, microwave, and sink. The bathrooms are spacious. Each one-bedroom villa has a king-size bed in the master bedroom and a queen-size sleeper sofa in the living room; the master bath has a whirlpool tub, sink, and shower. The two-bedroom villa features a king-size bed in the master bedroom, two queen-size beds in the second bedroom, a living room with a queen-size sleeper sofa and a VCR, a dining room, and a spacious kitchen with a refrigerator, dishwasher, toaster, and coffeemaker, plus dishes, silverware, cooking utensils, and more.

The master bathroom is split into two separate rooms with an extra-large whirlpool tub and a sink in one and an oversize shower, sink and vanity, and toilet in the other.

Disney Vacation Club

Imagine a club that gives members the convenience of ready-made vacations from year to year, with the flexibility of choosing when and where to visit, how long to stay, and the type of accommodations. It starts with the purchase of a real estate interest in a Disney Vacation Club property. For a one-time price and annual dues, members garner vacation stays that can be enjoyed at Disney's Old Key West Resort and Disney's Board-Walk Villas Resort at Walt Disney World, Disney's Vero Beach Resort in Florida, and Disney's Hilton Head Island Resort in South Carolina.

Disney's Vero Beach Resort is a two-hour drive from Walt Disney World. It has villa-type accommodations comparable to those at Disney's Old Key West Resort—with lush surroundings, an endless uncrowded beach, and lots of local sights. The proximity makes it easy to tack a beach vacation onto a WDW visit. Members can also elect to stay at their choice of nearly 200 resorts worldwide, including select Disney resorts and the Disney Cruise Line. Visit the DVC Web site at *www.disneyvacationclub.com*.

There's a terrace off the living room and bedroom, and ceiling fans in each room. The configuration of the two-story three-bedroom Grand Villas is similar to that of the two-bedroom models, but adds a third bedroom with two double beds. As for capacity, the studios and one-bedroom villas sleep 4 people, the two-bedroom villas sleep 8, and two-story three-bedroom villas accommodate 12.

WHERE TO EAT: In addition to the restaurant and snack bar here, there are grills and picnic tables available for meals outdoors.

Guests can also make a short boat journey to Downtown Disney. Pizza delivery is available from Dixie Landings from 4 P.M. to midnight.

Good's Food to Go: Pick up continental breakfast or burgers, conch fritters, salads, sandwiches, and snacks at this casual spot by the main pool.

Olivia's Cafe: This casual full-service restaurant serves Key West favorites plus more traditional items for breakfast, lunch, and dinner. Menus change seasonally. A Winnie the Pooh character breakfast is held on Monday, Wednesday, and Sunday.

WHERE TO DRINK: The watering holes at Old Key West are as laid-back as they come.

Gurgling Suitcase: Near the main pool area, this bar serves specialty drinks, cocktails, wine, beer, and soft drinks. Sit at outdoor tables or on stools inside.

Turtle Shack: In the recreation area located off Turtle Pond Road, this poolside spot serves pizza, salads, sandwiches, and snacks (seasonal).

WHAT TO DO: An activities director is on hand to schedule events for guests and members alike. At Conch Flats Community Hall, table tennis, board games, playing cards, a large-screen television set, video rentals, and planned activities are on hand. Basketball, shuffleboard, and volleyball courts are located throughout the resort, and equipment is available from Hank's Rent 'N Return.

Biking: A variety of bicycles may be rented from Hank's.

Boating: Pedal boats, rowboats, and pontoon boats are available for rent at Hank's.

Health Club: The R.E.S.T. health club features Nautilus and cardiovascular machines, a sauna, and massage (by appointment).

Playground: The kids' play area is located between the main swimming pool and the tennis courts.

Shopping: Conch Flats General Store stocks groceries, books, magazines, sun care products, and Disney character merchandise.

Swimming: The sprawling main pool, with a large whirlpool nearby, is located behind the Hospitality House. The children's pool and play area resembles a giant sand castle. Additional pools are found around the resort.

Tennis: There are two lighted courts located near the main pool. A third court, in a more removed area, is not equipped for night play.

Video Arcade: The Electric Eel Arcade is located in the Hospitality House.

TRANSPORTATION: Buses go to the Magic Kingdom, Epcot, the Disney-MGM Studios, Animal Kingdom, Blizzard Beach, Typhoon Lagoon, and Downtown Disney. Water launches also make the trip between the resort and Downtown Disney.

Animal Kingdom Area

All-Star Movies, All-Star Music, & All-Star Sports

The first Disney entries into the value-priced hotel market, the All-Star Movies (opening in early 1999), All-Star Music, and All-Star Sports resorts are the most startlingly themed at Walt Disney World. Each resort has 1,920 rooms housed in ten buildings devoted to five Disney movies, five types of music, and five sports respectively.

Sports fans will find themselves in a world of baseball, football, tennis, surfing, or basketball at the All-Star Sports resort. Brightly colored larger-than-life football helmets, surfboards, tennis balls, basketball hoops, and baseball bats adorn the buildings. Stairwells in the shape of three-story soda cups, lifeguard shacks, and tennis ball cans lead guests to the second and third floors.

At the All-Star Music resort, Broadway, country, jazz, rock, and calypso are the themes. A walk-through, neon-lit jukebox, a three-story pair of cowboy boots, and a Broadway theater marquee are among the giant icons.

The brand-new All-Star Movies resort celebrates five classic Disney films: *Toy Story*, *The Mighty Ducks*, *Fantasia*, *101 Dalmatians*, and *The Love Bug*. Buildings are adorned with such icons as 40-foot dalmatians, duck-shaped hockey masks, and wildly oversize versions of Buzz Lightyear and Woody.

As value resorts, the All-Star properties offer few frills, but the service and whimsical atmosphere are pure Disney.

Guests check in at Cinema Hall for All-Star Movies, Melody Hall for All-Star Music, or Stadium Hall for All-Star Sports. Each building houses a food court, arcade, shop, and Guest Services. To reach All-Star Movies, call 939-7000; to contact All-Star Music, call 939-6000; to reach All-Star Sports, call 939-5000.

ROOMS: The guestrooms, measuring 260 square feet, are rather small compared with the rooms at Port Orleans and Dixie Landings, which are 314 square feet. Each room has two double beds (with the exception of rooms designed for travelers with disabilities, which have one king-size bed), a vanity area with a single sink, a separate bathroom, a small dresser, and a small table with chairs.

WHERE TO EAT: Three food courts: **World Premiere** in Cinema Hall, **Intermission** in Melody Hall, and **End Zone** in Stadium Hall. Each features a bakery, convenience market, and several stands geared to barbecue, pizza and pasta, and burgers. Each food court has a common seating area with a central beverage bar.

For entertainment, the End Zone offers children's movies during the day and showcases big games on its enormous big-screen TV. The All-Star resorts all deliver pizza, salads, beer, and wine to rooms from 4 P.M. to midnight.

WHERE TO DRINK: There are no lounges at the All-Star resorts; however, the **Silver Screen Spirits**, **Singing Spirits**, and **Team Spirits** pool bars serve drinks throughout the day and evening. The bars are in the main pool areas.

WHAT TO DO: Swimming gets top priority in these parts. Note that guests may swim in any of the three main pools. All-Star guests may rent boating equipment at any of the Walt Disney World resorts.

Playground: A playground is located in each hotel's courtyard area.

Shopping: Maestro Mickey's in Melody Hall, and Sport Goofy Gifts and Sundries in Stadium Hall, and a shop in Cinema Hall all feature magazines, books, sun care products, character merchandise, and sundries.

Swimming: Each hotel has two pools and one kiddie pool. The main pool at All-Star Movies has a *Fantasia* theme. (Look for Sorcerer Mickey.) The smaller Duck Pond Pool is based on *The Mighty Ducks*. At the All-Star Music resort, the Calypso Pool is in the form of a giant guitar, while the Piano Pool is designed to look like—you guessed it—a grand piano. At the All-Star Sports resort, Surfboard Bay has a soothing ocean motif. The smaller Grand Slam Pool pays tribute to our national pastime—it's shaped like a baseball diamond (Goofy is on the mound).

Video Arcades: The Reel Fun Arcade (at All-Star Movies), Notable Arcade (at All-Star Music), and Game Point Arcade (at All-Star Sports), offer a large selection of current and classic games. In addition to points, some games yield tickets that can be redeemed for prizes.

TRANSPORTATION: Buses make pickups at Cinema Hall, Melody Hall, and Stadium Hall for trips to each of the four theme parks, Blizzard Beach, Typhoon Lagoon, and Downtown Disney. Each resort has its own bus line.

A word about All-Star resort transportation: The bus service at these "value" resorts tends to be slightly *more efficient* than the service at other locations. The combination of fewer stops and connections makes for a nice bonus for guests here.

All-Star Resort Trivia

- It would take all the water at Typhoon Lagoon's wave pool to fill one of the Coca-Cola cups at the baseball-themed Home Run hotel.
- The tennis racquet at Centre Court would practically cover an entire regulation tennis court.
- It would take 9,474,609 tennis balls to fill one of Centre Court's giant tennis ball cans.
- The gold star in front of Melody Hall, one of 727 stars there, is one-fourth the size of Epcot's Spaceship Earth.
- The jukeboxes at Rock Inn could hold 4,000 compact discs, enough to supply music for 135 days straight.
- The cowboy boots doing the two-step at Country Fair would fit a size 270 foot.
- The car on top of The Love Bug building isn't a traditional compact car. It's four times the size of a real one.
- The 40-foot dalmatian was constructed in California. To do it, workers created a special Pongo mold from a foam base. Now it'll be easy to make another one. Or a hundred and one, if need be.

Coronado Springs

This resort reveals its southwestern-Mexican theme in such elements as a tiled stucco lobby with a fountain, and a pyramid with water tumbling down from it that appears to have created the Mayan ruin–themed pool. The hotel's 1,967 rooms are found in three guest areas that stretch around Lago Dorado, a 15-acre lake. The food court, restaurant, and lounge are located near the lobby. A convention center offers access to business services. The telephone number for Coronado Springs is 939-1000.

ROOMS: Standard rooms are smaller than those at Disney's deluxe hotels, but adequate for a family of four; each has two double beds (some king-size beds are available). In-room amenities include a coffeemaker, hair dryer, and modem port. Decor varies in each section but is characterized by yellow, blue, and scarlet accents. In the Casitas area, where most of the suites are located, terra-cotta guest buildings occupy a citylike landscape. In the pueblo-style Ranchos, scattered along a dry streambed, rooms have a rustic feel. Cabanas, located along the rocky palm-lined beach, reflect the casual feel of their namesake. Walkways link guestroom areas with the recreational facilities.

WHERE TO EAT: In addition to a full-service restaurant and food court, limited room service is available for breakfast and dinner.

Maya Grill: A casually elegant specialty restaurant, open for breakfast and dinner, this spot offers seafood, steaks, lamb, and pork cooked over an open-pit wood-fired grill.

Pepper Market: High ceilings make this nontraditional food court feel like an open-air market. The fare includes tacos, tostadas, pizza, pasta, and omelettes made to order.

WHERE TO DRINK: There are two places to wet your whistle at Coronado Springs.

Francisco's: A colorful lounge providing cocktails and evening entertainment is located in the main building.

Siesta's: In the Dig Site area, this poolside bar lets swimmers and archaeologists enjoy a variety of cocktails and light snacks.

WHAT TO DO: The resort's recreation area, called the Dig Site, features a huge pyramid with a water slide that spills into a pool. There is an array of water sports in which to participate, as well as volleyball, and a short nature trail. For more information, see *Sports*.

Biking: Bikes may be rented at La Marina.

Boating: A variety of boating equipment is available for rental at La Marina.

Health Club: La Vida health club offers a full range of fitness equipment.

Playground: The Explorer's Playground is part of the Dig Site area and includes a sandbox stocked with Mayan carvings waiting to be excavated.

Salon: The Casa de Belleza salon, located near La Vida health club, offers a large variety of spa services.

Shopping: Panchitos Gifts & Sundries is the place to pick up pottery, jewelry, and other items with a southwestern flavor, Disney character merchandise, film, and basic necessities.

Swimming: The main pool can be found in the Dig Site area. It surrounds a Mayan pyramid and features a towering water slide. There is a 22-person whirlpool and a kiddie pool nearby. Each of the guestroom areas features a quiet unguarded pool.

Video Arcades: The Jumping Bean Arcade is found in the main building and the Iguana Arcade is in the Dig Site area.

TRANSPORTATION: Buses take guests to the Magic Kingdom, Epcot, the Disney-MGM Studios, Animal Kingdom, Typhoon Lagoon, Blizzard Beach, BoardWalk, and Downtown Disney.

Disney Cruise Line

In the summer of 1998, the *Disney Magic* officially joined the ranks of the world's finest oceangoing vessels. The custom-built cruise ship is the first in Disney history. Its sister ship, the *Disney Wonder*, makes its debut in spring of 1999. (Although the cruise experience is essentially the same on both ships, restaurant names and some theming do differ.)

A Disney Cruise Line vacation begins with a three- or four-day stay at a WDW resort. After that, guests simply retain the same room keys for their staterooms. Disney staffers remove luggage from the resort and move it into the appropriate shipboard stateroom. There is no second check-in on the ship, ensuring a seamless land-sea vacation. (Staterooms closely match the category of the resort accommodations, from Moderate to Deluxe.)

After transferring via private motor coach to Port Canaveral, the departure point for all cruises, guests board a 1,750-passenger ship for a three- or four-day journey. From the innovative ship design to entertainment options, families, teens, and adults without kids all have their own comfort zones—without ever having to say bon voyage to Mickey. (In addition to the Mouse, the usual cast of characters is on board.) The itinerary includes a stop at the port of Nassau in the Bahamas, plus a daylong stay on Disney's private Bahamian island, Castaway Cay. Back at Port Canaveral, guests are transported to Orlando International Airport.

The *Disney Magic*'s classic exterior recalls the majesty of early ocean liners. Guests enter a three-story atrium, where traditional definitions of elegance expand to include a demure bronze statue of Mickey as helmsman and subtle cutout Disney character silhouettes along the grand staircase. There's even a 15-foot, topsy-turvy statue of a decidedly "goofy" painter hanging off the ship's stern.

Disney Cruise Line vacations can be booked through travel agents or by calling Disney Cruise Line reservations at 566-7000.

ROOMS: All 875 staterooms aboard both ships are a cut above the standard cruising cabin. Overall, each offers about 25% more space, most have a bath and a half, and 73% are outside rooms with ocean vistas—many with verandas. All feature telephones with "land lines," minibars, televisions, hair dryers, and safes. There are rooms equipped for guests with disabilities, and nonsmoking rooms are available.

There are 12 stateroom categories that correspond to WDW resorts with comparable room rates. The seven-day land and sea vacations range from $1,229 to $4,225 per person, double occupancy. Package prices include airfare to Orlando from major U.S. cities, transfers, accommodations, unlimited admission to the theme parks, shipboard meals and recreation, and more. Depending on availability, guests may opt for a three- or four-day sea-only vacation. Note that proper ID is required in the Bahamas—pack a passport or birth certificate.

WHERE TO EAT: There are three themed dining rooms (and one picturesque adults-only alternative dining room), in addition to 24-hour room service on each ship; guests rotate, spending a night in each of the three main rooms, enjoying a different dining experience each time.

Note: The restaurants, clubs, and shipboard activities described below focus on the *Disney Magic*. However, their counterparts on board the *Disney Wonder* deliver comparable experiences.

Animator's Palate: Here the restaurant and the food—California cuisine—are works of art. As in the movie *The Wizard of Oz*, everything begins in black and white—from the checked floors to the waiters' attire and even the appetizers. As the meal progresses, color slowly begins to creep into the picture. By the time dessert arrives, the room is awash in a sea of brilliant hues.

Parrot Cay: In a colorful Caribbean setting complete with Sebastian wall sconces, this restaurant features tasty tropical cuisine.

Lumière's: Continental food, chandeliers, and *Beauty and the Beast* trompe l'oeil effects characterize this casually elegant dining room. An abundance of roses completes the theme.

Palo: A dining room reserved for adults, Palo is a romantic restaurant perched atop the vessel. Chefs prepare contemporary Italian cuisine in an exhibition kitchen. Picture windows provide ocean views.

Topsider Buffet: An indoor-outdoor cafe serving breakfast, lunch, snacks, and a buffet dinner for kids.

WHERE TO DRINK: Among the options are a variety of lounges, including a sports bar, and a number of clubs. Beat Street, like Pleasure Island, is an adults-only cluster of nighttime entertainment venues:

Offbeat: An anything goes, improvisational comedy club.

Rockin' Bar "D": A dance club with a split personality—one night it's rock 'n' roll, the next it's country.

Sessions: An intimate piano bar lounge.

WHAT TO DO: In addition to shuffleboard, basketball, and paddleball, there are many sporting activities to enjoy aboard the *Disney Magic* and the *Disney Wonder*. Recreational areas on each ship, as well as at its ports of call, are strategically located to attract families, teens, and adults to different areas, with nearly an entire deck devoted to kids.

Biking: Bikes are available for rent at Castaway Cay.

Buena Vista Theater: A 270-seat cinema, this theater features a variety of first-run movies and classic Disney films.

Children's Programs: A huge area dedicated exclusively to kids offers supervised, age-specific programs for kids ages 3 through 12 from 9 A.M. until 1 A.M. The Oceaneer Club provides engaging activities for the 3- through 8-year-old set. The Oceaneer Lab, designed for children 9 through 12, is a science-based interactive play area. This amusement center keeps older kids entertained for hours at a time.

Golf: Golfers can practice their swings in a safely netted area aboard the ship.

Health Club and Salon: Guests get in ship-shape a this modern facility, which offers exercise equipment and spa treatments, educational and enrichment programs, sauna, steam room, whirlpool, and massage. The salon offers many services, including haircuts, manicures, and pedicures (for an extra fee).

Shopping: In addition to the colorful shipboard shops—Radar Trap, Mickey's Mates, Treasure Ketch, Shutters, and ESPN Locker Room—guests can indulge their shopping fantasies while exploring Nassau.

Studio Sea: At this family lounge, guests participate in live entertainment, such as cabaret acts and a family game show, in a setting that looks like a television studio.

Swimming: There are several whirlpools and three swimming pools on the ship: a family pool, a sports-activity pool, and an adults-only pool. Guests may also swim off the sandy shores and lagoon of Castaway Cay.

Teen Entertainment: In a coffee bar called Common Ground, teenagers can hang out, watch movies, and listen to music.

Volleyball: Guests can play water volleyball in the ship's pool, and sand volleyball at Castaway Cay.

Walt Disney Theatre: A tribute to the grand theatrical palaces of long ago. Guests can see a different musical show each night.

Anchors Aweigh!

Every Disney Cruise Line trip culminates in a visit to Castaway Cay (pronounced *key*). Disney has maintained the island's natural beauty while providing a host of outdoor activities, including volleyball, snorkeling, biking, and hiking. The island has a beach for families, and a mile-long stretch of secluded sand—complete with massage cabanas—for adults seeking less action and more privacy.

As guests awaken on the final day of their Disney Cruise Line vacation, they find their ship already docked at Castaway Cay's private pier. The pier allows for easy access to and from the ship.

Castaway Cay, a 1,000-acre tropical island, is located in the Bahamas, due east of Fort Lauderdale. Trams and other transportation are available for guests who wish to explore the island. All of the architecture, including a bar, restaurant, straw market, and even a post office, is in true Bahamian style.

Resorts on Hotel Plaza Boulevard

These seven hotels—the Hilton, Buena Vista Palace, Travelodge, Grosvenor, Doubletree Guest Suites, Royal Plaza, and Courtyard by Marriott—occupy a unique position among Orlando-area accommodations not owned by Disney: They are inside Walt Disney World. In fact, they've been here since the park first opened, in 1971, or soon thereafter, accommodating Mickey enthusiasts from the very beginning. The hotels feature Disney-run shops; the three largest (Hilton, Buena Vista Palace, and Grosvenor) have meals hosted by Disney characters.

Often referred to as the Downtown Disney Resort Area Hotels, they line mile-long Hotel Plaza Boulevard. The Hilton, Buena Vista Palace, and Grosvenor are across the street from the Downtown Disney Marketplace, with its tempting shops, restaurants, and nightlife, and the other four properties are a 10- to 25-minute stroll away. They are also close to the Crossroads of Lake Buena Vista shopping center, home to inexpensive eateries and Gooding's 24-hour grocery.

Privileges of staying in one of these hotels include:
- Preferred access to all Disney golf courses
- Preferred seating at Planet Hollywood before 5 P.M.
- 20% discount on Pleasure Island admission when you present a receipt showing that you have eaten dinner at one of the hotels' restaurants on the same evening

- Complimentary bus service to the four theme parks, with limited service to Downtown Disney, Typhoon Lagoon, and Blizzard Beach. Transportation notes: Buses that service these resorts are not part of the Disney transportation network. Be sure to build in extra time for bus travel. The loop, which includes a stop at each of the resorts on Hotel Plaza Boulevard, can be time-consuming.
- On-premises Disney gift shop
- Free Disney Channel and ESPN for in-room viewing
- Flexibility to book tickets for both on- and off-WDW-property attractions
- Car rental available on premises (at all but Travelodge)

To book a room, call the individual hotel's toll-free number or WDW Central Reservations at W-DISNEY (934-7639). The resorts on Hotel Plaza Boulevard are included in several Walt Disney Travel Company packages. Internet users can access information via *www.downtowndisneyhotels.com*.

All of the following hotels offer nonsmoking rooms and accommodations for travelers with disabilities. To get to the hotels from the airport, take Exit 27 off I-4.

HILTON: This hotel, with a splashy salmon, aqua, and beige facade and palm-lined drive, gets high marks for its 23 well-groomed acres, laid-back ambience, impressive pool area, and upscale shops selling resort and golf apparel. The 814 rooms feature minibars and phones with voice mail and computer hookups. Among the seven restaurants and lounges, casual Finn's Grill offers dinners of seafood and steaks, wines by the glass, themed evenings, and bread served in a unique way; Chatham House has New England decor and serves breakfast (with characters in attendance on Sunday), lunch, and dinner (choose from assorted salads, pastas and other entrées, and sandwiches; outdoor seating is available on The Terrace); Rum Largo Pool Bar & Cafe serves hamburgers, salads, sandwiches, and tropical drinks alfresco. The Old-Fashioned Soda Shoppe has ice cream; Mainstreet Market is part gourmet deli, part country store. For light meals, snacks, or cocktails, drop by John T's Sports Bar in the lobby; specialty coffees and wines by the glass are served at Mugs.

Recreational facilities include two whirlpools and heated swimming pools, a children's wading pool, and a fitness room. The Vacation Station Kids' Hotel, designed for children 4 through 12 years old, has a video room, play area, and scheduled recreational activities supervised by a trained staff. The cost is $6 for the first child, with a $1 discount for each additional child. Rates range from $200 to $365; suites are $459 to $759. Hilton; 1751 Hotel Plaza Blvd.; Lake Buena Vista, FL 32830; 827-4000 or 800-782-4414; *www.hilton-wdwv.com.*

BUENA VISTA PALACE & SPA: The tallest resort at Walt Disney World and the largest of the resorts on Hotel Plaza Boulevard (it's actually at the intersection of Hotel Plaza Boulevard and Buena Vista Drive) is a cluster of towers set on 27 acres beside Lake Buena Vista. Each of the 1,014 rooms has a ceiling fan, two phones (with voice mail, speakerphone, and computer hookup), two queen beds or a king, and spa-inspired amenities; most have a balcony or patio. Concierge accommodations and one- and two-bedroom suites are also available.

The resort's European-style spa features myriad treatments and services (including a variety of massages), a full-service salon, fitness center, and private lap pool. Bustling Recreation Island has two swimming pools, a kiddie pool, whirlpool, sauna, three lighted tennis courts, sand volleyball court, marina with boat and bike rentals, and children's playground. Kids' Stuff is a year-round recreational program for children 4 through 12.

The hotel also provides 24-hour room service, and it has boutiques, a guest laundry, and two Family Calling Centers (booths with speaker-phones for communal chatting). Dining spots include the lakeside Watercress Cafe, which serves all meals, with breakfast and dinner buffets available (characters are in attendance on Sunday morning); the Watercress Pastry Shop, open 24 hours for counter-service baked goods and sandwiches; Arthur's 27, with an international menu and undeniably gorgeous view; The Outback restaurant (not part of the chain), for hefty portions of seafood and steaks; and the Courtyard Mini-Market, serving snacks and smoothies in a tranquil outdoor setting.

The Laughing Kookaburra Good Time Bar, nicknamed "The Kook," features live entertainment and dancing; ladies imbibe for free on Thursday nights. Noise from the restaurants can flow through the atriums and penetrate the solid oak doors, so if silence is golden, stay in the 27-story tower or the Palace Island Suites complex. The Top of the Palace lounge provides the perfect perch to gaze at the sunset or fireworks over a glass of fine wine. For the allergy prone, 65 EverGreen Rooms provide filtered air and water. Rooms range from $129 to $294 per night (no charge for kids under 18); suites are $229 to $529. Buena Vista Palace Resort & Spa; 1900 Buena Vista Dr.; Lake Buena Vista, FL 32830; 827-2727 or 800-327-2990; *www.bvp-resort.com.*

DOUBLETREE GUEST SUITES: Striking outside and in, this 229-unit property has a stellar staff, low-slung facade reminiscent of a Mayan temple, public areas with bright colors and whimsical patterns, and an aviary in the lobby, where a child's check-in desk adjoins the "grown-up" one. Young guests receive a bag of goodies, and everyone gets an oversize cookie. The only all-suite hotel at Walt Disney World, it features roomy (625-square-foot) units, which were renovated last year. Each has a living room (with sleeper sofa), dressing area, and separate bedroom. Each can sleep up to six persons; there are some two-bedroom suites as well. Most bedrooms have two double beds, though some kings are available. Room amenities include two remote control TVs, wet bar, refrigerator, coffee and tea, microwave oven, hair dryer, and safe ($2.50 daily charge). The bath has a full vanity area, small TV, and night-light.

Recreational facilities include a heated pool and whirlpool in a landscaped area with two hammocks; there is also a children's play area, sand volleyball court, and two lighted tennis courts (with pro instruction available). The children's playroom has a big-screen TV, toys, games, and special seasonal activities.

PHOTO BY ALICE GARRARD

Streamers restaurant features American classics and a breakfast buffet; it's also the source for more of those habit-forming cookies. Streamers Market sells snack items and groceries. The hotel's arcade doubles as an ice cream parlor. Rates range from $129 to $289. Doubletree Guest Suites; 2305 Hotel Plaza Blvd.; Lake Buena Vista, FL 32830; 934-1000 or 800-222-8733; *www.doubletreehotels.com/ DoubleT/Hotel141/44Main.htm.*

GROSVENOR: British in name (pronounced GROVE-nor) and ambience, this hotel attracts many international guests. Each of the 626 rooms is located in a mauve 19-story tower and two wings framing two large, formal courtyards with griffin centerpieces. Each room has voice mail, a coffeemaker, and a

VCR; movie rentals are available. Extensive recreational facilities include an exercise room, two lighted tennis courts, shuffleboard courts, basketball court, volleyball court, two heated pools, children's pool, large play area, and arcade. Baskervilles, the hotel's main restaurant, incorporates a Sherlock Holmes museum and serves breakfast and dinner buffets; characters are in attendance for breakfast on Tuesday, Thursday, and Saturday, and for dinner on Wednesday. Baskervilles also becomes the stage for the Murder Watch

Mystery Theatre on Saturday at 6 P.M. and 9 P.M. Crumpet's Cafe, open 24 hours, serves continental breakfast, snacks, and light fare. Crickets lounge provides occasional entertainment. Rates range from $170 to $220 for two guests, year-round; suites are $345 to $940. Grosvenor; 1850 Hotel Plaza Blvd.; Lake Buena Vista, FL 32830; 828-4444 or 800-624-4109; *www.grosvenor.com.*

TRAVELODGE: This 18-story, almost entirely leisure-oriented hotel is surrounded by pines, with an entry lined with oaks draped in Spanish moss. Each of its 325 spacious rooms and suites has new windows (ensuring a quiet stay), either one king-size bed and a queen sofabed or two queen-size beds, as well as voice mail, minibar, free coffee and tea, safe, hair dryer, iron and ironing board, and private balcony (floors 7 through 16 provide a WDW view). EverGreen rooms feature filtered air and water. Two rooms, called Sleepy Bear Dens, are specially themed for children. The four suites, on the 18th floor, offer a fine view of the other resorts on Hotel Plaza Boulevard and the fireworks at the Disney theme parks.

The hotel also has an arcade, small heated pool, kiddie pool, landscaped playground, and coin-operated laundry. Other amenities include room service, overnight film processing, and free local calls. Traders restaurant serves breakfast and dinner, and the Parakeet

Cafe offers light entrées for breakfast, lunch, and dinner, as well as snacks and made-to-order pizza. Besides views of Downtown Disney and Epcot, Toppers lounge, on the 18th floor, has dart machines, pool tables, and music videos. Flamingo Cove is the lobby-level cocktail lounge, with adjacent screened porch. Note that the hotel may undergo a name change. Rates range from $119 to $199 for guestrooms; $299 to $399 for suites. Travelodge; 2000 Hotel Plaza Blvd.; Box 22205; Lake Buena Vista, FL 32830; 828-2424 or 800-348-3765.

COURTYARD BY MARRIOTT: This pleasant hotel appeals especially to adults. Its 323 guestrooms, some of the most spacious on Hotel Plaza Boulevard, are situated in a 14-story tower and 6-story annex. They feature sitting areas, modem ports, marble vanities, voice mail, movies and Nintendo, coffeemakers with china mugs, irons, ironing boards, and safes. The bathrooms are a little on the small side. In the inviting atrium lobby, you'll find tables topped with colorful umbrellas, the 2 Go breakfast bar, and the Tipsy Parrot lounge. The Courtyard Cafe & Grille is a full-service restaurant with a breakfast buffet; the

Village Deli serves snacks, muffins, fruit, sandwiches, TCBY yogurt, and Pizza Hut pizza. Room service is available. There are three heated pools, including one for kids; a whirlpool; playground; arcade; and exercise room. The pool bar is open seasonally. Rates range from $139 to $179 year-round. Courtyard by Marriott; Box 22204; 1805 Hotel Plaza Blvd.; Lake Buena Vista, FL 32830; 828-8888 or 800-223-9930.

ROYAL PLAZA: A pineapple motif, a symbol of hospitality, permeates this extensively renovated hotel. The 394 guest units, all with enlarged baths, are divided between a 17-story main tower (with two concierge floors and a glass-enclosed elevator scaling the facade) and 2-story lanai wings with gated patios or small balconies. The buildings enclose the pool, poolside bar, and courtyard, creating a cloistered area for guests. Each appealing

tower room has a sitting area, desk, dresser, double armoire with closet space, oversize bathtub, safe, and minibar. Baths have marble counters and corner tubs (whirlpools on the concierge level); baths in the enormous rooms with king-size beds have a separate shower stall. All rooms have VCRs, hair dryers, and free coffee and tea. There are 22 suites.

Recreational facilities include a large heated pool with nearby whirlpool, two saunas, an arcade, and four lighted tennis courts. The hotel has a restaurant (where kids eat breakfast free before 8 A.M.) and a small, casual lounge. Depending on the season and the view, room rates range from $99 to $179 for up to five in a room; suites, $139 to $650. The hotel is across the street from the national headquarters of the Amateur Athletic Union. Royal Plaza; Box 22203; 1905 Hotel Plaza Blvd.; Lake Buena Vista, FL 32830; 828-2828 or 800-248-7890; *www.royalplaza.com*.

Off-Property Accommodations In Lake Buena Vista

A full lineup of accommodations, from laid-back to luxurious, abuts the crossroads at I-4 and S.R. 535 in the heart of Lake Buena Vista. Most offer free transportation to the four main Disney parks. The following listings are arranged according to standard room rates, from highest to lowest starting price. All offer nonsmoking rooms and accommodations for guests with disabilities unless otherwise indicated.

GRAND CYPRESS: Not far from the hotels that line Hotel Plaza Boulevard, and just three miles from Epcot, the Hyatt Regency Grand Cypress is flush with plants and artwork. It has a dramatic 18-story atrium lobby and 750 Florida-inspired guestrooms and suites with wicker furniture, ceiling fans, and shutters, as well as four bars and five restaurants, including the popular Hemingway's, which serves game, seafood, and steaks, and La Coquina, where the lavish Sunday brunch is legendary.

The secluded Villas of Grand Cypress provide Mediterranean-style accommodations. Each club suite features a spacious bedroom with a separate sitting area, large luxury bath with separate shower and tub, and sundeck, patio, or veranda. The villas themselves are even larger, with a substantial living room, dining room, and fully equipped kitchen. The Villas area has three dining possibilities of its own: the sophisticated Black Swan restaurant, the casual Fairways, and the Poolside Snack Shop.

The Hyatt Regency Grand Cypress and the Villas of Grand Cypress share 1,500 acres, incorporating a half-acre free-form swimming pool with 12 waterfalls, 2 water slides, and 3 whirlpools (the Villas also has its own pool and whirlpool); a 21-acre lake with rental boats; and a tennis complex with 12 courts. Add to that racquetball and volleyball courts, a playground, bicycling, 4.7-mile jogging trail, 45-acre nature area, health club, and arcade.

Forty-five holes of Jack Nicklaus–designed golf separate the Hyatt Regency from the Villas (they are actually 1½ miles apart, connected by a 24-hour shuttle). The superb North South course features two Scottish-style shared greens, grassy dunes, elevated tees, and a greens fee that will set you back $140 ($100 in the summer). The Grand Cypress Academy of Golf, Equestrian Center, and Racquet Club offer still more activities.

Shuttle service to the four Disney theme parks costs $6 round-trip. Rates at the Hyatt Regency range from $205 to $395; suites start at $650. Rates at the Villas range from $200 to $400 for a club suite, $300 to $500 for a one-bedroom villa, and $400 to $800 for a two-bedroom villa. Hyatt Regency Grand Cypress; One Grand Cypress Blvd.; Orlando, FL 32836; 239-1234 or 800-233-1234; Villas of Grand Cypress; One N. Jacaranda; Orlando, FL 32836; 239-4700 or 800-835-7377; *www.grandcypress.com.*

SUMMERFIELD SUITES LAKE BUENA VISTA: A half mile from the Crossroads of Lake Buena Vista, this popular all-suite hotel has 150 units, most of which feature two separate bedrooms with a king-size bed in the master bedroom, each with a private bath; living room; three TVs; VCR; and good-size, fully equipped kitchen with full-size refrigerator. An arcade, guest laundry, and deli–convenience store are on the property. The staff will even do your grocery shopping for you if you provide them with a list early in the day. Nearby restaurants offer takeout. The good-size pool is in an enclosed courtyard. Scheduled complimentary shuttle service to the Disney theme parks is provided.

Rates range from $119 to $249 for a one-bedroom unit (for up to four guests), and $159 to $319 for a two-bedroom trio unit (for up to eight guests), and include a sumptuous continental breakfast buffet. Ask about the company's new Sierra Suites studio apartments with full kitchens, located nearby and priced up to $50 lower, with weekly rates available. Summerfield Suites Lake Buena Vista; 8751 Suiteside Dr.; Orlando, FL 32836; 238-0777 or 800-830-4964; *www.summerfield-orlando.com.*

PERRIHOUSE BED & BREAKFAST INN:

Staying in this ranch-style house in a country setting is as habit forming as visiting Walt Disney World, which is less than two miles away. The accommodations (eight rooms off a cedar-paneled central library) rival well-appointed lodging in major hotels, and Nick and Angi Perretti are truly gracious hosts. Each guestroom has a private entry, king or queen bed (one room has two queens), TV, telephone (local calls are on the house), and robes. Complimentary fruit, tea, coffee, and juice are always available. Guests have their own refrigerator and laundry ($4 charge for the latter); they can use the whirlpool and small swimming pool 24 hours day.

A welcome board in the kitchen lists current guests by first names and hometowns, and a small hallway gallery is filled with mementos of (and from) past visitors. The library has leather couches and gliders, books, games, Angi's birdhouse collection, and a bird-sighting journal. This is a peaceful place, filled with the songs of birds and crickets. Room rates are $89 to $139, including a continental breakfast buffet; $10 for an extra adult; $5 for a child. Ask about their romantic new birdhouse cottages. PerriHouse Bed & Breakfast Inn; 10417 Centurion Court; Box 22005; Lake Buena Vista, FL 32830; 876-4830 or 800-780-4830; *www.perrihouse.com*.

HOLIDAY INN SUNSPREE–LAKE BUENA

VISTA: Pretty and pink, this 507-unit hotel, about 1½ miles from the Downtown Disney Marketplace, has a most obliging staff, an innovative children's program, and an atmosphere of nonstop activity reminiscent of a busy shopping mall. Its unique Kidsuites (pictured below) provide privacy for adults and kids, who get a soundproof, themed room

within a room. Among the options: Sesame Street, Noah's Ark, an igloo, a circus tent, and a space capsule—complete with two to four beds, TV, VCR, Nintendo, and cassette player. Some Kidsuites, designed to appeal to older kids, have movie, music, and sports theming, full-size twin bunk beds, a desk, and a vanity with a makeup mirror. Family King Rooms are similar to Kidsuites, only semiprivate. Each standard guestroom comes with a refrigerator, microwave, coffeemaker (with free coffee packet daily), hair dryer, electronic safe, and VCR. Most of the rooms have two queen-size beds, although some have king-size beds and sleeper sofas.

Camp Holiday, an activity program for children 3 through 12, is open every evening at no charge—a real bargain. Parents can rent a beeper for $5 so they can be reached at any time. Children receive a special surprise when they register at the Kids' Check-In Desk, and a free bedtime tuck-in from Maxx, the hotel's mascot, on request. A child under 13 eats all meals for free (ordered from a special menu) when accompanied by a paying adult.

Recreational facilities include a heated pool, two whirlpools, a basketball court, playground, fitness center, and the CyberArcade (the cadillac of hotel arcades). Maxine's Food Emporium serves a buffet breakfast and features outlets of national fast-food chains. Pinky's Convenience Court sells microwavable and refrigerated items. Free scheduled transportation to the four Disney theme parks is provided. Rates run $88 to $113, depending on the season; add an additional $39 to $49 for Kidsuites or $24 to $29 for King Family Rooms. Anyone who's 100 years old (or older) stays free; for "youngsters" 50 and over, the Senior Fun Club represents savings of $20 to $60. Holiday Inn SunSpree–Lake Buena Vista; 13351 S.R. 535; Lake Buena Vista, FL 32821; 239-4500 or 800-366-6299; *www.kidsuites.com*.

COURTYARD BY MARRIOTT PARK

SQUARE: Across the street from the Vista Centre shopping complex, the hotel, totally renovated in 1998 and popular with families, is less than a five-minute drive from the Downtown Disney Marketplace. Its 222 rooms and 86 suites all offer lake or courtyard settings. The guestrooms have two double beds, and the bathrooms are a decent size for the price. Each suite has a microwave oven–refrigerator unit and a coffeemaker, as well as a sleeper sofa. Recreational facilities include two large heated pools, a whirlpool, children's pool, two playgrounds, a pool table, and an arcade. The Courtyard Cafe serves a buffet breakfast; one child under 12 eats free with one paying adult. The lobby lounge has a big-screen TV, and a gift shop is on site.

By early 1999, the hotel will offer a fitness area, and all rooms will have coffeemakers, hair dryers, irons, and free newspaper delivery on weekdays. Complimentary shuttles carry guests to the four Disney theme parks. Room rates range from about $75 to $125; suites are $90 to $140, depending on the season. Courtyard by Marriott Park Square; 8501 Palm Pkwy.; Box 22818; Lake Buena Vista, FL 32830; 239-6900 or 800-635-8684.

In Orlando

Some of Orlando's top hotels are on International Drive, or I-Drive, as it is known locally. This famous thoroughfare has two distinct sectors: the more orderly south end, which stretches from Sea World, past the Orange County Convention Center and the dynamic new Pointe Orlando shopping, dining, and entertainment complex, to Sand Lake Road. From here north, it becomes a strip crammed with restaurants, T-shirt shops, and outlet stores.

Old-fashioned I-Ride trolleys travel back and forth along a three-mile stretch of I-Drive daily from 7 A.M. to midnight, from Sea World to the Belz factory outlet stores, stopping every two blocks. The fare is only 75 cents per ride or $7 for seven days; a transfer costs 10 cents, and children 12 and under ride free. Exact change is required.

The following hotels—all located at the southern end of I-Drive—are arranged by standard room rates, from the highest to the lowest starting price. All offer nonsmoking rooms and accommodations for guests with disabilities unless otherwise indicated.

PEABODY ORLANDO: The sister property to the famed Peabody in Memphis, this 27-story, 891-room hotel is International Drive's most luxurious establishment. It's also home to the famous Peabody ducks, which every day at 11 A.M. waddle into the lobby, down a red carpet, then settle into a marble fountain; they waddle back at about 5 P.M. Each of the Peabody's guestrooms has a hair dryer, two telephones, two TVs (including one in the bathroom), and turndown service on request. Facilities include a heated pool, four lighted tennis courts (lessons available), tennis and golf pro shops, arcade, and health club with personal trainers. Baby-sitting is available.

Dux (where no duck is served) is the hotel's—and Central Florida's—premier restaurant. Capriccio showcases northern Italian cuisine and mesquite-grilled specialties in an exhibition kitchen, and offers a champagne brunch on Sunday; the B-Line Diner, the perfect re-creation of a fifties-style diner, serves entrées, sandwiches, and homemade confections 24 hours a day (try the vegetable soup). Afternoon tea is served Monday through Friday in the Dux foyer. There are also four bars, including the elegant Mallard.

The hotel's whimsical Double-Ducker bus provides shuttle service to the four Disney theme parks for guests and the general public for $7 round-trip. Room rates are $270 to $330; $475 to $1,400 for suites. Peabody Orlando; 9801 International Dr.; Orlando, FL 32819; 352-4000 or 800-732-2639; *www .peabody-orlando.com.*

Note: The Peabody Orlando is building 700 more guestrooms and additional meeting space on an adjacent site, opening in 2000.

EMBASSY SUITES INTERNATIONAL DRIVE SOUTH: Popular with families, this eight-story hotel has a lobby lined with gleaming marble, a tropical atrium with waterfalls, and a small pond. Guest quarters include 143 king suites, 94 suites with two double beds, 4 conference suites, and 1 two-bedroom suite. Each unit offers a private bedroom with a separate living-dining room, as well as a wet bar, coffeemaker, microwave, refrigerator, and sleeper sofa.

Facilities include indoor and outdoor swimming pools, and a whirlpool, sauna, steam room, health club, arcade, laundry, and gift shop. The hotel provides room service, car rental, and laundry and valet service, and the staff can arrange for baby-sitting and tickets for attractions and entertainment. There is a restaurant and lounge; guests receive a complimentary, cooked-to-order breakfast and are invited to a free cocktail reception daily. Free shuttle service to the four Disney theme parks is provided. Rates range from $139 to $199. Embassy Suites International Drive South; 8978 International Dr.; Orlando, FL 32819; 352-1400 or 800-433-7275; *www.embassy-suites.com.*

CLARION PLAZA: This 810-room hotel attracts guests with its lively ambience, large outdoor heated pool, spacious accommodations, and location next to the convention center and across the street from Pointe Orlando. Each of the rooms is newly painted and redecorated in rich colors and offers voice mail, Nintendo, a safe, separate vanity area, and movies. The property also has a whirlpool, arcade, guest laundry, three restaurants, concierge, gift shop, baby-sitting service, car rental, and business center.

Sardi's-style Jack's Place, named after the owner's dad, specializes in steak, seafood, and memorable desserts. Cafe Matisse serves outstanding buffet and à la carte meals, Rossini's Pizza has calzones and chicken wings, and Lite Bite is a 24-hour bakery-deli. Backstage, the hotel's nightclub, stays open until 2 A.M. and features a deejay and a generously long happy hour daily. Shuttle service to Walt Disney World costs $11 round-trip. Rates for up to four people range from $135 to $155 for doubles, although special-value rates as low as $79 are usually available during select periods of the spring and fall; suites are $310 to $680. There's no charge for children under 18. Clarion Plaza; 9700 International Dr.; Orlando, FL 32819; 352-9700 or 800-627-8258; *www.clarionplaza.com.*

THE CASTLE: This turreted edifice conjures up visions of Renaissance times, outside and in, where European chandeliers and fountains predominate. The nine-story hotel (a Doubletree resort) has 216 rooms, including 7 junior suites, each with a large

PHOTO BY ALICE GARRARD

mirror reminiscent of a court jester's cap, hair dryer, refrigerator, electronic safe, and iron, coffeemaker, makeup mirror, and tiled bath. Most rooms have two queen beds; a few kings are available.

Medieval music and sounds of nature are piped throughout the property, even out to the striking circular pool, with a playful fountain centerpiece and nearby whirlpool. Austin's Texas Steakhouse & Saloon and Cafe TuTu Tango are on-site, along with a poolside bar and lobby lounge. The ninth-floor Moon and Stars Terraces are pure whimsy. Complimentary shuttle service to the four WDW theme parks is provided. Rates are $115 to $195, depending on the season; junior suites are $10 to $30 more (kids stay free in their parents' room). The Castle; 8629 International Drive; Orlando, FL 32819; 345-1511 or 800-952-2785.

WYNFIELD INN WESTWOOD: Weather-beaten shutters give this three-story motel, which is right off I-Drive, the look of an inn, and the landscaped grounds make it even more appealing, especially to families with young children. Each of the 300 rooms is pleasantly decorated and features two double beds, voice mail, coffeemaker, separate vanity, free local calls, and a safe (for a nominal fee). Request a poolside room to avoid expressway noise. There are two heated swimming pools,

Hot Tip

Driving to the WDW theme parks from the southern end of I-Drive usually takes about 15 minutes, but figure on an extra 15 minutes during rush hour and when large conventions are in town.

two wading pools, and a pool bar that serves beer, wine, soft drinks, and snacks. An arcade is situated off the lobby. Although there is no place to eat on the premises, the adjacent Village Inn serves breakfast, lunch, and dinner, and offers a 10% discount and room service. Complimentary shuttle service to the four theme parks is provided. Rates run from $69 to $109. Wynfield Inn Westwood; 6263 Westwood Blvd.; Orlando, FL 32821; 345-8000 or 800-346-1551; *www.orlando.com/wynfield.*

COUNTRY HEARTH INN: This is the kind of place you'd expect to find in Savannah, not Orlando. Rocking chairs line the porch, and a patterned tin ceiling, hardwood floors, and half a dozen chandeliers grace the lobby. The Country Parlor restaurant, in a corner of the lobby, serves a complimentary continental breakfast, Sunday brunch with champagne and live jazz, and a cozy à la carte dinner.

The beautifully maintained property is across the street from the convention center (though you'd hardly know it), and while it does attract conventioneers, it also maintains a loyal following among vacationers, wedding parties, and locals. Each of the 150 guest-rooms has French doors, polished cherry furniture, colorful drapes and bedspreads, a veranda, cable TV, refrigerator, safe, and coffeemaker. Most rooms have two double beds, although a few have king-size beds.

Movie rental is available. A good-size heated pool is set in a lush, landscaped courtyard with a gazebo. The inn offers room service, and its popular cocktail lounge, the Front Porch, serves free hors d'oeuvres every afternoon. Rates range from $59 to $139. Country Hearth Inn; 9861 International Dr.; Orlando, FL 32819; 352-0008 or 800-447-1890.

In Kissimmee

U.S. 192, also known as Irlo Bronson Memorial Highway, intersects I-4 in Kissimmee, and the hotels and motels here are closer to Disney's theme parks than the flashier accommodations along Orlando's better known International Drive. The area itself is less appealing, but it represents a bargain for budget travelers. Rooms go for $90 or less a night, and as low as $30 off-season.

The following listings are arranged by standard room rates, from highest to lowest starting price. All offer nonsmoking rooms and accommodations for guests with disabilities. They are within a couple of miles of Walt Disney World, a large drugstore, a 24-hour grocery, a discount shopping mall, a one-hour dry cleaner, numerous eateries, and Celebration, the incorporated town that Disney founded in 1997 (see page 196).

HOWARD JOHNSON MAINGATE EAST: The world's largest Howard Johnson has other notable attributes: an outstanding staff, inviting lobby, large guest services desk, enormous gift shop, up-to-date arcade, fenced-in playground, guest laundry, two heated pools, whirlpool, and 24-hour security. Set back from the street, its 567 rooms, in seven two- and three-story buildings (note: there are no elevators in the former), are spacious, quiet, and newly decorated in mauve and burgundy; entry is via key cards. Most rooms have two double beds, though there are rooms with king-size beds; suites and efficiency units with microwaves and mini-refrigerators are available.

Guests enjoy in-room movies, Nintendo, Sky Mall (catalog) shopping, and express check-out. There is no dining on the premises, but the hotel is flanked by IHOP and the Waffle House, and is less than a half mile from the town of Celebration and more dining choices. The hotel sends three buses to the Magic Kingdom each morning, and three pick up there and at Epcot in the afternoon. Rates range from $75 to $90. Howard Johnson Maingate East; 4840 W. Irlo Bronson Memorial Hwy.; Kissimmee, FL 34746; 396-8282 or 800-288-4678; *www.hojomge.com.*

KISSIMMEE/ORLANDO KOA CAMPGROUND AND CABINS: One alternative to WDW's Fort Wilderness is the well-maintained Kissimmee/Orlando KOA campground five miles east of I-4. It's got a heated pool, tennis court, miniature golf, shuffleboard, playground, pond stocked with bass, arcade, laundry, hot showers, convenience store, and resident cranes. Inexpensive eateries and a grocery store are nearby. Besides tent and RV sites, there are 33 air-conditioned, hibiscus-bordered cabins that sleep four or six people. Pets and kids are welcome, and free shuttle service to the Magic Kingdom is provided. Rates for two adults and any children under 18 are $18 for tent sites; $28 to $34 for RV hookups; $29 to $54 for cabins; $5 more, each additional adult; no charge for pets. Kissimmee/Orlando KOA campground; 4771 W. Irlo Bronson Memorial Hwy.; Kissimmee, FL 34746; 396-2400 or 800-562-7791; *www.koacampgrounds.com.*

ORLANDO/KISSIMMEE RESORT HOSTEL: In a renovated motel on 2½ acres beside Lake Cecile and a real find for budget travelers, this "resort hostel" provides spacious private rooms for families and couples, each with a telephone, TV, private bath, and closet. Dormitory rooms accommodate up to six people in extra-wide bunk beds with foam mattresses; sheets are complimentary.

Other amenities include a kitchen, modern laundry, common room, TV and video room, outdoor pool, tiled fountain, volleyball court, barbecue area with picnic tables, and free pedal boats for guests' use. Jet Skis may be rented nearby. Evening activities take place here regularly. A pharmacy and grocery store are across the street; local buses bound for WDW stop out front.

Private rooms run from $27 to $47; dormitory rates are $14 to $17. Hostelling International Orlando/Kissimmee Resort Hostel; 4840 W. Irlo Bronson Memorial Hwy.; Kissimmee, FL 34746; 396-8282 or 800-909-4776 (for reservations only; access number 33); *www.hiayh.org.*

Room Service

Every type of accommodation, from all-suite hotel to budget motel, is represented in Orange County, the largest hotel market in the United States. If you arrive in the area without lodging, go to the Official Visitor Information Center, at 8723 International Dr., Suite 101 (383-5872), and ask what's available in the "black book" that day.

Note: You have to show up in person for this service, but it can save time and money in the long run.

Magic Kingdom

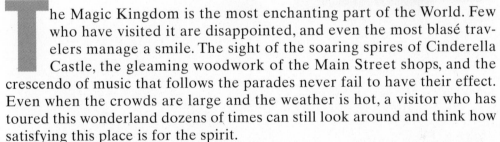

The Magic Kingdom is the most enchanting part of the World. Few who have visited it are disappointed, and even the most blasé travelers manage a smile. The sight of the soaring spires of Cinderella Castle, the gleaming woodwork of the Main Street shops, and the crescendo of music that follows the parades never fail to have their effect. Even when the crowds are large and the weather is hot, a visitor who has toured this wonderland dozens of times can still look around and think how satisfying this place is for the spirit.

What makes the Magic Kingdom timeless is its combination of the classic and the futuristic. Both childhood favorites and space-age creatures have a home here. Every "land" has a theme, carried through from the costumes worn by the hosts and hostesses and the food served in the restaurants to the merchandise sold in the shops, and even the design of the trash cans. Thousands of details contribute to the overall effect, and recognizing these touches makes any visit more enjoyable.

But the delight most guests experience upon first glimpse of the Magic Kingdom can disappear when disorientation sets in. There are so many bends to every pathway, so many sights and sounds clamoring for attention, it's too easy to wander aimlessly and miss the best the Magic Kingdom has to offer. So we earnestly suggest that you study this chapter before your visit.

Unless otherwise noted, all phone numbers are in area code 407.

MAIN STREET, U.S.A.

1 Main Street Vehicles
2 Walt Disney World Railroad

ADVENTURELAND

3 Jungle Cruise
4 Pirates of the Caribbean
5 Swiss Family Treehouse
6 The Enchanted Tiki Room—Under New Management

MICKEY'S TOONTOWN FAIR

27 Donald's Boat
28 Mickey's Country House
29 Minnie's Country House
30 Toontown Hall of Fame
31 The Barnstormer
32 Walt Disney World Railroad Station

LIBERTY SQUARE

14 The Hall of Presidents
15 The Haunted Mansion
16 Liberty Belle Riverboat

FANTASYLAND

17 Cinderella's Golden Carrousel
18 Dumbo the Flying Elephant
19 It's a Small World
20 Mad Tea Party
21 Mr. Toad's Wild Ride
22 Peter Pan's Flight
23 Legend of the Lion King
24 Skyway to Tomorrowland
25 Snow White's Adventures
26 Ariel's Grotto

FRONTIERLAND

7 Big Thunder Mountain Railroad
8 Country Bear Jamboree
9 Frontierland Shootin' Arcade
10 Splash Mountain
11 Tom Sawyer Island
12 Diamond Horseshoe Saloon Revue
13 Walt Disney World Railroad Station

TOMORROWLAND

33 Astro Orbiter
34 Buzz Lightyear's Space Ranger Spin
35 The ExtraTERRORestrial Alien Encounter
36 Tomorrowland Speedway
37 Space Mountain
38 The Timekeeper
39 Walt Disney's Carousel of Progress
40 Skyway to Fantasyland
41 Tomorrowland Transit Authority

·········· Parade Route

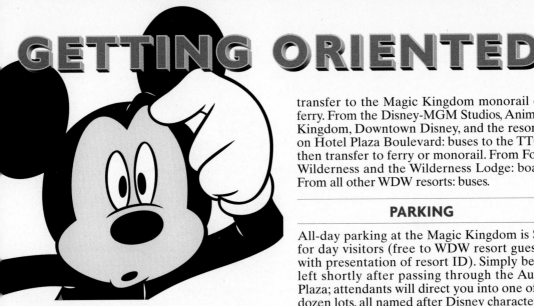

GETTING ORIENTED

When you visit Walt Disney World's original theme park, it's vital to know the lay of the lands. The Magic Kingdom has seven "lands"—Main Street, U.S.A.; Adventureland; Frontierland; Liberty Square; Fantasyland; Mickey's Toontown Fair; and Tomorrowland. Main Street begins at Town Square, located just inside the park gates, and runs directly to Cinderella Castle. The area in front of the castle is known as the Central Plaza, or, more aptly, the Hub. Bridges over the several narrow waterways here serve as passages to each of the lands.

As you enter the park, the first bridge on your left goes to Adventureland; the next, to Liberty Square and Frontierland. On your right, the first bridge heads to Tomorrowland, the second to Fantasyland and Mickey's Toontown Fair. The end points of the pathways leading to the lands are linked by a street that is roughly circular, so that the layout of the Magic Kingdom resembles a wheel. All attractions, restaurants, and shops are found along the wheel's rim and spokes.

Free guidemaps are available just inside the turnstiles, at City Hall in Town Square, and at many shops throughout the park. Be sure to pick one up as soon as possible. You'll find it an invaluable navigational and scheduling resource.

HOW TO GET THERE

Take Exit 25 off I-4. Continue about four miles to the Auto Plaza and park; walk or take a tram to the main entrance complex, known as the Transportation and Ticket Center (TTC). Choose a five-minute ferry ride or a slightly shorter trip by monorail for the last leg of an anticipation-filled journey.

By WDW Transportation: From the Grand Floridian, Contemporary, and Polynesian: monorail (Contemporary also has a walkway). From Epcot: monorail to the TTC, then transfer to the Magic Kingdom monorail or ferry. From the Disney-MGM Studios, Animal Kingdom, Downtown Disney, and the resorts on Hotel Plaza Boulevard: buses to the TTC, then transfer to ferry or monorail. From Fort Wilderness and the Wilderness Lodge: boat. From all other WDW resorts: buses.

PARKING

All-day parking at the Magic Kingdom is $5 for day visitors (free to WDW resort guests with presentation of resort ID). Simply bear left shortly after passing through the Auto Plaza; attendants will direct you into one of a dozen lots, all named after Disney characters. Minnie, Sleepy, and Dopey are within walking distance of the TTC; other lots are served by trams. Be sure to note the section and aisle in which you park. Also, know that the parking ticket allows for re-entry to the parking area throughout the day.

HOURS

The Magic Kingdom is generally open from 9 A.M. to 7 P.M. However, during busy seasons, it is open later than usual. It's best to plan on reaching the park entrance at least half an hour before the posted opening time. Another way to avoid the morning crush is to put off your visit until 1 P.M. or later. Call 824-4321 for up-to-the-minute schedules.

GETTING AROUND

Walt Disney World Railroad steam trains make a 21-minute loop of the park, stopping to pick up and discharge passengers at stations on the edge of Main Street, Frontierland, and Mickey's Toontown Fair. Horseless carriages, a fire engine, and horse-drawn trolleys take turns offering one-way trips down Main Street. And while the Skyway aerial tram is not necessarily the quickest commute between Tomorrowland and Fantasyland, the five-minute ride nets a fine bird's-eye view of the park.

Hot Tip

Wednesdays tend to be the least crowded days at the Magic Kingdom.

PARK PRIMER

BABY FACILITIES

The best place in the Magic Kingdom to take care of little ones' needs is the Baby Care Center. This center, equipped with changing tables and facilities for nursing mothers, is located at the Hub end of Main Street next to the Crystal Palace restaurant. Disposable diapers are kept behind the counter at many Magic Kingdom shops; just ask. Restrooms are also equipped with baby facilities.

CAMERA NEEDS

The Kodak Camera Center on Main Street proffers disposable cameras as well as the requisite film and batteries. Two-hour film processing is available here and wherever you see a Photo Express sign. Film is also sold in most Magic Kingdom shops.

DISABILITY INFORMATION

Most shops and restaurants, and many attractions, are accessible to guests in wheel-chairs. Convenient parking is reserved for guests with disabilities. Additional services are available for guests with visual or hearing disabilities. The *Guidebook for Guests with Disabilities* provides a detailed overview of all services available, including transportation, parking, and attraction access. For more information, refer to the "Travelers with Disabilities" section of the *Getting Ready to Go* chapter.

EARLY-ENTRY DAYS

On Monday, Thursday, and Saturday, guests staying at WDW resorts may enter the Magic Kingdom up to 1½ hours before

Hot Tip

The theme parks are the busiest on their respective early-entry days. WDW resort guests should "hop" to another park once the general public is admitted. Day guests should avoid early-entry days at all costs.

the official opening time to head for Space Mountain and Fantasyland attractions. Early-entry days and attractions are subject to change.

FERRY VS. MONORAIL

For guests arriving by car or bus, it's necessary to decide whether to travel to the Magic Kingdom by ferry or monorail. The monorail makes the trip from the Transportation and Ticket Center (TTC) in about five minutes. During busy seasons, the ferry will often get you there more quickly (long lines can form at the monorail, and most people simply don't make the short extra walk to the ferry landing). Vacationers who use wheelchairs should note that while the monorail platforms are accessible, the ramp leading to the boarding area is a bit steep.

FIRST AID

A registered nurse tends to minor medical problems at the First Aid Center, located near the Crystal Palace restaurant at the Hub end of Main Street.

INFORMATION

City Hall, located just inside the park entrance in Town Square, serves as the Magic Kingdom's information headquarters. Guest Relations representatives can answer questions. Park guidemaps, updated weekly (including details about entertainment, as well as character greeting times and locations), are available here, and all kinds of arrangements can be made, including priority seating for restaurants. Should you have problems with your park pass or a question about the number of unused days remaining on a pass, City Hall is the place to go.

LOCKERS

Attended lockers are located at Station Break, underneath the Main Street Railroad Station just inside the park entrance. Lockers are also available at the TTC. Cost is $5 per day (plus a $1 refundable deposit) for unlimited use. Items too big to fit into the larger units can be checked at the Station Break desk.

LOST & FOUND

On the day of your visit, report lost articles at City Hall or at the TTC. Recovered items can also be claimed at these locations. After your visit, call 824-4245.

LOST CHILDREN

Report lost children at City Hall or the Baby Care Center, or alert a Disney employee to the problem.

MONEY MATTERS

The Magic Kingdom has three ATMs: under Main Street's train station, near the Diamond Horseshoe Saloon in Frontierland, and at the Tomorrowland Light & Power Co. (near Space Mountain). Most foreign currency can be exchanged at City Hall.

Credit cards (American Express, Visa, MasterCard, and The Disney Credit Card) are accepted as payment for admission, merchandise, and meals at all full-service restaurants and fast-food locations. Traveler's checks and WDW resort ID cards are also accepted. Some food carts accept cash only.

Disney Dollars are available at City Hall in $1, $5, and $10 denominations. They are accepted for dining and merchandise throughout Walt Disney World and can be exchanged at any time for U.S. currency.

PACKAGE PICKUP

Individual shops can arrange for large or heavy purchases to be transported to a location next to Main Street's Emporium

for pickup after noon and until two hours before the Magic Kingdom closes. The service is free. (Disney resort guests may have packages delivered to their rooms at no extra charge.)

SAME-DAY RE-ENTRY

Be sure to have your hand stamped and to retain your ticket upon exiting the park if you plan to return later the same day.

STROLLERS & WHEELCHAIRS

Stroller and Wheelchair Rental, on the right, inside the Magic Kingdom entrance, offers one-day rentals of strollers, wheelchairs, and Electric Convenience Vehicles (ECVs). The cost for strollers and wheelchairs is $5, with a $1 refundable deposit; $30 for ECVs, with a $10 refundable deposit. Quantities are limited. Remember to keep your rental receipt; it can be used on the same day to obtain a replacement stroller or wheelchair at Epcot, the Disney-MGM Studios, Animal Kingdom, or at the Magic Kingdom.

TIP BOARDS

Located at the end of Main Street, U.S.A., closest to Cinderella Castle; in Tomorrowland; and in Frontierland; tip boards are an excellent source of information on waiting times for attractions, as well as showtimes and other entertainment information. Check the boards throughout the day.

Admission Prices

ONE-DAY TICKET

(Restricted to use only in the Magic Kingdom. Prices include sales tax and are subject to change.)

Adult...$44.52
Child*..$36.92

*3 through 9 years of age; children under 3 free

MAIN STREET, U.S.A.

Stepping onto Main Street, U.S.A., is like jumping through a time portal. Welcome to turn-of-the-century America! Horse-drawn trolleys are the transportation of choice, peppy marching bands underscore the bustle of merry, moving masses, and the tantalizing aroma of fresh-baked cookies constantly perfumes the air.

A rose-colored retrospective? Maybe. But this is Disney's version of a small-town Main Street—and the charm of this nostalgic land is lost on no one. Anchored by the old-fashioned train station at one end and a fairy-tale castle at the other, Main Street, U.S.A., whisks you from reality to fantasy in a few short blocks. Literally.

All of the addresses here feature just-dried coats of paint, curlicued gingerbread moldings, and pretty details. Add to that the baskets of hanging plants and genuine-looking gaslights, and Main Street, U.S.A., becomes a true showplace—both in the bright light of high noon and after nightfall, when the tiny lights edging all of the rooflines are flicked on.

The street represents an ideal American town. Although such a town never really existed, many claim to have served as the inspiration for it. Chances are Walt Disney got the idea from Marceline, Missouri, the tiny rural town that was his boyhood home.

Most of the structures along the thoroughfare are given over to shops, and each one is different. Some emporiums are big and bustling, others are relatively quiet and orderly; some are spacious and airy, others are cozy and dark. Inside and out, maintenance and housekeeping are superb.

White-suited sanitation workers patrol the street to pick up litter and quickly shovel up any droppings from the horses that pull the trolley cars from Town Square to the Hub. As in the rest of the Magic Kingdom, the pavement here is washed down every night with fire hoses. There's one crew of maintenance workers whose sole job is to change the little white lights around the roofs; another crew devotes itself to keeping the woodwork painted. As soon as these people have worked their way as far as the Hub, they start all over again at Town Square. The greenish, horse-shaped cast-iron hitching posts are repainted 20 times a year on average—and totally scraped down each time.

The "attractions" along Main Street, U.S.A., are relatively minor compared to the really big deals such as Tomorrowland's Space Mountain, Frontierland's Splash Mountain, or The Haunted Mansion in Liberty Square. But each and every shop has its own quota of merchandise that is meant as much for show as for sale. It's almost as entertaining to watch the cooks stir up batches of peanut brittle at the Main Street Confectionery as it is to actually savor a sweet sample. The shop windows, particularly at the Emporium, are also worth a look.

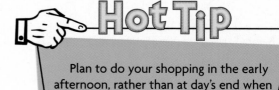

Plan to do your shopping in the early afternoon, rather than at day's end when the shops are normally jammed.

Once you start to meander along Main Street, be sure to notice the names on the second-story windows. Above the Main Street Confectionery is that of Walt's brother, Roy O. Disney; above The Shadow Box, that of Dick Nunis, chairman of Walt Disney Attractions. And you'll see Walt's name above the ice cream parlor. Other names are those of people connected with the Walt Disney Company.

Note: Attractions in Main Street, U.S.A., are described in the order that they are encountered upon entering the park.

WALT DISNEY WORLD RAILROAD: The best introduction to the layout of the Magic Kingdom, the 1½-mile journey on this rail line is as much a must for the first-time visitor as it is for railroad buffs. It offers an excellent orientation, as it passes by most of the park's major lands.

The 1928 steam engine happens to be exactly the same age as Mickey Mouse. Walt Disney himself was a railroad afficionado. During the early years of television, viewers watched films of him circling his own backyard in a one-eighth-scale train, the *Lilly Belle* (named for his wife).

The Walt Disney World Railroad also has a *Lilly Belle* among its quartet of locomotives. The others are named *Roy O. Disney*, *Walter E. Disney*, and *Roger E. Broggie* (a Disney Imagineer who shared Walt Disney's enthusiasm for antique trains). All of them were built in the United States

around the turn of the century and later taken to Mexico to haul freight and passengers in the Yucatán, where Disney scouts found them in 1969. The United Railways of Yucatán was using them to carry sugarcane. Brought north once again, they were completely overhauled, and even the smallest of parts were reworked or replaced.

All aboard: The Walt Disney World Railroad circles the park in 21 minutes, making stops in Frontierland, Mickey's Toontown Fair, and Main Street, U.S.A. Trains generally arrive in each station every 4 to 10 minutes. The lines are usually shortest at Mickey's Toontown Fair, but there's rarely a long wait at any station.

Note: The Walt Disney World Railroad does not run during fireworks presentations.

MAIN STREET VEHICLES: A number of these can be seen traveling up and down Main Street—horseless carriages and jitneys patterned after turn-of-the-century vehicles (but fitted with Jeep transmissions and special mufflers that make the putt-putt-putting sound); a spiffy scarlet fire engine, which is on display near the firehouse adjoining City Hall when not in operation; and a troop of trolleys drawn by Belgians and Percherons, two strong breeds of horse that once pulled plows in Europe. These animals—between six and ten years old, weighing in at about a ton each, and shod with plastic (easier on their hooves)—pull the trolley the length of Main Street about two dozen times during each of their three to four working days; afterward, they're sent back to their homes at the barn at the Fort Wilderness campground (where you can visit them). After their shift, the horses are often hosed down next to the firehouse. Kids love to watch.

DID YOU KNOW...

Before Disney World opened in 1971, Roy O. Disney changed the resort's official name to *Walt* Disney World. Why? He wanted everyone to know that it was his brother's dream.

ADVENTURELAND

Adventureland seems to have even more atmosphere than the other lands. That may be a result of its neat separation from the rest of the Magic Kingdom by the bridge over Main Street on one end and by a gallerylike structure (where it merges with Frontierland) on the other, or possibly it's because of the abundance of landscaping.

As for the architecture, although it was inspired by areas as diverse as the Caribbean, Polynesia, and Southeast Asia, it gives one the sense of being in a single place, a nowhere-in-particular that is both familiar and distinctly foreign, smacking of island idylls and tropical splendor. Shops offer imports from India, Thailand, Hong Kong, Africa, and the Caribbean islands.

As guests stroll away from Main Street, they just may hear the sound of beating drums, the squawks of parrots, the regular boom of a cannon. Paces quicken. And the wonders soon to be encountered do not disappoint.

Note: The Adventureland attractions are described in the order that they are encountered upon entering the land from the Hub and heading away from Cinderella Castle.

SWISS FAMILY TREEHOUSE: "Everything we need is right at our fingertips," said the father in Disney's 1960 rendition of the classic story *Swiss Family Robinson*. He was describing the treehouse that he and his kids built for the family after their ship was wrecked in a storm. When given a chance—several adventures later—to leave the island, all but one son decided to stay on. That decision is not hard to understand after a tour of the Magic Kingdom's version of the Robinsons' banyan-tree home. This is everybody's idea of the perfect treehouse, with its many levels and comforts—patchwork quilts, lovely mahogany furniture, candles stuck in abalone shells, even running water in every room. (The system is ingenious.)

The Spanish moss draping the branches is real; the tree itself—unofficially christened *Disneyodendron eximus*, a genus that is translated roughly as "out-of-the-ordinary Disney tree"—was constructed entirely by the props department. Some statistics: The roots, which are made of concrete, poke 42 feet into the ground, and about 300,000 lifelike polyethylene leaves "grow" on the tree's 1,400 individual branches.

JUNGLE CRUISE: Inspired in part by the 1955 documentary *The African Lion*, this ten-minute adventure is one of the crowning achievements of Magic Kingdom landscape artists for the way it takes guests through

surroundings as diverse as a Southeast Asian jungle, the Nile Valley, and an Amazon rain forest. Along the way, passengers encounter zebras, giraffes, lions, impalas, vultures, and headhunters (all of the Audio-Animatronics variety); they also see elephants bathing, and tour a Cambodian temple—while listening to an amusing, though corny, spiel delivered by the skipper. (Bet you didn't know that Schweitzer Falls was named after the famous doctor Albert . . . Falls.)

For most passengers, this is all just in fun. Gardeners, however, are always especially impressed by the variety of species coexisting in such a small area. To keep some more sensitive subtropical specimens alive, gas-fired heaters and electric fans concealed in the rocks pump hot air into the jungle when temperatures fall to 36 degrees (a rarity). This adventure, which is best enjoyed by daylight, is one of the Magic Kingdom's more popular

attractions, and it tends to be crowded from late morning until late afternoon.

As you exit the attraction, consider navigating your own miniature jungle boat at Shrunken Ned's Junior Jungle Boats. Note that park passes do not include use of the boats; there is an additional charge here.

THE ENCHANTED TIKI ROOM—UNDER NEW MANAGEMENT: Though cherished for their historical significance (the Tiki Birds were the first Audio-Animatronics attraction ever), the Tiki show was growing a bit tiresome. Now, thanks to clever new costars and zippy new tunes, the Tiki Room is rockin' once again.

The nine-minute show still features Michael, Pierre, Fritz, and

José (who is pining for his beloved Rosita)—plus some 225 birds, flowers, and tiki statues singing up a tropical storm. But before long, their sweet serenade is interrupted by an unimpressed Iago (Jafar's partner in crime from *Aladdin*).

It seems that Iago, along with Zazu from *The Lion King*, is a new owner of the Tiki Room—and he has big changes in store for the show. In a fractured version of "Friend Like Me," the bratty Iago warns the Tiki Birds that they'd "better get hip, or the audience will disappear." In a welcome twist, it is Iago who disappears, leaving the Tikis to prove just how hip they really are.

The fun-loving spirit of the revised rendition is downright infectious. While it helps to have seen the old show to appreciate all of the humor, veterans and newcomers alike are sure to get a kick out of The Tiki Room—Under New Management.

PIRATES OF THE CARIBBEAN: One of the very best of the Magic Kingdom's classic adventures, this ten-minute cruise is a Disneyland original, added to Walt Disney World's Magic Kingdom (in revised form) due to popular demand. Here guests board a simple boat and set sail for a series of scenes depicting a pirate raid on a Caribbean island town, dodging cannon fire and weathering one small, though legitimate, watery dip along the way. There are singing marauders, plastered pigs, and wily wenches; the observant will note that the leg of one rum-swilling swashbuckler, dangled over the edge of a bridge, is actually hairy.

While it's not the most politically correct attraction on-property, the rendition of "Yo Ho, Yo Ho; a Pirate's Life for Me"—the attraction's theme song—makes what is actually a rather brutal scenario into something that comes across as good fun. Before entering the queue area, stop and give a nod to the parrot dressed in the pirate costume, near the Pirates of the Caribbean sign.

FRONTIERLAND

With the Rivers of America lapping at its borders and Big Thunder Mountain rising up in the rear, this re-creation of the American Frontier encompasses the area from New England to the Southwest, from the 1770s to the 1880s. Hosts and hostesses wear denim, calf-length cutoffs, long skirts, or similar garb. Additionally, the shops, restaurants, and attractions have unpainted barn siding or stone or clapboard walls, and outside there are several wooden sidewalks of the sort Marshal Matt Dillon used to stride along. The Walt Disney World Railroad makes a stop here.

Note: Attractions are described as they are encountered upon entering the land from the Hub, heading away from Cinderella Castle.

DIAMOND HORSESHOE SALOON REVUE: Singing cowboys, dancing girls, silly jokes—this western dance hall has it all. Each 30-minute show features a madcap mix of melodies and mirth.

The Prohibition-style saloon (translation: no alcohol) serves soft drinks, sandwiches, and snacks. There's no table service, so you'll have to belly up to the bar should you wish to indulge. See *Good Meals, Great Times* for details.

Reservations are not required and guests may drop in at any point during a performance. The entertainment varies from show to show. Check a guidemap for details and showtimes. (Get there about 15 minutes early to snag a seat.)

FRONTIERLAND SHOOTIN' ARCADE: This arcade is set in an 1850s town in the Southwest Territory. Gun positions overlook Boothill, a town complete with bank, jail, hotel, and cemetery. But bullets have given way to electronic beams at this shooting gallery.

Genuine Hawkins .54-caliber buffalo rifles have been refitted, and when an infrared beam strikes any of the targets, an interesting result is triggered. Struck tombstones rise, sink, spin, or change their epitaphs; hit the cloud and a ghost rider gallops across the sky; a bull's-eye on a gravedigger's shovel causes a skull to pop out of the grave. Sound effects—howling coyotes, creaking bridges, and shooting guns—are created by a digital audio system. Note that admission passes do not include use of the Frontierland Shootin' Arcade; there is an additional charge here.

COUNTRY BEAR JAMBOREE: The Country Bears may never make it to Broadway, but they don't seem to mind. Disney's brood of banjo-strummin' bruins have been playing to packed houses in Grizzly Hall for more than a quarter century. Judging by all the toe tappin' and hand clappin' that accompany each performance, the show remains a countrified crowd pleaser. As for the few folks who aren't charmed by the backwoods ballads and down-home humor, well, they just have to grin and *bear* it.

As guests are settling into their seats (all of which provide a decent view of the show), Buff, Max, and Melvin are already beginning to grumble. Despite their status as permanent fixtures in the theater, the mounted animal heads would rather not "hang around all day" waiting for the show to get going. The 17-minute review opens with a rousing ditty by the Five Bear Rugs. The wheels set in motion, the remaining songs come fast and furious. Together, they capture the spirit of a genre that has a tendency to celebrate and lampoon itself simultaneously.

For example, Bunny, Bubbles, and Beulah bemoan "All the Guys That Turn Me On Turn Me Down"; Henry, the emcee who sports a coonskin cap (which is still attached to the coon), belts out "The Ballad of Davy Crockett"; and Big Al, the tone-deaf piéce de résistance, woefully croons "Blood on the Saddle," much to the delight of the giggle-prone audience.

Timing Tip: Lines can get long during busy periods. It's worth noting, however, that huge groups of people are admitted together so that once a line starts moving, it dwindles rather quickly.

TOM SAWYER ISLAND: This small patch of land in the middle of the Rivers of America has hills to scramble up; a working windmill, Harper's Mill, with an owl in the rafters and a perpetually creaky waterwheel; and a few pitch-black (and scary) caves. To reach the island, guests take a raft across the river. (It's the only way to get there and back.)

Paths wind this way and that, and it's easy to get disoriented, especially the first time around. Keep an eye out for the large mounted maps scattered about the island.

There are two bridges here—a suspension bridge and a so-called barrel bridge, which floats atop some lashed-together wooden barrels. When one person bounces, everybody lurches—and all but the most chickenhearted laugh. Both bridges are easy to miss, so keep your eyes peeled and ask an employee for directions if the path eludes you.

Across the suspension bridge is Fort Langhorn. Inside the fort, there are about a dozen air guns for youngsters to fire in a ceaseless cacophony. Keep poking around and you'll discover a twisting, dark, and occasionally scary escape tunnel. Walk along the pathway on the banks of the Rivers of America and you'll find your way back to the bridges.

The whole island seems as rugged as backwoods Missouri, and, probably as a result, it actually feels a lot more remote than it is—enough to be able to provide some welcome respite from the bustle.

One particularly pleasant way to relax here is over lemonade and a snack at Aunt Polly's Dockside Inn. (The pickles are quite popular.) Restrooms are located at the main raft landing and inside Fort Langhorn.

Timing Tip: This attraction closes at dusk.

SPLASH MOUNTAIN: On the day this attraction made its official 1992 Walt Disney World debut, *everyone* got soaked—thanks in part to a particularly potent Florida rain cloud. But the rain wasn't entirely responsible for the sea of soggy Magic Kingdom guests. The five-story drop into an aqueous briar patch was. And a steady stream of thrill seekers have been taking the plunge ever since.

In this guaranteed smile inducer, guests enjoy a waterborne journey through brightly colored swamps and bayous, down waterfalls, and are finally hurtled from the peak of the mountain to a briar-laced pond five stories below.

Splash Mountain is based on the animated sequences in Walt Disney's 1946 film *Song of the South*. The scenery entertains as the story line follows Brer Rabbit through a variety of exploits as he tries to reach his "laughin' place." It's tough for a first-time rider to take in all the details, since the tension of waiting for the big drop is all-consuming.

It is a bit terrifying at the top, but once back on the ground, it seems most riders can't wait for another trip—even though they may get drenched! (Water-wary guests are often seen wearing rain ponchos on this attraction. On the other hand, if you *want* to get wet, try to sit up front; seats in the back provide a smaller splash.)

By the second or third time around, it's possible to relax a bit, enjoy the interior scenes, and take in the spectacular views of the Magic Kingdom from the top of the mountain. At this point you may even manage to keep your eyes open for the duration of the final fall—or at least part of it.

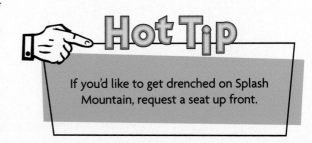

If you'd like to get drenched on Splash Mountain, request a seat up front.

Splash Mountain's designers not only borrowed characters and color-saturated settings from *Song of the South* but also used quite a bit of the film's Academy Award–winning music in this attraction. As a matter of fact, the song in Splash Mountain's final scene, "Zip-A-Dee-Doo-Dah," has become something of a Disney anthem over the years.

Note: You must be at least 40 inches tall to ride Splash Mountain.

BIG THUNDER MOUNTAIN RAILROAD:

It's certainly not hard to spot Big Thunder, the lone red rock formation this side of the Mississippi. Even newcomers to the Magic Kingdom will be able to distinguish the landmark from its two famed counterparts—Splash and Space Mountains—because it's the only one that actually looks like a mountain range. The designers took Utah's Bryce Canyon as their inspiration, and the resemblance is remarkable.

According to Disney legend, the 2.5 acre mountain is chock-full of gold. Unfortunately for the residents of Tumbleweed, the local mining town, a flood has ruined any chance of uncovering the remainder of it. Before these gold diggers find drier land, they are having one last party at the saloon to celebrate their riches. Even though in danger of washing away, they don't seem too worried, and guests who decide to take a trip on the Big Thunder Mountain Railroad have nothing to worry about either.

As passengers board the 15-row train they are advised to "hang on to your hats and glasses 'cause this here's the wildest ride in the wilderness." Do heed the warning, but don't despair. The ride, though thrilling, is relatively tame, so relax and enjoy the sights. Note that passengers seated nearest the caboose experience a bit more turbulence than those up front.

A bleating billy goat atop a peak, a family of possums hanging overhead, and a dark cavern full of bats, not to mention chickens, donkeys, and washed-up miners, can be spotted along the way. Be sure to keep an eye out for the not-yet-sunken saloon—it's easy to miss the first time around.

A continuous string of curves and dips around Big Thunder's pinnacles and caverns is sure to please thrill seekers of all ages, but the adrenaline surge is caused by more than just the speed of the trip. The added sound of a rickety track, a steam whistle that blows right before the train accelerates into a curve, and an unexpected earthquake all compound the passengers' anticipation, making this attraction one of the Magic Kingdom's most popular.

Timing Tip: Plan to visit early in the morning, during an evening parade, or just before park closing, when lines are generally shorter.

LIBERTY SQUARE

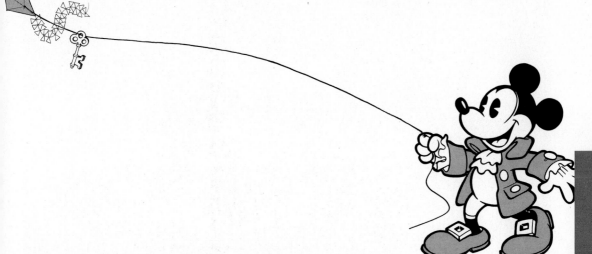

The transition between Frontierland on one side and Fantasyland on the other is so smooth that it's hard to say just when you arrive at Liberty Square, yet ultimately there's no mistaking the location. The small buildings are clapboard or brick and topped with weather vanes; the decorative moldings are Federal or Georgian in style; the glass is sometimes wavy, and there are flower boxes in shop windows, brightly colored gardens, neatly trimmed borders of Japanese yew, and masses of azaleas in a number of varieties and shades of white, pink, and red. There are a number of good shops, most notably The Yankee Trader and Ye Olde Christmas Shoppe; plus two of the park's most popular attractions, The Haunted Mansion and The Hall of Presidents; and the Liberty Tree Tavern, one of the most charming full-service restaurants in the Magic Kingdom.

Liberty Square is also home to one of the most delightful nooks in all the Magic Kingdom — the small, secluded area just behind Ye Olde Christmas Shoppe. There are tables with umbrellas, plenty of benches, and big trees to provide shade — and the sound of the crowds seems a million miles away.

Note: Liberty Square attractions are described in the order they are encountered upon entering the land from the Hub and heading away from Cinderella Castle.

THE HALL OF PRESIDENTS: This is not one of those laugh-a-minute attractions, like Pirates of the Caribbean or the Country Bear Jamboree; it's long on patriotism and short on humor. But the detail of this 20-minute show certainly is fascinating. After a film (presented on a sweeping 70mm screen) discusses the importance of the Constitution from the time of its framing through the dawn of the space age, the curtain goes up on what some guests have mistakenly called the "Hall of Haunted Presidents." A portion of today's presentation of The Hall of Presidents derives from the Disney-designed Illinois Pavilion's exhibition Great Moments with Mr. Lincoln, from New York's 1964–65 World's Fair.

At the Magic Kingdom show, Bill Clinton and Abraham Lincoln have speaking roles. All 42 chief executives are announced in a roll call and each responds with a nod; careful observers will note the others swaying and nodding, fidgeting, and even whispering to each other during the proceedings.

Costumes were created by two famous film tailors coaxed out of retirement. Not only are the styles those of the period in which each president lived, but so are the tailoring techniques and the fabrics. Some had to be specially woven for the show. Each of the Audio-Animatronics figures has at least one change of clothes; jewelry, shoes, hair texture, and even George Washington's chair are all re-created exactly as indicated by careful research of paintings, diaries, newspapers, and government archives. Perceptive viewers should be able to see the braces on Franklin Delano Roosevelt's legs. The effect is so lifelike that the figures look almost real, even at very close range.

Timing Tip: Planning to pop in on the presidents? Visit at a quarter past or a quarter till the hour. That's usually when the show starts.

LIBERTY BELLE RIVERBOAT: The *Liberty Belle*, built in dry dock at Walt Disney World, is a real steamboat. Its boiler turns water into steam, which is then piped to the engine, which drives the paddle wheel that propels the boat. It is not the real article in one respect, however: It moves through the half-mile-long, nine-foot-deep Rivers of America on an underwater rail. The pleasant 17-minute ride is a good way to beat the heat on steamy afternoons. En route, a variety of props create a sort of Wild West effect: moose, deer, a burning cabin, and the like.

Birnbaum's Best

THE HAUNTED MANSION: This eight-minute experience is among the Magic Kingdom's most enjoyable. However, guests who expect to be scared silly when they enter the big old house, modeled after those built in the Hudson River Valley in the 18th century, will be a tad unfulfilled. In deference to the small children and other easily frightened souls who tour the Magic Kingdom every day, The Haunted Mansion steers clear of anything too terrifying, and a good-spirited voice-over keeps the mood light.

Once inside the portrait hall, which you enter after passing through the front doors, it's amusing to speculate: Is the ceiling moving up—or is the floor dropping? It's also where you meet your "ghost host" and learn how he met his untimely demise.

The spooky journey through the mansion takes place in a "doom buggy." The attraction is chock-full of tricks and treats for the eyes; just when you think you've seen it all, there's something new: bats' eyes on the wallpaper, a plaque that reads "Tomb, Sweet Tomb," a suit of armor that comes alive, a terrified cemetery watchman and his mangy mutt, and the image of a creepy lady in a crystal ball.

One of the biggest jobs of the maintenance crews here is not cleaning up, but keeping things dirty. Since the mansion is littered with some 200 trunks, chairs, dress forms, harps, rugs, and assorted other knickknacks, it requires a lot of dust. This is purchased by the five-pound bagful and distributed by a device that looks as if it were meant to spread grass seed—sort of a vacuum cleaner in reverse. Local legend has it that enough dust has been used since the park's 1971 opening to bury the mansion. (Which begs the question: Where did it all go?) Cobwebs are bought in liquid form and strung up by a secret process.

When waiting to enter, take note of the amusing inscriptions on the tombstones in the overgrown cemetery.

FANTASYLAND

Walt Disney called this a "timeless land of enchantment," and his successors term it "the happiest land of all"—and it is, for some. Although it's not precisely a kiddieland, it is the home of a number of rides that are particularly well liked by children. The nursery rhyme cadences of "It's a Small World" appeal to them, as do the bright colors of the trash baskets, the flowers, and the tentlike rooftops; and they delight in the fairy-tale architecture and ambience, reminiscent of a king's castle courtyard during a particularly lively fair.

Note: Fantasyland attractions are described in the order that they are encountered upon entering the land via Cinderella Castle and proceeding roughly clockwise through the land.

CINDERELLA CASTLE: Just as the amiable mouse named Mickey stands for all the merriment in Walt Disney World, this storybook castle represents the hopes and dreams of childhood—a time in life when anything seems possible.

At a height of about 190 feet, Cinderella Castle is nearly twice the height of Disneyland's Sleeping Beauty Castle. It was inspired by the architecture of 12th- and 13th-century France, the country where the classic fairy tale originated, as well as the Bavarian King Ludwig's fortress and designs prepared for Disney's 1950 classic, *Cinderella*.

Unlike real European castles, this one is made of steel and fiberglass; in lieu of dungeons, it has service tunnels. Its upper reaches contain security rooms; there's even an apartment originally meant for members of the Disney family (but never occupied). From any vantage point, Cinderella Castle looks as if it came straight from the land of make-believe.

Mosaic Murals: The elaborate murals beneath the castle's archway rank among the true wonders of the World. They tell the story of the little cinder girl and one of childhood's happiest happily-ever-afters, using a million bits of glass in some 500 different colors, plus real silver and 14-karat gold.

Cinderella Wishing Well: This pleasant alcove, nestled along a pathway that leads to Tomorrowland, is the perfect spot to gaze at the castle. Any coins tossed into the water are donated to children's charities.

CINDERELLA'S GOLDEN CARROUSEL: Not everything in the Magic Kingdom is a Disney version of the real article. This carousel, discovered at the now-defunct Olympic Park in Maplewood, New Jersey, was built back in 1917. That was the end of the golden century of carousel building that began around 1825 (when the Common Council of Manhattan Island, New York, granted one John Sears a permit to "establish a covered circus for a Flying Horse Establishment"). During the Disney refurbishing, many of the original horses were replaced with horses made of fiberglass.

While waiting for the two-minute ride, it's worthwhile to take the time to study the animals carefully. No two are exactly alike. The band organ, which plays favorite music from Disney Studios (such as the Oscar winners "When You Wish Upon a Star," "Zip-A-Dee-Doo-Dah," and "Be Our Guest"), was made in one of Italy's most famous factories.

LEGEND OF THE LION KING: Based on the animated film *The Lion King*, this Fantasyland show combines 25 minutes of animation, puppetry, special effects, and music to make guests feel as if they walked into a cel from the film. In the pre-show area guests meet Rafiki, the wise baboon who serves as

the narrator. His voice is provided by stage and television actor Robert Guillaume. A clip from the film is shown and Rafiki recounts the legend that is about to unfold.

Once inside the 500-seat theater, visitors see the movie's Circle of Life scene presented on a stage. As the sun rises over Pride Rock, Mufasa assures his son, Simba, that he will always be with him. The characters are depicted by fully articulated puppets—when they speak, their mouths move accordingly. Some of the puppets require up to four people to coordinate their head, feet, ear, and mouth movements. The story advances to other scenes, introducing the assorted characters. Some of the more familiar voices you hear are those of Jeremy Irons as the evil Scar, James Earl Jones as Mufasa, Cheech Marin as Banzai, and Whoopi Goldberg as Shenzi.

Guests experience environmental effects, including warm winds during scenes in the Serengeti Plain, and mists of rain and cold winds during jungle nights. The climactic stampede scene begins on the screen; the noise builds and the theater shakes as smoke gives way to darkness. Note that small children may be frightened when the room goes dark.

PETER PAN'S FLIGHT: "Come on everybody, here we go!" So says Peter Pan at the start of this nonstop flight to Never Land. The three-minute adventure, which takes you soaring in a pirate ship, fancifully retells the story of Peter Pan—the boy with a knack for flying and an immunity to maturity. The effects in this classic attraction are simple, but enchanting.

The journey starts in the Darling family nursery—which Wendy, Michael, and John quickly abandon to follow Peter on a trip to his homeland. As in Disney's animated feature, one of the most beautiful scenes—and one that makes this attraction a treat for grown-ups as well as smaller folk—is the sight of nighttime London, dark blue and speckled with twinkling lights. Keep your eyes peeled for such landmarks as Big Ben and London Bridge.

By the time you spot your first mermaid, you're deep in the heart of Never Land. Alas, something is terribly wrong—Captain Hook and his buccaneer buddies have taken the Darling kids captive. It's all really a trap for Peter (Hook is still peeved at Pan for serving his hand to a hungry crocodile). Does everyone live happily ever after? We'll *never* tell.

Timing Tip: The slow-moving lines for this attraction can be daunting. To avoid the big crowds, plan to visit in the late evening or during any of the parades throughout the day.

SKYWAY TO TOMORROWLAND: This aerial tram transports guests one-way to Tomorrowland in about five minutes. En route it's possible to see the striped tent tops of Cinderella's Golden Carrousel, the Tomorrowland Speedway, and the not-so-wonderful rooftops of the buildings where many Magic Kingdom adventures take place.

This attraction is best boarded at its Tomorrowland station, where the lines are usually shorter. Guests with disabilities who are able to leave their wheelchairs may make a round-trip from the Fantasyland station.

IT'S A SMALL WORLD: *Hola! Guten Tag! Hello!* No matter what language you speak, what you look like, or where you live, you still have a lot in common with folks the world over (including an especially high

Many Fantasyland attractions are dark, and in some cases the special effects may be too intense for small children.

tolerance for a singsong melody that relentlessly reminds us that it's a small world after all). That's the message driving this ten-minute boat ride around the world.

Originally created for New York's 1964–65 World's Fair, the attraction is an oldie-but-goodie (and is quite popular with young children). The ride moves at slightly swifter than snail's pace, drifting past hundreds of colorfully costumed kids from around the world—all of whom know all the words to the ride's infectious theme song.

A showcase of diversity, the attraction is a simple celebration of human similarities. It's also a relaxing alternative to many of the park's higher-tech, longer-line attractions.

DUMBO THE FLYING ELEPHANT: This is purely and simply a kiddie ride—though such noted grown-ups as gymnast Nadia Comaneci and Muhammad Ali have loved it. A beloved symbol of Fantasyland, the ride is most popular with the two- to seven-year-old set. Inspired by the 1941 film classic *Dumbo*, the attraction lasts two memorable minutes. Consider stopping here during the afternoon parade, when the line—which is often prohibitively long—thins out a bit. Incidentally, the mouse that sits atop the hot air balloon at the center of the circle of flying elephants is Dumbo's faithful sidekick, Timothy Mouse.

MAD TEA PARTY: The theme of this two-minute ride—in a group of oversize pastel-colored teacups that whirl and spin wildly—was inspired by a scene in the Disney Studios 1951 movie production of Lewis Carroll's novel *Alice in Wonderland*. During the sequence in question, the Mad Hatter hosts a tea party for his un-birthday.

Unlike many rides in Fantasyland, this is not just for younger kids; the 9-to-20 crowd seems to like it best. Keep in mind that when the cups stop spinning, your head may continue to do so. Skip this ride if you suffer from motion sickness or if you've recently enjoyed a snack. Don't miss the woozy mouse that pops out of the teapot at the center of the platform full of teacups—he ignored our advice.

MR. TOAD'S WILD RIDE: Wild in name only, this three-minute attraction is based on the 1949 Disney release *The Adventures of Ichabod and Mr. Toad*, which itself derives from Kenneth Grahame's classic novel *The Wind in the Willows*. It seems that a gang of weasels have tricked Mr. J. Thaddeus Toad into trading the deed to his mansion for a motorcar that turns out to have been stolen.

In the attraction, flivvers modeled on this very car take guests zigging and zagging along the road to Nowhere in Particular, through dark rooms painted in neon colors and lit by black lights, where you witness

Mr. Toad trying to get out of the scrape. In the process, you crash through a fireplace, narrowly miss being struck by a falling suit of armor, hurtle through haystacks and a barn door and into a coop full of squawking

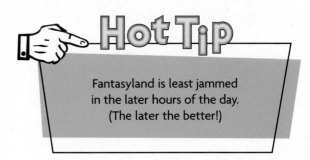

Fantasyland is least jammed in the later hours of the day. (The later the better!)

chickens, then ride down a railroad track on a collision course with a train. Some of this is scary enough for some younger children to end up momentarily frightened. By and large, though, this is a ride to be enjoyed with kids.

SNOW WHITE'S ADVENTURES: This three-minute attraction takes guests on a twisting, turning journey through a few happy moments and several scary scenes from the Grimm brothers' fairy tale, which Walt Disney made into the world's first full-length animated feature in 1937. Snow White makes several appearances, as do the seven Audio-Animatronics dwarfs. But the wicked witch—evil, long-nosed, and practically toothless—appears more than once with a suddenness that startles some youngsters. The adventure ends happily, as the dwarfs wave goodbye to Snow White and the prince.

Ariel's Grotto

The Little Mermaid's Ariel doesn't greet Magic Kingdom guests in the traditional way, since mermaids, like most fish, find it difficult to walk around theme parks. Instead, she invites folks of all ages to stop by her Fantasyland home away from home—a colorful grotto surrounded by starfish, coral, and waterfalls. Here guests can meet and pose for a picture with the popular Disney heroine (don't forget your camera). The area, which is especially popular with little ones, also features a soft-surface play zone filled with squirting fountains. Note that the line here is often long enough to scare Ursula herself.

MICKEY'S TOONTOWN FAIR

The newest neighborhood in the Magic Kingdom was built with little visitors in mind. Scaled-down buildings, vibrant colors, and an abundance of Disney characters make Mickey's Toontown Fair a veritable children's paradise. Not only do Mickey, Minnie, and their pals keep homes here, but the county fair is always in town. Tucked away behind Fantasyland, the area can be reached by taking a path from the Mad Tea Party or Space Mountain and via the Walt Disney World Railroad. Guests who arrive by stroller are advised to park their vehicles in the lot across from Pete's Garage. Keep in mind that the traffic here is the heaviest early in the day.

Note: Attractions are described in the order that they are encountered upon entering the area from Fantasyland and proceeding counterclockwise.

THE BARNSTORMER: At Goofy's Wiseacre Farm, guests of all sizes climb into crop dusters and follow the same fluky flight path taken by the Goof himself. The planes zip through the farm and crash through a barn, causing quite a ruckus among the chickens. Don't let the size fool you—this roller coaster proves that big thrills come in small packages. Although guests as young as three are allowed to ride, it may be too turbulent for some.

Take time to explore Goofy's Wiseacre Farm before lining up for the ride. Cotton, tomatoes, and other real crops have been spotted growing here. The observant may notice the unconventional parking spot that Goofy found for his plane (hint: look up). Plan to swing by the farmers market on your way out. In addition to souvenirs, the shop sells cupcakes, bananas, and other simple snacks. Feel like putting together your own strawberry shortcake? You're in luck. A buffet-style setup has everything you'll need. (No oven necessary. The cake's already baked.)

TOON PARK: Centrally located, this covered green provides a nice respite from the sun (or the rain). There are shaded benches surrounding a spongy, toddler-friendly surface and a small menagerie of topiary "bushes" (cushiony copies of the real thing) to climb on. The pig has even been known to oink when poked in the right place. Expect others to speak in their native tongues, too.

DONALD'S BOAT: If you're looking to cool off a bit, stop at Donald Duck's boat, the *Miss Daisy*. The vessel has sprung so many leaks, it looks like a fountain. It's almost impossible to walk across the "duck pond" without getting squirted once or twice. The ship's interior, though sparse, includes a captain's wheel and a whistle—pull it and water shoots out the top.

MICKEY'S COUNTRY HOUSE: Don't bother knocking—the door to Mickey's house is always open. Guests are welcome to peer inside each of the four rooms in this modest cottage. The kitchen is being remodeled, but it's worth a peek (after which you'll vow never to hire Donald Duck and Goofy to redecorate your own home). As the gameroom shows, the Mouse is quite a sportsman, dabbling in everything from table tennis to football. (Is that a Heisman trophy on the shelf?!)

Despite all there is to see, one thing is conspicuously missing from Mickey's house . . . Mickey himself. Don't despair. The head judge of the county fair is in the Judge's Tent, where he greets guests all day long. (It's the best place to meet Mickey in all of Walt Disney World.) To get there, slip out the back door of the house and follow the path toward the tent. (Others can exit through the garage, which packs some surprises of its own.) It's fun to check out the backyard, where Mickey's award-winning garden is bursting with giant vegetables, many of which have mouse ears. This is also the spot to take a peek at Pluto's doghouse.

JUDGE'S TENT: An absolute must for fans of the Mouse, this place is all Mickey all the time. The waiting area (and there's always a wait) features a pre-show video that highlights all of his county fair successes. All guests are treated to a private meeting with the star, so have those cameras ready! To get to the Judge's Tent, take a trip through Mickey's Country House. The line is usually shortest late in the day.

TOONTOWN HALL OF FAME: Just beyond Cornelius Coot Commons and across from Goofy's Wiseacre Farm is the Toontown Hall of Fame. The tent is stocked with Disney souvenirs as well as some of the prizewinning entries from the Toontown Fair. (Only the former are for sale.) Beyond this area, three different rooms offer guests the chance to meet any number of Disney characters. Stop in one room to meet the classic characters, including Goofy, Chip and Dale, and Pluto. Other rooms provide the opportunity to meet Pooh and his pals from the Hundred Acre Wood or some fairy-tale characters from Disney feature films past and present. Note that there is a separate line for each room, and characters vary throughout the day.

MINNIE'S COUNTRY HOUSE: Since Minnie and Mickey are neighbors here in the country, Minnie's house is merely a hop, skip, and a jump from Mickey's. Young kids will love it here because the special toon furniture is meant for climbing. As they explore, guests can push a button to listen to answering-machine messages, open the refrigerator (Minnie has cheese chip ice cream in the freezer, which is actually chilly inside), and try in vain to snatch some chocolate chip cookies (it's a clever mirror trick, courtesy of Minnie herself). The screen porch is quite lovely, and full of special plants. Don't miss the palm tree (it's made of hands), the Tiger Lilies (feline faces), and the Twolips (no explanation necessary). Minnie has been known to make appearances in the gazebo out back.

PETE'S GARAGE: This cleverly disguised restroom is the only place to make a pit stop in Mickey's Toontown Fair.

The original Tomorrowland attempted a serious look at the future. But as Disney planners discovered, it isn't easy to portray a future that persists in becoming the present. So the old Tomorrowland has given way to a friendlier, space-age town whose neighborhood atmosphere is more in keeping with the other lands in the Magic Kingdom. This is the future that never was, the fantasy world imagined by the science fiction writers and moviemakers of the 1920s and '30s. It's a land of sky-piercing beacons and glistening metal, where shiny robots do the work, whisper-quiet conveyances glide along an elevated highway, and even time travel is possible.

Note: All Tomorrowland attractions are described in the order that they are encountered upon entering the land from the Hub and heading (roughly counterclockwise) away from Cinderella Castle.

THE TIMEKEEPER: A fantastic 20-minute multimedia presentation combining a Circle-Vision 360 film with Audio-Animatronics characters and special in-theater effects is hosted by Timekeeper, a wacky mad scientist robot. Inspired by the likes of Jules Verne and H. G. Wells, who wrote about fantastic visions of the future, Timekeeper has created the world's first and only working time machine (at least as far as we know). Assisting Timekeeper in his time voyage demonstration is 9-Eye, a flying robot camera who is the test pilot for Timekeeper's invention. She has volunteered to fly through history and transmit pictures back to guests in the 360-degree time chamber. Guests are able to experience what it was like to hear the young Mozart play his first composition and to see Leonardo da Vinci working on a masterpiece, among many other exciting stops on this whirlwind trip through time and space.

In a sweep of the 1900 Paris Exposition, guests see Jules Verne and H. G. Wells. When Verne hitches a ride to the present and beyond, he gets to see some of his visions realized. Guests may recognize the voice of Timekeeper as that of Robin Williams. Other stars featured are Rhea Perlman as 9-Eye, Jeremy Irons as H. G. Wells, and Michel Piccoli as Jules Verne.

THE EXTRATERRORESTRIAL ALIEN ENCOUNTER: The Tomorrowland Interplanetary Convention Center is the home of the Magic Kingdom's scariest attraction. Created by Disney Imagineers and director George Lucas, Alien Encounter features some of the most elaborate special effects ever employed by a theme park.

The premise is this: The Convention Center is hosting X-S Tech, a mysterious corporation from a distant planet. X-S Tech's objective is to impress earthlings with its high-tech products. Following a brief pre-show, guests are shown to a circular auditorium with a large teleporter (a machine that

"beams" objects from place to place) in the center. Screens around the theater display a live transmission from their planet. Restraints are suddenly lowered onto guests' shoulders. (Don't panic—this is not rough, just scary.) Sit up straight as the restraint comes down. It will enhance your enjoyment of the show. Just then, X-S Tech's Chairman Clench volunteers to be teleported to the Magic Kingdom.

Special effects abound as guests await the arrival of Chairman Clench. But something goes wrong, and an angry alien is transported into the audience as the theater goes black. Next comes a series of creepy sensations designed to convince everyone that the monster has found its way to their side. (And, no, you are not imagining it—something really is breathing down your neck.)

Note: This 20-minute attraction may be too intense for some children. You must be at least 44 inches tall to enter Alien Encounter.

BUZZ LIGHTYEAR'S SPACE RANGER SPIN:

The Evil Emperor Zurg is up to no good. As soon as he swipes enough batteries to power his ultimate weapon of destruction—*KER-PLOOEY!*—it's curtains for the toy universe as we know it. It's up to that Space Ranger extraordinaire Buzz Lightyear and his Junior Space Rangers (that means you) to save the day.

Tomorrowland's newest attraction is a video game–inspired spin through toyland. The adventure is experienced from a toy's point of view. Guests begin their 4½-minute tour of duty as Space Rangers at Star Command Action Center. It's really a big "toy" play set with a Buzz Lightyear theme.

Star command is also where Buzz gives his team a briefing on the dangerous mission that lies ahead. Then it's off to the Launch Bay to board the ride vehicles, XP-38 Star Cruisers. The ships feature laser cannons, glowing lights, and a piloting joystick.

In addition to Buzz and the evil Emperor, you may recognize some other toy faces swirling about—the little green, multi-eyed alien squeaky toys, best known for their awe of "the claw." The squeakies have been enlisted to help in the fight against Zurg. (They and their counterparts were animated by Pixar, the creative team responsible for the groundbreaking set of *Toy Story* films. *Toy Story* director, John Lasseter, was also on board to shape the ride's storyline.)

Once Junior Space Rangers blast off, they find themselves surrounded by Zurg's robots, who are mercilessly ripping batteries from other toys. As Rangers fire cannons at the robots, beams of light and puffs of smoke fill the air. Hit a target and—*POW*—knock the robot's block off. For every target hit, you'll be rewarded with sight gags, sound effects, and points. The points, which are tallied automatically, are accumulated throughout the journey. Although the vehicles follow a rigid flight path (they're on a track), the joystick allows riders to maneuver the ships, arcing from side to side or spinning in circles while taking aim at surrounding targets.

When the star cruiser finally arrives at Zurg's spaceship, it's showdown time. Will good prevail over evil? Or has time run out for the toy universe? And, most important of all, will you score enough points to rank as a Space Ranger First Class?

TOMORROWLAND TRANSIT AUTHORITY:

Boarded near Astro Orbiter, these trains (formerly known as the WEDway PeopleMover) move at a speed of about seven miles per hour along almost a mile of track, beside or through most of the attractions in Tomorrowland. They are operated by a linear induction motor that has no moving parts, uses little power, and emits no pollution.

The peaceful excursion takes about ten minutes. There is almost never a wait to board.

ASTRO ORBITER:

Here, passengers fly around for two minutes in machine-age rockets designed to look more like oversize Buck Rogers toys than 1990s space shuttles. Riders are surrounded by vibrantly colored, whirling planets as they get an astronaut's-eye view of Tomorrowland.

WALT DISNEY'S CAROUSEL OF PROGRESS:
First seen at New York's 1964–65 World's Fair
and moved here in 1975, this 20-minute show
features a number of tableaux starring an
Audio-Animatronics family, and demonstrates the improvements in American life
that have resulted from the use of electricity.
The audience moves around the scenes as on
a carousel. An updated final scene has been
added, in which guests see what life might be
like in the near future: A grandmother plays
a virtual reality game and the oven talks.

SKYWAY TO FANTASYLAND: An aerial
cable car, this attraction transports guests
from Tomorrowland to a point near Peter
Pan's Flight in Fantasyland in five minutes.
The cable car, built in Bern, Switzerland, is
notable for being the nation's first con-
veyance of its type able to make a 90-degree
turn. If you're going to ride the Skyway, this
is the place to get on: The lines at the Fantasyland end are usually slightly longer.

SPACE MOUNTAIN: This attraction, which
blasted onto the Magic Kingdom scene in
1975, is a can't-miss crowd pleaser for throngs
of thrill seekers. Rising to a height of over 180
feet, this gleaming steel and concrete cone
houses an attraction that most people call a
roller coaster. It's the Disney version—a roller
coaster and then some.

While the 2-minute, 38-second ride doesn't
quite duplicate a trip into space, there are
impressive effects—shooting stars and flash-
ing lights among them—and the ride takes

If you have doubts about riding
Space Mountain, or would like to
assess the wait time, take a trip on the
Tomorrowland Transit Authority. It travels
through the queue area inside Space
Mountain and offers a view of the rockets
as they hurtle through the darkness.

place in an outer space–like darkness that gets
inkier and scarier as the journey progresses.

The rockets that roar through this blackness
attain a maximum speed of just over 28 miles
per hour. The Space Mountain experience is

wild enough to send eyeglasses, purses, wallets,
and even an occasional set of false teeth plum-
meting to the bottom of the track, so be sure to
find a safe place for your possessions before
the ride starts. It's also turbulent enough to
upset the stomachs of those so unwise as
to ride it immediately after eating—but not
so harrowing that knees shake for more than
a minute or two after "touchdown." (Those
who chicken out at the last minute have
their own exit from the queue area.)

Note: Guests under 44 inches are not permitted to ride, and as the signs at the attraction warn, you must be in good health and
free from heart conditions, motion sickness,
back or neck problems, or other physical
limitations to ride. Expectant mothers
should pass up the trip.

The Tomorrowland Light & Power Co., an
arcade by Space Mountain's exit, is a great
place to wait for your party if you skip the
ride. An ATM is available.

TOMORROWLAND SPEEDWAY: Little cars
that burn up the tracks at this attraction provide most of the background noise in Tomorrowland. Kids love the ride and will spend as
many hours driving the gas-powered cars
as they can.

Like true sports cars, the vehicles have rack-
and-pinion steering and disc brakes, but unlike
most sports cars, these run along a track. Yet,
even expert drivers have trouble keeping them
going in a straight line. (Don't panic when you
notice the lack of a brake pedal—when
you take your foot off the gas, the car comes to
a quick, if not screeching, halt.) The one-lap
trip takes about five minutes.

Note: You must be at least 52 inches tall to
drive the cars by yourself.

SHOPPING

No one travels all the way to the Magic Kingdom just to go shopping. But as many a first-time visitor has learned with some surprise, shopping is one of the most enjoyable pastimes here.

The Magic Kingdom's boutiques and stores stock much more than just Disneyana. Along with the more predictable items in Main Street shops, it's possible to find cookbooks and stoneware dishes, pirate hats and toy frontier rifles, 14-karat gold charms and filigreed costume jewelry. In Adventureland, you can buy imported items from around the world—hand-carved elephant statues from Africa, batik dresses from Indonesia, and more. Shops generally stock items that complement the themes of the various lands.

In some shops, you can watch people at work—a candymaker pouring peanut brittle in the Main Street Confectionery, a glassblower crafting wares in Main Street's Crystal Arts, and the like. And every store offers a selection of items from the inexpensive to the somewhat costly.

Finally, some advice. We recommend shopping in the early afternoon, rather than at day's end, when the shops are more crowded. However, keep in mind that Main Street shops do stay open a half hour after park closing, in case you need any last-minute gifts on the way out of the park. Also note that purchases can be stored for the day in lockers under the Walt Disney World Railroad's depot or, in the case of very large items, sent to package pickup. WDW resort guests may arrange for purchases to be sent to their hotel rooms free of charge. Purchases may be shipped on request.

Main Street

THE CHAPEAU: This Town Square shop is the place to buy Mouse ears and have them monogrammed, and to shop for straw hats, baseball caps, and assorted other headgear.

CRYSTAL ARTS: Pretty cut-glass bowls, vases, urns, glasses, and plates glitter in the mirror-backed glass cases of this crystal-chandeliered emporium. An engraver or a glassblower is always at work by the bright light that floods through the big windows. There is a crystal castle on display in the window out front. Presented by the Arribas Brothers.

DISNEY & CO.: The wallpaper at this lovely shop on Center Street (the cul-de-sac just off Main) is Victorian and the woodwork elaborate; old-fashioned ceiling fans twirl slowly overhead. This shop specializes in intimate apparel.

DISNEY CLOTHIERS: This shop features an array of clothing, including sweatshirts and flannel sleepwear, all of which incorporate Disney characters in some way. Bags, jewelry, watches, and other accessories round out the selection.

DISNEY'S WALK AROUND THE WORLD: This outdoor booth, located near the entrance to the Magic Kingdom, answers questions and processes applications for sponsorship of the personalized bricks used to build the walkway surrounding the Seven Seas Lagoon. For information about Disney's Walk Around the World, call 934-2990.

Where to Eat in the Magic Kingdom

A complete listing of all eateries—full-service restaurants, fast-food emporiums, and snack shops—can be found in the *Good Meals, Great Times* chapter. See the Magic Kingdom section beginning on page 216.

EMPORIUM: Framed by a two-story-high portico, this Town Square landmark, the Magic Kingdom's largest gift shop, stocks stuffed animals and toys, an array of dolls, sundries, film, T-shirts, and more.

The cash registers always seem to be busy, especially toward the end of the afternoon and before park closing. It's a good place to shop, though, since it's only a few steps from lockers (under the train station) where packages can be stowed.

Don't forget to peer into the windows, which usually feature elaborate displays ranging from seasonal themes to character tableaux from the latest Disney movie.

FIREHOUSE GIFT STATION: Authentic firefighting paraphernalia provides the backdrop for a variety of *101 Dalmatians* products, Mickey Mouse firefighter souvenirs, and reproductions of historical firefighting objects.

HARMONY BARBER SHOP: The quaint, old-fashioned setting for this working shop (complete with occasional appearances by a harmonizing quartet) merits a peek even if you have no need for a trim. It's open from 9 A.M. to 5 P.M. daily.

KODAK CAMERA CENTER: Having recently moved to a location next to Tony's Town Square restaurant, this is still the spot for film, batteries, photo albums, disposable cameras, two-hour film processing, and very minor camera repairs.

MAIN STREET ATHLETIC CLUB: Sports-related gifts and apparel are the hallmarks of this shop. The merchandise features images of Disney characters pursuing their favorite sports. The shop also stocks golf shirts with a small Mickey embroidered on the pocket.

Let It Rain

The show doesn't stop just because of a storm. Instead, shops all over the Magic Kingdom stock bright yellow Mickey ponchos to outfit guests who have left their own rain gear back home, at their hotel, or in the car.

MAIN STREET CONFECTIONERY: Tasty chocolates are sold in this newly expanded old-fashioned pink-and-white paradise. A delight at any time of day, but especially when the cooks in the shop's glass-walled kitchen are pouring peanut brittle onto a table to cool. Then the candy sends up clouds of aroma that you could swear were being fanned out onto the street. Several batches are made each day; the sweet product is for sale in small bags, along with jelly beans, marshmallow crispies, and dozens of other ways to satisfy a sweet tooth.

MAIN STREET GALLERY: The focus here is on Disneyana—including limited-edition Disney plates, cels from Disney movies, and other collectibles. (The store is located in the building formerly occupied by the bank.)

MAIN STREET MARKET HOUSE: An old-fashioned spot, with cookies, candy, and housewares, including specialty tins, napkin rings, and espresso cups. The floors are pegged oak, and the lighting emanates from brass lanterns.

NEWSSTAND: No newspapers are sold in the Magic Kingdom—even at its newsstand, which is near the park entrance. (It's to the left, just inside the turnstiles.) The stand sells a small selection of character merchandise and souvenirs.

THE SHADOW BOX: Watching Rubio Artist Co. silhouette cutters snip black paper into the likenesses of children is one of Main Street's more fascinating diversions.

STROLLER AND WHEELCHAIR RENTAL: Inside the turnstiles on the right as you enter the park, this rental concession offers a limited number of strollers and wheelchairs (available on a first-come, first-served basis). Souvenirs may also be purchased here.

UPTOWN JEWELERS: Modeled after a turn-of-the-century collectibles shop, this store specializes in jewelry, china, and other gift items. One counter stocks wonderful souvenir charms in 14-karat gold and sterling silver, among them Tinker Bell, Cinderella Castle, and the Walt Disney World logo (a globe with mouse ears). There's also a selection of Disney character figurines, priced from $3.50 to $3,500. Clocks and watches in all shapes and sizes are available here, including Mickey Mouse watches in a variety of configurations. There are even a few pocket watches to consider adding to your timepiece collection.

Adventureland

BWANA BOB'S: A colorful hut full of the critters you may have just observed on the Jungle Cruise or at The Enchanted Tiki Room.

ELEPHANT TALES: A variety of women's and men's clothing with a safari theme is featured at this shop. Women's accessories and safari plush toys are also available.

ISLAND SUPPLY: This tropical surf shop features a vast assortment of surfing clothing and accessories.

TRADERS OF TIMBUKTU: Located in a marketlike complex opposite The Enchanted Tiki Room, this shop displays a selection of the sort of handsome (but inexpensive) trinkets that travelers find in parts of Africa—carved

wooden giraffes and antelope, ethnic jewelry (including carved bangles and malachite-and-elephant-hair baubles), and khaki shirts.

Caribbean Plaza

HOUSE OF TREASURE: A good spot to pick up pirate hats, this swashbuckler's delight adjoins Pirates of the Caribbean on the west and stocks nautical gifts and pirate merchandise—toy rifles, a Pirate's Creed of Ethics, Jolly Roger flags, rings, pirate dolls, sailing-ship models, ships in a bottle, and eye patches.

PLAZA DEL SOL CARIBE BAZAAR: Located next to the Pirates of the Caribbean attraction, this market sells candy and snacks, a variety of straw hats (including colorful oversize sombreros), piñatas, pottery, straw bags, clothing, and artificial flowers.

Frontierland

BIG AL'S: Named for the most popular (and least talented) member of the Country Bear Jamboree, this riverfront shop is the place to acquire a variety of leather goods, coonskin caps, and assorted six-shooters.

BRIAR PATCH: Cuddly creatures from The Hundred Acre Wood—Winnie the Pooh and all of his pals—are featured at this shop, located near the exit to Splash Mountain.

FRONTIER TRADING POST: Outfit a child like a true youngster of the Great Frontier. Cowboy hats or feathered headdresses and moccasins, sleeve garters, sheriff's badges, gold nugget and turquoise jewelry, and reproduction rifles should do the trick.

FRONTIER WOOD CARVING: The spot for wooden gifts with personalized carvings.

PRAIRIE OUTPOST & SUPPLY: Stop by this turn-of-the-century general store for candy, coffee, and cookies. Decorative items such as candles are also for sale.

TRAIL CREEK HAT SHOP: Hats of all kinds plus feathered hatbands and leather goods are on sale at this small shop tucked away near the Diamond Horseshoe Saloon Revue.

Liberty Square

HERITAGE HOUSE: Early American reproductions predominate in the stock of this store next to The Hall of Presidents. Parchment copies of famous American documents are popular with youngsters. Collectors might be tempted to snap up busts of the presidents, souvenir spoons, mugs in Early American motifs, or documents signed by famous figures from American history. Campaign buttons, flags, T-shirts, and Statue of Liberty items are also available.

ICHABOD'S LANDING: This small Liberty Square shop gives guests on their way to The Haunted Mansion a taste of things to come, with horrific monster masks and assorted ghoulish goodies. It's also the place to pick up an invisible pooch. Operates seasonally.

LIBERTY SQUARE PORTRAIT GALLERY: In the midst of Liberty Square, next to The Hall of Presidents, guests can sit to have their portraits drawn in this open-air studio.

THE YANKEE TRADER: This quaint little shop, near The Haunted Mansion, is crammed with kitchen items. There are Mickey waffle irons and Mickey-shaped pasta, among other Disney-themed goods. The shop also stocks jams and jellies, cooking oils and sauces, pots, dishes, and other creative kitchenware.

YE OLDE CHRISTMAS SHOPPE: A wide variety of decorative Christmas items, including tree-top dolls, automated display characters, angel figurines, and souvenir ornaments—Disney-themed and traditional—is available year-round.

Fantasyland

THE KING'S GALLERY: This shop, inside Cinderella Castle, features a line of knight-wear and other medieval items such as swords and shields. In addition, it stocks items related to Cinderella herself, as well as her castle (including glass slippers).

KODAK KIOSK: A convenient location to buy film and other photo supplies.

SEVEN DWARFS' MINING CO.: This souvenir stand next to Snow White's Adventures sells assorted Disney-motif key chains, candies, and stuffed animals, plus a colorful collection of Snow White merchandise.

SIR MICKEY'S: Expect to find all sorts of Disney souvenirs in this shop with a theme based on the "Brave Little Tailor"—the cartoon in which Mickey defeats a giant to win the hand of Princess Minnie. (It was one of the most elaborate and expensive Mickey Mouse cartoons ever made.) Notable items include embroidered denim jackets, character sweatshirts, and videos.

TINKER BELL'S TREASURES: One of the more wonderful boutiques in the Magic Kingdom. For sale are character clothing and costumes for kids, princess hats, stuffed animals, character toys, and an impressive array of Madame Alexander and other collector dolls. A must.

Mickey's Toontown Fair

COUNTY BOUNTY: Disney character memorabilia, featuring all the favorites, can be found in this merchandise location under the big tent. Look for costumes, children's apparel, autograph books, key chains, candy, and more. Don't miss the doll-making exhibit or the winning entries from previous fairs, including the "most upside-down cake," baked by Daisy Duck.

Tomorrowland

GEIGER'S COUNTER: This small shop near the Tomorrowland Speedway features a variety of souvenir hats, pins, and neon glow jewelry. It also monograms Mouse ears.

MERCHANT OF VENUS: The kinds of gifts and collector items that sci-fi enthusiasts love can be found here: futuristic toys, games, clothing, airbrushed shirts, and other such items. This is also the only shop that carries a selection of Alien Encounter merchandise.

Hot Tip

Merchandise found in shops at Walt Disney World is also available through mail order. Call 407-363-6200 for information.

MICKEY'S STAR TRADERS: This is one of the best places to go in the Magic Kingdom for Disney-themed items. Sunglasses and sun care products are also available.

URSA'S MAJOR MINOR MART: A small spot tucked away near the terminus of the Skyway to Fantasyland that's great for Disney souvenirs and Space Mountain T-shirts.

ENTERTAINMENT

In this most magical corner of the World, a tempting slate of live performances ranks among the more serendipitous discoveries. The Magic Kingdom's entertainment mix includes dazzling high-tech shows and old-fashioned numbers alike. To keep apprised of the offerings on any given day, stop at City Hall upon arrival at the park to pick up a current guidemap.

While the specifics are subject to change, the following listing is a good indication of the Magic Kingdom's extensive repertoire. As always, we advise calling 824-4321 to confirm entertainment schedules. For information on special events at the Magic Kingdom, see the "Holidays & Special Events" section of *Getting Ready to Go.*

ALL-AMERICAN COLLEGE MARCHING BAND: During weekdays in summer, this band, which features college students from around the country, performs throughout the Magic Kingdom in the afternoon and early evening.

CASEY'S CORNER PIANO: A pianist tickles the ivories of a snow-white upright daily at the centrally located Casey's Corner restaurant on Main Street.

DAPPER DANS: A barbershop quartet is likely to be encountered while strolling down Main Street. Conspicuously clad in straw hats and striped vests, the Dapper Dans tap-dance and let one-liners fly during their short four-part-harmony performances.

DIAMOND HORSESHOE SALOON REVUE: A dance hall such as might have been found in 19th-century Missouri hosts this lively old-time show with cancan dancers several times daily. Guests may drop in at any time during the performances.

DISNEY'S MAGICAL MOMENTS PARADE: This 15-minute dazzler has an interactive twist: cameo appearances by about 900 randomly selected Magic Kingdom visitors. (Guests are selected for participation and given a sticker by park employees walking along the parade route, beginning about 45 minutes before starting time.) The parade, which has six floats inspired by Disney films, as well as every character imaginable, begins at 3 P.M. in Frontierland and winds its way to Main Street, stopping eight times en route for special participatory sequences.

FANTASY IN THE SKY: This pyrotechnic extravaganza is presented during peak seasons and select weekends. The program opens (often at 10 P.M.) with Tinker Bell's Flight, a dramatic sprinkling of pyrotechnic pixie dust over Cinderella Castle. The seven-minute fireworks presentation is ideally viewed from Main Street, but there are good viewing locations in Fantasyland, Tomorrowland, and Frontierland. It is presented rain or shine.

FLAG RETREAT: At about 5:10 P.M., patriotic music fills the air as a color guard marches to Town Square, takes down the American flag that flies from the flagpole, and releases a flock of snow-white homing pigeons symbolic of the dove of peace. Watch carefully: They flap away toward their home (behind the castle) practically before you can say "Cinderella." The entire flight takes 20 seconds.

GALAXY SEARCH: The outdoor Galaxy Palace Theater in Tomorrowland hosts this talent show in search of unique entertainment, starring Mickey and his pals.

J. P. AND THE SILVER STARS: This group surfaces from time to time to play familiar tunes on steel drums, bringing a bit of the Caribbean islands to the area near Adventureland's Pirates of the Caribbean.

KIDS OF THE KINGDOM: Performing often in front of Cinderella Castle, this group puts on a lively show, featuring singing and dancing to Disney tunes—plus appearances by such characters as the portly Winnie the Pooh and Mickey Mouse himself.

RHYTHM RASCALS: Specialty songs and comic ditties from the Roaring Twenties on washboards and banjos are their trademark; they usually perform on Main Street.

SWORD IN THE STONE CEREMONY: Several times each day, a child is appointed temporary ruler of the realm by pulling the magical sword, Excalibur, from the stone in front of Cinderella's Golden Carrousel. Merlin the Magician presides over the ceremony.

WALT DISNEY WORLD BAND: This traditional concert band often performs during the flag retreat in Town Square and in front of the castle on select mornings and afternoons.

Holiday Happenings

It's a rare holiday that passes quietly in the Magic Kingdom. During certain holidays, such as Christmas, New Year's Eve, and the Fourth of July, this Kingdom usually breaks curfew, staying open extra late and stepping up its nighttime entertainment. On these occasions, special performances of SpectroMagic and the Fantasy in the Sky fireworks are often in store. Of course, entertainment plans are subject to change, so it's important to call 824-4321 for current schedules.

EASTER: A nationally televised holiday parade on Main Street makes Easter an especially delightful, if a bit crowded, time to visit the Magic Kingdom.

FOURTH OF JULY: The busiest day of the summer—and with reason: There's a double-size fireworks display whose explosions light up the skies not only above Cinderella Castle but also over Seven Seas Lagoon.

CHRISTMAS: A towering Christmas tree goes up in Town Square, and the entire Magic Kingdom is decked out as only Disney can do it. On select evenings, the Magic Kingdom hosts a special-admission nighttime celebration called Mickey's Very Merry Christmas Party. The festivities, complete with hot chocolate and snow, include Mickey's Very Merry Christmas Parade and other holiday shows. There are also special holiday performances during the day.

NEW YEAR'S EVE: It has always been true that on December 31 the throngs are practically body to body. For a celebration of this nature, that can be lots of fun. Expect double-size fireworks and holiday decorations. There's plenty of nip in the air as the evening goes on, so dress accordingly.

Where to Find the Characters

Mickey and his pals appear near City Hall on Main Street throughout the day. Adventureland is a good spot to find Rafiki and Timon from *The Lion King*. Alice and her Wonderland friends show up in Fantasyland, as does Ariel. The Fantasyland Character Festival is an excellent spot to see characters. (Be sure to check the nearby character greeting information board, too.) The character meals at Crystal Palace, Cinderella's Royal Table, and Liberty Tree Tavern offer guests a chance to meet their favorites. But the best character place is at Mickey's Toontown Fair, where guests can meet Mickey, Minnie, and others. Check a guidemap for updated information.

The Night Sparkles with SpectroMagic

Since its premiere during Walt Disney World's 20th anniversary celebration, this parade has gotten rave reviews and taken its place among WDW's must-sees.

Fiber-optic cable and threads are conduits for shimmering lights that create everything from the "hair" on King Triton's beard on one float to daisy petals on another. Some 600,000 miniature bulbs

of the Walt Disney World Railroad depot.

The next-best viewing points are the curbs along Main Street. It gets very crowded there, so you must claim your foot of curb as much as 1½ hours ahead of time (particularly for the first running).

light in wild, changing patterns, moving in perfect concert with sound effects and musical score.

SpectroMagic follows the traditional parade route (heading from Main Street, U.S.A., to Frontierland); of all the spots along the way, the best (though very popular) vantage point is the platform

The parade lights up the Kingdom during peak seasons and select nights. If there are two shows, the first parade is always more crowded than the second.

Note: SpectroMagic may be canceled due to inclement weather.

HOT TIPS

- Allow plenty of time to sample the Magic Kingdom in small bites. Trying to see it all in a day (or even two) is like eating a rich ice cream sundae too quickly.

- Each day, sections of one park are open up to 1½ hours early for WDW resort guests only. But keep in mind that the parks can get crowded on these days—that's when a park hopper pass comes in handy.

- If you are not staying at a Walt Disney World resort, still plan to start out early. Most people arrive between 9:30 A.M. and 11:30 A.M., and the roads and parking lots are jammed. If you're coming at Easter, Christmas, or in summer, plan to arrive before 8:30 A.M. or wait until late afternoon, when things are less hectic. Be at the gates to the Magic Kingdom when they open, and then be at the end of Main Street when the rest of the park opens.

- Wear very comfortable shoes: You'll be spending a lot of time on your feet. (Note that no bare feet are permitted in the park.)

- WDW resort guests can have packages delivered to their hotels for free. (Keep in mind that it's often next-day delivery.)

- Check out the Tip Boards for information on the waiting times for the most popular attractions.

- You can usually get in line for an attraction right up until the minute the park closes.

- Avoid the mealtime rush hours by eating early or late: before 11 A.M. or after 2 P.M., and before 5 P.M. or after 8 P.M.

- At busy times, take in these not-so-packed attractions: Walt Disney World Railroad, Liberty Belle Riverboat, Carousel of Progress, and Tomorrowland Transit Authority.

- Break up your day. Go to one of the water parks, or head back to your hotel (if it's not too far) for some swimming. Be sure to have your hand stamped and hold on to your admission pass and your parking stub, so you can re-enter the Magic Kingdom.

- If your party decides to split up, set a meeting place and time. Avoid meeting in front of Cinderella Castle, since this area can become quite congested.

- Many Magic Kingdom attractions have two lines. The one on the left usually will be shorter, since most visitors automatically head for the one on the right.

- For a full-service meal in the Magic Kingdom, make advance priority seating arrangements by calling WDW-DINE (939-3463).

- There are picnic facilities at the TTC.

- If you want to be part of Disney's Magical Moments parade, choose your spot at least 45 minutes early. Guests are randomly picked to participate from the parade route.

Epcot

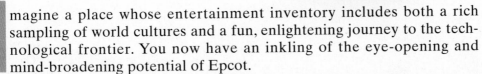

magine a place whose entertainment inventory includes both a rich sampling of world cultures and a fun, enlightening journey to the technological frontier. You now have an inkling of the eye-opening and mind-broadening potential of Epcot.

Walt Disney suggested the idea back in October 1966: "Epcot will be an experimental prototype community of tomorrow that will take its cue from the new ideas and new technologies that are now emerging from the creative center of American industry." It would never be completed, he said, but would "always be introducing and testing and demonstrating new materials and systems." Now, more than ever, Walt Disney's dream is a reality. Innoventions, an ever-evolving showplace of the near future, is continually bounding into new territory in its mission to close gaps with technological destiny. A transformed Universe of Energy has emerged. And with the addition of Test Track, Epcot guests have a (thrilling) inside track on the fast and perilous world of automobile testing.

The theme park, which opened in 1982, consists of two distinct areas of exploration: Future World and World Showcase. The former examines the newest and most intriguing ideas in science and technology in ways that make them seem not only comprehensible but downright irresistible. The latter celebrates the diversity of the world's peoples, portraying a stunning array of nations with extraordinary devotion to detail.

Think of Epcot as Disney's playground for the curious and the thoughtful. The experiences it delivers—all of them wonders of the real world—never fail to amaze, delight, inspire, and (rest assured) entertain.

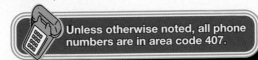
Unless otherwise noted, all phone numbers are in area code 407.

World Showcase

MOROCCO

FRANCE

JAPAN

INTERNATIONAL GATEWAY

THE AMERICAN ADVENTURE

AMERICA GARDENS THEATRE

UNITED KINGDOM

WORLD SHOWCASE LAGOON

Future World

ITALY

GERMANY

CANADA

JOURNEY INTO IMAGINATION

THE LAND

CHINA

SHOWCASE PLAZA

INNOVENTIONS WEST

INNOVENTIONS EAST

THE LIVING SEAS

NORWAY

MEXICO

TEST TRACK

SPACESHIP EARTH

To Buses

HORIZONS

Entrance Plaza

WONDERS OF LIFE

UNIVERSE OF ENERGY

N

GETTING ORIENTED

Double the Magic Kingdom and you have an idea of the size of Epcot. As for layout, the park is shaped something like a giant hourglass. The nine pavilions of Future World fill the northern bulb, while the international potpourri called World Showcase occupies the southern bulb. Future World is anchored on the north by the imposing silver "geosphere" dubbed Spaceship Earth.

As you pass through Epcot's main Entrance Plaza, Spaceship Earth looms straight ahead. Pathways curve around either side of the 180-foot-tall geosphere, winding up at Innoventions Plaza. Here, in addition to a huge show fountain, you see signposts for Innoventions, whose two buildings cradle the east and west sides of the plaza. Beyond this central area, there are two roughly symmetrical north–south avenues; these are dotted with the eight pavilions that form the outer perimeter of Future World. Test Track, Horizons, Wonders of Life, and Universe of Energy flank Spaceship Earth on the east, while Journey into Imagination, The Land, and The Living Seas lie to the west.

In World Showcase, the 11 international pavilions are arranged around the edge of sparkling World Showcase Lagoon, with The American Adventure directly south of Spaceship Earth on the lake's southernmost shore. A walkway from Future World leads to Showcase Plaza and World Showcase Promenade, a 1.2-mile thoroughfare that wraps all the way around the lagoon, winding past each World Showcase pavilion in the process. Proceeding counterclockwise around World Showcase, countries are encountered in the following order: Canada, the United Kingdom, France, Morocco, Japan, the United States of America (the host pavilion is called The American Adventure), Italy, Germany, China, Norway, and Mexico.

HOW TO GET THERE

Take Exit 26B off I-4. Continue along to the Epcot Auto Plaza; take a tram from the parking lot to the park's main entrance.

By WDW Transportation: From the Grand Floridian, Contemporary, and Polynesian: hotel monorail to the Transportation and Ticket Center (TTC), then switch for the TTC-Epcot monorail. From the Magic Kingdom: express monorail to the TTC, then switch for the TTC-Epcot monorail. From Fort Wilderness and Downtown Disney: buses to the TTC, then change for the TTC-Epcot monorail. From the Disney-MGM Studios, Animal Kingdom, all other WDW resorts, and the resorts on Hotel Plaza Boulevard: buses.

Note: A second Epcot entrance, called the International Gateway, provides entry directly to World Showcase. This gateway, which may be reached via walkways and water launches from the Swan, Dolphin, Yacht and Beach Club, and BoardWalk resorts, deposits guests between the France and United Kingdom pavilions.

PARKING

All-day parking at Epcot is $5 for day visitors (free to WDW resort guests with presentation of resort ID). Attendants will direct you to park in one of several lots named in honor of Future World pavilions. Trams circulate regularly, providing transportation between the lots and the main entrance. Be sure to note the section and aisle in which you park. Also, know that the parking ticket allows for re-entry to the area throughout the day.

HOURS

Future World is usually open from 9 A.M. to 9 P.M. World Showcase hours are 11 A.M. to 9 P.M. During certain holiday periods and the summer months, hours are extended. It's best to arrive at the park at least a half hour before the posted opening time, particularly during these busy seasons. Call 824-4321 for up-to-the-minute schedules.

GETTING AROUND

Water taxis, called *FriendShip* launches, ferry guests across the World Showcase Lagoon. Docks are located near Mexico, Canada, Germany, and Morocco. (The only other way to traverse the area is on foot.)

Admission Prices

ONE-DAY TICKET

(Restricted to use only in Epcot. Prices include sales tax and are subject to change.)

Adult...$44.52
Child*.......................................$36.04

*3 through 9 years of age; children under 3 free

PARK PRIMER

EPCOT

BABY FACILITIES

Changing tables and facilities for nursing mothers can be found at the Baby Care Center in the Odyssey Center, between Test Track and Mexico. Also, disposable diapers are kept behind the counter at many Epcot shops; just ask.

CAMERA NEEDS

The Camera Center on the west side of the Entrance Plaza and World Traveler in International Gateway stock film, batteries, and disposable cameras. Two-hour film processing is available here and wherever you see a Photo Express sign. A third camera shop is found in Journey into Imagination. Film is sold in most Epcot shops. Attendants may be able to assist with minor camera repairs.

DISABILITY INFORMATION

Nearly all attractions, shops, and restaurants are barrier-free. Parking for guests with disabilities is available. Additional services are available for guests with sight and hearing disabilities. The *Guidebook for Guests with Disabilities* is available at Guest Relations. It provides a detailed overview of all services. For more information, turn to *Getting Ready to Go*.

EARLY-ENTRY DAYS

On Tuesday and Friday, WDW resort guests may enter Epcot up to 1½ hours before the posted opening time and enjoy selected attractions at Future World—usually Honey, I Shrunk the Audience, The Living Seas, The Land, Spaceship Earth, and Test Track. Days and attractions are subject to change.

FIRST AID

Minor medical problems can be handled at the First Aid Center, located in the Odyssey Center, between Test Track and Mexico.

INFORMATION

Guest Relations, next to Spaceship Earth, is equipped with guidemaps, a helpful staff, and WorldKey Information Service terminals. Other terminals are near Germany and on the pathway to World Showcase.

LOCKERS

Lockers are found immediately west of Spaceship Earth. Cost is $5 plus a $1 refundable deposit for unlimited use all day.

LOST & FOUND

The Lost and Found department is on the west side of Epcot's main Entrance Plaza at the Gift Stop. To report lost items after your visit call 824-4245.

LOST CHILDREN

Report lost children at Guest Relations or the Baby Care Center, or alert a Disney employee.

MONEY MATTERS

There are ATMs on the east side of the Entrance Plaza, on the path between Future World and World Showcase, and near Germany. Currency exchange is handled at Guest Relations or at the American Express Travel Office on the west side of the Entrance Plaza. Credit cards (American Express, Visa, MasterCard, and The Disney Credit Card), traveler's checks, and WDW resort IDs are accepted for admission and merchandise, as well as meals at all full-service and fast-food restaurants.

PACKAGE PICKUP

Epcot shops can arrange for bulky purchases to be transported to the Gift Stop on the west side of the Entrance Plaza for later pickup. There is no charge for this service.

SAME-DAY RE-ENTRY

Be sure to have your hand stamped upon exiting the park and to retain your ticket if you plan to return later in the same day.

STROLLERS & WHEELCHAIRS

Strollers, wheelchairs, and Electric Convenience Vehicles (ECVs) may be rented from venues on the east side of the Entrance Plaza and at the International Gateway entrance. Wheelchairs are also available at the Gift Stop. Cost is $5 for strollers and wheelchairs, plus a $1 refundable deposit; and $30 for ECVs, plus a $10 refundable deposit. Quantities are limited. Keep your rental receipt; it can be used that same day to obtain a replacement stroller or wheelchair at Epcot or at any of the other theme parks.

TIP BOARD

Check this digital board in Innoventions Plaza throughout the day to learn current waiting times for the most popular attractions.

FUTURE WORLD

A wise alternative is to choose two or three pavilions from those described in this section, and then to head for World Showcase as soon as it opens at 11 A.M., moving clockwise around the lagoon on the first day of your visit and counterclockwise on the next. Then, in the afternoon, when many guests have shifted over to World Showcase, return to Future World. Innoventions is not only a fascinating spot to pass the exceptionally busy hours after lunch, but also a cool refuge when high temperatures prevail outdoors. And although queues can be found during peak seasons at Journey into Imagination, The Land, Horizons, Wonders of Life, and Test Track throughout most of the late morning and afternoon, the period from late afternoon until park closing is usually less hectic. But don't forget to make it back to World Showcase in time for the evening's fireworks and laser spectacular.

Future World pavilions are described here as a visitor encounters them while moving counterclockwise (from right to left, which is west to east, around the area).

A mere listing of the basic themes covered by the pavilions at Future World—agriculture, communications, car safety, the ocean, energy, health, and imagination—tends to sound a tad academic, and perhaps even a little forbidding. But when these serious topics are presented with that special Disney flair, they become part of an experience that ranks among Walt Disney World's most exciting and entertaining.

Some of these subjects are explored in the course of lively and unusual Disney "adventures," involving a whole arsenal of remarkable motion pictures, special effects, and Audio-Animatronics figures so lifelike that it is hard to remain unmoved. And Innoventions offers an invitation to sample cutting-edge technology. The basic elements are also appealing in their own right, from the palm-dotted Entrance Plaza and the massive buildings of Innoventions to the stupendous fountain just past Spaceship Earth and the many-faceted "geosphere" that has become the universal symbol of Epcot.

There is so much to see and enjoy that it's hard to know just what to do first. Many guests simply stop at Spaceship Earth on their way into Epcot and proceed to wander at random from one pavilion to the next through the morning. As a result, many of the pavilions are frustratingly crowded early in the day—especially Spaceship Earth.

Guest Relations

Located adjacent to Spaceship Earth, this is not only the principal source of Epcot information, but the spot to make restaurant priority seating arrangement via the easy-to-use touch-sensitive screens. (For more information, turn to page 247 in the *Good Meals, Great Times* chapter.)

When the terminals are not being used to arrange tables, they can be used to get an overall picture of Epcot, to learn about each pavilion in considerable detail, and to discover nearly everything else that a guest could conceivably want to know about Epcot. If the system's electronic A-to-Z index of shops, restaurants, attractions, and services does not answer a question, it's possible to communicate with a specially trained host or hostess (who is able to hear and see the querying guest with the aid of a microphone and video camera adjacent to the screen). Hosts and hostesses also manage the message service for Epcot guests and keep records of any lost children who may be at the Baby Care Center or Guest Relations.

Spaceship Earth

As it looms impressively just above the earth, this great faceted silver structure—visible on a clear day from an airplane flying along either Florida coast—looks a little bit like a spaceship ready to blast off. It appears large from a distance, and it seems even more immense when viewed from directly underneath. It's no surprise that some visitors simply stop beneath it and gawk. The show inside, which explores the continuing search by human beings for ever more efficient means of communication, remains one of Epcot's most visually compelling.

A common misconception about Spaceship Earth is that it is a geodesic dome. Not so. It's a *geosphere*. A geodesic dome is only half a sphere, while Spaceship Earth is almost completely round. Presented by AT&T.

SPACESHIP EARTH RIDE: The noted science fiction writer Ray Bradbury, together with a number of consultants from the Smithsonian Institution, the Los Angeles area's prestigious Huntington Library, the University of Southern California, and (among others) the University of Chicago, collaborated with Disney designers in developing this memorable 14-minute journey. It begins in an inky black time tunnel complete with a musty smell that suggests the dust of ages, and continues through history from the days of Cro-Magnon man (30,000 or 40,000 years ago) to the future.

The attraction features remarkable special effects, such as the flickering candles in the scene where a monk has nodded off, and the smell of smoke coming from the fall of Rome. Every scene is executed in exquisite detail. The symbols on the wall of that Egyptian temple really are hieroglyphics, and the content of the letter being dictated by the pharaoh was excerpted from a missive actually received by an agent of a ruler of the period.

All these sights are enough to keep heads turning as the "time machines" wend their way upward. The most dazzling

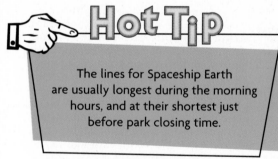

The lines for Spaceship Earth are usually longest during the morning hours, and at their shortest just before park closing time.

scene is the ride's finale, when the audience is placed in the heart of a communications revolution amid interactive global networks that tie all the peoples of the world together.

In the Global Neighborhood exhibit at the end of the journey, guests interact with emerging technologies such as voice-activated television and telephones with wacky sound effects.

GATEWAY GIFTS AND CAMERA CENTER: These two shops are located near the entrance to Spaceship Earth. The former sells Epcot souvenirs—shirts, mugs, toys, etc.—as well as sunscreen, tissues, and the like. Film and various other Kodak products, including disposable cameras, are sold at the Camera Center. Same-day film processing is available.

Innoventions

Imagine being able to get your hands on technological goodies fresh off the drawing board—gadgets that will one day change the way you live and work. At Innoventions, you can see, touch, and test products. The pavilion is one of Epcot's most experiential

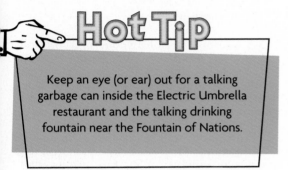

Keep an eye (or ear) out for a talking garbage can inside the Electric Umbrella restaurant and the talking drinking fountain near the Fountain of Nations.

areas. Equally important, it offers an unintimidating environment where you needn't know how to program a VCR to be able to try out supercomputers, experiment with virtual reality, and see a fully automated home in action.

Within the 100,000-square-foot area, diverse exhibits are presented by major manufacturers. Computers, games, telephones, and appliances are among the wide variety of products on display. Exhibits change constantly, making one of Walt Disney's original dreams for Epcot a reality. Well-informed employees are on hand to answer questions from curious—or even skeptical—visitors. It's also possible to register via computer terminals around the area to receive information about many new products at home.

Innoventions is separated into two buildings, referred to as Innoventions East and West. The outside area between the pavilions is filled with color, light, spinning mobiles, and sidewalks glistening with fiber-optic lighting effects. Inside, areas are divided by company (a sampling is described below). Since exhibits change often, there may be many different technologies available when you visit.

A "pre-show" hosted by Tom Morrow, a mini-robot and "a friend to technology" is a useful way to kick off the Innoventions experience. Above all, count on spending quite a while exploring the exhibit areas (at least an hour or two). There's so much to see and do that curiosity will often get the better of any schedule here.

INNOVENTIONS WEST: Exhibitors on the west side of Innoventions include **Sega**, which occupies a very large space. Kids love

to try out the numerous new and proposed video games here. There is also an actual "pay-as-you-play" arcade.

At the **AT&T** area, interactive exhibits deliver a straightforward introduction to the Internet.

IBM features new ways to think, work, and play with your computer. Try out some of IBM's newest technologies, such as speech recognition—kids love getting a cartoon puppy to sit, roll over, and fetch. (He understands several languages, too!) At the IBM Internet Postcards stations, visitors may have their picture taken and superimposed on a cool background, and then send it to friends and family across the Internet. (Remember to bring some e-mail addresses with you.)

Silicon Graphics has an all-new exhibit showcasing the latest advances in "visualization technology." A brief show in which computers spring to life is presented in the Visualization Theater.

INNOVENTIONS EAST: Exhibits shown on the east side of Innoventions include the entertaining House of Innoventions, presented by **Honeywell**. In a sample kitchen, living room, laundry room, bathroom, and bedroom, representatives demonstrate the latest ideas to help make home life a little easier by automating daily tasks. Some of the products include home security systems and a remote control toilet (with a heated seat). But our favorite is the Total Home—a computer that fully automates all of the above, plus the lighting, heating, and cooling systems, most appliances, and more.

At **Motorola**, an Audio-Animatronics figure named Sky Cyberguy hosts an amusing show, inviting guests to choose one of

three paths for a trip on Motorola's Information Skyway. It's also possible to try out hand-writing recognition software and two-way radios that allow you to talk to your family at the other end of the exhibit. But the big attraction here is the virtual reality exhibit, where guests line up to be immersed in a virtual game world while others watch on monitors.

GE displays its newest products, from home appliances to jet engines. GE TechnoLab is a multimedia educational exhibit featuring live shows and interactive demonstrations. In the NBC area, guests can exchange quips with "The Tonight Show" host Jay Leno, join the cast of "Saved by the Bell," or broadcast an NBC Sports Update.

Family PC sponsors an exhibit showcasing multimedia technologies. The themed activity areas include preschool, creativity, fun and games, reference and education, and families-on-line. Among the highlights for kids are interactive animated storybooks, including CD-ROMs reprising the latest Disney animated features.

The **General Motors** display allows guests to "test drive" a new electric vehicle called EV1, enhanced by surround sound and scenery, and see the inner workings of the technology in a cutaway model.

CENTORIUM: This enormous, recently expanded shop stocks a vast selection of Disney character memorabilia and souvenirs—watches, books, candy, key chains, T-shirts, pencils, hats, and much more—making this the number one source for character merchandise in Epcot. There are also many items related to the park itself, such as Spaceship Earth picture frames and Figment dolls, along with a large selection of Disney-themed apparel and children's clothing. A must.

THE ART OF DISNEY EPCOT GALLERY: Upstairs from Centorium is Epcot's spot for a unique assortment of Disney collectibles. The shop showcases a wide variety of Disney animation art, including production cels, hand-painted limited-edition cels, sericels, maquettes (character models), fine-art serigraphs, and lithographs. In addition, a large selection of decorative items include renditions of Disney characters by such well-known companies as Lladró.

The Living Seas

The Living Seas is the largest facility ever dedicated to humanity's relationship with the ocean, and was designed by Disney Imagineers, in cooperation with a board of some of the world's most distinguished oceanographic experts and scientists.

At The Living Seas, breakfast is usually served at 10 A.M. — for the fish! Stop by and watch the feeding frenzy.

A 2½-minute multimedia presentation provides an introduction saluting ocean research, beginning with early ships, diving bells, and submarines. The show also features a seven-minute film about how Earth's oceans were formed and about the diversity of the life that calls them home.

From there, a ride through a simulated Caribbean coral reef environment and the hands-on activities of Sea Base Alpha combine to prolong a visitor's stay.

CARIBBEAN CORAL REEF RIDE: To reach the sea cabs that make the trip to the coral reef, visitors enter "hydrolators," elevator-like capsules that create the illusion of diving deep under the sea while actually descending only about an inch. The man-made reef exists in an enormous tank that holds about six million gallons of water and more than 65 species of sea life. Among the 8,500 or so inhabitants are sea turtles, barracuda, angelfish, sharks, dolphins, and diamond rays.

Guests sometimes get to see scuba divers testing and demonstrating the newest diving gear and underwater monitoring equipment as they carry on training experiments with dolphins. Following the three-minute ride, guests are deposited at Sea Base Alpha.

EPCOT

Under the Sea

Two behind-the-scenes tours offer guests a closer look at life in The Living Seas underwater environs. DiveQuest gives certified scuba divers the opportunity to explore one of the world's largest aquariums. Dolphins in Depth offers guests the chance to learn about dolphin behavior as they closely observe researchers and trainers interacting with dolphins. Reservations for either tour can be made by calling WDW-TOUR (939-8687). For more information on both of these programs, turn to page 200 of the *Everything Else in the World* chapter.

SEA BASE ALPHA: This prototype undersea research facility, spread over two levels, includes a visitors center and six rooms, each dedicated to a specific subject. One focuses on ocean ecosystems and shows various forms of adaptation, including camouflage, symbiosis, and bioluminescence.

A 6,000-gallon tank displays another coral reef where Bermuda morays, barracuda, and bonnethead sharks swim about. Another room is dedicated to the study of porpoises and manatees. A tank features a step-in port, where guests can see the mammals up close.

At another station, a show stars an Audio-Animatronics submersible named Jason who describes for visitors the history of robotics and its use in underwater exploration. Guests can try a cutaway suit and test its maneuverability by doing tasks as part of a game. There are also video screens to test and expand your knowledge of oceanography.

Adjacent to the six rooms of Sea Base Alpha, the Sea Base concourse features three displays. The diver lockout chamber is where the crew enters and exits the ocean environment. Visitors can see divers enter, ascend, and disappear through the ceiling.

The Land

Occupying six acres, this enormous skylighted pavilion examines the nature of one of everybody's favorite topics—food. A film, *The Circle of Life*, uses characters from *The Lion King* to deliver an entertaining yet inspirational message about humanity and the environment. A boat ride explores farming in the past and future.

Guided tours give visitors the chance to learn about the experimental agricultural techniques being practiced in the pavilion. In addition, the subject of nutrition is touched upon in one of Epcot's wackiest attractions, a musical show called Food Rocks. The pavilion is presented by Nestlé.

Timing Tip: During peak seasons, lengthy queues build up for the boat ride and *The Circle of Life*. It's best to visit early in the morning and have a quick breakfast at the food court. Or wait until late afternoon, when many people have moved on to World Showcase.

LIVING WITH THE LAND: The 13½-minute boat ride through the rain forest and greenhouses in this pavilion opens with a dramatic storm scene. Guests sail through tropical rain forests, prairie grain fields, and a family farm. As the boat passes through each realistic setting, the guide offers commentary on humanity's ongoing struggle to cultivate and live in harmony with the land. Note some of the details that make each setting so convincing, such as sand blowing over the desert, and light flickering from the television set in the farmhouse window.

In the next segment, guests enter a plant research laboratory–solarium. Here, our planet's major food crops are being grown in research projects along with rare new crops that may someday help meet Earth's ever-growing dietary needs.

The guide on each boat provides information on the crops being grown. Also of interest are the experiments being conducted to explore the possibilities of raising fish like other farm products, and a desert farm area, where plants get nutrients through a drip irrigation system that delivers just the right amount of water—important in a dry climate.

As fantastic and unreal as they appear, all the plants on view in the experimental greenhouses are living. In contrast, those in the biomes (the ecological communities viewed from the boat ride) were made in Disney studios out of lightweight plastic that simulates the cellulose found in real trees. The trunks and branches were molded from live specimens; the majestic sycamore in the farmhouse's front yard, for example, duplicates one that stands outside a Burbank, California, car wash. Hundreds of thousands of polyethylene leaves were then snapped on.

THE CIRCLE OF LIFE: This 20-minute film uses animation and live action to illustrate some of the dangers to our environment, as well as potential solutions. Presented as a fable featuring *The Lion King* favorites Simba, Timon, and Pumbaa, the film takes an optimistic approach to a serious subject. It is shown in the Harvest Theater, just inside the entrance to The Land.

Soon after the film begins, Simba is startled by the shout of "Timber!" and is drenched by the splash of a fallen tree in the water. The culprits are none other than his friends Timon and Pumbaa, who are clearing the savanna for the development of the Hakuna Matata Lakeside Village. Simba seizes the opportunity to tell them a tale about creatures who sometimes forget that everything is connected in the Circle of Life: humans.

Simba demonstrates to Timon and Pumbaa the consequences of progress, as his lessons are driven home by visual evidence of humans' mistreatment of the air, water, and land. (Timon: "And everybody was *okay* with this?") The effect is a compelling mix of entertainment and a valuable message about environmental responsibility.

FOOD ROCKS: Classic songs have been humorously altered to deliver a nutritional message at this 15-minute mock rock concert. The show is set in a kitchen of cartoonish proportions, and life-size characters make this an entertaining show. It is hosted by Füd Wrapper, who was inspired by rap artist Tone Loc.

The opening number, performed by a "heavy metal" group—giant kitchen utensils atop a cartoon stove—is Queen's "Bohemian Rhapsody" with new lyrics. Musical guests include the Peach Boys, Neil Moussaka, Chubby Cheddar, the Get-the-Point-Sisters, and (Little) Richard.

It's interesting to note that Tone Loc, Chubby Checker, Neil Sedaka, Little Richard, and The Pointer Sisters actually recorded the parodies of their music.

BEHIND THE SEEDS: For guests who are interested in a more detailed look at the growing areas at The Land, one-hour guided tours take place throughout the day. The tour travels through four themed greenhouses where plants are grown hydroponically (without soil).

Different areas of the greenhouses showcase pioneering research projects undertaken in cooperation with NASA and the U.S. Department of Agriculture. Because this walking tour is an expanded version of the Living with the Land boat ride, the ride is suggested as a prerequisite.

Reservations, which are required, can be made in person on the day of the tour, inside the Green Thumb Emporium. Cost is $6 for adults and $4 for children ages three through nine. Call WDW-TOUR (939-8687) for information.

GREEN THUMB EMPORIUM: This little shop between the Sunshine Season Food Fair and Food Rocks stocks land-related merchandise such as hydroponic plants, seeds, books, and topiaries, as well as kitchen accessories.

Journey into Imagination

The oddly shaped glass pyramids that house Journey into Imagination (immediately to your right as you face World Showcase Lagoon) are striking. But they pale in comparison with the experiences inside, which are easily among the most whimsical at Epcot. The crown jewel here is a dazzling 3-D movie called Honey, I Shrunk the Audience. There's also a guided tour of the imagination, hosted by Dreamfinder, a jolly, professorial figure, and his sidekick, Figment. Another pavilion highlight is the electronic fun house known as Image Works. Not to mention the quirky fountains

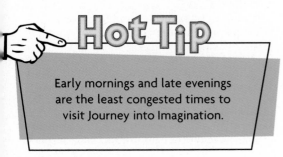

Early mornings and late evenings are the least congested times to visit Journey into Imagination.

outside—the Jellyfish Fountains, which spurt streams of water that spread out at the top, looking for an instant like their namesake sea creature, and the Leap Frog Fountains, which send out smooth streams of water that arc from one garden plot to another in the most astonishing fashion. Kids love them. Presented by Kodak.

Timing Tip: During peak seasons, the queue outside seems to be longest from about 10 A.M. to noon and remains fairly lengthy throughout most of the day. Count on spending an hour at the very least at this pavilion.

JOURNEY INTO IMAGINATION RIDE: It is here that Dreamfinder creates Figment out of a lizard's body, a crocodile's nose, a steer's horns, two big yellow eyes, two small wings, and a pinch of childish delight—and commences the visitor's journey into the world of imagination.

Together, Dreamfinder and Figment guide visitors on a 14-minute exploration of imagination. First there is a visit to the Dreamport, the area of the human mind to which the senses are constantly sending data to be stored for later use by the imagination. Subsequent scenes depict the way imagination suffuses the worlds of the visual and performing arts, science and technology, and literature. In the course of all this, laser beams dance, lightning crackles, and letters come pouring out of a gigantic typewriter like notes from an organ. The images are as fanciful as the imagination itself.

IMAGE WORKS: It's a rare Image Works visitor who doesn't experience at least some of the emotion felt by one four-year-old girl who cried every time her parents tried to take her home. That's not surprising, because Image Works is filled with activities that give every visitor the chance to use his or her imagination.

For instance, at Dreamfinder's School of Drama, near the entrance to Image Works, visitors have the opportunity to be in a video play. Guests step onto a small stage and, thanks to a Chroma-Key video-effects technique involving foreground and background matting, perform in short video stories. Spectators and performers alike see the results as they happen via video screens. It's always fun to watch the groups of people jumping crazily around onstage following on-screen instructions from Dreamfinder.

Another exhibit here is Figment's Coloring Book, where guests use computer technology to paint giant coloring-book images. Upon entering the Rainbow Corridor, you'll find a tunnel of neon tubes in all the hues of the rainbow. Another feature is Making Faces, a

set of screens that allow you to capture electronically your own image and then apply different features, hairstyles, even accessories.

Stepping Tones is like hopscotch with a musical twist. Hexagonal splotches of colored light on the floor correspond to sounds— a drumroll, a flourish on the harp, a couple of chords sung by a men's chorus, a snippet of hoedown fiddling, and such—emitted when the area is trod upon. The floor was "orchestrated" so that all possible combinations sound interesting at the very least—and the more the merrier.

Other activities include Light Writer, which involves drawing geometric patterns with laser beams, and the Magic Palette, where a special stylus and a touch-sensitive control surface can be used to create all kinds of images, mostly in Day-Glo colors. People often queue up to try these, while the huge kaleidoscopes and the unusual pin screens nearby are practically overlooked. Manufacturing the latter involved putting thousands of straight pins through a screen illuminated with colored lights from below (visitors run their hands across the bottom, thereby creating sweeping patterns of color).

The Electronic Philharmonic, one of the most amusing sections of Image Works, allows guests to take turns conducting an orchestra. Here's how this works: Each patch of light on the console represents a group of instruments (strings, woodwinds, brass, percussion). Moving one's hand above that patch of light increases and decreases the volume of the sound produced by that section of the "orchestra." The faster the movement, the louder they play.

Just outside Image Works, note the terrific photography display. The images are winners of Kodak's International Newspaper Snapshot Awards, and well worth a look.

HONEY, I SHRUNK THE AUDIENCE: Welcome to the Imagination Institute, workplace of Professor Wayne Szalinski, the featured character in the three hit "Honey" movies: *Honey, I Shrunk the Kids*; *Honey, I Blew Up the Kid*; and *Honey, We Shrunk Ourselves*. Rick Moranis, Marcia Strassman, and the kids reprise their film roles at this 25-minute attraction.

In the pre-show area, guests see a movie about the imagination. Then they are welcomed to the Imagination Institute and given an overview of what they will see inside the theater. Szalinski is to be presented with the Inventor of the Year Award, and will demonstrate several of his inventions. On the

way into the theater, guests are given "protective goggles" (3-D glasses), to shield their eyes from flying debris that can come loose during new-product demonstrations.

Once the audience is seated, Szalinski is nowhere to be found. Then he zooms off the screen in his new HoverPod, out of control and miniaturized by his shrinking machine. Szalinski's son Nick steps in to demonstrate the "Dimensional Duplicator," a machine that can make exact copies of anything. As Nick switches on the machine, his little brother Adam drops his pet mouse into the duplicating chamber and hits the number 999. Suddenly hundreds of mice pour out of the screen in an almost 4-D effect that leaves guests squirming.

Nick quickly gets rid of the mice with Professor Szalinski's No-Mess Holographic Pet System, which projects a 3-D cat out into the audience to scare away the mice. The cat morphs into a lynx and finally into a ferocious lion before overheating and exploding. Just then, Szalinski returns, blows himself up to normal size, and demonstrates his new, more powerful, shrinking machine. The machine spins out of control and accidentally shrinks the audience and Nick. While the audience is miniaturized the theater shakes with every on-screen footstep. When apparent giants crouch down to ogle guests in the theater, it's a rare person who doesn't feel diminished to ant proportions. The effects are very believable, particularly when Adam picks up the theater and shows it to his mom. Motion effects in the theater add to the realism, as does the full-size pet snake that gets loose. The audience is eventually brought back to normal size, of course, although not without incident. The attraction has one last surprise in store that we won't divulge.

Note: This attraction has been known to frighten small children and some adults (especially those afraid of snakes or mice).

CAMERAS AND FILM: A good selection of film is for sale here, along with disposable cameras and other photographic essentials.

Test Track

This new General Motors pavilion was among the most keenly anticipated in Epcot history (the official opening was delayed about a year). It is a thrill ride of the highest order, pushing Epcot to the fore of visitors' attention. Equally important, Test Track honors the park's mission to educate as well as entertain. It also happens to be one of the fastest rides in Disney history.

The industrial-looking pavilion puts guests through the frenetic motions of automobile testing. As vehicles progress along the track, they whiz down straightaways, hug hairpin turns, and face near-collisions—and not always in ideal road conditions. En route, riders learn how tests are performed in real facilities (called proving grounds) and discover why certain procedures are crucial to car safety.

Before developing the attraction, Disney Imagineers toured GM proving grounds around the country. The result: From the roll-up doors of its steely facade to the rows of authentic testing equipment inside, Test Track bears more than a passing resemblance to the real thing.

The experience begins with a 20-minute pre-show, a walking tour of the plant that reveals the incredible amount of component testing performed before automakers commit to production. Guests witness automotive testing vignettes, with everything from human interface (our courageous, crash-prone counterparts) to tires, brakes, air bags, and even seats being put through their paces.

The computer-controlled six-seater vehicles are equipped with video and audio, but no steering wheels or brake pedals. The roads bear the familiar lines and signage of the real world, adding to the attraction's realism.

The five-minute ride begins with an uphill acceleration test. Then the suspension gets a workout, as vehicles descend over a bumpy surface that puts the wheels at odds with one another. During environmental testing, riders feel the heat and get the shivers as vehicles pass first through a radiant heat chamber, then a cold chamber. Roadside robots pitch in by spraying the fenders and door panels with water to test for corrosion.

The ride takes a dramatic turn during the road-handling segment. Vehicles course along a winding road, complete with simulated mountain scenery, and into a darkened tunnel. Passengers hear a horn blast, see the blinding high beams of a tractor trailer, and swerve to avoid the truck. As they emerge and the light level picks up, there is a crash; guests round a corner to witness a barrier crash test. Their own vehicles then accelerate toward the same barrier.

A long straightaway feeds into a series of heavily banked turns and another straight shot that sends vehicles rocketing around the pavilion at top speed (up to 65 miles per hour). Strobe lights add to the effect.

Note: Children under seven years old must be accompanied by an adult; guests under 40 inches tall are not permitted to ride; passengers must be free of back problems, heart conditions, motion sickness, and other physical limitations to ride.

TEST TRACK SHOP: This retail spot features General Motors merchandise as well as items with a Test Track theme. Impulse buyers take note: There are no actual automobiles available for purchase here.

Horizons

For generations, visionaries have been making predictions about life in the future. Jules Verne forecast rockets that would fly to the moon. The 19th-century French artist Albert Robida envisioned subways and dirigible taxis and sketched what life in Paris would be like in 1950. And in the 1930s, pulp science fiction magazines circulated ideas about automatic barber chairs that would give their owners shoeshines and haircuts, air conditioners that would pipe in alpine chills, robots that would do housework, and suntan lamps and television.

The Horizons show, which draws on the wisdom of countless scientists, adds its own predictions in a pavilion located between Test Track and Wonders of Life. After a nod to the visions of earlier centuries, the continuously moving, four-passenger vehicles convey guests through a series of sets demonstrating aspects of life in the future. Among the displays are advanced transportation and communication systems (magnetic levitation trains and holographic telephones), high-tech farm methods (genetic engineering and desert farming), and innovative housing (cities that float at sea and in space).

The ride ends with a simulated trip to the ocean, the desert, or outer space. Visitors choose the destination by pressing a button in the ride vehicle. The 30-second experience that follows represents the choice made by the majority of your fellow riders.

Wonders of Life

The 72-foot-tall steel DNA molecule at the entrance to this popular pavilion beckons guests to humorous and informative experiences related to health. Housed in a geodesic dome and two attached buildings, this pavilion allows guests to enjoy both a serious and an amusing look at health, fitness, and modern lifestyles. Wonders of Life also boasts Body Wars, Epcot's first authentic thrill ride—a fast and furious journey through the human body.

Once inside the building, guests find themselves at the Fitness Fairgrounds. At the Fairgrounds, a variety of shows and activities for both children and adults are offered. *Goofy About Health* is an eight-minute multiscreen montage that sees Goofy go from a sloppy-living guy to a health-conscious fellow. Using old Goofy cartoons that haven't been seen for many years, the show traces Goofy's ups and downs, and winds up with new footage of Goofy at his doctor's office. The film is shown in an open theater where visitors can come and go as they please.

At the AnaComical Players Theater, a wacky (but nonetheless informative) show is presented by an improvisational theater group. Audience members are asked to participate, and it's all a lot of fun. This theater seats 100 people.

The third theater at the Fitness Fairgrounds is enclosed. The 14-minute film shown here, *The Making of Me*, is a story starring Martin Short as a man who wonders how he came into existence. To find out, he travels back in time to the birth of his parents, their first few years together, and their decision to have a child—him. Footage from an actual delivery is part of the film; it is sensitively presented and provides an accessible and touching view of childbirth. It was written and directed by Glenn Gordon Caron, who directed the TV show "Moonlighting."

Parents should be aware that the film is a bit graphic and so may not be suitable for some children. It also leaves a few key questions unanswered, thereby allowing parents to satiate their kids' appetite for knowledge on a case-by-case basis.

There are plenty of hands-on activities in areas surrounding the theaters. Guests can ride Wonder Cycles, computerized stationary bicycles that enable guests to pedal through a variety of locales, including Disneyland and the Rose Bowl Parade. At Coach's Corner, golf, tennis, or baseball swings are analyzed, and a professional knowledgeable in each sport offers free, albeit taped, advice to help you on your way. The Sensory Funhouse offers hands-on activities for the young and young at heart. It's the Disney version of a children's museum, where education and entertainment go hand in hand.

At the Met Lifestyle Revue, guests punch in such information as age, weight, height, exercise habits, whether they smoke, and perceived stress levels at an interactive computer terminal. The computer then processes the information and offers some advice on how to lead a healthier and less stressful existence.

Frontiers of Medicine, located toward the rear of the Fitness Fairgrounds, features the only completely serious segment of Wonders of Life. Here guests can see some scientific and educational exhibits of leading developments in medicine and health sciences. The exhibits change regularly. Presented by MetLife.

WELL & GOODS LIMITED: Located near Body Wars, this shop offers a selection of athletic wear, most of which features classic Disney characters participating in a variety of sports, as well as some educational materials.

CRANIUM COMMAND: This area of the Wonders of Life pavilion welcomes guests into the mind of a 12-year-old kid. The pre-show sets the mood as an animated film explains what you are about to see. General Knowledge is recruiting pilots for an assortment of new brains. There are jokes aplenty, many of which go right over the heads of young kids. Buzzy, our star pilot, fumbles through basic training and gets assigned to the most volatile brain of all, that of an adolescent boy.

Inside a 200-seat theater, the enormously exaggerated head of our 12-year-old subject is piloted by Buzzy, a delightfully goofy Audio-Animatronics figure. The two large eyes are actually rear-projection video screens, and it is through them that the audience gets an idea of how a young boy thinks and reacts. The other animated participant, General Knowledge, helps Buzzy learn which portion of the mind is required for a particular situation. The right and left sides of the brain, the stomach, the heart, and the adrenal gland are all represented by familiar celebrities. Our favorite is George Wendt (Norm from "Cheers"), operating the stomach. Other characters include Bobcat

BODY WARS: The same state-of-the-art technology that sends guests on a rollicking ride through space at the Star Tours attraction at the Disney-MGM Studios also exists at Wonders of Life in the form of this five-minute thrill ride. After boarding the vehicles, which are actually the same type of flight simulators employed by military and commercial airlines in pilot training, guests are whisked away on a bumpy, rocky, and exciting ride through the human body. (When instructed to fasten your seat belt, do so. This is a rough ride.) Movie buffs will think immediately of the films *Fantastic Voyage* and *Inner Space*. The queue area features exhibits from a fictional company specializing in the latest technology in the miniaturization of people. Guests pass through two special-effects portals and are declared ready to do a routine medical probe of the human body—from the inside.

During the course of this bumpy trip, a scientist is dispatched to remove a splinter that has made its way beneath the patient's skin. Guests go along for the ride but end up on a rescue mission when the scientist is attacked by a white blood cell. Of course, there are some problems along the way, making this trip seem out of control.

Note: This is a rougher ride than Star Tours at the Disney-MGM Studios. Signs posted outside Body Wars warn that passengers must be free of back problems, heart conditions, motion sickness, and other such physical limitations. Pregnant women are not permitted to board. Kids must be at least 40 inches tall to ride. Finally, if the sight of blood makes you woozy, this attraction may not be for you.

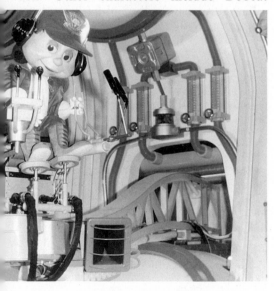

Goldthwait as the adrenal gland, Dana Carvey and Kevin Nealon (Hans and Franz of "Saturday Night Live" fame) as the heart, Charles Grodin as the left brain, and Jon Lovitz as the right brain.

Cranium Command is an altogether whimsical and entertaining show—one of the best at Epcot. This 17-minute show is fast-paced and packed with so many details that you'll notice new things even after seeing it many times.

EPCOT

Universe of Energy

Although it's easy to spot this pavilion's mirrored pyramid, the facade doesn't provide any clue at all to the 45 minutes of surprises in store. One of the most technologically complex experiences at Epcot, the show consists of several movies and a ride-through segment. None of these are exactly what guests might expect. This is especially true after the pavilion's 1996 renovation, which repackaged the attraction, placing its legendary Audio-Animatronics dinosaurs and lofty environmental message in a decidedly funny and much more personal context.

The show begins with a film (featuring a few familiar faces). In it, a character named Ellen is watching a TV game show. One of the contestants is Ellen's annoying college roommate Judy.

Ellen tries to play along but keeps striking out, particularly in the ENERGY category. As she watches, her neighbor Bill Nye, the Science Guy, pops in and is aghast at Ellen's ignorance. Shortly thereafter, Ellen falls asleep.

Ellen dreams she is on the game show competing against her friend Judy and Albert Einstein. This time, all of the questions are about energy. As Einstein ponders and Ellen fumbles, Judy is racking up points. Ellen, who has a negative score ("this nightmare game is a lot harder than the home version"), decides to freeze her dream and ask Bill Nye, the Science Guy, for help.

The second segment leads guests into a theater where Bill Nye vows to educate Ellen about the importance of energy. He persuades her to travel back in time to see where some of our energy sources came from. Suddenly, the whole seating area rotates, then breaks up into six sections that move slowly forward.

The vehicles embark with Ellen upon an odyssey through the primeval world. Enormous prehistoric trees crowd the forest. Apatosauruses wallow in the lagoon out front.

A lofty allosaurus battles with an armored stegosaurus, and an elasmosaurus bursts out of a tide pool with frightening suddenness—all under the vulturelike gaze of winged creatures known as pteranodons.

Next, guests move out of the forest and view a fast-paced montage of pictures capturing the history of human civilization, from cave dwellers to the present. (Keep your eyes peeled for the caveman who discovers fire—you just might recognize him.) The issue of alternative energy sources is raised, and the message is that there is no save-all energy source, but rather there are many possibilities with promise.

The attraction winds up with Ellen returning to the game show of her dreams. This time, she's beating her friend Judy, who is not at all happy about how much Ellen has learned during the commercial break. Ellen bets everything in the final round. In order to win, she must name the one energy source that will never be depleted. (We won't reveal the answer, but we're not too proud to brag about getting it right!)

Almost as intriguing as the attraction is the technology behind it. The vehicles weigh about 30,000 pounds when fully loaded with passengers, yet are guided along the floor by a wire only *one-eighth inch thick*. Some of the pavilion's energy is generated by two acres of photovoltaic cells mounted on the roof. The cells generate enough energy to run six average homes. Presented by Exxon.

Epcot is bigger than it seems, so allow plenty of time to get from place to place. (It takes about a half hour to walk from Spaceship Earth to Japan.)

WORLD SHOWCASE

Noble sentiments about humanity and the fellowship of nations, which have motivated so many world's fairs in the past, also inhabit World Showcase. But make no mistake about it: This area of Epcot is unlike any previous international exposition.

The group of pavilions that encircle World Showcase Lagoon (a body of water that is about the size of 85 football fields, with a perimeter of about 1.2 miles) demonstrates Disney conceptions about participating countries in remarkably realistic, consistently entertaining styles. You won't find the real Germany here; rather, the country's essence, much as a traveler returning from a visit might remember what he or she saw.

Shops, restaurants, and attractions are housed in a group of structures that is an artful pastiche of all the elements that give that nation's countryside and towns their distinctive flavor. Although occasional liberties have been taken when scale and proportion required, careful research governed the design of every nook and cranny.

Equally authentic is the cuisine. With no fewer than ten gourmet eateries to choose from, it's no wonder some guests come to World Showcase to do nothing but nosh.

In the shops, many of the wares represent the country in whose pavilion they are for sale. Craftspeople are occasionally on hand to demonstrate their arts. Thanks to special Walt Disney World cultural exchange programs and the personnel department's recruiting efforts, many of the World Showcase staffers hail from the countries the pavilions represent.

A diverse lineup of entertainment—from the sweet and simple to the sublime—ensures that all visitors experience more than a little culture, foreign or otherwise. The entertainment is as authentic as the Disney casting directors can make it, with native performers commonly featured and new festivities always in the works.

On the landscaping front, it is interesting to note that each pavilion's plantings closely approximate what would be found in the featured nation. All told, there are more than 10,000 tree roses, grandifloras, tea roses, and miniature roses planted at World Showcase.

Pavilions are described in the order that they would be encountered while moving counterclockwise around the World Showcase Lagoon after crossing the bridge from Future World.

Canada

Celebrating the many beauties of America's neighbor to the north, the area devoted to the Western Hemisphere's largest nation is complete with its own mountain, waterfall, rushing stream, rocky canyon, mine, and splendid garden massed with colorful flowers. There's even a totem pole, a trading post, and an elaborate, mansard-roofed hotel similar to ones built by Canadian railroad companies as they pushed west around the turn of the century. All this is imaginatively arranged somewhat like a split-level house, with the section representing French Canada on top, and another devoted to the mountains alongside it and below. From a distance, the Hôtel du Canada, the main building here, looks like little more than a bump on the landscape—as does Epcot's single Canadian Rocky Mountain. But up close they both seem to tower as high as the real thing.

The gardens were inspired by the Butchart Gardens in Victoria, British Columbia, a famous park created on the site of a limestone quarry. The hotel is modeled after Ottawa's Victorian-style Château Laurier. Lively, engaging entertainment is provided by a troupe of Canadian folk dancers called "Off-Kilter," and the Caledonia Bagpipe Band.

O CANADA!: This 17-minute motion picture, presented in Circle-Vision 360 inside Canada's mountain, portrays the Canadian confederation in all its coast-to-coast splendor—the prairies and plains, sparkling shorelines and rivers, and the untouched snowfields and rocky mountainsides surround you. The Royal Canadian Mounted

Police also put in an appearance. All the maritime provinces are pictured, with their covered bridges and sailing ships, as is Montreal, with its old-world cafes and churches; the scene in the Notre-Dame Basilica, with its organ booming and choirboys in attendance, is particularly stirring.

The great outdoors gets equal play. In one scene, snow geese take off all around the

Hot Tip

Don't try to fit all of the World Showcase movies into one day, especially if you are traveling with small children.

screen, and the beating of their wings is positively thunderous. Eagles, possums, mallards, bobcats, wolves, bears, deer, bison, and herds of reindeer were all filmed.

Filmed, too, were steers being roped at a rodeo and the chuck wagon race that takes place every year at that great provincial fair known as the Calgary Stampede. Skiers in the vast and empty Bugaboos, dogsledders, and ice-skaters are featured in the winter scenes; in a hockey game, the sound system almost perfectly conveys the scratch of skates on ice and the sharp whack of sticks slamming against the puck. And throughout, the motion picture provides a you-are-there feeling that makes all of this spectacular scenery still more memorable. Note that there are no seats in this theater.

NORTHWEST MERCANTILE: The first shop to the left upon entering the pavilion's plaza on the way to the Hôtel du Canada features heavy lumberjack shirts, maple syrup, Royal Canadian Mounted Police merchandise, and other wares that trappers might have purchased back in pioneering days. Skeins of rope, tin scoops, lanterns, and a pair of antique ice skates hanging from the long beams overhead set the mood, together with the structure itself.

Located to the store's rear are Indian artifacts and souvenirs—items like fur hats and sleek-lined sculptures (some carved in soapstone by the Inuit). Notable are handcrafted Canadian items that are seldom seen elsewhere in the American market.

LA BOUTIQUE DES PROVINCES: This small shop inside Hôtel du Canada, which features a variety of items with an Anne of Green Gables theme, also proffers jewelry, prints, ceramics, and giftware.

United Kingdom

In the space of only a few hundred feet, visitors to this pavilion stroll from an elegant London square to the edge of a canal in the rural countryside—via a bustling urban English street framed by buildings that constitute a veritable rhapsody of historic architectural styles. But one scene leads to the next so smoothly that nothing ever seems amiss. Here again, note the attention to detail: the half-timbered High Street structure that leans a bit, the hand-painted "smoke" stains that make the chimneys look as if they had been there for centuries. When a thatched roof is required, it's right where it should be—though the roof may be made of plastic broom bristles because fire regulations prohibit the real thing. Off to the side is a pair of scarlet phone booths identical to those that used to be found all around the U.K. And there are eight architectural styles characteristic of the streetscapes, from English Tudor to Georgian and English Victorian.

There is no major attraction in this pavilion; instead, it features half a dozen fine shops and a pub that serves a selection of beers and ales that would be the toast of any first-class "local" in London itself. There's also plenty of good entertainment, including a group of comedians called the World Showcase Players, who, when not engaged in general clowning on the World Showcase Promenade, coax audience members into participating in their farcical playlets. In the pub, a pianist plays, takes requests, and interacts with guests late into the evening. A mop-topped quartet known as the British Invasion occasionally plays Beatles tunes in the garden courtyard.

Characters, such as Mary Poppins and Winnie the Pooh, also appear in the garden courtyard throughout the day.

THE TOY SOLDIER: This delightful shop presents a variety of British toys, as well as a rather extensive selection of merchandise starring Winnie the Pooh, Piglet, Eeyore, and Tigger, too. Outside, the shop resembles a stone manor built during the last half of the 16th century.

THE CROWN & CREST: This shop looks like a backdrop for a child's fantasy of the days of King Arthur, with its high rafters decked out with bright banners, vast fireplace (and crossed swords above), and immense wrought-iron chandelier. Dart boards, fragrance products, "pub mugs," glasses that serve yards of beer, limited-edition chess sets, and coin and stamp sets are the stock-in-trade at this emporium adjoining The Toy Soldier.

PRINGLE OF SCOTLAND: On a sweltering summer day in Central Florida, trying on lamb's wool and cashmere may not hold terrific appeal. But the huge selection of styles and colors in men's and women's

Where to Eat *in Epcot*

A complete listing of all eateries—full-service restaurants, fast-food emporiums, and snack shops—can be found in the *Good Meals, Great Times* chapter. See the Epcot section beginning on page 221.

sweaters, knitted by Scotland's most famous maker, may well prove enticing despite the temperature outside. Tam-o'-shanters, socks, hats, ties, mittens, and kilts are only some of the items offered. Don't miss the tartan map on the wall across from The Crown & Crest; it identifies plaids from Glen Burn and Gordon to Langtree and St. Lawrence.

THE QUEEN'S TABLE: Sponsored by Royal Doulton, Ltd., this shop (opposite Pringle of Scotland) may be one of the loveliest in Epcot. This is particularly true of the store's elegant Adams Room, embellished with elaborate moldings, hung with a crystal chandelier, and painted in cream and robin's-egg blue. The setting is a lovely background for the selection of superbly crafted collector's statuettes. Perfumes and soaps and Royal Doulton china dinnerware are also available.

Don't forget to inspect small, serene Britannia Square just outside the shop entrance farthest from World Showcase Promenade. But for its somewhat reduced scale and the distinctively Floridian climate, it feels almost like London itself.

THE MAGIC OF WALES: This small emporium offers pottery, jewelry, souvenirs, and handcrafted gifts from Wales. Despite its modest size, it does the highest volume of business among the United Kingdom shops.

THE TEA CADDY: Fitted out with heavy wooden beams and a broad fireplace to resemble the Stratford-upon-Avon cottage of William Shakespeare's wife, Anne Hathaway, this shop, presented by R. Twinings & Company, Ltd., stocks English teas, both loose and in bags, in a variety of flavors. Other items include teapots, biscuits, and candies.

International Gateway

GATEWAY GIFTS: Disney memorabilia, fresh coffee, convenience items, and a package pickup depot are located at this spot near the France entrance.

WORLD TRAVELER: Disney fashions and character merchandise plus film and a drop-off for two-hour film processing are conveniently located here.

STROLLER AND WHEELCHAIR RENTAL: Strollers and wheelchairs are available for rent at this location. Remember to keep your rental receipt; it can be used on the same day in the Magic Kingdom, the Disney-MGM Studios, Animal Kingdom, or again in Epcot should you leave and return at a later hour.

France

The buildings here have mansard roofs and casement windows so Gallic in appearance that you expect to see some sad bohemian poet looking down from above. A canal-like offshoot of the World Showcase Lagoon seems like the Seine itself; the footbridge that spans it recalls the old Pont des Arts. There's a kiosk nearby like those that punctuate the streets of Paris and a bakery whose heavenly rich aromas announce its presence long before it's visible.

Shops sell perfumes, jewelry, crystal, and other luxury items. Their roofs are of real copper or slate, and the cabinetry is crafted finely enough to dazzle even the most skilled woodworker. Galerie des Halles—the iron-and-glass-ceilinged market that Paris once counted as one of its most beloved institutions—lives again (near the Palais du

Cinéma exit). But perhaps most special of all are the people. Hosts and hostesses who hail from Paris and the French provinces answer questions in lyrically French-accented English. It's fun to take in the shows put on by the The Living Statues, amazing white-robed performers who stand motionless and then suddenly change poses when you least expect it.

Some interesting background notes: The dusty rose–colored, lace-trimmed costumes that the hostesses wear were inspired by the dresses in *Le Bar aux Folies-Bergère* by the Impressionist painter Edouard Manet, and the main entrance to the pavilion recalls the architecture of Paris, most of which was built during the Belle Epoque ("beautiful age"), the last decades of the 19th century.

Don't miss the garden on the opposite side of this arcade. It is one of the most peaceful spots in World Showcase.

IMPRESSIONS DE FRANCE: Shown in the Palais du Cinéma, an intimate, elegant little theater that's not unlike the one at Fontainebleau, this enchanting 18-minute film takes viewers from one end of France to the other. The film shows off a beautiful tree-dotted estate, fields and vineyards at harvest time, a flower market and a luscious pastry shop, the ribbed tongue of a glacier, and a harbor full of squawking gulls. Viewers visit the Eiffel Tower; Versailles and its gilt Hall of Mirrors (just outside Paris); Mont St. Michel; the French Alps; and Cannes, the star-studded resort city on the Mediterranean coast. All this is even more appealing thanks to a superb sound track, consisting almost entirely of the music of French classical composers.

The exceptionally wide screen adds yet another dimension. This is not a Circle-Vision 360 film like the movies shown at China and Canada. The France film used only five cameras, and it is shown on five large projection surfaces—200 degrees around. It's a beautiful film, one of the park's best.

PLUME ET PALETTE: This is one of World Showcase's loveliest shops. The best of the Art Nouveau style is reflected in the curves that embellish the wrought-iron balustrade edging the mezzanine and the moldings that decorate cherry-wood cabinets and shelves.

The decor makes a fine backdrop for an array of merchandise that includes a number of collectible miniatures, perfume, small china boxes, and intricate tapestries. On the mezzanine level, a handful of fine oil paintings (by well-known French landscape artists) are for sale from $300 to $3,000 each, along with attractive prints of French countryside scenes. Prints of paintings by the likes of Monet, Renoir, and Toulouse-Lautrec are also available, as are original signed letters from such French luminaries as François Voltaire, Jules Verne, and Napoleon Bonaparte.

LA SIGNATURE: Another beautiful spot, with a chandelier, wallpaper that resembles watered silk, brass-and-crystal sconces, and velvet curtains, this boutique carries candles, china, and glassware.

GALERIE DES HALLES: Souvenirs—from Eiffel Tower statues to CDs with music by French composers to merchandise featuring the Hunchback of Notre Dame—are the stock-in-trade at this area located at the exit from the Palais du Cinéma. The area is based on Paris's now-demolished Les Halles, designed by the noted architect Victor Baltard.

LA CASSEROLE: This shop presents a selection of gifts themed to the artwork of French artists, such as Monet and Renoir. Mugs, tote bags, umbrellas, and picture frames are among the offerings.

LA MAISON DU VIN: Selections in this lovely wine shop range from the inexpensive to the pricey, from *vin ordinaire* going for several dollars to upward of $290 for a rare vintage. Wine tastings are held here to sample the offerings (a small charge is levied, but you get to make a souvenir of the glass). Those who don't want to carry their purchases may have them dispatched to Package Pickup for retrieval later in the day.

Morocco

Nine tons of tile were handmade, handcut, and shipped to Epcot to create this World Showcase pavilion. To capture the unique quality of this North African country's architecture, Moroccan artisans came to Epcot to practice the mosaic art that has been a part of their homeland for thousands of years. Koutoubia Minaret, a detailed replica of the famous prayer tower in Marrakesh, stands guard at the entrance. A courtyard with a fountain at the center leads to the Medina (Old City). Between the traditional alleyways and the more modern sections are the pointed arches and swirling patterns of the Bab Boujouloud gate, a replica of the one that stands in the city of Fez. An ancient working waterwheel irrigates the gardens, and the motifs repeated throughout the buildings include carved plaster and wood, tile, and brass. Festival Marrakesh takes over the courtyard, with belly dancing and Moroccan songs performed by native musicians.

GALLERY OF ARTS AND HISTORY: This museum houses ever-changing exhibits of Moroccan art, artifacts, and costumes.

MOROCCAN NATIONAL TOURIST OFFICE: An information center offers literature useful in planning a visit to Morocco, and the Royal Air Maroc desk makes it easy to book a trip if the mood strikes.

CASABLANCA CARPETS: Hand-knotted Berber carpets, Rabat carpets with brightly colored geometric designs, prayer rugs, wall hangings, and handloomed bedspreads and throw pillows are among the offerings here.

TANGIER TRADERS: This is the perfect place to buy a fez, plus woven belts, leather sandals, leather purses, and other traditional Moroccan clothing.

MARKETPLACE IN THE MEDINA: Hand-woven baskets, sheepskin wallets and bags, assorted straw hats, and split-bamboo furniture and lampshades are available.

THE BRASS BAZAAR: Interspersed among the decorative brass items in this waterside enclave are ceramic and glass pitchers, planters, pots, and serving sets.

BERBER OASIS: This shop on the promenade spills over with crafted brasswork. Baskets and leather goods abound.

MEDINA ARTS: Stop here for merchandise featuring characters from Disney's *Aladdin*.

Japan

Serenity rules in Japan. Except, of course, when the pavilion resounds with traditional Japanese music performed by a drum-playing duo or group.

The landscaping, designed in accordance with traditional symbolic and aesthetic values, contributes to the pavilion's peaceful mood. Rocks, which in Japan represent the enduring nature of the earth, were brought from North Carolina and Georgia (since boulders are scarce in the Sunshine State). Water, symbolizing the sea (which the Japanese consider a life source), is abundant; the Japan pavilion garden has a stream and pools inhabited by koi (fish). Evergreen trees, which in Japan are symbols of eternal life, are here in force.

Disney horticulturists created this very Japanese landscape using few plants native to that country because the climate there is so different from that of Florida. Among the few trees here native to Japan are the *sago* near the courtyard entrance to the Yakitori House; the two Japanese maple trees, identifiable by their small leaves, not far away (near the first stairway from the promenade on the left side of the courtyard as you face it); and the prickly monkey-puzzle trees near the walkway to the promenade, on The American Adventure side of the pagoda. Needle-sharp thorns make the latter the only species of tree that monkeys cannot climb.

The pagoda was modeled after an eighth-century structure located in the Horyuji Temple in Nara, Japan. The striking *torii* gate on the shore of World Showcase Lagoon derives from the design of the one at the Itsukushima shrine in Hiroshima Bay.

BIJUTSU-KAN GALLERY: Housing a changing cultural display, this small art museum has offered, among other exhibitions, "Netsuke—Historic Carvings of Old Japan," a showcase of traditional Japanese art forms that features carved miniatures (from a private collection).

MITSUKOSHI DEPARTMENT STORE: There are kimonos in silk, cotton, and polyester; attractive T-shirts bearing Japanese characters; expensive, almost sculptural traditional headdresses; and an excellent selection of bowls and vases meant for flower arranging. But on the whole, no one would ever apply the term *quaint* to this spacious store set up by Mitsukoshi—an immense, three-century-old retail firm that was once dubbed "Japan's Sears."

The shop features a large selection of kimonos, as well as chopsticks, bonsai, jewelry, china, paper fans, and origami products. There is also a bounty of snacks, candies, and tea. The pleasant atmosphere and variety of merchandise makes this establishment a rewarding experience for both the casual browser and the serious shopper.

The building's design was inspired by the Gosho Imperial Palace, which was constructed in Kyoto in 794 A.D.

The American Adventure

When it came to creating The American Adventure, the centerpiece of World Showcase, Disney Imagineers were given relatively free rein. So the 110,000 bricks of the imposing Colonial-style structure that houses a show, fast-food restaurant, and shop are of real brick—made *by hand* from soft Georgia clay. The show inside stands out because of its wonderfully evocative settings, its detailed sets, and the 35 superb Audio-Animatronics players, some of the most lifelike ever created by the Disney organization. A superb a cappella vocal group called The Voices of Liberty periodically serenades guests in the building's foyer.

Be sure to note the four luxuriant trees out front. They were originally planted in 1969 on Hotel Plaza Boulevard, and have been moved four times in the intervening years. The classic Disney characters often appear here. Presented by American Express.

THE AMERICAN ADVENTURE SHOW:
One of the truly outstanding Epcot attractions, this 26-minute presentation celebrates the American spirit from our nation's earliest years right up to the present. Beginning with the arrival of the Pilgrims at Plymouth Rock and their hard first winter on the western shore of the Atlantic, the Audio-Animatronics narrators—an amazingly lifelike Ben Franklin and a convincing, cigar-puffing Mark Twain—recall certain key people and events in American history: the Boston Tea Party, George Washington and the grueling winter at Valley Forge, the influential black abolitionist Frederick Douglass, the celebrated 19th-century Nez Percé chief Joseph, and many more. The Philadelphia Centennial Exposition is remembered, along with the contributions of women's rights campaigner Susan B. Anthony, telephone inventor Alexander Graham Bell, and the steel giant and philanthropist Andrew Carnegie. Naturalist John Muir converses onstage with Teddy Roosevelt. Charles Lindbergh, Rosie the Riveter, Jackie Robinson, Marilyn Monroe, and Walt Disney are represented. So are John Wayne, Lucille Ball, Margaret Mead, John F. Kennedy, Martin Luther King Jr., Muhammad Ali, and Billie Jean King.

The idea is to recall episodes in history, both negative and positive, which most contributed to the growth of the spirit of America, either by engendering "a new burst of creativity" (in the designers' words) "or a better understanding of ourselves as partners in the American experience."

Throughout the show, the attention to historical detail is meticulous. Every one of the rear-projected illustrations was executed in the painting style of the era being described. The Chief Joseph and Susan B. Anthony figures are speaking the originals' own words. The precise dimensions of the cannon balls in another scene were carefully investigated—then reproduced. In the Philadelphia Centennial Exposition scene, Pittsburgh's name is spelled without the *h* that subsequent years have added.

For information about how each of the various historical figures actually spoke during his or her lifetime, researchers contacted about half a dozen historians and cultural institutions—the Philadelphia Historical Commission, Harvard's Carpenter Center of Visual Arts, the State Historical Society of Missouri, the Department of the Navy's Ships Historical Branch, and others. When recordings were not available, educated guesses were made: Bell's voice was created on the basis of contemporary comments about his voice's clarity, expressiveness, and crisp articulation, coupled with the fact that his father taught elocution. To select Will Rogers' speeches for the Depression scene, whole pages of quotes were collected, reviewed, edited, and re-edited; the voice is the humorist's own, from an actual broadcast, as is that of FDR, here heard over the radio in the roadside gasoline-stand scene. That particular scene was suggested by a *Life* magazine photograph; details are accurate down to the price for a gallon of gasoline (18 cents).

A special highlight of the show is the majestic music played throughout by the Philadelphia Symphony Orchestra. The Golden Dreams sequence includes notable figures such as Muppet creator Jim Henson, Ryan White—the young hemophiliac who succumbed to AIDS after a courageous battle with the disease—and basketball star Earvin "Magic" Johnson.

Timing Tip: As one of the most compelling of all the World Showcase attractions, The American Adventure is often quite busy. Perhaps the best time to schedule a visit to the show is soon after World Showcase opens or in the early evening. If you have some time before the show, read the quotes on the walls.

HERITAGE MANOR GIFTS: Visit this shop for a variety of nostalgic Americana. Gifts include American flag–patterned men's and women's clothing, housewares, baseballs, coins, and books on American history.

AMERICA GARDENS THEATRE: An ever-changing slate of entertainment is presented throughout the week in this lakeside amphitheater in front of The American Adventure pavilion. Check your guidemap for details and exact times. Showtimes are also posted on the promenade at the east and west entrances to the amphitheater.

Italy

The arches and cutout motifs that adorn the World Showcase reproduction of the Doge's Palace in Venice are just the more obvious examples of the attention to detail lavished on the individual structures in this relatively small pavilion. The angel atop the scaled-down campanile was sculpted on the model of the original right down to the curls on the back of its head—then covered with real gold leaf, despite the fact that it was destined to be set almost 100 feet in the air. The other statues in the complex, including the sea god Neptune presiding over the fountain in the rear of the piazza, are similarly exact. And the pavilion even has an island like Venice's own, its seawall appropriately stained with age, plus moorings that look like barber poles, with several distinctively Venetian gondolas tied to them. St. Mark the Evangelist is also remembered, together with the lion that is the saint's companion and Venice's guardian; these can be seen atop the two massive columns that flank the small arched footbridge that connects the landfall to the mainland. The only deviation from Venetian reality is the alteration of the site of the Doge's Palace in reference to the real St. Mark's Square.

The sounds of opera, accompanied by an accordion and guitar, frequently fill the courtyard. Some of the most interesting entertainment at this pavilion is Rondó Veneziano from Venice, a contemporary string sextet performing classically inspired European music. The pavilion is equally interesting from a horticultural point of view. The island boasts kumquat trees, citrus plants typical of the Mediterranean, and a couple of olive trees that can be seen on both sidewalls of the Delizie Italiane; originally located in a Sacramento, California, grove, they arrived in Florida via flatbed truck a bit slimmer than when they started out. (Arizona border inspectors decreed that the trees be trimmed to the ten-foot width required by state law, and so, the ancient olives were shorn en route. The hardy trees survived, leaving only their scars to remind visitors of the ordeal; the darker bark is what remains of the original, while the lighter areas are new growth.) The tall, narrow trees that stand like dark columns in the pavilion are Italian cypresses, which are extremely common in Italy.

DELIZIE ITALIANE: This open-air market on the western edge of the piazza is a good spot for a sweet snack of tasty Italian chocolates and other goodies.

IL BEL CRISTALLO: The production of fine glassware has been a tradition in Italy for centuries, so a shop like this one (just off the promenade on the Germany side of the piazza) was a must for the pavilion. On display are Venetian glass paperweights and other items, their bright colors trapped in smooth spheres of clear or milky glass; small porcelain figurines and flower bouquets so

finely crafted that they look almost real; pastel flowers made of beads; and lead crystal bowls and candlesticks. The name of the shop means "the beautiful crystal."

LA CUCINA ITALIANA: This gourmet shop tempts with an assortment of Italian pastries and desserts. Expect to find wines from some of the finest vineyards in Italy. Pasta, olive oils, vinegars, and coffee are just a few of the other provisions available. An eclectic blend of decorative ceramics, cookware, and cutlery rounds out the selection.

LA GEMMA ELEGANTE: Located to the rear of the piazza on its eastern edge, this small shop focuses on Italian products such as ties, women's scarves, leather purses, and accessories.

Germany

There are no villages in Germany quite like this one. Inspired variously by towns in the Rhine region, Bavaria, and in the German north, it boasts structures reminiscent of those found in urban enclaves as diverse as Frankfurt, Freiburg, and Rothenburg. There are stair-stepped rooflines and towers, balconies and arcaded walkways, and so much overall charm that the scene seems to come straight out of a fairy tale. The beer hall to the rear is almost as lively as the one at Munich's famed Oktoberfest, especially late in the evening. The shops, which offer a range of merchandise from wine and sweets to ceramics and cuckoo clocks, toys, and books—and even art—are so tempting that it's hard to leave the area empty-handed.

The elements that constitute the Germany pavilion are described here as they would be encountered walking from west to east (counterclockwise) around the cobblestone-paved central plaza, which is formally known as the St. Georgsplatz, after the statue at its center. Saint George, the patron saint of soldiers, is depicted with a dragon that legend says he slew during a pilgrimage to the Middle East.

Try to time your World Showcase peregrinations to bring you to Germany on the hour, when the handsome, specially designed glockenspiel at the plaza's rear can be heard chiming in a melody composed specifically for the pavilion. Check the guidemap to see if a German trio will be performing outside the Biergarten restaurant.

DER BUCHERWURM: This two-story structure, whose exterior is patterned after a merchants' hall known as the Kaufhaus (located in the German town of Freiburg in Breisgau), stocks prints and books about Germany; handsome prints of German

cities; and an assortment of souvenir items, including ashtrays, vases, and more. (Film and sundries are also available.)

VOLKSKUNST: Small and exceptionally appealing, this establishment is full of a burgher's bounty of German timekeepers, plus a smattering of other items made by hand in the rural corners of the nation. The latter include beer steins in all sizes, from the petite to the enormous and expensive; wood carvings made in the German town of Oberammergau; nutcrackers; and a whole collection of "smokers" (carved wooden dolls with a receptacle for incense and a hollow pipe for the smoke to escape). As for cuckoo clocks, some are small and unobtrusive, while others are are so immense that they'd look appropriate only in some cathedral-ceilinged hunting lodge. A must.

DER TEDDYBAR: Located adjacent to Volkskunst, this toy shop would be a delight if only for the lively mechanized displays: Some of the stuffed lambs and the dolls wearing folk dresses (called dirndls) have been animated so that tails wag and skirts swirl in time to German folk tunes. The shop is also home to one of WDW's best selections of toys, including an assortment of expensive stuffed keepsakes from Steiff. Colorful wooden toys are tempting as well, along with all kinds of building blocks. Last but not least, the dolls are simply wonderful—you can even have one customized to your personal specifications.

KUNSTARBEIT IN KRISTALL: This shop to the left of the Biergarten features Austrian and crystal jewelry, tall beer mugs, wineglasses in traditional German tints of green and amber, and crystal decanters. Guests can have glassware etched on the spot.

SUSSIGKEITEN: It's a mistake to visit this tiny confectionery shop on an empty stomach: Chocolate cookies, butter cookies, and almond biscuits mix with caramels, nuts, and pretzels on the shelves, and there are boxes upon boxes of *Lebkuchen*, the spicy crisp cookies traditionally baked in Germany at Christmas, not to mention Gummy Bears (which the packages announce as *Gummibaeren*). Be sure to note the attractive display of old Bahlsen cookie tins by the door.

WEINKELLER: The Germany pavilion's wine shop, situated between the cookie shop and the Christmas shop toward the rear of St. Georgsplatz, offers about 250 varieties of German wine produced and bottled by H. Schmitt Söhne, one of Germany's oldest and largest vintners. Wine tastings are held here daily. The selection includes not only those vintages meant for everyday consumption, but also fine estate wines whose

prices run into the hundreds of dollars per bottle. These are white (with a few exceptions), because white wine constitutes the bulk of Germany's vinicultural output. (Only 20% of all German bottlings are red.) The setting itself is quite attractive—low-ceilinged and cozy, and full of cabinets embellished with carvings of vines and bunches of grapes.

DIE WEIHNACHTS ECKE: This is a shop that can set a visitor's mind to thoughts of Christmas—even in the dog days of summer. Ornaments, decorations, and gifts manufactured by various German companies line the shelves of this store.

GLAS UND PORZELLAN: Featuring glass and porcelain items made by the German firm of Goebel, this is an attractive establishment with rope-turned columns, curved moldings, delicate scrollwork, and tiny carved rosettes. But no matter how attractive the background, the stars of the show are the M. I. Hummel figurines that Goebel makes. Cherubic, rosy-cheeked children, shown carrying baskets, trays, umbrellas, and other items—depicted as in the drawings of a young German nun named Berta Hummel—are favorites of collectors around the world. There is always an elaborate showpiece at the center of the shop, and a Goebel artist is here to demonstrate the process by which Hummel creations are painted and finished.

China

Dominated by the Disney equivalent of Beijing's Temple of Heaven, and announced by a pair of banners that offer good wishes to passersby (the Chinese characters translate: "May good fortune follow you on your path through life and May virtue be your neighbor"), this pavilion conveys a level of serenity that offers an appealing contrast to the hearty merriment of the bordering Germany and the gaiety of nearby Mexico. Part of this quiet environment is the by-product of the soothing traditional Chinese music. Live flute, zither, or dulcimer music is performed inside the Temple of Heaven, while agile acrobats do tricks in the courtyard. The gardens also make a major contribution. They are full of rosebushes native to China, and there is a century-old mulberry tree (to the left of the main walkway into the pavilion), with a pomegranate tree and a wiggly-looking Florida native known as a water oak nearby.

The number of stones in the floor of the pavilion's main structure is not random; the center stone is surrounded by nine stones because nine is considered a lucky number in China. Around the edge of the outer room rise 12 columns—because 12 is the number of months in the year and the number of years in a full cycle of the Chinese calendar. Be sure to stand on the round stone in the center: Every whisper is amplified.

A spacious emporium is devoted to Chinese wares, and two Chinese restaurants add to the overall atmosphere. However, all this is secondary to the motion picture shown inside the Temple of Heaven—a Circle-Vision 360 film that is one of the most diverting World Showcase attractions.

WONDERS OF CHINA: LAND OF BEAUTY, LAND OF TIME: This 19-minute presentation shows the beauties of a land that few Epcot visitors have seen firsthand—and does it so vividly that it's possible to see the film over and over and still not fully absorb all the wonderful sights. The Disney crew was the first Western film group to shoot certain sites, and their remarkable effort includes such marvels

Village Traders

Located between Germany and China, this open-air shop sports a selection of gift items from Africa, India, and Australia. Browse through such souvenirs as boomerangs, handbags, hats, and, of course, T-shirts.

as Beijing's Forbidden City; vast, wide-open Inner Mongolia and its stern-faced tribespeople; the 2,400-year-old Great Wall; the Great Buddha of Leshan, and the 3,000-year-old city of Suzhou. Its location on the Grand Canal, which is believed to be the largest man-made waterway in the world, led Marco Polo to call it the Venice of the East. Note that there are no seats in the theater.

HOUSE OF THE WHISPERING WILLOWS:
When exiting, pass by the House of the Whispering Willows, an exhibit of ancient Chinese art and artifacts. Changed about every six months, it invariably includes fine pieces from well-known collections.

YONG FENG SHANGDIAN:
This vast Chinese emporium, located off the narrow, charming Street of Good Fortune at the exit to the film, offers a huge assortment of merchandise—silk robes, prints, paper umbrellas, embroidered items, and more. Trinkets, moderately priced items, and expensive antiques are available in an array that may be matched in few places in the United States. The calligraphy on the curtains wishes passersby good fortune, long life, prosperity, and happiness.

Norway

Set between the Mexico and China pavilions is Norway, the last pavilion added to the mix at World Showcase. Built in conjunction with many Norwegian companies, the pavilion celebrates the history, folklore, and culture of one of the Western world's oldest countries.

The cobblestone town square is an architectural showcase of the styles of such Norwegian towns as Bergen, Alesund, and Oslo. There's also a Norwegian castle fashioned after Akershus, a 14th-century fortress still standing in Oslo's harbor; the castle here houses the Akershus restaurant. Few can resist walking into the bakery for a taste of its treats. In a show of modernity, a statue of Norway's living legend, marathoner Grete Waitz, stands behind the bakery. Shops stock handicrafts and folk items: hand-knit woolens, wood carvings, and glass and metal artwork. The World Class Brass comic musicians put on a show in the courtyard.

MAELSTROM: Appropriately, visitors tour Norway by boat—16-passenger, dragon-headed longboats inspired by those Eric the Red and other Vikings used a thousand years ago. The ten-minute voyage through time begins in a tenth-century Viking village where a ship is being readied to head out to sea. Seafarers then find themselves in a mythical Norwegian forest, populated by trolls who cause the boats to plummet backward, through a maelstrom to the majestic grandeur of the Geiranger fjord, where the vessel narrowly avoids spilling over a waterfall. Ultimately, after a plunge through a rocky passage, the boats wind up in the stormy North Sea. Lightning flashes reveal an enormous oil rig; as the boat passes the concrete platform legs, the storm calms and a coastal village appears on the horizon.

Survivors disembark and enter a movie theater, where the journey continues on-screen for five additional minutes, giving visitors a sense of the scenic spectacles and unique personalities that make up modern Norway.

Timing Tip: Maelstrom is one of World Showcase's more popular attractions. It is least crowded in the late evening hours.

STAVE CHURCH GALLERY: Inside the wooden stave church, there is a small exhibit that explores Norwegian culture. It's interesting to note that only 28 stave churches remain in Norway today.

THE PUFFIN'S ROOST: A collection of Norwegian gifts, sweaters, activewear, jewelry, fine leather goods, pewter, candy, toys, and trolls are the wares for sale at this shop.

Mexico

The tangle of tropical vegetation surrounding the great pyramid that encloses this pavilion and the Mexican restaurant at the lagoon's edge on the promenade provide only the barest suggestion of the charming area inside.

Dominated by a re-creation of a quaint plaza at dusk, the pyramid's interior is rimmed by balconied, tile-roofed, colonial-style structures. Crowding a pretty fountain area is a quartet of stands selling Mexican handicrafts, and to the left is a shop stocked with other handsome wares. The Mariachi Cobre band keeps things lively. To the rear, the San Angel Inn, a corporate cousin of the famous Mexico City restaurant, serves authentic Mexican fare. Behind it, the pavilion's main show chronicles Mexican culture from earliest times right up to the present.

Take a look at the cultural exhibit inside the pyramid entrance on the way in. Note that the pyramid itself was inspired by Meso-American structures dating from the third century A.D.

EL RIO DEL TIEMPO: THE RIVER OF TIME: Over the course of this six-minute boat trip, sprinkled with vignettes of pre-Columbian, Spanish colonial, and modern Mexican life, visitors greet a Mayan high priest, watch performers dance, and are assailed by vendors at a market. A band dressed to look like skeletons entertains at one juncture (in a reference to the Day of the Dead, a holiday celebrated in Mexico with candies and sweets shaped like skulls and skeletons). The cheery montage of film, props, and Audio-Animatronics figures is reminiscent of the Magic Kingdom's It's a Small World.

Timing Tip: During peak seasons, long lines, which prevail from late morning on, usually thin out in the afternoon.

PLAZA DE LOS AMIGOS: Brightly colored paper flowers, sombreros, wooden trays and bowls, peasant blouses, baskets, and pottery make this *mercado* (market) at the plaza's center as bright and almost as lively as one in Mexico itself. The colorful papier-mâché piñatas that figure strongly in the scenery here are so popular that Epcot has to buy them from suppliers by the truckload.

ARTESANIAS MEXICANAS: This shop carries Mexican-made home decor items. Among the featured items are candles, glasses, and pottery.

EL RANCHITO DEL NORTE: Gifts and souvenirs from northern Mexico are the featured items at this spot.

LA FAMILIA FASHIONS: Mexican fashions and accessories for women and kids, malachite, plus silver and turquoise jewelry are available.

Showcase Plaza

PORT OF ENTRY: A children's shop carrying infants' and kids' clothing, girls' character dresses, plush dolls, and toys.

DISNEY TRADERS: Merchandise combining the charms of Disney characters and World Showcase themes is the primary stock-in-trade. Sunglasses, film, cigarettes, and sundries are also available.

ENTERTAINMENT

E pcot presents an intriguing array of live performances each day, making it important for guests to consult an entertainment schedule (on the park guidemap). The following listing offers an indication of Epcot's crowd-pleasing potential. For information about special events at Epcot, see the "Holidays & Special Events" section of *Getting Ready to Go*. For up-to-the-minute schedules call 824-4321.

AMERICA GARDENS THEATRE: The venue alongside the lagoon at The American Adventure hosts an ever-changing program of diverse live entertainment. Check a guidemap for current offerings.

FOUNTAIN OF NATIONS: This dramatic fountain in Future World's Innoventions Plaza breaks into a computer-choreographed water ballet every 15 minutes.

ILLUMINATIONS: A spectacular display of lasers, fireworks, and fountains to the accompaniment of music, this show is a highlight of any Epcot visit. The extravaganza, visible from anywhere on the World Showcase Promenade, takes place every night at closing time. Note that it will be replaced by a new show in October 1999. (See box below.)

KIDCOT FUN STOPS: There is a special play area in each of the countries of World Showcase. These fun stops allow young guests to play games and make crafts that are native to each country's culture.

WORLD SHOWCASE PERFORMERS: It's all but impossible to complete a circuit of World Showcase without catching a few

performances en route. Keep an eye on the schedule to take in live entertainment at each pavilion, often performed by natives of the country represented. Among the possibilities: worldly comedians, a Mexican mariachi band, Moroccan belly dancers, Chinese acrobats, Canadian bagpipers, African drummers, and more. A bus full of Caribbean musicians travels the promenade. For details, see descriptions in the "World Showcase" section of this chapter.

Holiday Happenings

During certain holidays, such as the Fourth of July, Christmas, and New Year's Eve, Epcot usually stays open extra late and presents added entertainment for the occasion.

Note, too, that World Showcase keeps an international holiday calendar. January visitors might celebrate Scottish Heritage Day or Chinese New Year. In February there's the Black Heritage Celebration, an Epcot signature event, at The American Adventure. Independence Day is celebrated in Norway during the month of May. July packs France's Bastille Day, Japan's Tanabata Festival, and Canada's Dominion Day, in addition to the USA's Fourth of July. Germany's Oktoberfest and Morocco's Independence Day get their turn in October. Call 824-4321 to confirm schedules.

CHRISTMAS: Epcot celebrates the holiday in a big way, with a nightly tree-lighting ceremony, a lighted archway that hugs the pathway to Showcase Plaza, a candle-light choral processional, and a special edition of the nightly fireworks show among the traditional elements of its Holidays Around the World festivities.

Coming Attraction

A new century is about to be born, and Epcot is celebration central. The party begins on October 1, 1999, and will remain in full swing until January 1, 2001.

Special millennium events, inspirational exhibits, and turn-of-the-twenty-first-century entertainment are all on tap, as is an all-new nighttime spectacular (it replaces IllumiNations). The show pulls out every pyrotechnic stop imaginable, enveloping World Showcase in a display of fireworks, lasers, and synchronized sound.

HOT TIPS

- Stop by Guest Relations or in any shop for a free guidemap. Consult the entertainment schedule first thing.

- The best time to visit World Showcase is as soon as it opens (usually at 11 A.M.). See Future World in the late afternoon until park closing. Remember that lines throughout Epcot are longest at midday and shortest in the early evening.

- During peak seasons, preferred priority seating times at Epcot's table-service restaurants book quickly—arrange for priority seating as far in advance as possible. However, all is not lost if you fail to secure priority seating arrangements—some tables are available on a first-come, first-served basis.

- Most World Showcase restaurants seat guests until park closing. Guests can make advance plans by calling WDW-DINE (939-3463).

- Check the Tip Board in Innoventions Plaza for current wait times for the most popular Epcot attractions, and adjust your plans accordingly.

- Save the shops in World Showcase for the afternoon, when just about everything else is very crowded.

- Guests staying at WDW resorts can have purchases delivered to their hotels for free.

- Although a *FriendShip* water taxi is unlikely to transport you across World Showcase Lagoon any faster than a brisk walk would, it is a peaceful foot-friendly way to make the half-mile-plus journey—especially at the end of a long day, or if you are traveling with small children.

- Be sure to allow extra time to explore the hands-on exhibits at Innoventions, Image Works at Journey into Imagination, and Fitness Fairgrounds at Wonders of Life.

Where to Find the Characters

Characters host each meal at The Land's Garden Grill restaurant (see *Good Meals, Great Times* for details). Also, find Goofy at Wonders of Life, and Dreamfinder and Figment at Journey into Imagination. Mickey often appears at the Centorium. In World Showcase, characters often favor the country of their literary origin. Discover *Snow White* characters in Germany, familiar faces from *Beauty and the Beast* and *The Hunchback of Notre Dame* in France, friends from *Aladdin* in Morocco, and the cast of *Mulan* in China. The United Kingdom is home to Winnie the Pooh, Alice in Wonderland, Mary Poppins, and others. Check a guidemap for locations or ask a park employee.

Disney-MGM Studios

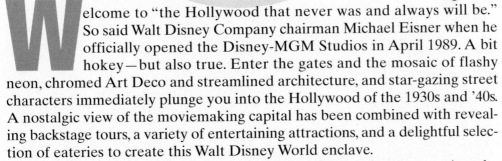

Welcome to "the Hollywood that never was and always will be." So said Walt Disney Company chairman Michael Eisner when he officially opened the Disney-MGM Studios in April 1989. A bit hokey—but also true. Enter the gates and the mosaic of flashy neon, chromed Art Deco and streamlined architecture, and star-gazing street characters immediately plunge you into the Hollywood of the 1930s and '40s. A nostalgic view of the moviemaking capital has been combined with revealing backstage tours, a variety of entertaining attractions, and a delightful selection of eateries to create this Walt Disney World enclave.

The Studios' water tower, known to punsters (for obvious reasons) as the "Earffel Tower," is reminiscent of the structures looming over most Hollywood studios of the Golden Age. Here, however, it gets that special Disney touch—it's capped by a Mouseketeer-style hat.

What makes this area of Walt Disney World different from other Disney theme parks is the extent to which guests can participate in the attractions. Our best advice is to volunteer, wherever and whenever possible. It's fun, and it adds enormously to the experience.

Even as the Studios marks its tenth anniversary, the park continues to expand and evolve. If the Magic Kingdom is the home of the classics, this park is the place where many of Disney's movie hits debut as creative shows, parades, and attractions. It's also where most of the contemporary characters make live appearances for the very first time.

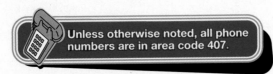

Unless otherwise noted, all phone numbers are in area code 407.

DISNEY-MGM STUDIOS

Ⓐ Beauty and the Beast Live on Stage
Ⓑ The Twilight Zone Tower of Terror
Ⓒ The Magic of Disney Animation
Ⓓ Voyage of The Little Mermaid
Ⓔ The Making of...
Ⓕ Backstage Pass to 101 Dalmatians
Ⓖ Disney-MGM Studios Backlot Tour
Ⓗ The American Film Institute Showcase
Ⓘ Honey, I Shrunk the Kids Movie Set Adventure
Ⓙ Disney's The Hunchback of Notre Dame—A Musical Adventure
Ⓚ Jim Henson's Muppet★Vision 3-D
Ⓛ Star Tours
Ⓜ Indiana Jones Epic Stunt Spectacular
Ⓝ ABC Sound Studio
Ⓞ Doug Rocks! (opening early 1999)
Ⓟ The Great Movie Ride
Ⓠ Fantasmic!
Ⓡ Rock 'n' Roller Coaster (opening summer 1999)

.... Parade Route

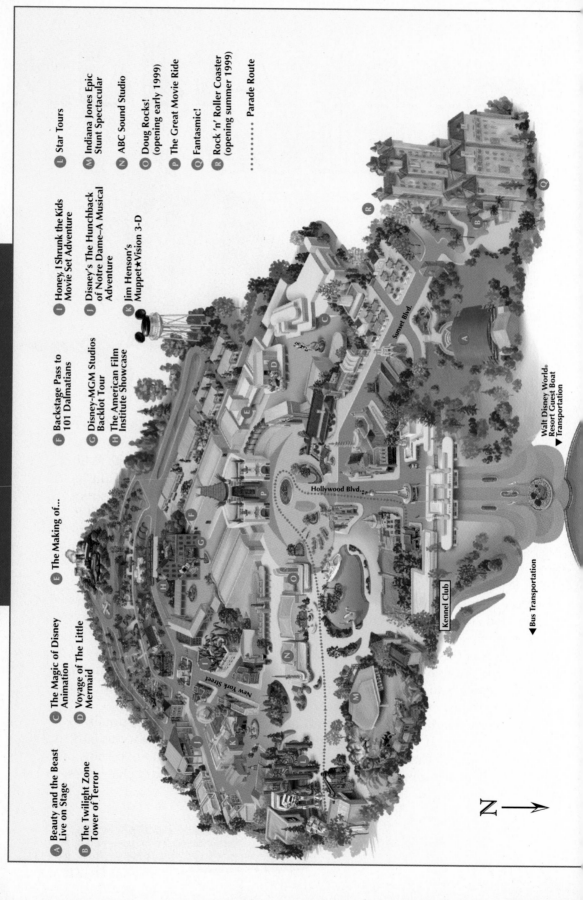

Kennel Club

Hollywood Blvd.

Sunset Blvd.

New York Street

▶ Bus Transportation

Walt Disney World® Resort Guest Boat ▶ Transportation

N →

GETTING ORIENTED

While the Disney-MGM Studios is considerably smaller than Epcot, the park has a sprawling layout with no distinctive shape or main thoroughfare. As such, the Studios can be a bit of a challenge to navigate. Be sure to study a guidemap as you enter.

The park entrance is at Hollywood Boulevard. This shop-lined avenue leads straight to Hollywood Plaza, address of the Studios' most central landmark, a replica of Mann's Chinese Theatre that doubles as the site of The Great Movie Ride. Walking along Hollywood Boulevard toward the plaza, you'll come to the first major intersection, Hollywood Junction. Here, a wide, palm-fringed thoroughfare known as Sunset Boulevard branches off to the right.

There are some new addresses on Sunset Boulevard: The Hollywood Hills Amphitheater, home of Fantasmic!, and, opening in summer 1999, Rock 'n' Roller Coaster. Anchoring the boulevard's far end is The Hollywood Tower Hotel, home of The Twilight Zone Tower of Terror. The strip is also graced with several shops, the Sunset Ranch Market, and the Theatre of the Stars amphitheater, where Beauty and the Beast Live on Stage is performed daily.

Stand in Hollywood Plaza facing the Chinese Theater, and you'll notice an archway just off to your right; this leads to Animation Courtyard, a self-contained area with a backstage feel to it. Mickey Avenue, the street veering off to the left of Animation Courtyard, leads to The Making of... and Backstage Pass to 101 Dalmatians.

If you turn left off Hollywood Boulevard and proceed past Echo Lake, you are on course for such attractions as ABC Sound Studio, Indiana Jones Epic Stunt Spectacular, and Star Tours. Just beyond Star Tours there is one more entertainment zone, near New York Street. The high-profile attractions here: Jim Henson's Muppet*Vision 3-D, Disney's The Hunchback of Notre Dame—A Musical Adventure, and the Honey, I Shrunk the Kids Movie Set Adventure.

HOW TO GET THERE

Take Exit 25 off I-4. Continue about a half mile to reach the parking area. Take a tram to the park entrance.

By WDW Transportation: From the Swan, Dolphin, Yacht and Beach Club, and BoardWalk: boat. From Fort Wilderness and Downtown Disney: bus to the Transportation and Ticket Center (TTC), then transfer to the Disney-MGM Studios bus. From the Magic Kingdom, Epcot, Animal Kingdom, all other WDW resorts, and the resorts on Hotel Plaza Boulevard: bus.

PARKING

All-day parking at the Studios is $5 for day visitors (free to WDW resort guests). Trams circulate regularly, providing transportation from the parking area to the park entrance. Be sure to note the section and the aisle in which you park. Also be aware that the parking ticket received allows for re-entry to the parking area throughout the day.

HOURS

The Disney-MGM Studios is usually open from 9 A.M. until about one hour after sunset. During certain holiday periods and summer months, hours are extended. It's best to arrive at least a half hour before the posted opening time, particularly during busy seasons. Depending on the season, some stage shows do not open until late in the morning.

Admission Prices

ONE-DAY TICKET

(Restricted to use only in the Disney-MGM Studios. Prices include sales tax and are subject to change.)

Adult	$44.52
Child*	$36.92

*3 through 9 years of age; children under 3 free

PARK PRIMER

BABY FACILITIES

Changing tables and facilities for nursing mothers can be found at the Baby Care Center, in the Guest Relations lobby near the park entrance. Disposable diapers are available at many Studios shops; just ask.

CAMERA NEEDS

The Darkroom on Hollywood Boulevard stocks film, batteries, and disposable cameras. Two-hour film processing is offered here and wherever you see a Photo Express sign. Film is sold in most Studios shops.

DISABILITY INFORMATION

Most attractions, restaurants, shops, and shows are accessible to guests using wheelchairs. Additional services are available for guests with visual or hearing disabilities. For a detailed overview of the services offered, including transportation, parking, attraction access, and more, pick up a copy of the *Guidebook for Guests with Disabilities* at Guest Relations. For more information, see the "Travelers with Disabilities" section of *Getting Ready to Go.*

EARLY-ENTRY DAYS

On Wednesday and Sunday, WDW resort guests may enter the Disney-MGM Studios up to 1½ hours before the official opening time to enjoy such attractions as Tower of Terror, Jim Henson's Muppet*Vision 3-D, The Great Movie Ride, and Star Tours. Early-entry days and attractions are subject to change.

FIRST AID

Minor medical problems can be handled at the First Aid Center, located next to Guest Relations at the park entrance.

INFORMATION

Guest Relations, located just inside the park entrance, has free guidemaps and an ever-resourceful staff. To make same-day dining arrangements for certain Studios eateries, go to the booth at the junction of Hollywood and Sunset boulevards.

LOCKERS

Lockers, found at Oscar's Super Service near the entrance, cost $5 per day (plus a $1 refundable deposit) for unlimited use.

LOST & FOUND

Located near the park entrance, past the turnstiles on the right. To report lost items after your visit, call 824-4245.

LOST CHILDREN

Report lost children at Guest Relations or alert a Disney employee to the problem.

MONEY MATTERS

There is an ATM located outside the park entrance, on the right. In addition to cash, credit cards (American Express, Visa, The Disney Credit Card, and MasterCard), traveler's checks, and WDW resort IDs are accepted for admission, merchandise, and meals at all full-service restaurants and at fast-food locations.

PACKAGE PICKUP

Shops can arrange for cumbersome purchases to be transported to package pickup at the Lost and Found (near the park entrance), where they can be picked up later. There is no charge for this service.

SAME-DAY RE-ENTRY

Be sure to have your hand stamped upon exiting the park and to retain your ticket if you plan to return later in the same day.

STROLLERS & WHEELCHAIRS

Strollers, wheelchairs, and Electric Convenience Vehicles (ECVs) may be rented from Oscar's Super Service, located just inside the park entrance on the right. Cost for strollers and wheelchairs is $5, with a $1 refundable deposit. Cost for ECVs is $30, with a $10 refundable deposit. Remember to keep your receipt, which can be used on the same day for a stroller or wheelchair replacement at the Magic Kingdom, Epcot, Animal Kingdom, or at the Studios (at the In Character costume shop). Quantities are limited.

TIP BOARD

Check this board at the junction of Hollywood and Sunset boulevards to learn the current waiting times for the most popular attractions in the park. This is also the place to look for showtimes. Hosts and hostesses stand nearby to provide additional information.

THE MAIN ATTRACTIONS

The Disney-MGM Studios has a brand of attractions altogether unique. Some offer guests behind-the-scenes looks at the creative and technical processes that generate television, movies, and animation. Others go so far as to allow guests to gain a bit of showbiz experience along with the insight. Still others resurrect popular characters and stories in new forms—from stage shows to thrill rides.

Because many shows and attractions are presented at scheduled times, it's very important to consult a guidemap or the park's Tip Board for starting times. Attractions are described roughly in the order they might be visited in a sweep of the park's major sections: Sunset Boulevard, Mickey Avenue, and the area stretching from Hollywood Boulevard to the New York Street vicinity.

The Twilight Zone Tower of Terror

The Hollywood Tower Hotel is the decrepit home of an exhilarating thrill ride. On the facade of the 199-foot-tall building (the tallest attraction at any Disney theme park) hangs a sparking electric sign. As the legend goes, lightning struck the building during a storm on Halloween night in 1939. An entire guest wing disappeared, along with an elevator carrying five people.

The line for the ride winds through the lobby, where dusty furniture, cobwebs, and old newspapers add to the eerie atmosphere. As guests enter the library, they see a television set brought to life by a bolt of lightning. Rod Serling intones a monologue, inviting them to enter another part of the building—and The Twilight Zone.

Guests are led toward the boiler room to enter the ride elevator. (This is your only chance to change your mind about riding.) Once you're inside, the doors close and the elevator begins its ascent. At the first stop, the doors open and guests have a view down a hotel corridor. Among the many effects is a ghostly visit by the hotel guests who vanished. The doors close again and you continue your trip skyward.

At the next stop, you enter the Fifth Dimension, a combination of eerie sights and sounds reminiscent of "The Twilight Zone"

TV series. In fact, Disney Imagineers watched each of the 156 original "Twilight Zone" episodes at least twice for inspiration. Notice the clock that ticks incessantly as it hangs in midair, and the giant eyeball (watch it closely and you may see your image floating inside). This part of the ride is a disorienting experience, in part because the elevator is actually moving horizontally.

What happens next depends upon the whim of Disney Imagineers, who have programmed the ride so that the drop sequence can easily be changed. At press time the ride was taking an immediate plunge (of about eight stories) before traveling quickly back up to the 13th floor. At the top, (about 157 feet up) passengers can look out at the

BIRNBAUM'S Best

Rock 'n' Roller Coaster

The newest and fastest roller coaster in Disney history is guaranteed to rock your world. Opening in summer 1999, it's ideally suited for those who consider the Tower of Terror to be a little on the tame side.

The indoor attraction reaches a speed of 60 miles per hour—in 2.8 seconds flat. Other twists include two loops and a corkscrew—marking the first time Disney has ever turned guests upside down on American soil.

The ride's premise is this: A chart-topping band has invited you to a backstage party. The only thing standing between you and the big bash is . . . the Los Angeles Freeway—at rush hour!

To get to the party on time, you'll have to zip through the nighttime streets in a stretch limo. The ride vehicles are equipped with a high-tech sound system (five speakers per seat make for a mega-decibel ride), and the remainder of the journey features rockin' synchronized sound—adding a dramatic dimension to the roller coaster experience most daredevils have grown accustomed to.

Guests under 44 inches are not permitted to take this topsy-turvy tour, and you must be free of back, neck, and heart problems to ride. Expectant mothers are advised to skip this attraction.

Studios below. (The flash is a camera capturing your look of horror for posterity.) Once the doors shut, you plummet 13 stories. The drop lasts about 2½ seconds, but it seems longer.

Just when you think it's over, the vehicle launches skyward, barely stopping before it plunges again. As you exit, Rod Serling offers a tip: Next time, use the stairs.

From the time you are seated in the service elevator, the trip takes about five minutes. Note that you must be at least 40 inches tall to go on the ride. It is not recommended for pregnant women, those with a heart condition, or people with back and neck problems.

TOWER HOTEL GIFTS: Located near the attraction exit, this is the spot to shop for items featuring The Hollywood Tower Hotel.

Beauty and the Beast Live on Stage

Here's the show that gave birth to the Broadway musical. Several times a day, Belle, Gaston, Mrs. Potts, and the rest of the cast of the Disney film *Beauty and the Beast* come to life at the 1,500-seat Theatre of the Stars amphitheater on Sunset Boulevard.

The 20-minute show is as entertaining as they come. The staging is just right and the music simply addictive as it traces the classic tale—from Belle's dissatisfaction with her life in a small French town to the climactic battle between the staff of the Beast's castle and Gaston and the townspeople. Lumière and friends perform the song "Be Our Guest" with a delightful display of dancing flatware. A

happy-ending finale, complete with fluttering doves, is a delight. Although showtimes vary, the first performance of the day is usually in the morning.

The Magic of Disney Animation

This tour, which was recently revised and updated, gives guests an insider look at the creative process behind Disney's animated blockbusters. In each 40-minute tour (which runs continuously), guests learn about animation and watch Disney animators as they work their magic. (They're generally on duty weekdays, until about 5 P.M. or 6 P.M.)

Before the tour, you can mill about the lobby of the animation facility. Copies of some of the many Oscars won by the Disney animation team are on display, along with

drawings from famous films. Later, you'll get to see how animators manage to bring drawings like these to life.

The tour begins with a hilarious new version of a film featuring Robin Williams and Walter Cronkite. It offers a lesson in the basics of animation. The film is followed by a meeting with an actual Disney animator. Feel free to ask questions—this is an interactive, though informal, presentation.

Next stop: the recently expanded animation studio. Depending on when you visit, you may see animators at work on *Tarzan*, *Fantasia 2000*, or another film. Once inside the studio, guests visit the story room, where plot lines are developed for animated fea-

tures. Then it's off to the drawing boards, where characters undergo the metamorphosis from pencil sketch to moving picture. Working at their desks in full view of visitors, animators are seen creating the drawings that will later appear in real films.

A guide describes what the artists are doing at any given moment. To learn even more, just look up: Video monitors allow guests to view snippets of the films the animators are working on and other works in progress.

Before moving on, spend some time browsing at the Animation Gallery, where Disney animation cels, exclusive limited-edition reproductions, books, figurines, and many other collectibles are for sale.

Voyage of The Little Mermaid

One of the Studios' most popular attractions, this 17-minute live musical production, adapted from the Disney animated classic, is presented in a theater with an underwater feel. Many of the characters, such as Flounder and Sebastian, are brought to life by puppeteers.

Hot Tip

An elevated stage makes it tough for small children to see all the details in the Voyage of The Little Mermaid. Their best vantage point is from the lap of a grown-up.

The show opens with the lively song "Under the Sea"; then clips from the movie are shown as actors join the puppets onstage.

Ariel is the star and performs songs from the film. Prince Eric makes an appearance, and an enormous Ursula glides across the stage to steal Ariel's voice. Of course, the happy ending prevails. The story line is a bit disjointed and hops from scene to scene, and some of the signature songs are missing, but most viewers are familiar with the plot, so this doesn't detract from the show.

There are excellent special effects, including cascading water, lasers, and a lightning storm that may be a bit intense for younger children. Note that the effects are best seen from the middle to the rear of the theater.

The Making of . . .

What happens before a movie director yells action and after he or she screams cut? How do the stars prepare for their roles? Who is responsible for the musical score? And where do all the props come from? The answers to these questions and more are found here (at least as far as the latest live-action Disney films are concerned).

The Making of… begins with a walk through a working production facility and leads to a video screening that gives guests a behind-the-scenes glimpse of the intricacies of making a film. Typically, it introduces actors and directors, as well as composers, lyricists, and other folks whose names and titles we see as movie credits roll by.

The brief video yields interesting, and perhaps surprising, bits of information. Consider an interview with John Cleese, one of the stars of *George of the Jungle*, a film recently featured at this attraction. Cleese, who played Ape, revealed that he recorded his part of the movie in just two days. He provided Ape's voice only; another actor actually filled out the gorilla suit (which was created by Henson's Creature Shop).

This attraction is updated periodically to keep up with new Disney releases. The Lights! Camera! Action! Theater entrance is on Mickey Avenue. The show, which runs continuously, lasts about 15 minutes.

Disney-MGM Studios Backlot Tour

Guests go backstage to see—and experience—some little-known aspects of television and movie production on a tour of real sets and prop stations. Highlights of the 35-minute tour (which runs continuously) include two special-effects sequences in which guests learn how natural disasters and waterborne scenes are created on a studio set.

First stop is an outdoor special-effects area, where two guests are tapped to hit the high seas. The show demonstrates the effects that can be used to reproduce battle scenes at sea in a water tank. Pyrotechnics, simulated depth charges, and torpedo blasts combine in an action-packed display.

Guests then board the trams that travel to the backlot area. Each trip begins with a look at the wardrobe department. More than 100 designers produce the costumes for all of Disney's movie, TV, and other entertainment projects—and with 2.5 million garments, Walt Disney World has the world's largest working wardrobe. Famous costumes are on display.

The tram then passes through the camera, props, and lighting departments. A look into the scene shop reveals carpenters at work on sets that are later finished on the soundstages.

The tram turns into the backlot residential street, where empty, hollow facades give the outward appearance of a lovely neighborhood. Used mainly for exterior shots, the houses on this street include Vern's home from *Ernest Saves Christmas* and the treehouse featured in *George of the Jungle*. In addition, there's the facade of "The Golden Girls" home and the house from "Empty Nest."

Where in Central Florida can you find an active oil field in the middle of a dry, rocky, barren desert canyon prone to flash floods? In Catastrophe Canyon! As the guide will tell you, crews are filming a movie in which a backstage tram gets stuck in the canyon during a flash flood. But supposedly it's safe to go in because they're not filming today.

In a series of special effects, a rainstorm begins; then there's an explosion, complete with flames that are so hot, even riders on the right side of the tram feel them; followed by a flash flood that is so convincing, it forces everyone to lean the other way. The road underneath the tram shifts and dips, lending even more reality to the adventure.

Hot Tip

Guests who sit on the left side of the tram sometimes get wet at Catastrophe Canyon, while those on the right stay dry. Choose accordingly.

From Catastrophe Canyon, the tram rides by New York Street, where meticulously reproduced facades line the urban street. Though the brickwork looks authentic, these backless facades are constructed mostly of fiberglass and Styrofoam. The skyscrapers, including the Empire State Building and the Chrysler Building, are actually painted flats. Forced perspective (the same technique that makes Cinderella Castle appear much taller than it is) makes the 4-story Empire State Building appear as if it were the actual 104-story structure. After the tour, if crews are not filming, guests can explore New York Street on foot.

Timing Tip: Crowds seem to thin out during the late-afternoon hours, so if the line is long, consider coming back later.

Backstage Pass to 101 Dalmatians

This 25-minute behind-the-scenes look at moviemaking is a walking tour that begins with a funny video clip about the process of casting dogs for roles in the featured live-action film. Guests are then led into a room called the Special Effects Creature Shop, where they see all kinds of props that were used to produce Disney's *101 Dalmatians*. The guide explains how certain props, such as Audio-Animatronics puppies, helped filmmakers create action scenes that otherwise would have been impossible to shoot.

Before the tour proceeds to the Special Effects Stage, a guest is randomly picked to participate as an actor. The crowd learns how film shot against a blue screen can be superimposed onto any background. Then

the actor is filmed while performing in front of the blue screen. The footage is quickly edited into a scene from the movie and shown to guests.

Then it's on to the soundstages, where specially designed, soundproof catwalks allow visitors to gawk and talk all they want. The tour takes in three soundstages, where filming may be in progress for movies or television shows. It is also possible, however, that nothing will be happening on the set. In this case, guests will view a short video about the challenges of orchestrating action scenes involving hundreds of puppies (each of which had its own trainer).

From this area, guests are led into a walkway, where they see a short film introducing the character Cruella de Vil (played by actress Glenn Close). At the film's conclusion, guests visit a large room overflowing with props and sets used to create Cruella's world, and the guide explains how these elements helped establish her lusciously villainous character.

The American Film Institute Showcase

Costumes, props, and set pieces used in recent as well as classic movies and TV shows are on display in this ever-changing exhibit.

Although showcased items may be different when you visit, displays have included Barbara Stanwick's costume from *Sorry, Wrong Number*, the police car from *Dick Tracy*, an Academy Award won by the film *My Fair Lady*, concept artwork from *Toy Story*, and live-action sets and stop-motion puppets from *James and the Giant Peach*. Other props have come from *Star Wars, Evita, Flubber*, and *George of the Jungle*. An interactive area demonstrates the five phases of moviemaking.

The Great Movie Ride

Housed in a full-scale reproduction of historic Mann's Chinese Theatre, this 22-minute attraction captivates guests' imaginations from the start. The queue area winds through the lobby and into the heart of filmmaking, where guests will see some famous movie scenes on a large screen. The guided tour begins in an area reminiscent of the hills of Hollywood (which as the famous, now abbreviated sign indicates, was then known as Hollywoodland) in its heyday. As a ride vehicle whisks guests under a vibrant marquee, they are transported to the celluloid world of yesteryear.

More than 60 dancing mannequins atop a cake greet guests in a replay of the "By a Waterfall" scene from the Busby Berkeley musical *Footlight Parade*. Gene Kelly's memorable performance from *Singin' in the Rain* is the next scene, in which rain seems to drench the soundstage but does not dampen the spirits of the Audio-Animatronics representation of Mr. Kelly. (Gene Kelly personally inspected his likeness.) Then Mary Poppins and Bert the chimney sweep entertain, as Mary floats from above via her magical umbrella and Bert sings "Chim Chim Cher-ee" from a rooftop.

From the world of musical entertainment, guests segue to adventure. James Cagney re-creates his role from *Public Enemy* as the ride proceeds along Gangster Alley. A mob shootout begins and puts guests in the midst of an ambush. An alternate route leads to a western town, where John Wayne can be seen on horseback eyeing some would-be bank robbers. When the thieves blow up the safe and flames pour from the building, heat can be felt from the trams.

As the ride vehicle glides into the spaceship from *Alien*, Officer Ripley guards the corridor while a slimy monster threatens riders from overhead. (Note that this and other scenes are presented in a dark setting and may be upsetting to young children.)

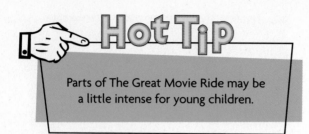

Hot Tip

Parts of The Great Movie Ride may be a little intense for young children.

The legendary farewell from *Casablanca* is also depicted, complete with a lifelike Rick and Ilsa. (Ingrid Bergman's daughter Isabella Rossellini has brought her kids here to "see Grandma.") Guests are moved from the airfield to the swirling winds of Munchkinland, where a house has just fallen on the Wicked Witch of the East. Her sister, as portrayed by Margaret Hamilton, appears in a burst of smoke. This Audio-Animatronics figure is impressively realistic (and scary). But happy endings prevail, and guests follow Dorothy and company along the Yellow Brick Road to the Emerald City of Oz. As the ride draws to a close, guests view a montage of memorable moments from classic films.

Timing Tip: If the queue extends outside the building, you're in for a long wait. It takes about 25 minutes to reach the ride vehicles once you've entered the theater.

ABC Sound Studio

What would a movie be without the usual battery of bumps, booms, and in some cases, barks? *Boring!* Sound effects are the shining stars of every show. Hear for yourself at this attraction, which spotlights the role of sound in filmmaking. It does so by allowing guests to create the sound effects for a short film clip.

The pre-show begins outside the theater with a series of short scenes from Disney's current lineup of programming. Upon entering the theater, the host chooses several "Foley" artists from the audience. (Foley is the Hollywood sound-effects system named for its creator, Jack Foley.) Volunteers are asked to step in to create the necessary sound effects for a scene from an ABC television show.

As the clip is shown, the amateur crew does its best to match the proper sound effects to the action on the screen. In the finished product, nothing really bumps or boinks exactly when it's supposed to, but that's all part of the fun.

Afterward, don't miss SoundWorks, in the post-show area—it's one of WDW's true hidden gems. It offers hands-on noise-making fun for everyone. Soundsations is our absolute favorite. This "3-D Audio" experience puts guests in a room filled with sound so realistic that the wind from a hair dryer can almost be felt.

Radio Disney fans take note: The "Just Plain Mark and Zippy Show" is broadcast out of the studio next to the ABC Sound Studio. Guests can catch a glimpse of Mark and Zippy while they are on the air (weekdays 4 P.M. to 9 P.M.).

Coming Attraction

The 12-year-old animated hero Doug and his alter ego Quailman are coming to town and coming to life in a brand-spanking-new show at the Disney-MGM Studios. Joining Doug will be his pooch, Porkchop, and his pals Skeeter and Patti. The evil Dr. Rubbersuit will be on hand to stir up trouble, of course.

Doug Rocks!, scheduled to open in early 1999, will replace SuperStar Television.

Star Tours

The attraction, which was inspired by George Lucas' Star Wars film trilogy, offers guests the chance to board StarSpeeders that are actually the same type of flight simulator regularly employed by the military and commercial airlines to train pilots. By synchronizing a stunning film with the virtually limitless motion of the simulator, the ride allows guests to truly feel what they see.

Visitors enter an area where the famed *Star Wars* characters R2D2 and C-3PO are working for a galactic travel agency. They spend their time in a bustling hangar area servicing the Star Tours fleet of spacecraft. Riders board the craft for what is intended to be a leisurely trip to the Moon of Endor, but the five-minute ride quickly develops into a harrowing flight into deep space, including encounters with giant ice crystals and laser-blasting fighters. The flight is out of control from the start, as the rookie pilot comically proves that Murphy's Law applies to the entire universe.

This is an extremely turbulent trip through the galaxy. Signs at Star Tours warn that passengers must be free of back problems, heart conditions, motion sickness, and other physical limitations. Pregnant women are not permitted to board. There is a minimum height requirement of 40 inches, and children under seven must be accompanied by an adult; children under three are not permitted to ride.

Indiana Jones Epic Stunt Spectacular

Earthquakes, fiery explosions, and assorted other dramatic events give guests some insight into the science of movie stunts and special effects at this impressive 2,000-seat amphitheater. Stunt men and women re-create scenes from Indiana Jones films to demonstrate the skill required to keep audiences on the edge of their seats. Show director Glenn Randall, who served as stunt coordinator of such films as *Raiders of the Lost Ark*, *Poltergeist*, *Never Say Never Again*, *E.T.*, and *Jewel of the Nile*, calls the show "big visual excitement."

But the 30-minute show isn't all flying leaps. Guests also see how the elaborate stunts are pulled off — safely — while the crew and an assistant director explain what goes on both in front of and behind the camera.

In one segment, a scene from *Raiders of the Lost Ark* is staged. A 12-foot-tall rolling ball chases a Harrison Ford look-alike out of the temple. The steam and flames are so intense that the audience can feel the heat. The crew then dismantles the set, revealing the remarkable lightness of movie props, as two assistants roll the ball uphill for the next show.

In a scene at a busy Cairo street market, "extras" chosen from the audience play out the famous scene in which Indiana Jones pulls a gun while others are fighting with swords. The explosive action continues, and leads to a desert finale in which the hero and his sweetheart make a death-defying escape.

There are moments during this presentation when the audience might wonder if something has actually gone wrong. But by revealing tricks of the trade, the directors and stars show that what appears to be very dangerous is actually a safe, controlled bit of movie magic.

Jim Henson's Muppet*Vision 3-D

One of the most entertaining attractions at the Disney-MGM Studios, this 3-D movie is quite remarkable. As with so many other Disney attractions, much of the appeal is in the details. A funny 12-minute pre-show gives clues about what's to come. Once inside the theater, many will notice that it looks just like the one from the television series "The Muppet Show." Even the two curmudgeonly fellows, Statler and Waldorf, are sitting in the balcony, bantering with each other and offering their typically critical commentary on the show.

The production comes directly from Muppet Labs, presided over by Dr. Bunsen Honeydew — and his long-suffering assistant, Beaker — and introduces a new character, Waldo, the "Spirit of 3-D." Among the highlights is Miss Piggy's solo, which Bean Bunny turns into quite a fiasco. Sam Eagle's grand finale leads to trouble as a veritable war breaks out, culminating

BIRNBAUM'S Best

BIRNBAUM'S Best

157

with a cannon blast to the screen from the rear balcony, courtesy of everyone's favorite Swedish Chef.

The 3-D effects, spectacular as they may be, are only part of the show: There are appearances by live Muppet characters, fireworks, and lots of funny details built into the walls of the huge theater. Including the pre-show, expect to spend about 25 minutes with Kermit and company. Shows run continuously.

Disney's The Hunchback of Notre Dame—A Musical Adventure

A 32-minute musical based on Disney's animated feature *The Hunchback of Notre Dame* is performed in the shaded comfort of the Backlot Theater—a canopied bleacher-style theater located just beyond New York Street. The show takes guests to the catacombs of 15th-century Paris, where gypsies reprise the tale of the bell ringer Quasimodo and his struggle to find love and happiness.

Clopin, the King of the Gypsies, is the narrator. It is he who parts the curtains for this play within a play, inviting guests to watch as a troupe of gypsies re-enact the bittersweet story of Quasimodo and Esmeralda. While gypsy magic plays a part throughout, the show is characterized by an imaginative simplicity akin to street theater. Runway ramps that bring characters into the audience enhance the feeling of being part of the show.

The curtain opens on a gypsy campsite beneath the city. Here, Clopin and the gypsies create a colorful set filled with such treasures as Persian rugs and jewels. The gypsies impart the details of Quasimodo's life in the cathedral's bell tower, telling the story through song, costumes, masks, puppets, and dance. As the show evolves, the gypsies' theatrics reveal Quasimodo's oppression at the hands of Judge Claude Frollo, his love for Esmeralda, and the kindness of Phoebus, the guard who helps the lonely bell ringer.

Lest there be too much sorrow, the set again transforms and a wonderfully lively scene steals away to the streets of Paris for a thoroughly rambunctious revival of the Festival of Fools. Comic relief is provided by the gargoyles, Victor, Hugo, and Laverne, who act as Quasimodo's collective conscience. A point of interest: The first two gargoyles' namesake is author Victor Hugo, while Laverne's is the Andrews Sister of the same name. The show features many of the film's tunes, including "Topsy Turvy," "A Guy Like You," and, of course, "God Help the Outcasts."

Timing Tip: The first show of the day, usually in the late morning, is often the least crowded.

Honey, I Shrunk the Kids Movie Set Adventure

The set for the backyard scenes of the popular Disney movie has been re-created as an imaginative, oversize soft-surface playground. Enter it and experience the world from an ant's perspective.

Blades of grass soar 30 feet high, paper clips are as tall as trees, and Lego toys are practically big enough to live in. There are caves to explore (under the giant mushrooms) and many climbing opportunities (tremendous tree stumps and sprawling spiderwebs are among the better ones). Kids love to crawl into the discarded canister of film and slide out along an oversize piece of film.

A leaky hose also provides entertainment as it squirts in a slightly different location each time. It's great fun, and the props make kids and adults look and feel as they were indeed shrunk by Professor Wayne Szalinski.

SHOPPING

Hollywood Boulevard

CELEBRITY 5 & 10: Modeled after a 1940s Woolworth's, this large shop carries Disney-MGM Studios logo merchandise, frames, clothing, and backpacks, as well as movie-themed items.

COVER STORY: Just through The Darkroom, this is where guests can have their images put on the front cover of a large selection of magazines. If you've had your picture taken by any of the park photographers, this is the place to pick it up.

CROSSROADS OF THE WORLD: In the middle of the entrance plaza, Mickey Mouse keeps watch from atop this Hollywood Boulevard landmark. The small kiosk deals in souvenirs, sunglasses, film, rain gear, sundries, and guidemaps.

THE DARKROOM: The Art Deco facade of this shop allows guests to enter through an aperture-like doorway. Cameras (including the disposable kind), film, and camera accessories are sold.

KEYSTONE CLOTHIERS: Women's fashions and accessories are the specialties of the house. A favorite item here is a Mickey Mouse umbrella that sprouts two ears when opened. There is also a large selection of character ties.

L.A. CINEMA STORAGE: A great source for kids' stuff, with a variety of clothing, including costume pajamas. Many items feature characters from recent animated films, but classic characters, especially Winnie the Pooh and friends, have a presence as well.

MICKEY'S OF HOLLYWOOD: The place to find character T-shirts, sweatshirts, hats, plush toys, watches, socks, wallets, tote bags, books, mugs, and sunglasses, plus items emblazoned with the Disney-MGM Studios logo or Walt Disney Studios logo.

MOVIELAND MEMORABILIA: Located just to the left of the main entrance, this kiosk stocks stuffed toys, hats, books, sunglasses, film, key chains, and other souvenirs.

OSCAR'S CLASSIC CAR SOUVENIRS & SUPER SERVICE: The 1949 Chevrolet Tow Truck parked out front gets plenty of attention. Automotive memorabilia, mugs, models, and key chains are for sale. (The truck, by the way, is not.) Services offered here include stroller and wheelchair rental, lockers, plus a stamp machine.

SID CAHUENGA'S ONE-OF-A-KIND: Unique antiques and curios are the stock-in-trade here. Autographed photos of past and present matinee idols, old movie magazines and posters, and assorted Hollywood memorabilia, such as Clark Gable's pants, are among the many celebrity-oriented collectibles with which Sid is willing to part— for a price. For movie buffs, a stop at Sid's is an absolute must.

Sunset Boulevard

LEGENDS OF HOLLYWOOD: A tribute to Disney's animated legend, Winnie the Pooh. Expect to find an abundance of shirts, hats, books, and other colorful merchandise featuring everyone's favorite chubby little cubby.

MOUSE ABOUT TOWN: The best source for casual men's apparel featuring the famed mouse subtly embroidered onto sportswear, button-down shirts, polo shirts, and jackets. The Mouse also purveys golf-related apparel and accessories.

ONCE UPON A TIME: The exterior of this shop replicates the Carthay Circle Theatre in Hollywood, where *Snow White* premiered in 1937. The shop specializes in decorative gifts and Disney houseware items. For $25, a Disney artist will customize a character sketch for you.

PLANET HOLLYWOOD SUPERSTORE: This spot offers Planet Hollywood brand items such as T-shirts, sweatshirts, caps, and jackets. It also has "Celebrity Edition" artwork and memorabilia.

SUNSET CLUB COUTURE: A sophisticated selection of mostly Mickey watches includes many limited-edition pieces and great pocket watches. A Disney artist can customize character watches on the spot. Jewelry highlights stylized Mickey designs.

SUNSET RANCH: This open-air shop carries Disney character hats, totes, and apparel, plus sunscreen, film, and sundries.

SUNSET VILLAINS: All bad guys, all the time. That's the motto of this new shop, which has a killer selection of merchandise featuring the dark side of Disney—the characters we love to hate.

Beyond the Boulevards

ANIMATION GALLERY: Don't overlook this entertaining shop in the Animation Building, where limited-edition figurines, Disney animation cels, and other colorful collectibles ensure great browsing, even if buying isn't on your mind.

BUY THE BOOK: This cozy nook next to the Sci-Fi Dine-In Theater has coffees, stationery, and, of course, books. Ask about recent—and future—book signings by authors. Even if you miss an author appearance, you may find an autographed copy of a book on the shelves. There's also a counter offering fresh-baked cookies and other tempting deserts.

ENDOR VENDORS: The shop near the exit of Star Tours offers intergalactic souvenirs tied to the *Star Wars* films and the Star Tours attraction. Among the wares are hats, T-shirts, and action figures, as well as Chewbacca masks, Darth Vader mugs, and talking C-3PO pens.

GOLDEN AGE SOUVENIRS: Between ABC Sound Studio and Doug Rocks!, this shop stocks items such as ESPN and ABC products, a variety of hats and sunglasses, film, and disposable cameras.

IN CHARACTER: In front of Voyage of The Little Mermaid, this costume shop has everything a child needs to dress up like his or her favorite Disney character.

INDIANA JONES ADVENTURE OUTPOST: Right next to the Indiana Jones attraction, you'll discover an assortment of adventure clothing, as well as hats, shirts, and other memorabilia emblazoned with the Indy insignia.

IT'S A WONDERFUL SHOP: Tucked away in a corner behind Muppet*Vision 3-D, this "snow-covered" shop—with Disney ornaments galore—feels like Christmastime all year-round.

STAGE 1 COMPANY STORE: Near the exit of Muppet*Vision 3-D, guests can find plush toys, shirts, figurines, and other merchandise with the likenesses of Muppet characters in addition to a variety of items featuring Disney characters.

THE STUDIO STORE: In the Animation Courtyard, expect to find T-shirts, hats, and accessories inspired by new and classic Disney films here. Items featuring the Disney-MGM Studios logo are available, too.

TOY STORY PIZZA PLANET GIFTS: Adjacent to Toy Story Pizza Planet, this spot is second only to Andy's room when it comes to stocking *Toy Story* collectibles.

Where to Eat at the Studios

A complete listing of eateries at the Studios—full-service restaurants, fast-food emporiums, and snack shops—can be found in the *Good Meals, Great Times* chapter. See the Disney-MGM Studios restaurant section, which begins on page 228.

ENTERTAINMENT

As you might expect from a park fashioned in the image of Hollywood's heyday, the Disney-MGM Studios knows how to put on a show. Celebrity appearances are a distinct possibility as well. Basically, in these parts, it's always showtime. So be sure to pick up a free guidemap (at Guest Relations, or any shop), not only to check attraction starting times, but also to find out what other entertainment is on tap.

While specifics may change, the following listing is a good indication of the Studios' stage presence. As always, we advise calling 824-4321 for entertainment schedules. For information on special events, see the "Holidays & Special Events" section of *Getting Ready to Go*.

MULAN PARADE: The star of *Mulan*, Disney's 36th animated feature, leads a parade down Hollywood Boulevard every afternoon. The colorful 25-minute procession features music and characters from the film, from the lovable Mushu to the nasty villain Shan Yu (who has no choice but to participate in the parade—he is tied to a bed of skulls).

STREETMOSPHERE CHARACTERS: This troupe of performers infuses Hollywood Boulevard with old-time Tinseltown ambience. Would-be starlets searching for their big break, fans seeking guests' autographs, and gossip columnists chasing leads entertain daily.

Holiday Happenings

The Disney-MGM Studios usually stays open extra late to mark holidays such as New Year's Eve, the Fourth of July, and Christmas. During these times, a slew of special entertainment is often in store. Call 824-4321 for up-to-the-minute schedules.

CHRISTMAS: The Osborne Family Spectacle of Lights is the Studios' brilliant, twinkling homage to the season. An extraordinary luminous holiday display featuring about four million lights (owned by Little Rock businessman Jennings Osborne and his family) sets the backlot area of the Studios aglow. The display, which is lit nightly throughout the season, is truly spectacular. Check a park guidemap for exact times.

Trip the Light Fantasmic!

Fantasmic!, a lavish musical extravaganza, recently opened to rave reviews in the new Hollywood Hills Amphitheater on Sunset Boulevard. A spectacular mix of fireworks, fountains, lasers, special effects, and dozens of Disney characters, the show invites you to take a peek into the dream world of Mickey Mouse.

Though conceptually similar to its Disneyland counterpart, half of this 26-minute production is original. The action follows Mickey through a series of imaginative dream sequences. In the first, he appears on a mountain, shoots fireworks from his fingertips, and conducts an orchestra of colorful fountains. (Note that guests seated up front may get spritzed.) Endearing Disney characters drop by to perform the peppy musical numbers that follow. Soon Mickey is plagued by nightmares as Disney villains take over his dreams. In a classic good-versus-evil finale, the Mouse and his pals prevail (of course!).

Seating begins approximately one hour before showtime. Check a park guidemap for exact times. While all 6,900 seats afford a good view, we recommend sitting toward the back of the theater. Note that there is standing room for 2,600 guests.

Timing Tip: On nights when Fantasmic! is presented more than once, take in the last show. Afterward, as the masses file through the park's exit, take some time to browse the shops on Hollywood Boulevard that keep after-hours hours.

HOT TIPS

- Arrive at the Disney-MGM Studios before the posted opening time. The gates usually open at about 8:30 A.M.

- Check the Studios Tip Board often to get an idea of showtimes and crowds.

- See Muppet*Vision 3-D, Voyage of The Little Mermaid, and Star Tours early in the day, before the crowds build up.

- Snag a spot along Hollywood Boulevard about 30 minutes before the parade.

- Tower of Terror is a popular attraction with very long lines. Ride it very early or later in the day—and never right after eating a meal.

- The line for the Great Movie Ride is generally the longest early in the morning and immediately following the afternoon parade.

- For a full-service meal, make priority seating arrangements when you arrive at the park, at either Hollywood Junction at the corner of Sunset and Hollywood boulevards or the desired eatery: 50's Prime Time Cafe, Hollywood Brown Derby, Sci-Fi Dine-In Theater, or Mama Melrose's Ristorante Italiano. Or make advance plans by calling WDW-DINE (939-3463) up to 60 days ahead.

- Sorcery in the Sky, the Studios' top-notch fireworks display, is presented on special occasions throughout the year. If it's scheduled during your visit, don't miss it.

- Many of the attractions and shows stop admitting guests prior to the park's official closing time. (Check a guidemap for schedules.) Attractions that you may enter up until the very last minute include The Twilight Zone Tower of Terror, The Great Movie Ride, Jim Henson's Muppet*Vision 3-D, Star Tours, and Backstage Pass to 101 Dalmatians.

- Park hoppers take note: There is a water taxi link between the Disney-MGM Studios and Epcot. The boat docks to the left, as you exit the Studios. Epcot, as well as all other parks, may also be reached by bus.

- The shops on Hollywood Boulevard are open a half hour past park closing.

Where to Find the Characters

You'll often find Disney characters—such as Buzz Lightyear and Woody from *Toy Story*—strolling down Mickey Avenue. Look for Aladdin and Jasmine, Donald and Daisy, and many of their friends in the festive Animation Courtyard. Mickey Mouse, Goofy, and Winnie the Pooh often appear at the Beverly Sunset Theatre on Sunset Boulevard. Another good way to meet the characters is at the Soundstage restaurant. As always, check the guidemap or with a park employee for current details.

Disney's Animal Kingdom

With a mix of lush landscapes, thrilling attractions, and spine-tingling encounters with exotic animals, this is clearly a theme park raised to another level of excitement. Here guests do more than just watch the action—they live it. They become paleontologists, explorers, and students of nature. And if, by doing so, they leave with nothing more than a great big smile, Disney will have accomplished one of its major goals. But most guests will come away with a little bit more: a renewed sense of respect for our planet and for the lifeforms we share it with (not to mention a few boffo souvenirs).

The attractions at Disney's Animal Kingdom are meant to engage, entertain, and inspire. They immerse guests in a tropical landscape and introduce them to wondrous creatures from the past and present—as well as a few that exist only in our collective imagination.

The park, which opened in April 1998, is home to more than 1,000 animals representing 200 different species. Most of the creatures are of the animate variety, as opposed to the Audio-Animatronics kind. Despite that, you won't see beasts behind bars here. Instead, you'll see a menagerie of wild critters living in spacious habitats, with virtually no separations visible to the naked eye.

The following pages will help you get the most out of your visit to Disney's Animal Kingdom. It is, after all, a jungle out there.

Unless otherwise noted, all phone numbers are in area code 407.

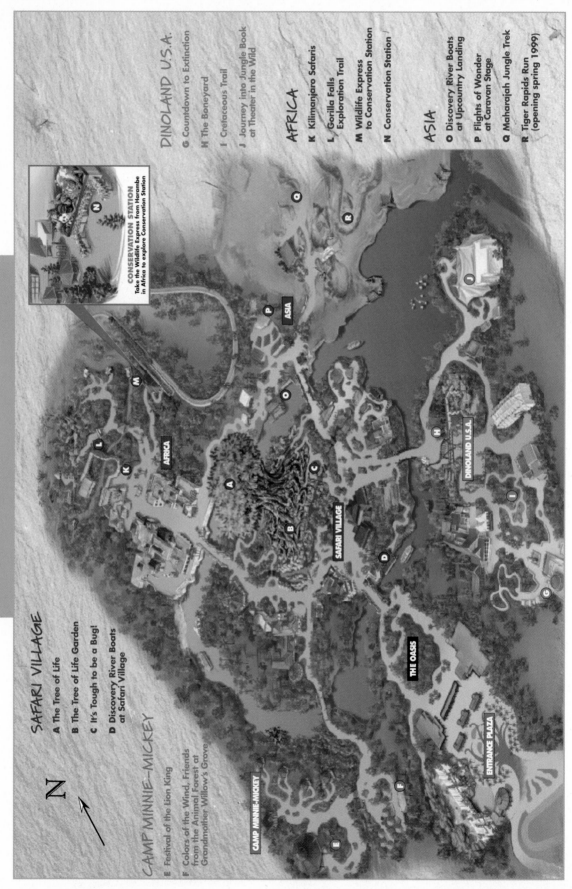

SAFARI VILLAGE
A The Tree of Life
B The Tree of Life Garden
C It's Tough to be a Bug!
D Discovery River Boats at Safari Village

CAMP MINNIE–MICKEY
E Festival of the Lion King
F Colors of the Wind, Friends from the Animal Forest at Grandmother Willow's Grove

DINOLAND U.S.A.
G Countdown to Extinction
H The Boneyard
I Cretaceous Trail
J Journey into Jungle Book at Theater in the Wild

AFRICA
K Kilimanjaro Safaris
L Gorilla Falls Exploration Trail
M Wildlife Express to Conservation Station
N Conservation Station

ASIA
O Discovery River Boats at Upcountry Landing
P Flights of Wonder at Caravan Stage
Q Maharajah Jungle Trek
R Tiger Rapids Run (opening spring 1999)

CONSERVATION STATION
Take the Wildlife Express from Harambe in Africa to explore Conservation Station

N

CAMP MINNIE–MICKEY

THE OASIS

ENTRANCE PLAZA

SAFARI VILLAGE

AFRICA

ASIA

DINOLAND U.S.A.

GETTING ORIENTED

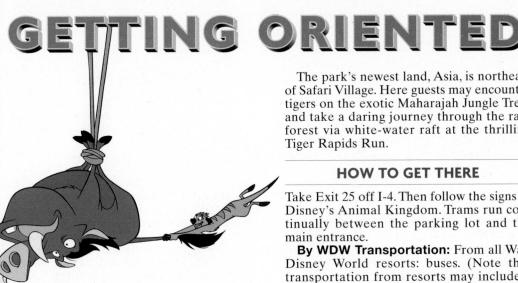

Though Disney's Animal Kingdom encompasses about five times the area of its Magic counterpart, one need not be in training for the Olympics to tackle it. By all estimates, pedestrians rack up about the same mileage in one day here as they do in a day at Epcot. (If you *want* to pack the hiking boots, by all means do—there are plenty of pretty trails to explore.)

The park's layout is reminiscent of the Magic Kingdom's: a series of sections, or "lands," connected to a central hub. In this case, the hub is Safari Village, an island surrounded by Discovery River, and home to The Tree of Life, the park's icon. A set of bridges connect Safari Village with other lands: The Oasis, DinoLand U.S.A., Africa, Asia (scheduled to begin opening in stages by early 1999), and Camp Minnie-Mickey.

As you pass through Animal Kingdom's entrance plaza, you approach The Oasis. Feel free to meander at a leisurely pace, absorbing the soothing ambience of a thick, elaborate jungle, or to proceed more quickly, and plan to revisit this relaxing region later on. Each of several pathways deposits you at the foot of a bridge leading to Safari Village. As you emerge from The Oasis, you'll see the awe-inspiring Tree of Life, a 14-story Disney-made banyan tree, looming ahead. The tree,which stands near the middle of the island, is surrounded by The Tree of Life Garden. Off to the southwest is the character-laden land known as Camp Minnie-Mickey.

To the southeast lies DinoLand U.S.A., home of countless prehistoric animals, a fossil dig, and an attraction that's sure to induce a mammoth adrenaline surge: Countdown to Extinction. Behind Safari Village and to the northwest is Africa, where guests can go on an African safari, explore a nature trail, and take a train to Conservation Station, the park's research and education center.

The park's newest land, Asia, is northeast of Safari Village. Here guests may encounter tigers on the exotic Maharajah Jungle Trek, and take a daring journey through the rain forest via white-water raft at the thrilling Tiger Rapids Run.

HOW TO GET THERE

Take Exit 25 off I-4. Then follow the signs to Disney's Animal Kingdom. Trams run continually between the parking lot and the main entrance.

By WDW Transportation: From all Walt Disney World resorts: buses. (Note that transportation from resorts may include a stop at Blizzard Beach.) From Downtown Disney: bus to the Transportation and Ticket Center (TTC), then transfer to the Animal Kingdom bus. From Magic Kingdom, Epcot, the Disney-MGM Studios, and the resorts on Hotel Plaza Boulevard: buses.

PARKING

All-day parking at Animal Kingdom is $5 for day visitors (free to WDW resort guests with presentation of resort ID). Trams circulate regularly, providing transportation from the parking area to the park entrance. Be sure to note the section and aisle in which you park. Also, be aware that the parking ticket allows for re-entry to the parking area throughout the day.

HOURS

Although hours are subject to change, Animal Kingdom is open daily from 7 A.M. until about one hour after dusk. During certain holiday periods and the summer months, hours are subject to change. It's best to arrive at the park at least a half hour before the official opening time. Call 824-4321 for current schedules.

Admission Prices

ONE-DAY TICKET
(Restricted to use only in Disney's Animal Kingdom. Prices include sales tax and are subject to change.)

Adult..$44.52
Child*...$36.92

*3 through 9 years of age; children under 3 free

PARK PRIMER

BABY FACILITIES

Changing tables and facilities for nursing mothers can be found at the Baby Care Center in Safari Village, behind Creature Comforts. Also, disposable diapers are kept behind the counter at many Animal Kingdom shops; just ask.

CAMERA NEEDS

Film may be dropped off for processing at Garden Gate Gifts near The Oasis, Disney Outfitters in Safari Village, Duka La Filimu and Mombasa Marketplace in Harambe, and Chester and Hester's Dinosaur Treasures in DinoLand U.S.A. The photo pickup location is at Disney Outfitters. Film is sold in most shops.

DISABILITY INFORMATION

Nearly all of the Animal Kingdom attractions, shops, and restaurants are accessible to guests using wheelchairs. Additional services are available for guests with visual or hearing disabilities. The *Guidebook for Guests with Disabilities* provides a detailed overview of the services available, including transportation, parking, and attraction access. (For additional information, refer to the *Getting Ready to Go* chapter.)

FIRST AID

Minor medical problems can be handled at the First Aid Center, located in Safari Village on the northwest side of The Tree of Life, near Creature Comforts.

INFORMATION

Guest Relations, located just inside the park entrance in The Oasis, is equipped with guidemaps and a helpful staff. Free guidemaps are also available in most shops.

LOCKERS

Lockers are found in two locations just inside the main entrance area: near Garden Gate Gifts and Guest Relations. Cost is $5 plus a $1 refundable deposit for unlimited use all day.

LOST & FOUND

The department is located near the Baby Care Center, behind Creature Comforts in Safari Village. To report lost items after your visit call 824-4245.

LOST CHILDREN

Report lost children at Guest Relations, near the park entrance, or alert a Disney employee to the problem.

MONEY MATTERS

There is an ATM at the entrance to the park. It's just before the turnstiles and to the right, next to the kennel. Currency exchange can be handled at Guest Relations. Disney Dollars, in $1, $5, and $10 denominations, are also available at Guest Relations. (The bills feature Mickey, Goofy, and Minnie, respectively.) In addition to cash, credit cards (American Express, Visa, MasterCard, and The Disney Credit Card), traveler's checks, and WDW resort IDs are accepted for admission and merchandise, and for meals at all full-service restaurants and fast-food spots. Many snack carts accept cash only.

PACKAGE PICKUP

Animal Kingdom shops can arrange for bulky purchases to be transported to Garden Gate Gifts for later pickup (purchases will be ready for pickup three hours after purchase). The service is free. WDW resort guests can arrange for packages to be delivered to their resort at no extra charge.

SAME-DAY RE-ENTRY

Be sure to have your hand stamped upon exiting the park and to retain your ticket if you plan to return later the same day.

STROLLERS & WHEELCHAIRS

Strollers, wheelchairs, and Electric Convenience Vehicles (ECVs) may be rented at Garden Gate Gifts (the first shop on the right inside the park entrance, near the entrance to The Oasis). The cost is $5 for strollers and wheelchairs, with a $1 refundable deposit; $30 for ECVs, with a $20 refundable deposit. Quantities are limited. Keep your receipt; it can be used that same day to obtain a replacement at the Magic Kingdom, Epcot, the Disney-MGM Studios, or here at Animal Kingdom.

TIP BOARDS

There are two Tip Boards in Safari Village. Check them throughout the day to learn the current wait times for the most popular attractions at Disney's Animal Kingdom.

THE OASIS

Traditionally, one has to travel across a long, sunbaked stretch of desert in order to experience the soothing atmosphere of a tropical oasis. With that in mind, think of the Animal Kingdom parking lot as a concrete version of the Sahara. Once you've trekked across it, your journey takes you through the park's front gate and entrance plaza. What's that up ahead? Could it be a kangaroo clinging to a towering tree limb? Here in central Florida? It must be a mirage.

But no. Within seconds you arrive at The Oasis, a thriving tropical garden filled with waterfalls, running streams, and lush vegetation. The transition is by no means a subtle one. You are immediately enveloped in a world of nature and animals. The setting is idyllic.

Though not a full-fledged "land" per se, this small jungle simply oozes atmosphere. It is thick and elaborate and crawling with critters. (Some are more difficult to spot than others. When searching for wildlife, remember to look up occasionally.) As visitors walk along the pathways, they will catch glimpses of all kinds of animals, from deer and iguanas to anteaters and kangaroos. As in the rest of Animal Kingdom, there is the illusion that guests are walking among the wildlife.

The Oasis is at once an exciting and calming experience. It sets the stage for what's to come. Guests have several options once they've entered The Oasis. They can continue on a northerly path, making tracks toward The Tree of Life and across a bridge to Safari Village. They can proceed at a more snail-friendly pace, keeping a tally of the various lifeforms that slither by. Or they can simply take time to stop and smell the flowers.

"I have learned from the animal world. And what everyone will learn who studies it is a renewed sense of kinship with the earth and all of its inhabitants."

—Walt Disney

Timing Tip: Making a trip through The Oasis is the only way to get into (and out of) Disney's Animal Kingdom. Therefore, some of the smaller paths can become a bit congested during the hours closest to opening and closing time. To beat the crowds, use the paths farthest to the left when you enter and exit the park.

SAFARI VILLAGE

Once you've passed through The Oasis, you will come to a bridge spanning Discovery River. The bridge leads to Safari Village, an island at the center of Animal Kingdom and the hub from which all other realms of the park may be reached.

Safari Village is defined by the brilliant colors, tropical surroundings, and equatorial architecture of Africa and the South Pacific. The facades of the buildings are all carved and painted, based on the art of nations from around the world. Don't fail to notice all of the bright, whimsical folk-art images representing various members of the animal kingdom.

This island is the shopping and dining center of Animal Kingdom. Many of the park's fast-food restaurants can be found here, including Pizzafari and Flame Tree Barbecue.

By far the most striking element in Safari Village is The Tree of Life. It is on the map, but chances are you'll have no trouble finding it. Rising from the middle of the island and as tall as a 14-story building, The Tree of Life is hard to miss.

The Tree of Life

The majestic Tree of Life is the dramatic 145-foot icon of Animal Kingdom. The imposing banyan-like tree, with its swaying limbs and gnarled trunk, looks an awful lot like the real thing—from a distance. Up close, it's apparent that this is a most unusual bit of greenery. Completely covered with more than 325 animal images, it is a swirling tapestry of carved figures, painstakingly assembled by a team of Disney artisans. The tree, though inorganic, stands as a symbol of the connected nature of life on Earth. Joyce Kilmer would approve.

THE TREE OF LIFE GARDEN: Walkways that snake around The Tree of Life allow guests to get a close-up view of the trunk and even play a game of "spot the animals." (The spiraling animal images go all the way to the top of the tree. You'll need a pair of binoculars if you hope to see them all.)

Scattered about the tree's base are a variety of animal exhibits. Animals can be seen in a very open, somewhat traditional parklike setting, with lush grass, trees, and other vegetation. Among the creatures you may recognize are toucans, otters, and storks. Others to which you may be introduced for the very first time as you meander through the exhibits include capybaras (huge rodents with an affinity for swimming) and ring-tailed lemurs (not quite monkeys' uncles, but more like cousins). The garden is accessible from several points around the tree.

IT'S TOUGH TO BE A BUG!: Inside the trunk of The Tree of Life is a 450-seat auditorium featuring an eight-minute, animated 3-D movie augmented by some surprising "4-D" effects. The stars of the show are the world's most abundant inhabitants—insects. They creep, crawl, and demonstrate why, someday, they just might inherit the earth. It's a bug's-eye view of the trials and tribulations of their multi-legged world.

As guests enter "The Tree of Life Repertory Theater," the orchestra can be heard warming up amid the sounds of chirping crickets. When Flik, the emcee (and star of *A Bug's Life*), makes his first appearance, he dubs audience members honorary bugs and instructs them to don their bug eyes (3-D glasses). Then the mild-mannered ant introduces some of his not-so-mild-mannered cronies, including the black widow spider, dung beetles, and "the silent but deadly member of the bug world"—the stink bug. What follows is a manic, often hilarious, revue.

Anyone who's leery of spiders, roaches, and their ilk is advised to skip the performance, or risk being seriously bugged.

Discovery River Boats

Safari Village is surrounded by the free-flowing Discovery River. Guests can cruise along it by boarding a Discovery River Boat at one of two docks: The first is located along the banks of Safari Village, near DinoLand U.S.A.; the second, called Upcountry Landing, is located across Discovery River, near Asia. Launches are dispatched, on average, every ten minutes. Each open-air cargo-like vessel has its own skipper, who deftly describes the landmarks and scenery as they are passed.

The cruise offers a great orientation to the park, passing along the edge of each land. The trip includes a close-up view of birds and other animals along the riverbanks. Expect a few entertaining surprises, including an encounter with a water dinosaur and a steaming geyser pit.

Also on board for each scenic voyage is an animal expert (of the human variety) and a few misunderstood members of the animal world: tarantulas, scorpions, geckos, or some of their equally underappreciated counterparts.

Note that these seven-minute "critter cruises" are one-way adventures. You'll be asked to disembark when the vessel stops at the next dock.

DID YOU KNOW...

The napkins in Disney's Animal Kingdom might look dirty even before you use them. Fear not. Their sandy color is a natural one—no bleach was used in the manufacturing process. It's a much more environment-friendly approach to cleaning up all those sticky faces and fingers.

AFRICA

The largest section of Animal Kingdom, Africa is bigger than the Magic Kingdom all by itself. This 110-acre, truer-than-life replica of an African savanna is packed with pachyderms, giraffes, hippos, and other jungle beasts. Guests enter Africa through Harambe, a village based on a modern East Kenyan coastal town. It is the dining and shopping center of Animal Kingdom's Africa.

The instant you cross the bridge to Harambe, you are transported to Africa. Everything is authentic, from the architecture to the landscaping to the merchandise in the marketplace. The result was achieved after Disney Imagineers made countless trips to the continent. After seven years of observing, filming, and photographing the real thing, they recreated it here in North America.

The animals, however, are not re-creations. They are quite real, most varied, and extremely abundant. In fact, this chunk of land puts the *animal* in Animal Kingdom.

Kilimanjaro Safaris

The Kilimanjaro Safaris, Africa's big attraction, has something for everyone: breathtaking landscapes, free-roaming animals, and a thrilling adventure. It's everything you'd expect from a trip to Africa, and more.

The 18-minute safari begins with a brief introduction from a guide who does double duty as your driver. Note that many of the guides actually come from various parts of the African continent.

The brown, camouflaged vehicle has a roof but no windows. Once you've boarded, look at the plates on the back of the seat in front of you. They'll help you identify the animals you see. And have those cameras ready!

As the open-air vehicle travels along dirt roads, you'll spot a number of exotic animals: zebras, gazelles, hippos, elephants, lions, warthogs, rhinos, and more. Some of the animals wander near your vehicle, and others cross its path. (Relax. Only the harmless creatures approach. Others, such as lions and cheetahs, only *appear* to invade your space.)

The majesty of the Serengeti may lull you into a state of serenity, but it's merely a calm before the storm. You'll soon be jostled and jolted as the vehicle crosses pothole-filled terrain and rickety bridges—one of which puts you close to a horde of sunbathing crocodiles.

The ride takes a sudden, even more dramatic, turn when a band of renegade ivory poachers is discovered searching for elephants. Your guide chooses to chase the outlaws, and takes you along for the ride. The mad pursuit that follows is a brief but wild adventure.

BIRNBAUM'S *Best*

Gorilla Falls Exploration Trail

This self-guided walking trail winds past communities of gorillas and other rare African animals. It can be accessed at the end of the Kilimanjaro Safaris or by its entrance located in Harambe.

The first major stop on the trail, which is as dense and lush as any other area of Animal Kingdom, is the Research Station. The station contains several exhibits, including naked mole rats. Just outside are a free-flight aviary and an aquarium teeming with exotic fish. Not far away is the hippo exhibit, which provides close-up views of hippopotamuses both in and out of water. Farther along the trail there is a scenic overlook point, where you can get an unobstructed view of the African savanna. This is also known as the "Timon" exhibit, featuring a family of perky meerkats. Afterward, you may catch an up-close glimpse (through a glass wall) of a cavorting gorilla or two.

As you come to the end of the suspension bridge, you'll find yourself in a beautiful green valley. Congratulations! You've finally reached the gorilla area—an experience well worth the wait. (Note that you may have to wait a little bit longer for that first gorilla sighting. Our evolutionary cousins have been known to play hide-and-seek in the lush vegetation.)

Wildlife Express to Conservation Station

On the east side of Harambe, bordering Asia, is the Harambe Train Station. Here you board the Wildlife Express and enjoy a tour of Africa, as well as an interesting behind-the-scenes look at a Disney park.

As part of the 5½-minute tour, you'll glide past the buildings where elephants, rhinos, and giraffes sleep at night. You will also see the animal care facilities at Conservation Station and get a backstage view of the Kilimanjaro Safaris. A guide narrates throughout the trip. All guests disembark at Conservation Station. (You must reboard the train to return to Harambe.)

Conservation Station

While Animal Kingdom's stories often carry a conservation theme, this part of the park really brings the message home. A veterinary lab, this facility is the park's conservation headquarters. It's also the research and education hub. Here guests get a look at the way animals are cared for.

Note: The only way to get to Conservation Station is by taking the Wildlife Express.

"Much of the world's wildlife is in imminent danger," says Judson Green, Walt Disney Attractions president. "Disney is working directly to save endangered animals, but we also hope to motivate our guests to support wildlife programs that are in urgent need of support." After spending time at Conservation Station, visitors just might have the motivation they need. Exhibits are geared to spark curiosity and wonder about wildlife and conservation efforts around the world. Here are a few highlights of the area.

Affection Section: A large animal encounter area with accessible, friendly animals to see and touch. Most of the animals are exotic breeds of familiar petting zoo types: goats, sheep, pigs, etc. However, this is still a not-to-be-missed experience for kids.

Animal Cams: Guest-operated video monitors that observe animals throughout the park as they go about their daily business.

Animal Health & Care: A tour of veterinary labs and research facilities.

Eco Heroes: A set of touch-sensitive video kiosks that allow guests to interact with famous biologists and conservationists.

EcoWeb: A computer link to conservation organizations around the world. Printouts are available.

Rafiki's Planet Watch: An interactive video, hosted by Rafiki, that connects guests to information about endangered animals.

Song of the Rainforest: A not-to-be-missed "3-D" audio show that surrounds guests with the sounds of the rain forest.

Get Involved!

When it comes to conservation efforts, the folks at the Walt Disney Company want you to do as they say—and as they do: The Disney Wildlife Conservation Fund helps nonprofit groups protect and study endangered and threatened animals and their habitats. Among those groups are the ASPCA, Dian Fossey Gorilla Fund, Jane Goodall Institute, and the Wildlife Conservation Society. To date, Disney has contributed more than $4 million to programs in 24 countries.

Of course, as a trip to Animal Kingdom makes clear, there are many ways to help our planet's wild inhabitants. Be sure and stop by Conservation Station during your visit. There you can get information about conservation efforts in your neck of the woods. Don't leave your enthusiasm behind when you leave the park!

ASIA

On the far side of a Himalayan-style bridge, beyond an ancient temple, lies the tranquil village of Anandapur (Sanskrit for "place of delight"). The buildings' design was inspired by structures in Thailand, Indonesia, and other Asian regions known for their rich architectural history.

A product of Disney Imagineering, the village epitomizes the complex, enduring relationship between the animals and ecosystems of the Asian continent. The village borders an elaborate re-creation of a Southeast Asian rain forest. As such, Disney's Asia is an ideal location for trekking through the jungle, shooting the rapids on a raging river, and gazing upon the multi-hued inhabitants of this treasured terrain. This land, which is the newest in Disney's Animal Kingdom, was scheduled to begin opening in stages by early 1999.

Maharajah Jungle Trek

Welcome to the jungle! The Maharajah Jungle Trek is a self-guided walking tour of a tropical paradise, complete with roaming tigers, gushing waterfalls, and dense greenery. Throughout the expedition, trekkers encounter a deluge of flora and fauna typically found in the rain forests of Southeast Asia. Gibbons, Komodo dragons, and a conglomerate of colorful birds call this corner of Animal Kingdom home. Majestic Bengal tigers can be spotted stalking ancient ruins, strategically separated from would-be prey. Deer and antelope graze and frolic nearby, blissfully oblivious of their fearsome neighbors' proximity.

Approximately midway through the thicket stands a rustic, tin-roofed assembly hall. Step inside to witness the breathtaking sight of giant fruit bats showing off their six-foot wingspans. As you look through the windows, thinking that the crystal-clear glass was cleaned by a super-diligent window washer, think again. There is no glass in some windows—and, therefore, *nothing* separating you from the giant creatures fluttering about on the other side. What keeps the big bats from getting up close and personal with guests? They're a lot less interested in humans than humans are in them. (Can't say that we blame them.) Note that some viewing areas are adorned with wire or glass—for guests who are more comfortable with a bat buffer.

Tiger Rapids Run

Before guests board rafts at Tiger Rapids (opening in spring 1999), a wise voice admonishes that "the river is like life itself, full of mysterious twists and turns." What the voice *doesn't* say is that the river is also full of drastic drops, waterfalls, and at least one blazing inferno. This may be business as usual for some daring souls, but for the rest of us, these elements make for one hair-raising adventure.

All guests begin the journey in the offices of Tiger Rapids Expeditions, a river rafting company. A slide show provides information on the sometimes unscrupulous business of logging—how it has ravaged the rain forest and deprived many animals of their habitats. However, thanks to ecotourism (among other things), there is hope. Peaceful voyages, like the one you'll

BIRNBAUM'S *Best*

take, give people a renewed appreciation and sense of responsibility for this precious endangered land.

A vibrant 12-seater raft whisks "eco-tourists" up a watery ramp and through an arching tunnel of bamboo. It proceeds onward, through a hazy mist and past remnants of an ancient shrine. As the raft moves along curves of the river, guests enjoy spectacular views of undisturbed rain forest.

The tranquillity is shattered by a startling sight. A huge chunk of forest has been gutted by loggers. On both sides of the river, the forest has vanished. As guests absorb the image, they are besieged by more disturbing sights and sounds. Straight ahead, the river is choked with a tangled arch of burning logs—and the raft is headed straight for it. Suddenly, the rain forest isn't the only thing that is endangered.

The perils that follow come at a rapid (make that *rapids*) pace. Be prepared to plummet down cascading slopes of rushing white water, teeter at the top of a waterfall, and find yourself on the receiving end of a thundering avalanche of lumber.

An exhilarating five-minute thrill ride, Tiger Rapids Run can be a drenching one. It is the rare guest that leaves the ride completely dry.

Note: This is a wild ride. In order to experience it, you must be at least 46 inches tall. It is not recommended for pregnant women, those with a heart condition, or people with back and neck problems.

Flights of Wonder

A 700-seat, open-air theater, the Caravan Stage features performances by actors wearing nothing but feathers and the occasional crown. Members of more than 20 different bird species have starring roles in Flights of Wonder, a high-flying celebration of the winged wonders of the world. Hawks, falcons, and even chickens awe spectators as they swoop, soar, and strut their stuff in each 20-minute performance. Some demonstrate how they hunt. Others display the fine points of pulverizing prey. And a few simply show off. (Case in point: Groucho the parrot. Expect him to belt out a rousing medley of such ditties as "How Much Is That Doggie in the Window?")

In order to accommodate the airborne antics of the performers, the theater is uncovered—so don't forget the sunscreen. Although performances are scheduled throughout the day, some may be canceled due to inclement weather. Check a park guidemap for showtimes.

DID YOU KNOW...

The benches in Disney's Animal Kingdom are made of recycled plastic milk jugs. It takes 1,350 jugs to make a single bench!

DINOLAND U.S.A.

If the look and feel of DinoLand U.S.A. seems familiar, there's a reason: It was designed to capture the flavor of roadside America. It is a delightful mixture of culture and kitsch—the likes of which you might stumble upon during a cross-country road trip. Here you'll come face-to-face with fossil fanatics, jump into gigantic footprints, and browse through a typically tacky roadside souvenir stand, where you can pick up some dinosaur mementos for the folks back home.

This self-contained corner of Animal Kingdom is a park within a park, complete with its own dramatic entrance: a 50-foot skeleton of a brachiosaurus. As guests stroll beneath the bones, they find themselves smack in the middle of a paleontological dig. Here, guests of all ages have the chance to play paleontologist as they dig through a fossil-packed pocket of dino discovery.

The dinosaurs that dwell here, though often quite animated, are all of the inanimate variety. But do keep your eyes peeled for the prehistoric life forms that actually *live* in this land. That is, for real creatures that exist in the here and now, but whose ancestors kept company with the likes of the carnotaurus and its dinosaur cousins from the Cretaceous era: alligators, turtles, and prehistoric birds.

The Boneyard

The Boneyard gives guests—especially younger ones—an opportunity to dig for fossils in a discovery-oriented playground. They will excavate the ancient bones of a mammoth in this imaginative re-creation of a paleontological dig. They'll also unearth clues that will help them solve the mystery of how and when the creature died.

For serious "boneheads" who just aren't satisfied with simple digging, there are plenty of other bone-related activities. You can play a bony xylophone, zip down prehistoric slides, and work your way through a fossil-filled maze. While exploring, watch your step: If you accidentally wander into a giant dinosaur footprint, you'll be greeted with a tremendous roar. Be sure to check out the OldenGate Bridge, too. It's a gateway structure made from the giant skeleton of a dinosaur. The bridge links one end of The Boneyard with the other.

Countdown to Extinction

This thrilling attraction is dramatic with a capital *D*. The dizzying adventure begins with guests being strapped into high-speed vehicles and catapulted back in time to complete a dangerous, albeit noble, mission: to locate the last living iguanodon—a 16-foot plant-eating dinosaur—and bring him back to the present. The iguanodon, which lived more than 65 million years ago (during the Cretaceous period) just might hold the answer to the mysterious disappearance of his dino brethren.

Throughout the frenetic quest to find the iguanodon, you cling to an out-of-control vehicle while dodging meteors and a mix of friendly and ferocious dinosaurs. Soon you encounter the carnotaurus—a fearsome, carnivorous dinosaur. The carnotaurus, which has horns like a bull, a face like a toad, and squirrel-like arms, is an unsightly specimen.

All of the dinosaurs are especially fierce-looking and move as though they were alive. Even their nostrils move as they "breathe."

This 3½-minute attraction offers much more than a thrill a minute. You rocket through time, get pelted by fiery meteors, and narrowly escape becoming dinner as a dinosaur turns the tables and chases after *you*.

Guests reach the Countdown to Extinction attraction through the Dino Institute, a museumlike building inside DinoLand U.S.A. Here you will see a dinosaur skeleton, asteroid fragments, and an assortment of fossils and other artifacts.

Note: This is an *extremely* intense attraction. You must be at least 48 inches tall to experience it. It is not recommended for pregnant women, those with a heart condition, or people with back or neck problems.

For a slightly less turbulent ride on Countdown to Extinction, request an inside seat toward the front of the vehicle.

Cretaceous Trail

Looking for something totally different from the high drama of Countdown to Extinction? We recommend the decidedly calmer Cretaceous Trail. This short and simple walking path is filled with living plants and some animals (like Chinese alligators, red-legged seriema birds, and Florida softshell turtles) that have survived from the Cretaceous period, the last time dinosaurs ruled the land.

Many of the land plants of the Cretaceous period were much like those that lived in the Jurassic period, the time that immediately preceded it, with a notable exception: the presence of angiosperms, or flowering plants. These and many other prehistoric flora evolved into the plants we see today.

Journey into Jungle Book

The huge, covered Theater in the Wild seats 1,500 guests at a time. Here, audiences are treated to a rousing 25-minute show featuring songs, dances, and characters based on those in Disney's *Jungle Book* film.

The familiar story follows Mowgli the man cub through the challenges of jungle life. Bagheera, the boy's trusty panther guardian, knows that Mowgli must move to the man village, where he'll be safe. He assigns that big lug, Baloo, to escort him there. When that doesn't work out, they must rescue the kid from the clutches of King Louie of the Apes and from the jaws of Shere Khan, the tiger.

Show-stopping numbers include "The Bare Necessities" and "I Wanna Be Like You." In addition to live vocals and creative costumes, the performance features innovative choreography and acrobatics.

Journey into Jungle Book runs throughout the day, on most days. Check a guidemap for exact times.

CAMP MINNIE-MICKEY

What would a theme park be without a gregarious cast of handshaking characters? You will find the patented Disney character experience in all of its animated glory in Camp Minnie-Mickey. Set deep in a dense forest, this land is really a summer camp frequented by Mickey Mouse and all of his pals.

To find the characters, guests follow one of four short trails. Each one leads to an open-air hut, occupied by the likes of Mickey, Minnie, Winnie the Pooh, Tigger, Timon, and Rafiki. Different characters make appearances at these meet-and-greet pavilions throughout the day.

Keep in mind that, with the exception of the character meals at DinoLand's Restaurantosaurus, this is the only place in Disney's Animal Kingdom to shmooze with the characters. Therefore, if you are traveling with small children, this area is not to be missed.

Camp Minnie-Mickey is also the home of two engaging theater shows, starring the cast of *The Lion King* and the heroine of the Disney film *Pocahontas*. Both shows are presented daily. Check a guidemap for times.

Festival of the Lion King

In addition to meeting, greeting, and rustling up grubs in Camp Minnie-Mickey, the cast of *The Lion King* performs a 28-minute stage show in the Lion King Theater.

Presented in the round, this lavish outdoor revue is as bright and boisterous as they come. The dramatic opening features a parade of performers in colorful animal costumes. What follows is an intriguing, energetic interpretation of the film, including songs, dances, and acrobatics. With the exception of Timon, who plays himself, the lead characters are portrayed by humans draped in bold African costumes. The rolling stages come courtesy of Disneyland. They were used in the park's *Lion King* parade.

Songs include Scar's nasty version of "Be Prepared," as well as "Can You Feel the Love Tonight?," "The Circle of Life," and a rousing audience-participation rendition of "The Lion Sleeps Tonight."

Timing Tip: Although this covered theater accommodates 1,000 guests at a time, we recommend arriving at least 45 minutes before the scheduled performance time—since the show is extremely popular.

Colors of the Wind, Friends from the Animal Forest

The forest is in trouble, and Pocahontas is worried. "It is being cut down limb by limb," she tells Grandmother Willow (the wise old tree from Disney's *Pocahontas*). "They are leaving nothing in their path."

And so the stage is set for this 12-minute presentation in Grandmother Willow's Grove. The grim premise soon gives way to a more positive outlook, as Grandmother Willow reminds Pocahontas that there is one creature of the forest who has the power to protect it. But which one?

Pocahontas begins a quest to find that creature. Along the way, she learns that many forest dwellers have special talents. Among them are possums, porcupines, skunks, bunnies, and even snakes. Her encounters with these real live critters are interspersed with heartfelt verses of the song "Colors of the Wind." At the end of this sweet and simple musical fable, she learns a very important lesson about preserving the forest—as do many members of the audience.

Note: The small theater space, though surrounded by trees, is uncovered. Wear sunscreen. Also, because live animals star in the production, no food is permitted in the seating area. The cast includes a few live rats and one live snake (just a warning).

SHOPPING

Entrance Area

GARDEN GATE GIFTS: Located near the entrance to The Oasis, this is the place to rent strollers and wheelchairs. Film and disposable cameras are for sale, as is a selection of shirts, hats, and other merchandise. This is also the park's package pickup location.

OUTPOST: This small shop, located just outside the park entrance, features a variety of character merchandise and Animal Kingdom souvenirs.

Safari Village

BEASTLY BAZAAR: Safari hats with Mickey, Pooh, or Pluto ears; Disney's Animal Kingdom logo watches; character figurines; and plush toys clad in safari garb are among the wares offered in this shop designed as a celebration of aquatic animals.

CREATURE COMFORTS: This open-air shop offers items for kids—toys, clothes, costumes, hats, and more.

DISNEY OUTFITTERS: This spot features men's and women's apparel, jewelry, and hats, plus candles, bags, Tree of Life souvenirs, and a variety of Animal Kingdom logo merchandise, including mugs, plates, photo albums, and umbrellas. Make a point of checking out the authentic carved animal totem poles in the center room—they are most impressive.

ISLAND MERCANTILE: This sprawling shop is themed as a shipping company that celebrates working animals—camels, elephants, beavers, and others. Here you'll find character merchandise, clothing, candy, and Disney paraphernalia. Note that it stays open a half hour after the park closes for the day.

Africa

DUKA LA FILIMU: Situated near the entrance to Kilimanjaro Safaris, this is an ideal location to load up on film for your trip. You'll find it comes in handy when you need to develop the film after your trip to the African savanna, too.

MOMBASA MARKETPLACE AND ISWANI TRADERS: An African marketplace and trading company, these connected shops feature animal toys, safari clothing, T-shirts, books, and Africa-themed gifts such as pottery, masks, and musical instruments.

DID YOU KNOW...

Many of the costumes worn by Animal Kingdom workers are made of wood! A natural fabric called lyocell is made from wood pulp. The pulp is harvested from trees grown specifically for this purpose.

OUT OF THE WILD: Located just outside the exit of Conservation Station, this open-air shop stocks souvenirs with a conservation theme, including shirts, hats, books, toys, and even items for the bath.

DinoLand U.S.A.

CHESTER AND HESTER'S DINOSAUR TREASURES: Themed as an American roadside souvenir stand, this shop pays homage to all reptiles and prehistoric animals. Its dinosaur focus is reflected in an assortment of wacky dino-inspired items.

177

ENTERTAINMENT

AFRICAN ENTERTAINMENT: Contemporary sounds of Africa often fill the air as live bands serenade guests passing through the village of Harambe. Storytellers perform animal tales throughout the day.

ANIMAL ENCOUNTERS: Enjoy up-close encounters with some of the smaller members of the animal kingdom as they wander the park with their human keepers.

DINOLAND U.S.A. ENTERTAINMENT: There's a bunch of loud-mouthed dinosaur-groupies on the loose in DinoLand U.S.A. This raucous troupe of improv performers will stop at nothing to get your attention—and make you dig 'em.

MARCH OF THE ANIMALS: A vivid musical procession of fanciful creatures great and small celebrates the world of animals in this 15-minute parade. Beginning in Safari Village, near Pizzafari, the march proceeds through the village, along the edge of Asia and past DinoLand U.S.A.

The parade is designed to show off the talents of Safari Village artists, such as painters, sculptors, and weavers. Visual inspiration for the costumes and five rolling stages comes from European artist Rolf Knie, who designs with color, modern style, and a whole lot of imagination.

Cockroaches, tigers, and bees are among the creatures featured. Not coincidentally, its musical score includes "La Cucaracha," "Hold That Tiger," and "Flight of the Bumble Bee."

The parade is presented twice a day. Check a guidemap for exact times.

HOT TIPS

• Arrive at the park at least 45 minutes before the posted opening time.

• Check the Animal Kingdom Tip Boards often to get an idea of showtimes and crowds.

• See Kilimanjaro Safaris very early in the day, when the animals are liveliest.

• There is a footpath connecting Asia with Africa. All other lands can be reached only by a bridge from Safari Village.

• Make priority seating arrangements *in advance* for the character breakfast at Restaurantosaurus in DinoLand U.S.A.

• Island Mercantile in Safari Village stays open a half hour after the park closes.

• If the skies seem threatening, take the Wildlife Express to Conservation Station.

• WDW resort guests can have packages delivered to their hotels free of charge.

Where to Eat in Animal Kingdom

A complete listing of eateries at Disney's Animal Kingdom—table-service restaurants, fast-food spots, and snack stands—can be found in the *Good Meals, Great Times* chapter of this book. See the Animal Kingdom restaurant section, which begins on page 231.

Everything Else in the World

W hile the total turf of the World comprises 47 square miles, the theme parks cover less than 1,000 acres. Much of the remaining Walt Disney World terrain is crammed with irresistible activities of a variety and quality seldom found anywhere else.

There's superb golf and tennis, beaches for sunbathing, lakes for speedboating and sailing, canoes for rent and winding streams to paddle along, bicycles for hire, campfire sites, nature trails, and picnic grounds. The recreation options continue with River Country, Disney's old-fashioned swimming cove; Typhoon Lagoon, a state-of-the-art water park complete with surfing lagoon; and Blizzard Beach, a thrilling watery wonderland that translates the hallmarks of a ski resort to the realm of swimming.

Add to all that Downtown Disney, a dining, shopping, and amusement district encompassing Pleasure Island, an after-dark entertainment complex; the Downtown Disney Marketplace, a colorful assortment of shops and restaurants; and Downtown Disney West Side, a cluster of themed eateries, unique shops, and interactive entertainment experiences. A host of programs invite guests to slip behind the scenes and learn about the workings of WDW. Finally, the Disney Institute gives guests a different way to vacation in the World. A resort geared to discovery, it offers the opportunity to dabble in animation, the culinary arts, and many other areas. As Michael Eisner said at the 1996 dedication, "It's like putting the cherry on top of the cake at Walt Disney World."

Unless otherwise noted, all phone numbers are in area code 407.

DOWNTOWN DISNEY

Sprinkled across 120 waterfront acres are the shops, nightclubs, restaurants, and entertainment sites that collectively comprise Downtown Disney. Like the downtown area of any thriving metropolis, Disney's Downtown is made up of several distinct neighborhoods. In this case, they are the Marketplace, Pleasure Island, and the West Side (which opened in fall 1997). Unlike a typical downtown, however, the Disney depiction dispenses with the downside. You won't see litter on the streets, unsightly storefronts, or weary workers rushing home at 5 o'clock. You *will* see a series of spirited spots designed solely for your dining, shopping, and partying pleasure.

Based on the throngs that descend upon this place, Downtown Disney is *the* place to be after dark. That said, it can get a tad congested—especially on the roads leading here. Whether you are traveling by bus or car, allow plenty of extra time to get to and from this fun zone. Note that all three sections are connected by walking paths and the West Side and Marketplace are linked by water taxi service.

Downtown Disney Essentials

GUEST SERVICES: Next to Toys Fantastic in the Marketplace, and at the AMC Theatres on the West Side, these information centers are also the place to go for priority seating assistance, Lost and Found, stroller and wheelchair rental, theme park ticket purchase, and more. There is an ATM at Guest Services in the Marketplace, next to Forty Thirst Street on the West Side, and near the Rock 'n' Roll Beach Club at Pleasure Island.

HOW TO GET THERE: Downtown Disney is accessible from Exit 26B off I-4.

By WDW Transportation: From the Disney Institute: walkway or bus. From Port Orleans, Dixie Landings, and Old Key West: boats or buses. From the Magic Kingdom, Epcot, Grand Floridian, Contemporary, and Polynesian: monorail to the Transportation and Ticket Center (TTC), then transfer to a Downtown Disney bus. From the Disney-MGM Studios, Animal Kingdom, Wilderness Lodge, and Fort Wilderness: bus to the TTC, then switch for a Downtown Disney bus. From all other WDW resorts: buses. For more information, turn to the *Transportation & Accommodations* chapter.

By Taxi: Yellow cabs, operated by several different companies, service the Downtown Disney area. The cost to most WDW resorts is usually $5 to $15. **Note:** We recommend sticking with the authorized yellow cabs, and avoiding the independent "gypsy" cabs. Their fees are not regulated.

West Side

Pleasure Island

Downtown Disney Marketplace

Located on the shores of Lake Buena Vista, the Marketplace is a relaxing setting for shopping, dining, and much more. The waterside enclave is sprinkled with gardens, including whimsical topiaries. Kids enjoy seeking out the interactive fountains scattered about the area. And adults may enjoy a drink at the outdoor area known as Sunset Cove.

While many guests choose to lunch in one of the themed restaurants, others may grab a bite from the Gourmet Pantry and eat at one of many waterfront tables. (Refer to the *Good Meals, Great Times* chapter for lounge and restaurant information.) Afterward, some gravitate toward the marina for boating or fishing. (See *Sports* for details.)

Shopping

The descriptions below suggest the types of wares each store offers. Most shops are open daily from 9:30 A.M. to 11 P.M. Note that delivery of purchases to a WDW resort is free.

THE ART OF DISNEY: Disney animation cels, porcelain figures, ceramics, and collectibles are the goods available at this gallery next to 2R's Reading and Riting.

DISNEY AT HOME: This new shop has an eclectic selection of items for the bedroom and bath. Among the wares recently on display were Pooh sheets, bathroom carpets shaped like Mickey's head, and lamps, rocking chairs, and even beds with a Mickey theme (some designs are more subtle than others).

DISNEY'S DAYS OF CHRISTMAS: Here's the best place to deck the halls Disney-style—it's the largest Christmas shop on Disney property. In addition to character items, the shop, which smells of cinnamon, boasts a large assortment of handcrafted ornaments. Other items to look for: Christmas cards, candles, Santa hats with mouse ears, pajamas, and books. Many items can be personalized.

EUROSPAIN: This shop sells handcrafted items from Spanish artisans and designers. Large cut-glass bowls and vases are available, along with mugs, sculptures, and other wares, all of which can be engraved. Presented by Arribas Brothers.

GOURMET PANTRY: Though escargots and smoked oysters can be found here, there are also breads and pastries, meats and cheeses, beer, wine, soft drinks, and much more. Unusual teas and specially blended coffees are available, as are chocolates, sandwiches, and salads. Guests staying at the nearby villas, take note: Purchases can be delivered to your room; if you aren't going to be there, the delivery person will even stash perishable items in your refrigerator. To order by phone, call 828-3886.

HARRINGTON BAY CLOTHIERS: Designed to have the appearance of a Bermuda plantation home, this shop boasts a sizable stock of traditional and casual men's clothing from designers such as Nautica, Ralph Lauren, and Tommy Hilfiger. It is located near Toys Fantastic.

Marketplace

LEGO IMAGINATION CENTER: World of Disney's next-door neighbor, this shop is a showcase for larger-than-life Lego models, including dinosaurs and aliens. It also invites guests to flaunt their creativity in an outdoor play area. The store stocks a variety of Lego products and educational toys. By the way, that fire-breathing sea serpent in Lake Buena Vista is also made of Legos.

POOH CORNER: Searching for that perfect plush Pooh? You'll find him here, along with his pals from the Hundred Acre Wood. Also on hand are kitchen items, stationery, books, sweatshirts, T-shirts, and other clothing for adults and kids. The shop itself is quite soothing, with the ceiling painted to look like a blue sky with puffy clouds drifting by. Pooh videos are shown on screens behind the counter.

RESORTWEAR UNLIMITED: An excellent source of bright and classy fashions for women. An assortment of sportswear is enhanced by bold jewelry and bags. Lancôme cosmetics are available.

STUDIO M: Here guests can have a professional portrait taken with Mickey Mouse, have their image "magically" added to photos of Disney characters, and watch as robotic artists decorate colorful apparel.

SUMMER SANDS: A beach lover's delight, this shop stocks swimwear, kids' clothing, sun care products, straw hats, and bags.

TEAM MICKEY'S ATHLETIC CLUB: A cavernous store with a locker-room motif, this shop is the perfect setting for sports clothing, activewear, and sports equipment.

You'll find many items with Disney characters in sporting poses emblazoned on them. There is also a large selection golf apparel.

TOYS FANTASTIC: This fun spot stocks a wide variety of Mattel toys and games, including the newest playthings featuring Disney characters, a full line of Hot Wheels action toys, and Barbie fashions.

2R'S READING AND RITING: Books on many subjects can be found here. Located near the bus stop, at the far end of the Marketplace, the shop also has greeting cards and stationery. You can sip cappuccino while browsing.

VILLAGE TOWER: This shop boasts a broad selection of Disney merchandise, which changes several times a year.

WORLD OF DISNEY: A sprawling space stuffed with a tremendous selection of Disney merchandise, this is the place for one-stop shopping. In fact, it's the largest Disney character shopping experience in the world. Twelve themed rooms provide the backdrop for the huge array of goods. The enchanted dining room from *Beauty and the Beast* was the inspiration for the culinary section; Disney villains are celebrated in a room that's filled with items such as clocks, watches, candles, and frames; and fairies from *Cinderella* and *Sleeping Beauty* can be seen floating through the intimate apparel department. Disney characters are available on everything from hats and shirts to sleepwear and bags.

Engraving and personalization services are available for many items. A concierge can help locate any item in the store, then arrange for delivery home or to a WDW resort.

Where to Eat *at Downtown Disney*

A complete listing of restaurants, bars, and snack spots can be found in the *Good Meals, Great Times* chapter. See the Downtown Disney restaurant listing, beginning on page 233. Most restaurants here are open from about 11:30 A.M. to midnight. Planet Hollywood serves until 1 A.M. West Side spots serve as late as 2 A.M.

Pleasure Island

A six-acre nighttime entertainment complex, Pleasure Island delivers a wealth of options that nicely top off a day in the parks. In addition to clubs, there are several restaurants and shops here in the central area of Downtown Disney.

Most clubs open at 7 P.M. or 8 P.M. and don't close until 2 A.M. There is no fee to explore Pleasure Island before clubs open or to eat at its restaurants. A single admission of $20.09 (including tax) allows access to clubs and the nightly street party. Length of Stay Passes and All-In-One Hopper Passes include Pleasure Island admission. An annual pass costs $54.01 ($43.31 for a renewal). Guests under age 18 must be accompanied by a parent or legal guardian. Valet parking is available for $6. Guidemaps provide showtime information.

Cocktails and soft drinks are available at all of the clubs. The drinking age in Florida is 21. Guests who are 18 and older will be admitted to the clubs (except Mannequins and BET SoundStage) but will not be served alcohol. A valid U.S., foreign, or international driver's license with a photo, an active U.S. military identification card, or a passport must be presented as proof of age.

Clubs

ADVENTURERS CLUB: "Explore the unknown, discover the impossible" states the credo posted at the entrance. The place is modeled after the paneled libraries and elegant salons of similar clubs of the 19th century, and is jam-packed with memorabilia. Just about all the items on display were collected at garage sales, antiques shows, and shops from around the world by Disney Imagineers.

The two-story club is littered with "stuff," so stroll around and snoop all you like. If you have a seat at the bar, ask the bartender to work some magic; your stool may slowly sink toward the floor. In the library, a haunted organ sets the scene for outrageous storytellers. The show is a little silly, but entertaining.

BET SOUNDSTAGE CLUB: Live performances, celebrity appearances, dancing and other audience-engaging activities combine to make BET Soundstage Club a unique entertainment experience. Located in the space previously occupied by the Neon Armadillo Music Saloon, the club opened in summer 1998. (It's operated by BET Holdings, Inc., which owns Black Entertainment Television.)

In keeping with the BET musical tradition, the club features the best in jazz, rhythm and blues, soul, and hip-hop. Early in the evening, a veejay cues up videos by contemporary urban artists from Mariah Carey to Sean "Puffy" Combs, chats with guests, and encourages everyone to take to the dance floor. Most evenings are highlighted by live performances and dancing—by guests and BET's own energetic troupe of dancers. Appetizers are available.

Although big-name talent does perform here on occasion, a Pleasure Island pass is all you need to enter. Shows are often announced several months ahead. Call 934-7781 for information. Note that BET SoundStage is restricted to guests 21 and older.

COMEDY WAREHOUSE: A comedy troupe performs five times each evening from 7 P.M. to 1 A.M. There are five comedians and one musician. It's a funny, entertaining show that features improvisational comedy based on audience suggestions. Every seat offers a good view, even if the stools are a little tough on bad backs. Popcorn is the snack of choice.

8TRAX: Got a penchant for the Partridge Family? Do the Bee Gees have a special place in your heart? If so, make tracks for 8TRAX. Music from the early seventies and the disco era fills this dance spot. To keep things in a 1970s mode, the staff even dresses in polyester. The club also has eighties nights for the seventies-challenged.

MANNEQUINS: This is the place to head to dance the night away. Guests enter through an elevator that rises to the third floor. Lights, contemporary dance music, and an overall exuberant atmosphere dominate the scene. The name of the club comes from the many mannequins serving as props.

The main dance floor is actually a big turntable, and the music is provided by a deejay. The lighting is a major attraction, with 60 robotically controlled lighting instruments and a matrix of lights behind the stage.

Note that guests must be at least 21 years old to enter Mannequins.

PLEASURE ISLAND JAZZ COMPANY:
Reminiscent of jazz clubs from the 1930s, the interior of this one resembles an old warehouse. There is live entertainment nightly, featuring jazz from the 1930s to the present. Guests sit at tables. The music is not too loud, so conversation is possible. Tapas-style appetizers are served.

ROCK 'N' ROLL BEACH CLUB: A combination of dancing and surfer-style decor awaits guests here. The dance floor is on the lowest level of the building, and there are billiard tables and games on the other two floors. Live bands perform hits from the 1960s to the present. The atmosphere is a little frenetic but nonetheless exciting. Light snacks are available.

Note that during the refurbishment a second staircase was added out front, allowing for quicker entrances and exits.

WILDHORSE SALOON: A dance club, restaurant, and concert hall all wrapped up in one, Wildhorse appeals to the fun-lovin' cowpoke in all of us. With an emphasis on new country, the daytime deejay cues up everyone from Garth Brooks to the Dixie Chicks. The atmosphere is casual even into the night (they may blame it all on your roots if you *don't* show up in boots), and live music keeps the joint jumpin'.

Free dance lessons are offered daily, beginning at about 4:30 P.M. There is no admission charge prior to 7 P.M. After that, guests have three options. They can purchase a Pleasure Island pass, which includes admission to Wildhorse; purchase a Wildhorse-only pass, which can be upgraded to include the rest of Pleasure Island; or buy a ticket to a premium concert—a show by a big name such as LeeAnn Rhimes or Vince Gill—which includes admission to the club. Call 827-4947 for ticket information.

Open from 10:30 A.M. to 2 A.M., the kitchen serves lunch and dinner. Priority seating is not available. For more information, turn to the *Good Meals, Great Times* chapter.

Entertainment

LATE-NIGHT STREET PARTY: At Pleasure Island, every night is New Year's Eve. There's a fireworks display, special-effects lighting and confetti, and a troupe of dancers entertaining on the streets.

WEST END STAGE: Bands, including some top-name groups, perform here nightly. The Island Explosion, Pleasure Island's own dance troupe, also entertains.

Shopping

The following Pleasure Island shops are all open from 11 A.M. to 1 A.M.

AVIGATOR'S SUPPLY: The latest in men's and women's casual attire is featured here.

CHANGING ATTITUDES: This shop reveals its hip young style with an assortment of shirts, accessories, jewelry, bags, and other goods.

DTV: A collection of fun and colorful contemporary fashions featuring Mickey Mouse and his friends is available here.

ISLAND DEPOT: The shop features surfwear and activewear, including shirts, shorts, backpacks, and hats, plus watches and jewelry.

MUSIC LEGENDS: CDs, T-shirts, and music memorabilia are available at this location. There are three sections, highlighting different types of music.

REEL FINDS: Movie- and TV-themed memorabilia constitute the stock here. Items once owned by celebrities are for sale.

SUPERSTAR STUDIOS: Guests lip-sync to favorite songs to create video recordings. A particular favorite with teens.

SUSPENDED ANIMATION: Posters, prints, lithographs, cels, and original Disney animation art are sold here.

Shopping at Crossroads

Constructed by the WDW folks, the Crossroads of Lake Buena Vista shopping center, near the resorts on Hotel Plaza Boulevard, is a convenient dining and shopping area. The center is anchored by a Gooding's supermarket, which is open 24 hours a day. In addition to the many shops and services, there's a miniature golf course dubbed Pirate's Cove Adventure Golf.

Downtown Disney West Side

When Disney's shopping and entertainment district underwent its recent growth spurt, it did so in true American style: It went west. The West Side, which made its debut in late 1997, boasts a wide variety of restaurants, shops, movies, and clubs. Although it does not have an admission fee, some venues may charge a cover.

AMC THEATRES: The most popular multi-screen movie theater complex in the state of Florida is also the largest. The 24 screens show an impressive selection of current movie releases. The seats are roomy and comfortable, and the sound system is first-rate. (It was developed by George Lucas, the creative force behind the trilogy of *Star Wars* blockbusters.) For current schedules, call 298-4488.

BONGOS CUBAN CAFE: Situated across from the AMC Theatres on the edge of Lake Buena Vista, Bongos echoes the style of clubs in Miami's sizzling South Beach. Created by Gloria Estefan and her husband, it features the flavors and rhythms of Cuba and other Latin American countries. The bold design is dramatic, yet whimsical. Guests dine and, if the mood strikes, even dance amid the colorful, tropical decor (and one remarkably oversize pineapple, which houses a multi-level cocktail lounge).

There is entertainment nightly. The food here moves to a Latin beat as well, with its slate of traditional and nouvelle Cuban dishes. (For more information, refer to *Good Meals, Great Times*.)

CIRQUE DU SOLEIL: The building that towers over all the others at Downtown Disney West Side is actually a tent—a circus tent. It's the home of a most extraordinary circus experience: Cirque du Soleil. This original show premiered for Walt Disney World resort guests in fall 1998.

Known for its high energy and artistic performances, Cirque du Soleil features a unique mix of acrobatics and modern dance combined with outrageous costumes, magical lighting, and dramatic original music. A cast of more than 70 international performers showcase their extraordinary physical talents on a daily basis.

Tickets for the show can be purchased up to a year in advance. Call 934-7639 for information or to order tickets. If you have not already purchased tickets, stop by the Cirque box office at Downtown Disney—some seats may be available. Note that the show is quite popular. Get your seats as early as possible.

DISNEYQUEST: This wildly imaginative entertainment complex features high-tech activities that engage kids and grown-ups alike. Best described as a self-contained theme park, the space under the DisneyQuest roof is divided into four distinct "zones": Explore, Score, Create, and Replay.

Each zone features interactive games from the simple (classic video games like Asteroids, in Replay) to the most technologically advanced (e.g., Explore's CyberSpace Mountain, in which guests not only design gravity-defying roller coasters but actually get to "ride" their creations).

Other stops on the tour include Buzz Lightyear's AstroBlaster (wacky bumper cars that shoot volleyballs at other drivers), Mighty Ducks Pinball Slam (which transforms players into human joysticks), Sid's Make-a-Toy (an interactive computer terminal that allows guests to assemble twisted toys), and the family-oriented Virtual Jungle Cruise (a turbulent trip into a primeval world).

Note that this is a "pay-as-you-play" environment—each activity has an individual fee. It's best to pre-pay select dollar amounts (stored on a DisneyQuest card) when you purchase admission at the entrance (about $7, which can be used as credit toward activities). Simply swipe the card at the attractions of your choice and the fee is deducted. Additional credit can be added to the card at any time.

Hunger pangs can be quelled in two areas run by The Cheesecake Factory: The Wired Wonderland Cafe, featuring snacks, drinks, and an Internet-based attraction; and FoodQuest, which has sandwiches and salads.

Expect to be fully engaged for two to three hours at a stretch (or until sensory overload sets in). Due to DisneyQuest's popularity, there may be a line to get in when you arrive. (It's worth the wait.)

HOUSE OF BLUES: A combination restaurant–music hall with seating for 2,000, House of Blues (HOB) was inspired by one of America's most celebrated musical traditions. Lest too much of the blues bring you down, there is a lively dose of jazz and country, plus a little bit of R & B and some rock 'n' roll thrown into the music mix. The promise of old-fashioned southern cooking lures diners here—especially on Sunday mornings, when the chefs prepare an all-you-can eat buffet feast, complemented by live gospel music. Concert tickets can be purchased through TicketMaster (839-3900; *www.ticketmaster.com*) or the HOB box office (394-2583). Prices range from about $5 to $30, depending on the performer.

The House of Blues restaurant features an interesting melange of Delta-inspired cuisine, including jambalaya, étouffée, and homemade bread pudding. (Refer to the *Good Meals, Great Times* chapter for additional information.)

Shopping

ALL STAR GEAR: This shop specializes in sports gear, hats, sweatshirts, and other items stamped with the logo of the Official All Star Cafe.

COPPERFIELD MAGIC UNDERGROUND—THE STORE: It's no illusion—this mysterious emporium is the very first shop of its kind. It features an array of magic-making merchandise for beginners and professionals, as well as signature clothing and gift items.

CELEBRITY EYEWORKS STUDIO: Looking to change your eyeglass image? Slip into some shades that have been sported by the stars—or at least convincing replicas of their shades. Celebrity Eyeworks has designer styles modeled in the movies.

DISNEY'S CANDY CAULDRON: Stop here for some homemade southern-style sweets in an open candy kitchen.

GUITAR GALLERY BY GEORGE'S MUSIC: Whether you prefer it plugged or unplugged, this spot can satisfy all of your guitar needs. A vintage guitar display entices buyers and browsers alike.

HOYPOLOI: The glass, ceramics, sculpture, jewelry, and other decorative items on display here make this shop seem more like an art gallery. Designed as a "soothing retreat," it is meant to communicate an ambience of harmony, balance, and serenity.

MAGNETRON: Your fridge will never be the same once you've visited this specialty magnet shop with its eclectic assortment of 20,000 collector-quality magnets.

SOSA FAMILY CIGARS: In addition to offering premium cigars, this shop showcases the art of hand-rolling.

STARIBILIAS: The spotlight here is on memorabilia—music, television, movie, political, and historical—allowing you to bring a piece of Hollywood to the folks back home.

WILDHORSE STORE: Before you step onto the Wildhorse dance floor, you might want to step into this shop. It has a variety of western-style duds, including denim shirts and bandannas. Also for sale: baseball caps, leather jackets, and Wildhorse logo merchandise.

VIRGIN MEGASTORE: This store stocks a selection of music, from classical to contemporary. Much of it can be sampled with headphones at one of many CD listening stations. Videos and books are also available. Outside, an elevated stage is used for live performances.

BOARDWALK

A stroll at Disney's BoardWalk is a journey back in time. Inspired by the Middle Atlantic seaside attractions of the early 1900s, BoardWalk recaptures the carefree atmosphere of that bygone era. The resort is surrounded by restaurants, clubs, and amusements similar to those enjoyed by beachgoers of yesteryear. It's bordered by a wood-planked walkway, which hugs the shore of Crescent Lake. By day, BoardWalk is a peaceful place to soak up sun, enjoy lunch, or simply walk the boards. After dark, the place turns into a twinkling center of nighttime activity—some of it elegant, some of it downright raucous.

The Wyland Galleries, which features the world's foremost marine environmental art, is one of the more calming diversions. Wild-Wood Landing challenges onlookers to test their luck and skill at a collection of classic carnival games. And strolling performers enchant passersby of all ages with magic shows, balloon tricks, and more.

BoardWalk is open to everyone. Although there is no admission price, individual venues may charge a cover. There is a $6 charge for valet parking after 5 P.M. for guests who are not staying at a Walt Disney World resort. Self-parking is free. (For additional restaurant information, refer to *Good Meals, Great Times*.)

Clubs

ATLANTIC DANCE: As the name implies, the main attraction at this big elegant boardwalk address is dancing. A deejay cranks up tunes from the seventies, eighties, and nineties on a nightly basis, tempting guests to twist and shout on the spacious dance floor. Live bands play on select occasions.

In additional to traditional cocktails, the club offers 25 specialty drinks. Sample one at a table in the "big room" or on the more private waterfront balcony.

You can dance here from 8 P.M. until 2 A.M. nightly. Guests must be 21 or older, with a legal ID, to enter.

Note that a deejay often spins discs just outside the club, turning the boardwalk into a rockin' dance party. Guests of all ages are welcome to join the fun.

ESPN CLUB: This club aims to please sports enthusiasts of all kinds, from the casual armchair quarterback to the most rabid fanatic. It includes a multimedia center (complete with an Internet connection), broadcasting facility, arcade, and table-service restaurant and bar.

More than 80 televisions broadcast live sports events, so guests always know the score. (Need to make a pit stop at a crucial moment of the game? Don't sweat it—there are even TVs in the bathrooms.)

The ESPN Club has three sections. As you enter, you're on the 50-yard line at The Sidelines. You can catch a game on a television monitor above the "penalty box" bar or sit at a nearby table (from which you can pick up the sound of any TV in the room). Beer, wine, and soft drinks are available, as is the usual pub fare.

Sports Central, the main dining area, has a big screen, showing—what else—the big game. The kitchen is open until 11:30 P.M. for meals, 1 A.M. for appetizers.

The Yard Arcade, a gameroom with an "urban playground" motif, lets you play the latest sports-themed video games while listening to the big game of the moment.

JELLYROLLS: You might want to warm up your vocal cords before crossing the threshold. They don't call it a sing-along bar for nothing: Guests are expected to sing, clap, and join in the fun at this rollicking warehouse, home of dueling pianos. You'll hear everything from Gershwin to *Grease!* The piano players take requests, so plan ahead. Write the request—a cocktail napkin will do—and slip it onto the piano. (Although it's not required, we recommend slipping a tip along, too. It will increase the odds of your hearing the request *and* help the musicians pay their rent.)

Jellyrolls is open from 7 P.M. until 2 A.M. nightly. There is usually a $3 to $5 cover charge on weekends, none on weekdays. (Note that the cover charge may vary.) To get in, you must be at least 21 and willing to prove it.

WATER PARKS
Typhoon Lagoon

A furious storm once roared 'cross the sea,
Catching ships in its path, helpless to flee,
Instead of a certain and watery doom,
The winds swept them here to Typhoon Lagoon!

So reads the legend that guests see as they approach Typhoon Lagoon, a 56-acre aquatic park. The watery playground was inspired by an imagined legend: A typhoon hit a tiny resort village many years ago, and the storm—plus an ensuing earthquake and volcanic eruption—left the village in ruins. The locals, however, were resourceful and rebuilt their town as best they could.

The centerpiece of Typhoon Lagoon is a huge watershed mountain known as Mt. Mayday. Perched atop its peak is the *Miss Tilly*, a marooned shrimp boat originally from Safen Sound, Florida. *Miss Tilly*'s smokestack erupts every half hour, shooting a 50-foot flume of water into the air.

The surf lagoon is huge: Thrilling slides snake through caves, tamer ones offer twisting journeys, and tiny slides entertain small kids. Note that children under ten must be accompanied by an adult.

SURF POOL: The main swimming area contains nearly three million gallons of water, making it one of the world's largest wave pools. The Caribbean-blue lagoon is surrounded by a white-sand beach, and its main attraction is the waves that come crashing to the shore every 90 seconds. The less adventurous can loll about in two relatively calm tide pools, Whitecap Cove and Blustery Bay.

CASTAWAY CREEK: This 2,100-foot circular river that winds through the park offers a lazy, relaxing orientation to Typhoon Lagoon.

Tubes are free and are the most enjoyable way to make the trip along the three-foot-deep waterway. The ride takes guests through a rain forest, where they are cooled by mists and spray; through caves and grottoes that provide welcome shade on hot summer days; and through an area known as Water Works, where "broken" pipes from a water tower unleash showers on helpless passersby. The current is calm, and aside from a few floating props, the journey is unimpeded. There are exits along the way, where guests can hop out for a while and do something else, or just dry off a bit and then jump right back into the water. It takes 25 to 35 minutes to ride around the park without taking a break.

Modest maidens beware!
A one-piece suit is far safer than a two-piece on many of the more adventurous water slides—especially Typhoon Lagoon's Humunga Kowabunga and Blizzard Beach's Summit Plummet.

GANGPLANK FALLS, KEELHAUL FALLS, AND MAYDAY FALLS: These three whitewater rides offer guests a variety of slippery trips, two of them in inner tubes. All of the slides course through caves and waterfalls, and past intricate rockwork, making the scenery an attraction in itself. Gangplank Falls gives families a chance to ride together in a three- to five-passenger craft.

HUMUNGA KOWABUNGA: These two speed slides, reported to have been carved into the landscape by the historic earthquake, will send guests zooming through caverns at speeds of 30 miles per hour. The 214-foot slides each offer a 51-foot drop, and the view from the top is a little scary. But it's over before you know it, and once-wary guests hurry back for another try. Guests are also warned that they should be free of back trouble, heart conditions, and other physical limitations to take the trip. Pregnant women are not permitted to ride.

STORM SLIDES: The Jib Jammer, Rudder Buster, and Stern Burner body slides send guests off at about 20 miles per hour down winding fiberglass slides, in and out of rock formations and caves, and through waterfalls. It's a somewhat tamer ride than Humunga Kowabunga, but still offers a speedy descent. The slides run about 300 feet, and each offers a different view and experience.

SHARK REEF: Guests obtain free snorkel equipment for a swim through a coral reef, where they come face-to-face with sharks and fish. The reef is built around a sunken tanker (where guests who don't care to swim among the fish can get a close look from the port-holes). The sharks, by the way, leopard, nurse, and bonnethead, are all passive members of the species. Guests must shower before entering the reef's depths.

KETCHAKIDDEE CREEK: Open only to those four feet tall or under, this area has small rides for pint-size visitors. Children must be accompanied by an adult. There are slides, fountains, waterfalls, squirting whales and seals, a mini rapid ride, an interactive tugboat, and a grotto with a veil of water that kids love to run through.

SURFING: Surf clinics are offered on select mornings before the park opens. For information, call WDW-PLAY (939-7529).

Essentials

WHEN TO GO: Typhoon Lagoon gets very crowded early in the day. When the park reaches peak capacity, no one will be admitted until crowds subside (usually after 3 P.M.). Hours vary seasonally, but the park is generally open from 10 A.M. to 5 P.M., with extended hours in the summer months. All of the pools are heated in the winter. Note that Typhoon Lagoon is usually closed for refurbishment during certain winter months, typically November and December. The park may also close due to inclement weather. Call 824-4321 for schedules.

HOW TO GET THERE: Buses are available from the TTC and all WDW resorts, except the Grand Floridian, Contemporary, Polynesian, Wilderness Lodge, and Fort Wilderness (which require transfers at the TTC).

LOCKER ROOMS: Restrooms with showers and lockers are located near the entrance. Other restrooms are available farther into the park. These are labeled "Buoys" and "Gulls." Small lockers cost $3 plus a $2 deposit to rent for the day, while large lockers cost $5 plus a $2 deposit. Towels rent for $1, and life jackets are available with a $25 refundable deposit.

WHERE TO EAT: There are two restaurants at Typhoon Lagoon, both offering similar fare and outdoor seating at tables with colorful umbrellas. Leaning Palms, which was known as Placid Palms before the typhoon hit, was renamed to fit its somewhat unorthodox architecture. Burgers, hot dogs, salads, ice cream, and assorted snacks are sold here. Typhoon Tilly's offers a similar menu and has a separate area just for ice cream and frozen yogurt. Let's Go Slurpin offers frozen drink specialties and spirits. Also on hand are picnic areas, where guests can bring their own food or enjoy a sampling from the restaurants. Note that no alcoholic beverages or glass containers can be brought into the park.

FIRST AID: A first-aid station capable of handling minor medical problems is located just to the left of Leaning Palms.

BEACH SHOP: Singapore Sal's, located to the right of the park's main entrance, is set in a ramshackle building left a bit battered by the typhoon. Bathing suits, sunglasses, hats, towels, sunscreen, souvenirs, thong sandals, and beach chairs are among the wares for sale here.

Admission Prices

ONE-DAY TICKET
(Prices include sales tax and are subject to change.)

Adult	$26.45
Child*	$20.67

ANNUAL PASS

Adult	$93.45
Child*	$74.73

Note: Admission is included with a Length of Stay, All-In-One Hopper, or Premium Annual Pass.

*3 through 9 years of age; children under 3 free

Blizzard Beach

A wintery, watery wonderland, Blizzard Beach is said to be the result of a freak storm that dropped a mountain of snow onto Walt Disney World, prompting the quick construction of Florida's first ski resort. When temperatures soared and the snow began to melt, designers prepared to close the resort. But when they spotted an alligator sliding down the slopes they realized that they had created an exhilarating water adventure park! The slalom and bobsled runs became downhill water slides. The ski jump is now the world's tallest (120 feet), fastest (60 miles per hour), free-fall speed slide.

The centerpiece of Blizzard Beach is the snow-capped Mt. Gushmore and its Summit Plummet. Most of the more thrilling runs are found on the slopes of this mountain, which tops out at 90 feet. At the summit, swimmers have a choice of speed slides, flumes, a white-water raft ride, and an inner-tube run. There is also an observation tower that offers a spectacular view. Guests reach the top of Mt. Gushmore via chairlift. The lift is equipped with a gondola for guests with disabilities. There are also three sets of stairs for those who prefer to scale the mountain on foot.

This is the most action-packed Disney water park yet, with enough activities for the entire family to fill at least a day. Note that kids under ten must be accompanied by an adult.

MELT-AWAY BAY: This one-acre pool at the base of Mt. Gushmore is equipped with its own wave machine. No tsunamis here, however—just a pleasant bobbing wave.

CROSS COUNTRY CREEK: This meandering 3,000-foot waterway circles the entire park. A slow current keeps visitors moving along. Inner tubes, which are free, are the most pleasant way to travel. The ride includes a

Hot Tip

The early birds get the lounge chairs around these parts. If you want to snag a chair at any of Disney's three water parks, arrive long before noon.

trip through a bone-chilling ice cave, where guests are splashed with the "melting ice" from overhead.

SUMMIT PLUMMET: The big thrill ride begins 120 feet in the air on a platform built 30 feet above the top of Mt. Gushmore. (In other words, it's high! If you suffer from vertigo, pass on this plummet.) Brave souls travel about 60 miles per hour down a 350-foot slide. Near the top, guests pass through a ski chalet. To those watching from below, riders seem to disappear into an explosion of mist.

SLUSH GUSHER: This relatively tame, double-humped water slide offers a brisk journey through a snow-banked mountain gully. Topping out at 90 feet, Slush Gusher is the tallest slide of its kind. You'll find it on Mt. Gushmore, next to Summit Plummet.

TEAMBOAT SPRINGS: The longest family white-water raft ride in the world takes five-passenger rafts down a twisting, 1,200-foot series of rushing waterfalls.

TOBOGGAN RACERS: An eight-lane water slide sends guests racing over a number of dips. They lie on their stomachs on a mat and travel headfirst down the 250-foot route.

SNOW STORMERS: A trio of flumes descends from the top of the mountain. Guests race down on a switchback course that includes ski-type slalom gates.

RUNOFF RAPIDS: On this inner-tube run, guests careen down three different twisting, turning flumes, one completely in the dark.

DOWNHILL DOUBLE DIPPER: Guests travel down these two parallel 230-foot-long racing slides at speeds of up to 25 miles per hour. The partially enclosed water runs feature ski-racing graphics, flags, and time clocks.

SKI PATROL TRAINING CAMP: An area designed specifically for preteens. Frozen Pipe Springs looks like an old pipe and drops sliders into eight feet of water. The Thin Ice Training Course tests agility as kids try to walk along broken "icebergs" without falling into the water. Snow Falls' "wide" slides allow a parent and child to ride together. At the Ski Patrol Shelter, guests grab on to a T-bar for an airborne trip. At any point in the ride they can drop into the water below. Ski patrol participants also experience Cool Runners, where riders can bank on hurtling and whirling over lots of moguls on twin inner-tube slides. No bunny slopes for these brave daredevils.

TIKE'S PEAK: A kid-size variation of Blizzard Beach, this attraction features miniature versions of Mt. Gushmore's slides and a snow-castle fountain play area.

Essentials

WHEN TO GO: As the World's largest water park, Blizzard Beach becomes very crowded early in the day. When the park reaches peak capacity, no one is admitted until crowds subside (usually after 3 P.M.). Hours vary seasonally, but the park is generally open from 10 A.M. to 5 P.M., with extended hours in summer. All pools are heated in winter. Blizzard Beach is often closed for refurbishment during certain winter months, typically January and February. It may also close due to inclement weather. For schedules, call 824-4321.

HOW TO GET THERE: Buses are available from the TTC and all WDW resorts.

LOCKER ROOMS: Restrooms with showers are located near the main entrance. Other restrooms and dressing rooms are located around the park. Small lockers cost $3 plus a $2 deposit to rent for the day, while large lockers cost $5 plus a $2 deposit. Towels rent for $1, and life jackets are available with a $25 refundable deposit.

WHERE TO EAT: Burgers, hot dogs, fruit salads, and drinks are available at Lottawatta Lodge, a fast-food restaurant in the main village area. Two other snack stands with limited offerings are located in more remote areas: Avalunch and The Warming Hut. Frostbite Freddie's Frozen Frosty Freshments offers drink specialties and spirits. There are also picnic areas for those who prefer to pack their own. No alcoholic beverages or glass containers are permitted in the park.

FIRST AID: Minor medical problems are handled at this station near the main entrance.

BEACH SHOP: The Beach Haus, near the main entrance, stocks bathing suits, T-shirts, shorts, sunglasses, hats, suntan lotion, beach towels, and all the other accoutrements needed for a day in the park. Logo merchandise is in large supply.

Admission Prices

ONE-DAY TICKET
(Prices include sales tax and are subject to change.)

Adult	$26.45
Child*	$20.67

ANNUAL PASS

Adult	$93.23
Child*	$74.73

Note: Admission is included with a Length of Stay, All-In-One Hopper, or Premium Annual Pass.

*3 through 9 years of age; children under 3 free

River Country

It's next to impossible to go through childhood reading such classic books as *The Adventures of Tom Sawyer* and *The Adventures of Huckleberry Finn* (and other great tales of growing up) without developing a few fantasies about what it would be like to swim in the perfect swimming cove. A group of Imagineers concocted a Disney version on a somewhat larger scale at River Country, a water-oriented playground that occupies a corner of Bay Lake near Fort Wilderness campground.

Fred Joerger—the same Disney rock builder who created Big Thunder Mountain, Schweitzer Falls at the Jungle Cruise, and the caves of Tom Sawyer Island in the Magic Kingdom—also helped design the rocks used to landscape one of the largest swimming pools in the state. The rocks, scattered with real pebbles acquired from streambeds in Georgia and the Carolinas, look so real that it's hard to believe they aren't.

More to the point, the place is great fun. Slipping and sliding down the curvy water chutes at top speed, floating along White Water Rapids, and slamming into the water from the swimming pool's high slides make even careworn grown-ups smile, grin, giggle, chortle, and roar with delight. People who climb to the top of the Raft Rider Ridge with trepidation may be surprised to find themselves rushing back for more. Line-haters queue up—over and over again. Those who associate lakes with muck and weeds get ecstatic over the way the soft sand on the River Country bottom squishes between their toes. Kids under ten must be accompanied by an adult.

WHAT TO DO: There are several sections to River Country: the 330,000-gallon swimming pool; Bay Cove, the big walled-off section of Bay Lake that most people consider the main (and best) part of River Country; Kiddie Cove, an adjoining junior version of the above for small children, with its own beach; and the grassy grounds, with picnic tables and Indian Springs, a squirting fountain in which to play. On the edge of the lake there's also Cypress Point, a boardwalk nature trail through a lovely cypress swamp, and a wide (if not terribly long) white-sand beach.

The large swimming pool that's known as Upstream Plunge is heated in winter. It has a pair of Slippery Slide Falls water slides that begin high enough above the water to make an acrophobe climb right down again. They plunge at such an angle that it's impossible to see the bottom of the slide from the top. Daredevils who don't chicken out are shot into the water from a height of about

seven feet—hard enough, as one commentator observed, to "slap your stomach up against the roof of your mouth." Gutsy kids adore the experience; those who like their thrills a bit tamer might prefer to watch.

The heart of River Country, Bay Cove, is actually a part of Bay Lake (and quite chilly during cooler months). It's fitted out with a rope climb, a ship's boom for swooping and plunging, and other constructions designed to put hearts into throats as swimmers plunge from air to water. The big deals, however, are the two flume rides—one 260 feet long and a smaller one, 100 feet shorter (accessible by a stairway to the left)—and a white-water raft ride called White Water Rapids.

The flumes, which are steep-sided water slides, corkscrew through the greenery at the top of the ridge, sending even the most stalwart shooting into the water, usually like greased lightning. White Water Rapids involves a more leisurely trip through a series of chutes and pools in an inner tube from the crest of Raft Rider Ridge (adjoining Whoop-'N-Holler Hollow) into Bay Cove. It's not a high-speed affair like the flumes, but some people like it better.

Essentials

WHEN TO GO: Daytime temperatures in Florida are such that it's possible to enjoy River Country almost all year round, though it is perhaps most pleasant in spring, when the weather is getting hot but the water is still on the cool side. In summer, the place can be very busy indeed. When the park reaches capacity, no one will be admitted until the

crowds subside. Things usually quiet down after 3 P.M. Although hours vary, River Country often opens at 10 A.M. and closes at 5 P.M. During the summer it's open till 7 P.M. River Country is usually closed for refurbishment during off-peak months, typically September and October. Call 824-4321 for up-to-the-minute schedules. Note that the park may also close due to inclement weather.

The warmer months are especially festive here. Independence Day is celebrated from late spring through early September. The All-American Water Party features character appearances, special games, and a parade. For details, call 934-2760.

HOW TO GET THERE: From the TTC, buses drop off passengers within walking distance of River Country. It's also possible to go by boat. Launches leave regularly from the dock near the gates of the Magic Kingdom. Guests arriving at River Country by car may take a bus from the Fort Wilderness visitor parking lot to the entrance.

LOCKER ROOMS: Dressing rooms with showers and lockers are available. Small lockers cost $3 plus a $2 deposit to rent for the day; large lockers cost $5 plus a $2 deposit. Towels are available for rent at $1 each at the concession window, but they're small, so you'll probably want to bring a beach towel.

WHERE TO EAT: Pop's Place has barbecued chicken, pork, and beef; baked beans; brownies; ice cream; apple pie; and peanut butter and jelly sandwiches. The Waterin' Hole offers a limited selection during peak seasons. Picnicking is permitted (no alcohol or glass containers can be brought into the park). Eat on the beach or at a shaded table.

FIRST AID: A first-aid station capable of handling minor medical problems is located near the locker rooms.

BEACH SHOP: Film, towels, sand pails, sunscreen, and other beach essentials are available at the River Relics stand.

Admission Prices

ONE-DAY TICKET
(Prices include sales tax and are subject to change.)
Adult $17.95
Child* $14.50

ANNUAL PASS
Adult...$59.31
Child* $47.17

RIVER COUNTRY/DISCOVERY ISLAND TICKET
Adult...$19.95
Child* $14.50

Note: Admission is included with a Length of Stay, All-In-One Hopper, or Premium Annual Pass.

*3 through 9 years of age; children under 3 free

FORT WILDERNESS

In a part of the state where campgrounds tend to look like pastures—barren and very hot—the Fort Wilderness campground, located almost due east of the Contemporary resort, is an anomaly—a forested 700-acre wonder of tall slash pines, white-flowering bay trees, and ancient cypresses hung with streamers of Spanish moss. Seminole Indians once hunted and fished here.

There are more than a thousand campsites arranged in several campground loops; among them, Wilderness Cabins and Homes are available for rent, completely furnished and fitted with all the comforts of home. For information about lodging options, see *Transportation & Accommodations*.

Scattered throughout the campground loops are sporting facilities, including two tennis courts, and many tetherball, basketball, and volleyball courts. Fort Wilderness has riding stables, two swimming pools, a marina full of boats, a canoe livery, a beach, bikes and golf carts for rent, and a nature trail. Some facilities are available to campground guests only; some are open to guests at WDW-owned resort hotels and villas as well; some can also be enjoyed by guests lodging at the establishments at the resorts on Hotel Plaza Boulevard as well as off the property.

There's also a petting farm and a barn that's home to the horses that pull the Magic Kingdom's Main Street trolleys. The barn houses a small museum that celebrates horses and the role they've played in Disney history.

Two stores—the Settlement Trading Post and the Meadow Trading Post—stock campers' necessities, groceries, and souvenirs. And then there's Pioneer Hall, the home of the Hoop-Dee-Doo Musical Revue dinner show (described in *Good Meals, Great Times*). This rustic structure (made of white pine shipped all the way from Montana) also has a buffet-style restaurant and a lounge.

Last but not least in the Fort Wilderness neighborhood is River Country. The eight-acre expanse of water-oriented recreation embodies everyone's idea of a perfect old-fashioned swimming area. Note that it's a separate attraction, with its own hours and admission fee.

BEACHES AND SWIMMING: The beach on the shore of Bay Lake is a delightful spot for sunning or snoozing in a hammock. There are also two pools for campers' use. Note that beaches and pools are open to Fort Wilderness guests only.

BIKE RENTALS: A variety of bikes can be rented at the Bike Barn for trips along the bike paths and roadways of Fort Wilderness—or just for getting around. Bikes cost $5 per hour or $12 per day.

BLACKSMITH SHOP: The pleasant fellow who shoes the draft horses that pull trolleys in the Magic Kingdom is on hand most mornings to answer questions and talk about his job; occasionally guests can watch him at work, fitting the big animals with the special polyurethane-covered, steel-cored horseshoes that are used to protect the horses' hooves. This shop is located at the Tri-Circle-D Ranch.

BOATING: Fort Wilderness is ribboned with tranquil canals that make for delightful canoe trips of one to three hours—or longer if you take fishing gear and elect to wet your line. Canoe rentals are available at the Bike Barn for $6 per half hour or $10 per hour. Pedal boats ($6 per half hour or $10 per hour) can also be rented here for use in the canals. For a trip around Bay Lake, zippy little Water Mouse boats, canopy boats, and pontoon boats are available for rent at the marina, at the north end of the campground. (See the *Sports* chapter for details and fees.)

CAMPFIRE PROGRAM: Held nightly (weather permitting) near the Meadow Trading Post at the center of the campground, this evening entertainment program features Disney movies, a sing-along, and cartoons. It's open to WDW resort guests only (no charge). Also, Chip and Dale always put in an appearance.

ELECTRIC CART RENTALS: Available at the Bike Barn ($35 to $40 for 24 hours) for sightseeing or transportation. Renters must be 18 years old and have a valid driver's license. Reservations are necessary; call 824-2742 for reservations and additional information.

ELECTRICAL WATER PAGEANT: This twinkling cavalcade of lights (described in more detail in the *Good Meals, Great Times* chapter) can be seen from the beach here nightly at 9:45 P.M.

FISHING EXCURSIONS ON BAY LAKE: Walt Disney World's restrictive fishing policy means plenty of angling action—largemouth bass weighing two to eight pounds, mainly—for those who sign up for the special 8 A.M., 11:30 A.M., and 3 P.M. fishing excursions. The fee is about $150 for up to five people for a two-hour excursion (one additional hour is $50) and includes gear, a guide, and refreshments; no license is required. Note that all fishing is strictly catch-and-release. Call WDW-PLAY (939-7529) for reservations.

FISHING IN THE CANALS: In addition to largemouth bass, catfish and panfish can be caught here as well. Those without their own gear will find cane poles and lures for sale at the trading posts; equipment is also available for rent at the Bike Barn. Cane poles are $2 per hour or $4 for the whole day. Rods and reels are $4 per hour or $8 per day. Bait costs about $3.50. No license is required. Fort Wilderness resort guests may toss their lines in right from the shore.

HAYRIDES: The hay wagon departs from Pioneer Hall at 7 P.M. and 9:30 P.M., and carries guests on a trip through wooded areas near Bay Lake. Each ride lasts about an hour and concludes at Pioneer Hall. Purchase tickets from the hayride host: $6 for adults; $4 for children three through nine. Children under ten must be accompanied by an adult.

LAWN MOWER TREE: The tree that somehow, mysteriously, grew around a lawn mower is a Fort Wilderness point of interest worth hunting down. It's just off the sidewalk leading to the marina.

PETTING FARM: This fenced-in enclave just behind Pioneer Hall is home to some friendly goats, sheep, rabbits, chickens, and other assorted barnyard critters. (A colony of prairie dogs didn't work out because its members persisted in burrowing out of their compound; no sooner would their Disney caretakers try to thwart them—by digging a bigger hole and installing a below-ground-level wire fence—than the little creatures would gnaw through it.) Pony rides are available between 9 A.M. and 5 P.M. for $2. Note that the pony-ride weight limit is 80 pounds. Though designed with youngsters in mind, the Petting Farm is also fun for adults, and a good place to pass the time while waiting for seating at the Hoop-Dee-Doo Musical Revue.

TENNIS: Two tennis courts are available; play is on a first-come, first-served basis.

TRAIL RIDES: Guided horseback trips depart four times daily from the Trail Blaze Corral and take riders on a leisurely, meandering ride through the Florida wilderness, where it is not uncommon to see birds, deer, and even an occasional alligator. Galloping is

not part of the ride, so you don't need riding know-how to sign up. Cost is $23 per person. No children under nine are allowed to ride. There is a weight limit of 250 pounds. Reservations are necessary; call WDW-PLAY (939-7529) up to 30 days in advance.

TRI-CIRCLE-D RANCH: This corner of Fort Wilderness is the place that the world champion Percherons and the draft horses that pull trolleys down Main Street in the Magic Kingdom call home. You can watch them chomping on their food, and occasionally see young colts and fillies as well. The Tri-Circle-D insignia above the barn door—two small circles atop a large one with the letter *D* inside—is the WDW brand. The barn is also the site of a museum that pays tribute to horses and their role in Disney history.

VOLLEYBALL, TETHERBALL, AND BASKETBALL COURTS: Open only to guests at Walt Disney World–owned properties, these are scattered throughout the camping loops. No charge.

WATERSKI TRIPS: Ski boats with drivers and equipment can be hired (including instruction) for $105 an hour at the marina. There is a minimum of two people and a maximum of five. Reservations are necessary. They must be made at least 24 hours ahead and can be made up to 60 days in advance. Call WDW-PLAY (939-7529).

WILDERNESS SWAMP TRAIL: A three-quarter-mile trail, this smooth footpath into the woods skirts the marshes along the shore of Bay Lake, then plunges into a forest thick with tall, straight-standing cypress trees. It is near Marshmallow Marsh, at the northern end of the campground.

Essentials

HOW TO GET THERE: From outside the World, take Magic Kingdom Exit 25 off I-4 onto U.S. 192, go through the Magic Kingdom Auto Plaza, and, bearing to your right, follow the Fort Wilderness or River Country signs. This is the most expeditious way to go, even for WDW resort guests.

By WDW Transportation: There is a direct bus (or bicycle path) from the Wilderness Lodge to Fort Wilderness. From Epcot, the Contemporary, Polynesian, and Grand Floridian resorts, take the monorail to the Transportation and Ticket Center (TTC), and transfer for the bus to Fort Wilderness. From Disney-MGM Studios, Animal Kingdom, Downtown Disney, and the resorts on Hotel Plaza Boulevard, take a bus to the TTC. Change there to the bus to Fort Wilderness. From all other WDW resorts, take a bus to Downtown Disney, switch for the bus to the TTC, then take the Fort Wilderness bus. Allow yourself plenty of time to make transfers.

Boats are also available from Magic Kingdom marinas (about a 30-minute ride) and from the Contemporary and Wilderness Lodge resorts (about a 25-minute ride). For details about Walt Disney World Transportation, see the *Transportation & Accommodations* chapter.

WHERE TO EAT: For a description of the restaurant at the Fort Wilderness campground, see page 238 in the *Good Meals, Great Times* chapter. The Settlement Trading Post, located not far from the beach at the north end of the campground, and the Meadow Trading Post, located near the center of Fort Wilderness, also offer food staples.

It's a Celebration!

What happens when a little bit of Disney magic spills into the real world? A town called Celebration, Florida. Founded in 1996 by a subsidiary of the Walt Disney Company, the town is surrounded by 4,700 acres of protected greenland.

The homes, with their front porches and picket fences, hark back to a much simpler time. Built along a scenic lakeside promenade, Downtown Celebration is a pleasant place to relax outdoors. Guests may shop, stroll, skate, rent pedal boats, or simply enjoy a picnic by the lake. There are several village parks, miles of nature trails, and an 18-hole public golf course (rates range from $30 to $105). Near the par-72 course is a three-hole youth course.

The community's retail and business district invites visitors to enjoy a variety of dining, shopping, and entertainment spots, including a bookstore, antiques shop, ice cream parlor, diner, and movie theater.

Located southeast of the intersection of U.S. 192 and I-4 near Kissimmee, Celebration is about a ten-minute drive from Walt Disney World. For information, call 939-8666, or write: Celebration Information; 200 Celebration Place; Celebration, FL 34747-4600.

DISCOVERY ISLAND

This 11-acre island (an accredited member of the American Zoo and Aquarium Association) is a delightful place to go for a change of pace. Its lush scenery and Bay Lake island location create a mood different from anywhere else in the World. The sweet-smelling flowers that dot the landscape, the trees that canopy the footpaths, the butterflies, the dense thickets of bamboo, and the graceful palms, not to mention the animals themselves, provide all the distraction needed.

Each season offers its own rewards on the island. In the summer you'll find the flowers in full bloom. On a fall day, you might discover a vibrant peacock feather abandoned on a path, since these magnificent birds lose their long tail feathers every autumn. Come in winter and you'll get to see their new coats growing in. Spring is an especially nice time to visit because it's breeding season and the birds put on all of their courting displays. (Note that nesting birds can be a bit noisy and aggressive during this season.)

Discovery Island has always been known for its tropical birds, but the addition of many more mammals and reptiles has contributed to the diversity of the population here. Along your journey you'll find two Asian fishing cats, several kinds of South American primates, and large rabbit-like animals called Patagonian cavies. The Galápagos turtles on **Tortoise Beach** are always a treat to see, as are the native Florida gators in the **Alligator Swamp**. At **Crane's Roost** you'll find small demoiselle cranes, white-crested hornbills, and Asian muntjac deer. **Trumpeter Springs** offers trumpeter swans—the largest members of the waterfowl family. You'll encounter lemurs, endangered primates from Madagascar, at **Primate Point**. The **South American Aviary**, one of the largest walk-through aviaries in the world, houses the United States' most extensive breeding colonies of scarlet ibis. You'll also find some white ibis speckled among the Caribbean flamingos in **Flamingo Lagoon**. **Pelican Bay** is the home of several brown pelicans that were injured in the wild and, though healthy now, would not be able to survive on their own.

Discovery Island KidVenture offers kids age seven through ten a chance to explore Marshmallow Marsh and Discovery Island. **Discovery Island Explorers**, for kids 11 through 15, focuses on animal care. Each of the 3½-hour programs features hands-on nature activities and costs $59. For information, call 800-496-6337.

Essentials

WHEN TO GO: Discovery Island is open daily in the fall and winter from 10 A.M. to 5 P.M., and in the spring and summer from 9:30 A.M. to 6 P.M. The last boat to the island leaves 1¼ hours before closing.

HOW TO GET THERE: The island can be reached from the Magic Kingdom, the Contemporary, Wilderness Lodge, Fort Wilderness, and River Country by watercraft.

WHERE TO EAT: Thirsty Perch snack bar near the main entrance, and the Aviary Outpost, next to the aviary, both offer lunch items, snacks, and beverages. Picnic areas are located by each of these facilities, including on the beach near the handsome old shipwreck.

Admission Prices

ONE-DAY TICKET
(Prices include sales tax and are subject to change.)
Adult $12.67
Child* $6.89

DISCOVERY ISLAND & RIVER COUNTRY TICKET
Adult $19.95
Child* $14.50

Note: Admission is included with a Length of Stay Pass, an All-In-One Hopper Pass, or a Premium Annual Pass.

*3 through 9 years of age; children under 3 free

DISNEY INSTITUTE

Unlike its contemporaries that also include *institute* in their monikers, the Disney Institute does not impart wisdom in the traditional higher-ed style. True, there's a lot of learning going on here, but it doesn't happen inside a stuffy classroom. Instead, this creative center actively engages guests in a variety of innovative programs ranging from animation and wilderness exploration to topiary gardening, rock climbing, and the culinary arts.

Participants choose from a variety of different program areas, including one specially designed for youths, to create a customized vacation. The Disney Institute provides a creative environment that's meant to inspire guests to try something new. While some are cooking up a healthy feast, others are scrambling up a rock wall. As one member of the family is hosting a television show, another is making a topiary. Some guests hone their photography skills while others are improving their golf game or trying their hand at computer animation.

Contributing to the environment of experimentation are artists-in-residence, who bring their expertise to workshops during the day and sometimes perform at night. Inquire about special events that provide an opportunity to learn from celebrities in the areas of culinary arts, photography, gardening, and animation. Packages offer demonstrations, workshops, and hands-on programs.

Getting Oriented

Participants stay in the surrounding villas as part of an intimate lakeside community. The architecture is reminiscent of a quaint American village, with a town green as the center of activity. Facilities include a cinema, outdoor amphitheater, performance center, closed-circuit TV and radio station, 28 program studios, and a youth center. Note the inscriptions surrounding signs at the Disney Institute, which offer inspirational quotes.

Sports & Fitness Center: This 38,000-square-foot center boasts an indoor exercise pool, a basketball court, two large aerobics rooms, and a wealth of state-of-the-art Cybex weight-training equipment and cardiovascular machines. (Use of the center is complimentary to those participating in full-day programs.)

The Disney Institute also encompasses four lighted clay tennis courts, six swimming pools, and the Lake Buena Vista golf course. Within the fitness center, a full-service spa invites guests to indulge in an extensive array of facials, massage, aromatherapy, body therapies, and hand and foot treatments (all of which are priced à la carte). Locker rooms include a steam room, sauna, and whirlpool.

Note that there is an additional charge for the greens fees, golf and tennis clinics, and spa treatments.

The Programs

Here's the fun part. Participants get to design their own vacation by choosing from a menu of fascinating programs. Instructors are experts

in their field, and the small student–instructor ratio ensures plenty of personal attention. The idea is that participants get to try something different, taking home with them newfound skills, creations, and insights. Our advice: Bring a large suitcase. On one trip we came home with a topiary, rosemary-infused oil, a best-seller, a dried floral arrangement, and new perspective.

Animation: Learn the techniques behind Disney's animated hits from the artists themselves. No drawing skills are necessary to sketch a Disney character or learn about computer and clay animation techniques.

Behind the Scenes: For those who simply cannot get enough Disney, these programs explain the creative processes behind some of that magic. Journey to select Walt Disney World resorts or to Epcot's World Showcase and explore the Disney design concepts used to tell stories through architecture and design.

Culinary Arts: In these popular programs, guests can try preparing regional cuisine, party planning, pairing food and wine, or executing new techniques, all at individual cooking stations with chefs leading the way.

Gardening and the Great Outdoors: These programs celebrate nature. Guests might try climbing a 26-foot rock wall, paddling a canoe for a relaxing waterborne adventure, creating a container garden or topiary, or bringing the garden indoors through the creation of home decorations and gifts.

Television and Film: Learn production secrets from experts in the media. Participants may get to make a mini drama, learn how to shoot better portrait photographs, or discover the art of "seeing" while applying 35mm photography techniques to outdoor environments.

Camp Disney: Kids ages 7 through 15 have special programs just for them in many areas, plus behind-the-scenes theme park tours. Examples of the experiences offered include wildlife adventures, a "journey into imagination" that involves painting and sculpting, a backstage look at Disney stage shows, rock climbing, and comic strip illustration.

Entertainment

Accomplished musicians, dancers, writers, and filmmakers sometimes stay at the Disney Institute for a few days, holding workshops (and taking programs themselves) during the day and entertaining in the evening. Seeing one of their performances or watching a film in the on-site cinema is the perfect ending to any day, so be sure to check the program and events board (in the town green) to see what's on tap.

Essentials

Disney Institute guests stay in Bungalows and Townhouses at The Villas at the Disney Institute. For room configurations, see page 67 of *Transportation & Accommodations*.

Where to Eat: Seasons Dining Room offers full breakfast, lunch, and dinner menus for the convenience of guests. For a light bite, head to Reflections Gourmet Coffee & Pastries. See *Good Meals, Great Times* for details.

Shopping: Dabblers offers a selection of items related to Disney Institute programs.

Package Rates: Accommodations are per person, based on double occupancy; rates also cover unlimited programs, use of facilities including the Sports & Fitness Center (but excluding spa treatments and golf and tennis clinics), taxes, and baggage gratuities. Single rates are available. Packages including theme park tickets and a meal plan are available, as are spa packages.

Bungalows start at $529 for three nights, $705 for four nights, and $1,233 for seven nights. One-bedroom Townhouses start at $586 for three nights, $782 for four nights, and $1,370 for seven nights. Two-bedroom Townhouses start at $714 for three nights, $952 for four nights, and $1,666 for seven nights. Cost per additional person sharing the same accommodation is $297 for three nights, $396 for four nights, and $693 for seven nights. Rates are higher during peak seasons. All prices are subject to change.

Reservations: It's wise to register for Disney Institute programs up to six months in advance; however, changes can be made upon arrival (based on availability). For additional information, call 800-496-6337. To make reservations, call 800-282-9282.

Day Programs at the Disney Institute

If you can't spend a week, then at least come for the day. Full-day programs designed to offer a "day in the life" allow guests to sample two programs, use the Sports & Fitness Center, and, if scheduled, catch an evening performance for $99. Half-day programs are available for $69. Reservations are necessary; call 800-282-9282 up to 60 days in advance.

Another package offers a more literal taste of the Disney Institute, with dinner at Seasons Dining Room plus evening entertainment. Available on select nights. The cost is about $27 per person; call 939-3463 for reservations.

BEHIND-THE-SCENES TOURS

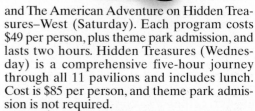

Disney Discoveries programs offer the opportunity to experience Walt Disney World from the inside out. These guided behind-the-scenes tours give visitors 16 and older a glimpse of the magic, and some of the logistics, that make up many of Disney's greatest creations. The following tours are subject to change; for current information or to make reservations call WDW-TOUR (939-8687).

Backstage Magic (Monday through Saturday): This is Walt Disney World's most popular program. Highlighting the seven-hour exploration of the Magic Kingdom, Disney-MGM Studios, and Epcot is an underground tour of the Magic Kingdom's Utilidors—Disney's hidden tunnel system. Lunch, the chance to paint an animated souvenir cel, and a few surprises are included along the way. Cost is $199 per person, and theme park admission is not required.

Keys to the Kingdom (daily): This 4½-hour tour offers an on-site orientation to the history and workings of the Magic Kingdom. Guests visit an attraction (waiting in the regular attraction line) and take a peek at the Production Center and the Utilidors. Cost is $45, plus theme park admission, per person.

Disney's Family Magic Tour (daily): Guests of all ages can participate in this two-hour Disney-themed scavenger hunt through the Magic Kingdom. The cost is $25 per adult, $15 per child age three through nine, plus theme park admission.

DiveQuest (daily): The highlight of the 2½-hour program is a 30-minute underwater adventure—complete with sharks, turtles, rays, and other tropical fish—in The Living Seas aquarium. Participants must present proof of current scuba "open water" adult certification. Cost per person is $140. Theme park admission is not required, and all gear is provided.

Dolphins in Depth (weekdays): This 3½-hour program teaches guests about dolphin behavior as they interact with the animals and observe researchers and trainers working with them. The cost is $140 per person, and theme park admission is not required. For more information, call 939-8687.

Hidden Treasures of World Showcase: There are three programs to choose from. Hidden Treasures–East (Tuesday) takes guests on a tour through Mexico, Norway, China, Germany, Italy, and The American Adventure. Participants uncover the mysteries of Canada, the United Kingdom, France, Morocco, Japan, and The American Adventure on Hidden Treasures–West (Saturday). Each program costs $49 per person, plus theme park admission, and lasts two hours. Hidden Treasures (Wednesday) is a comprehensive five-hour journey through all 11 pavilions and includes lunch. Cost is $85 per person, and theme park admission is not required.

Gardens of the World (Tuesday, Thursday): Hosted by a Disney horticulturist, this three-hour program guides guests through a study of the plants, flowers, and trees of Epcot's World Showcase. Cost is $49, plus theme park admission, per person.

Inside Animation (Tuesday, Wednesday, Thursday): This 2½-hour program takes place at the Disney-MGM Studios. Participants learn about the art of animation, discover how the classics are brought to life, and create their own Mickey Mouse cel. Cost is $49, plus theme park admission, per person.

Backstage Safari: (Monday, Wednesday, and Friday): This three-hour tour takes guests through backstage animal facilities such as the nursery and elephant barn at Disney's Animal Kingdom. The cost is $60 per person, plus park admission.

Just for Kids

There is also a selection of behind-the-scenes tours and programs designed especially for kids. They are offered by Camp Disney at the Disney Institute and cost $69 for a half-day program or $99 for a full-day program. For more information, call 800-496-6337.

Sports

SPORTS

Many first-time visitors don't realize that Walt Disney World provides a plethora of sporting opportunities. Within WDW's 27,000-plus acres there are more tennis courts than at most tennis resorts, and more holes of championship-caliber golf than at most golf centers, plus so many other diversions—from fishing and bicycling to boating, swimming, and horseback riding—that the quantity and variety are matched by few other vacation destinations.

So while the family golfers are pursuing a perfect swing on one of five first-rate 18-hole courses, tennis buffs can be wearing themselves out on the courts, sailors can be sailing, waterskiers can be skimming back and forth across powerboat wakes, and anglers can be dangling a cane pole in hopes of hooking a big bream. Those who prefer to spectate rather than participate can visit a virtual sports mecca at Disney's Wide World of Sports complex, an enormous state-of-the-art facility that hosts a staggering array of sporting events, both amateur and professional.

Instruction, as well as guides, drivers, and assorted supervisors, makes every sport as much fun for beginners as for hard-core aficionados. Moreover, the ready accessibility of WDW sporting activities—via an excellent system of public transportation (see *Transportation & Accommodations*)—means that no family member need curtail play time to chauffeur others around.

Note: Prices are subject to change and do not include applicable state tax.

Unless otherwise noted, all phone numbers are in area code 407.

A MATTER OF COURSES

Most people don't immediately think of Walt Disney World when they contemplate a golf vacation. Yet there are six superb courses here: The Magnolia, the Palm, and the Oak Trail are situated across from the Polynesian resort and extend nearly to the borders of the Magic Kingdom. Just a short drive away is the Lake Buena Vista course, whose fairways are framed by the Disney Institute and Old Key West resort. Osprey Ridge and Eagle Pines play from the Bonnet Creek Golf Club near Fort Wilderness.

While the original Joe Lee–designed courses (the Palm, Magnolia, and Lake Buena Vista) won't set anyone's knees to knocking in terror from the regular tees, all three are demanding enough to have merited the status of a stop on the PGA Tour tournament trail.

Tom Fazio designed Osprey Ridge to offer a reasonable challenge for beginners as well as more advanced players. Eagle Pines, designed by Pete Dye, is a low-profile layout built level with, or lower than, the surrounding land.

Depending on the tee from which a golfer opts to play, the Disney courses will prove challenging and/or fun, and all are constructed to be especially forgiving for the midhandicap player.

PALM & MAGNOLIA: The wide-open, tree-dotted Magnolia measures 5,232 yards from the front tees, 6,642 from the middle, and 7,190 from the back. The Palm is tighter, with more wooded fairways and nine water hazards; it measures 5,398 yards from the front, 6,461 from the middle, and 6,957 from the back. Both courses have received a four-star ("outstanding") rating from *Golf Digest* magazine. The Magnolia and Palm share two driving ranges and two putting greens.

Oak Trail: This nine-hole 2,913-yard layout, a walking course tucked in a corner of the Magnolia, was designed for beginners, but it has some tough holes, including two par 5s.

OSPREY RIDGE & EAGLE PINES: These two par-72 courses play from the Bonnet Creek Golf Club. The Tom Fazio–designed Osprey Ridge measures 5,402 yards from the front tees, 6,680 from the middle, and 7,101 from the back. It takes guests into remote areas of WDW property as it winds through wooded landscape near Fort Wilderness.

Dramatic contouring puts some tees 20 to 25 feet above the basic grade. In contrast, the Pete Dye–designed Eagle Pines is a low-profile layout. It plays 4,838 yards from the front tees, 6,309 from the middle, and 6,772 from the pro tees. Many fairways are bordered by scrub and pine needles; water comes into play as well. Osprey Ridge and Eagle Pines share a driving range and a putting green.

LAKE BUENA VISTA COURSE: This Joe Lee design measures 5,176 yards from the front tees, 6,268 from the middle, and 6,820 from the rearmost markers. Among the shortest of the 18-hole, par-72 courses, it has a fair amount of water, and its tree-lined fairways are Disney's narrowest. The course is well suited for beginners but equipped to challenge experienced players. A driving range and putting green are available. This is the location for the Disney Institute's extensive golf programs.

Essentials

WHEN TO GO: January through April is peak golfing season. To beat the crowds, play on a Monday or Tuesday, tee off in the late afternoon, or take advantage of low summer rates. Guests pay just $45 after 10 A.M. from May 1 through October 3. From May 1 through October 31, Classic Badges (available to Florida residents and Magic Kingdom Club members for $50) net steep discounts.

RESERVATIONS: Call WDW-GOLF (939-4653) to confirm rates and to secure tee-off times. From January through April, morning and early afternoon tee times should be reserved well in advance; starting times after 3 P.M. are often available at the last minute. Those buying a golf package can reserve tee times up to 90 days prior to their check-in date. Guests with confirmed reservations at a WDW resort or at one of the resorts on Hotel Plaza Boulevard can reserve 60 days ahead. Others can book tee times 30 days ahead. All reservations must be made with a major credit card. Cancellations must be made at least 48 hours in advance to avoid paying the full fee.

FEES: At the 18-hole courses, greens fees (including a required cart) vary with the course and season. Rates range from $90 to $120 for guests at WDW resorts and the resorts on Hotel Plaza Boulevard, and from $100 to $150 for day visitors. Twilight rates, usually in effect beginning at 3 P.M., are $45 to $75. Cost for adults to play Oak Trail is $24 for 9 holes, $32 for 18 holes; juniors (17 and under) pay $20 for 9 holes, $30 for 18 holes. Prices are subject to change.

INSTRUCTION: At the Walt Disney World Golf Studio at the Palm and Magnolia, private lessons cost $60 per half hour for

adults; $30 for juniors. Pros offer 45-minute video sessions; cost is $75. Nine-hole playing lessons in which a pro gives instruction in club selection, strategy, and more, cost $150 for adults or $100 for juniors. Reservations are necessary for lessons; call 939-4653. The Bonnet Creek Golf Club offers the Callaway Golf Experience: a system that lets golfers evaluate their swings, and compare various clubs and balls. The 45-minute session is free. For information, call 888-223-7842. Note, too, that the Disney Institute offers a first-rate golf instruction program at the Lake Buena Vista course (see page 198 for details on the Disney Institute).

DRESS: Proper golf attire is required. Shirts must have collars and any shorts must be Bermuda length.

EQUIPMENT RENTAL: Equipment can be rented at all courses; Callaway golf club rentals range from $35 to $45 for men and $25 to $35 for women depending on the season. A photo ID and major credit card (for the $500 refundable deposit) are required for club rentals. Range balls ($5 per basket) are also among the items available.

Tournaments

The National Car Rental Golf Classic is among the biggest spectator events on Walt Disney World's sports calendar. It features most of the PGA Tour's top players and takes place in mid-October. Guests who plan to golf during their WDW vacation are advised not to visit during tournament week. (You can, however, play with the pros if you are willing to pay for it.)

The Compaq World Putting Championship, by Dave Pelz, has also become an annual WDW event. For details on these and other special events, call WDW-GOLF (939-4653). Private tournaments may be arranged by calling the same number.

TENNIS EVERYONE

No one comes to Walt Disney World strictly for a tennis vacation; it just doesn't exude the country-club ambience of a tennis resort where everyone is totally immersed in the game. But the facilities and instruction programs here are extensive enough that such holidays are possible. Certainly, playing a couple of sets of tennis on one of the World's 25 resort courts is a good way to unwind after a mad morning in the parks.

With six courts and a professional shop, Disney's Racquet Club at the Contemporary resort is Walt Disney World's major tennis facility for guest use. Located just beyond the hotel's north wing, the club features state-of-the-art hydrogrid clay courts. Elsewhere on-property, The Villas at the Disney Institute, with four hydrogrid clay courts, merit attention. The Grand Floridian boasts a pair of clay courts. All other WDW tennis is played on hard courts. Fort Wilderness, Yacht and Beach Club, and BoardWalk have two; Old Key West has three; and the Swan and Dolphin share a four-court facility.

Essentials

WHEN TO GO: Courts are generally open from 7 A.M. to 7 P.M. daily (hours are seasonal, so call ahead for exact times); courts at the Swan and Dolphin are open 24 hours a day; lighted courts are available at each of the above-mentioned resorts. In February, March, April, June, and July the courts endure fairly heavy use, but there is usually a lull between noon and 3 P.M., and again from dinnertime until closing time. January, October, and November are considered prime months for tennis enthusiasts. Note that April is also an excellent month for watching tennis, as Disney's Wide World of Sports complex hosts the Men's U.S. Clay Court Championships.

RESERVATIONS: Courts may be reserved up to 90 days in advance for play at Disney's Racquet Club at the Contemporary, at the Grand Floridian, and at the Disney Institute, by calling WDW-PLAY (939-7529), and as far ahead as desired for courts at the Swan and Dolphin (934-4396). Other courts are available on a first-come, first-served basis. Individual players seeking partners can find them through the player-matching program at Disney's Racquet Club (824-3578). The amount of time a single group of players can occupy a court is restricted only during very busy periods—to two hours on any morning, afternoon, and evening.

FEES: Play is $15 per hour at the Contemporary, Grand Floridian, Swan, and Dolphin. Courts at the Disney Institute are often given over to programs, but are available with a $15 one-day health club pass. All other courts are free.

INSTRUCTION: The tennis program at WDW is under the direction of Peter Burwash International (PBI). PBI has trained pros staffing the resort programs (except at the Swan and Dolphin).

Pro Drill Sessions and Non-Stop Tennis are one-hour high-energy programs available for $15. One-and-a-half-hour daily clinics that focus on the fundamentals are $25. Private, semiprivate, and group lessons (3 to 5 people) are available for $50, $60, and $70 respectively. Special "hit with the pro" sessions are available for $40 per hour.

For information about tennis opportunities or to make reservations, call WDW-PLAY (939-7529). For details on the Disney Institute, see page 198.

TOURNAMENTS: Private tourneys may be arranged by calling 827-4433. For information on tournaments at Disney's Wide World of Sports complex, call 363-6600.

DRESS: Tennis whites are appropriate, but not required, for play on Disney's courts.

EQUIPMENT RENTAL: Ball machine rental is $12.50 per half hour; good-quality (adult or child) racquets may be rented for $5. New balls sell for about $5 per can.

LOCKERS: Lockers are available at the Contemporary and Grand Floridian resorts.

WATERS OF THE WORLD

Boating

Walt Disney World is the home of the country's largest fleet of pleasure boats. Cruising on Bay Lake and the Seven Seas Lagoon can be excellent sport, and a variety of boats are available for rent at WDW resort marinas. Bay Lake excursions originate from the Contemporary, on the lake's western shore; Wilderness Lodge, on the south shore; and Fort Wilderness, which occupies the lake's southeastern shore. The Polynesian and Grand Floridian resorts send boaters out from their marinas on the southern shore of Seven Seas Lagoon. The Caribbean Beach resort leases watercraft for use on its own 45-acre Barefoot Bay. The Yacht and Beach Club, BoardWalk, Swan, and Dolphin share a boating haven in 25-acre Crescent Lake. And marinas at Dixie Landings, Port Orleans, Old Key West, and the Downtown Disney Marketplace set guests up to cruise the waterways adjoining the 35-acre Lake Buena Vista. Guests at Coronado Springs may rent watercraft for use on the 15-acre Lago Dorado.

To rent, day visitors and resort guests alike must show a resort ID, a driver's license, or a valid passport. Rental of certain craft may carry other special requirements (described below). Note that no privately owned boats are permitted on any of the WDW waters. Also, all prices are subject to change.

CANOEING: A long paddle down the smooth, wooded Fort Wilderness canals is such a tranquil way to pass a misty morning that it's hard to remember that the bustle of the Magic Kingdom is just a launch ride away. Canoes are available for rent at the Bike Barn at Fort Wilderness ($6 per half hour, $10 per hour). Most trips last one to three hours; those with fishing gear can easily stay out longer. Canoes may also be rented at the Caribbean Beach, Port Orleans, The Villas at the Disney Institute, and Dixie Landings marinas. Ocean Kayaks (open-top kayaks) may be rented at La Marina at Coronado Springs and at the Bike Barn at Fort Wilderness ($6 per half hour, $10 per hour).

CANOPY BOATS: These 16-foot, V-hulled motorized boats with canopies are a good choice for relaxing cruises. They accommodate up to eight adults, and can be rented for about $20 per half hour at the Downtown Disney Marketplace, Polynesian, Contemporary, Grand Floridian, Wilderness Lodge, Yacht and Beach Club, Old Key West, Port Orleans, Caribbean Beach, Dixie Landings, and Fort Wilderness marinas.

PEDAL BOATS: These craft rent for $6 per half hour or $10 per hour at most WDW resort marinas. They're available for rent (to WDW resort guests only) at the Caribbean Beach, Port Orleans, Dixie Landings, Coronado Springs, Yacht and Beach Club, and Swan and Dolphin marinas. Watercraft are available to all guests at the Downtown Disney Marketplace and at the Fort Wilderness Bike Barn. For pedaling of a different sort, Hydro Bikes (boats resembling bicycles affixed to pontoons) may be rented at the Yacht and Beach Club and the Swan and Dolphin when it's not too windy; single-bike units cost $8 per half hour at each location; doubles, $13 per half hour at the Swan and Dolphin, $16 per half hour at the Yacht and Beach Club.

PONTOON BOATS: Motorized, canopied platforms on pontoons are perfect for families, inexperienced sailors, and visitors more interested in serenity than in thrills. Available at most resort marinas, the 20-foot craft hold up to ten adults and cost about $22 per half hour, $44 per hour.

SAILBOATS: The running room and usually reliable winds of Bay Lake and Seven Seas Lagoon make for good sailing, and the

Grand Floridian, Polynesian, Contemporary, and Wilderness Lodge marinas rent a variety of craft so that guests might get a little wind in their sails on the 650-acre expanse. Various types of sailboats are available; models accommodate two to six people and rent for $12 to $20 per hour. Experience is required for rental of catamarans, available at the Contemporary, Polynesian, and Grand Floridian.

Sailing conditions are usually best in March and April, and before the inevitable late-afternoon thundershowers in the summer—and that's when demand is greatest.

SPEEDBOATS: Particularly when the weather is warm, there are always dozens of small boats zipping back and forth across Bay Lake, Seven Seas Lagoon, Lake Buena Vista, Crescent Lake, and Barefoot Bay. These are called Water Mouse boats, and they're just as much fun as they look. The boats, which move as fast as 22 miles per hour, are so small that a rider feels every bit of speed, and they zip around quickly enough so that a lot of watery terrain can be covered in a half-hour rental period (about $18).

Water Mouse boats can be rented at the Grand Floridian, Polynesian, Wilderness Lodge, Contemporary, Yacht and Beach Club, Fort Wilderness, Caribbean Beach, and Downtown Disney Marketplace marinas. When the weather is warm, lines usually form at about 11 A.M. and remain fairly constant until about 4 P.M. The minimum rental age is 12, except at the Marketplace, where the minimum age is 14. Kids under the minimum age may ride as passengers but are not allowed to drive.

At the Contemporary marina, even zippier little boats called Searaiders may be rented for $35 per half hour. Accommodating up to three people, Searaiders can attain speeds up

to 30 miles per hour; riders must be 18 to drive. Spincraft speedboats (slightly slower than Water Mouse boats) may be rented at Coronado Springs ($10 per half hour, $16 per hour). The minimum age to rent is 12.

WATERSKIING AND WAKEBOARDING: Ski boats with Sammy Duvall instructors and equipment ($105 an hour, with a minimum of two guests and a maximum of five) are available for rent at the Contemporary, Polynesian, Grand Floridian, Wilderness Lodge, and Fort Wilderness resort marinas. Reservations must be made at least 24 hours in advance and can be made up to 60 days ahead; call WDW-PLAY (939-7529).

Fishing

The 70,000 bass with which Bay Lake was stocked in the mid-1960s have grown and multiplied as a result of WDW's restrictive fishing policy. (It's strictly catch-and-release.) No angling is permitted on Bay Lake or the Seven Seas Lagoon, except on the guided two-hour fishing expeditions. Largemouth bass weighing two to eight pounds are the most common catch. Excursions depart from the marinas daily at around 8 A.M., 11:30 A.M., and 3 P.M.; five people can be accommodated on a trip. The fee per boatload is $148.40 for two hours ($50 for one additional hour) and includes guide, gear, and refreshments (coffee and soft drinks). Guides will pick up guests at the Contemporary, Polynesian, Grand Floridian, Fort Wilderness, and Wilderness Lodge marinas.

Other trips depart from the Downtown Disney Marketplace marina at 6:30 A.M. and 9 A.M. for fishing on Lake Buena Vista and adjoining waterways. Guides will also pick up guests at Old Key West, Dixie Landings, and Port Orleans. Cost for up to five people, including guide, gear, and refreshments, is $137 for two hours per boat or $68.50 per person ($50 for one extra hour).

At Dixie Landings and Port Orleans, a two-hour fishing trip tours the Sassagoula River and Lake Buena Vista. The daily 6:30 A.M. excursion can accommodate four people; includes guide, gear, artificial bait, and soft drinks; and costs $50 per person. Kids under ten must be accompanied by an adult.

Anglers might also consider the two-hour trips that leave the Yacht and Beach Club and BoardWalk marinas at 7 A.M. and 10 A.M. daily for fishing on Crescent Lake and the adjoining waterways. The cost for up to five people, including guide, gear, and refreshments, is $148.40

Special kids' fishing excursions depart Monday through Friday from the Contemporary, Grand Floridian, Polynesian, Fort Wilderness, and Wilderness Lodge. The cost is $20 per child, ages 6 through 12. Light refreshments are provided, as is bait.

SPORTS

Reservations for all fishing excursions must be made at least 24 hours in advance and can be made up to 60 days ahead; call WDW-PLAY (939-7529).

Fishing on your own—again, strictly catch-and-release—is permitted off the dock at the Downtown Disney Marketplace and BoardWalk; in the canals near The Villas at the Disney Institute and at Fort Wilderness; and at the stocked fishing hole at Dixie Landings. Fort Wilderness guests may toss in lines from any campground shore. Licenses are not required. Canoes, rods and reels, and cane poles are available for rent at the Fort Wilderness Bike Barn. Bait (in the form of worms) can be purchased for $3.50. Poles may also be rented at Dixie Landings, BoardWalk, and the Downtown Disney Marketplace.

Swimming

Between Bay Lake and Seven Seas Lagoon, Walt Disney World resort guests have five miles of powdery white-sand beach at their disposal. Although the beaches are strictly for sunbathing, swimmers can get down to business in one of the many pools in every shape and size imaginable. River Country, Typhoon Lagoon, and Blizzard Beach (see *Everything Else in the World*) only add to the fun.

BEACHES: When Walt Disney World was under construction during the mid-1960s, Bay Lake had an eight-foot layer of muck on its bottom. It was drained and cleaned, and below the muck, engineers unearthed the pure, white sand that now edges WDW resort shorefronts, most notably at the Contemporary, Grand Floridian, Caribbean Beach, and Fort Wilderness. These four sections of beach, plus the ones at the Polynesian, Wilderness Lodge, Yacht and Beach Club, Coronado Springs, and Swan and

Dolphin, make up WDW's sandy areas. They aren't walk-forever strands, but they are long enough that most people don't bother to go to the end. Note that all Walt Disney World resort beaches are open only to those guests staying at the respective hotels.

POOLS: WDW resorts have at least one pool apiece. With the exception of the sister resorts (Yacht and Beach Club, Dixie Landings and Port Orleans, All-Star Movies, All-Star Music, and All-Star Sports, and Swan and Dolphin), which share some of their recreational facilities, WDW hotel pools are open only to guests staying at those resorts. This policy was initiated to prevent overcrowding. Note that most of the pools are heated in winter.

Featuring one pool apiece are the Grand Floridian, Wilderness Lodge, and Port Orleans. The Contemporary, Polynesian, Fort Wilderness, and the three All-Star resorts have two pools each. BoardWalk features three pools, Coronado Springs and Old Key West have four swimming holes each, Dixie Landings and The Villas at the Disney Institute have six apiece, and Caribbean Beach has seven. The Yacht and Beach Club resorts have between them two quiet, unguarded pools plus a small water park, called Stormalong Bay, that features slides, jets, and a sand-bottomed wading area. The Swan and Dolphin share a themed grotto pool with a slide, one huge rectangular pool, and a third smaller pool. For descriptions of the delightfully themed pools at WDW resorts, consult hotel listings in *Transportation & Accommodations*.

There are no diving boards at any of the pools; swimmers in search of a big splash should head for River Country, Blizzard Beach, or Typhoon Lagoon. Lifeguards are on duty during most daylight hours at the resort's main pools. In addition, each of the resorts on Hotel Plaza Boulevard has its own pool.

DISNEY'S WIDE WORLD OF SPORTS COMPLEX

Variety is the name of the game at Disney's Wide World of Sports complex. The multimillion-dollar complex invites athletes and spectators alike to dive into more than 30 types of sporting experiences. It's a grand slam for die-hard sports fans.

The 200-acre facility hosts amateur and professional events in everything from archery to wrestling. The home of the Amateur Athletic Union (AAU) is also the training site for Major League Baseball's Atlanta Braves and basketball's Harlem Globetrotters.

Designed as a modern vision of old-time Floridian building styles, the architecture harks back to the days when sports facilities were extensions of their neighborhoods; to that end there is even a town commons.

The complex includes a baseball stadium; a fieldhouse that accommodates basketball, wrestling, and volleyball; a track-and-field complex; tennis courts; and multipurpose fields fit for football, soccer, and more. Given the possibilities, sports-loving spectators have a world of choices on their hands.

For those looking to flex a muscle or two, the NFL Experience may be just the ticket. This interactive football playground, like those built in Super Bowl host cities, gives fans of all ages a chance to test their football ability in a series of skills challenges.

A general admission ticket costs $8 for adults and $6.75 for kids ages three through nine. Tickets can be purchased at the gate and allow guests to spend the day watching "nonpremium" events.

Tickets to premium events such as Atlanta Braves games (beginning in late February), the U.S. Men's Clay Court Championships (beginning April 17) and the NFL Quarterback Challenge may be purchased through Ticket-Master (839-3900; *www.ticketmaster.com*) and include general admission privileges. Premium tickets are available at the complex box office on the day of an event. Prices vary, depending on the event.

WHERE TO EAT: The big-ticket eatery here is the Official All Star Cafe. The colorful sports-themed restaurant is owned by a team of high-profile athletes, including Wayne Gretzky, Monica Seles, and Ken Griffey Jr. Don't worry about missing anything while you dine. TV monitors and a deejay will keep you posted with up-to-the-minute scores from the sports world.

There are more than 30 concessions for those seeking a lighter bite. They offer hot dogs, popcorn, and beer (not to mention peanuts and Cracker Jack) as well as a few more substantial, yet just as portable, snacks.

WHERE TO SHOP: D-Sports Shop, located just outside the baseball stadium (on the third base line side), features a powerful lineup of NBA, NFL, and NHL merchandise, as well as other sports-themed items. Disney's Clubhouse, which is inside the stadium, is a hit with the baseball-loving crowd. Foot Locker Superstore, scheduled to open in 1999, features every kind of athletic shoe imaginable.

Essentials

HOW TO GET THERE: WDW resort guests can take a bus to the Disney-MGM Studios and transfer to a bus headed for the complex from 10 A.M. to 6 P.M. From 6 P.M. to 11 P.M., take a bus to Downtown Disney and transfer there. Allow at least an hour for the bus commute. If you are driving, take the Magic Kingdom exit (25) off I-4. The complex is between U.S. 192 and Osceola Parkway. Parking is free.

Touch Base

Get the scoop on all the action at Disney's Wide World of Sports complex by calling 363-6600 or visiting the WDW Web site: *www.disneyworld.com*.

SPORTS

MORE SPORTING FUN

BIKING: Pedaling along the rustic pathways and lightly trafficked roads at Fort Wilderness and The Villas at the Disney Institute can be a pleasant way to spend a couple of hours. Both areas are sufficiently spread out so that bicycles are a practical means of getting around. Bikes are available for rent at Fort Wilderness, Old Key West, Wilderness Lodge, Port Orleans, Caribbean Beach, Dixie Landings, BoardWalk, The Villas at the Disney Institute, and Coronado Springs. The cost is about $5 an hour or $12 per day; tandem bicycles are offered at some locations. Bikes with training wheels or baby seats are also available. Helmets are free.

JOGGING: Except from late fall to early spring, the weather is usually too steamy in Central Florida for comfortable jogging. If you run very early in the morning in warm seasons, the heat is somewhat less daunting. The 1.4-mile promenade around the lake at the Caribbean Beach resort is ideal for jogging, as is the three-quarter-mile promenade surrounding Crescent Lake, the peaceful waterway that's bordered by the Swan and Dolphin, Yacht and Beach Club, and Board-Walk resorts, and the three-quarter-mile path around Coronado Springs' Lago Dorado. Fort Wilderness and the Wilderness Lodge share a three-quarter-mile path with exercise stations. Dixie Landings and Old Key West also have scenic routes. Courses range from one mile to about three.

MINIATURE GOLF: The Fantasia Gardens Miniature Golf complex, located near the Swan, Dolphin, and BoardWalk resorts, offers players two 18-hole courses themed to the Disney film. Disney's Fairways offers a difficult layout sure to tantalize serious golfers. It features traditional golf obstacles, such as sand traps, water hazards, doglegs, and roughs. Don't be fooled by the small size of the course—the challenges are big. (At press time, the record for the par-61 course was 50.)

Fantasia Gardens, on the other hand, is all in fun, with clever things (a dancing hippo, xylophone stairs, brooms dumping buckets of water) at every hole. The degree of difficulty varies from hole to hole, but overall this is an easy course to conquer. There are a few challenges out there, however. Hole 15, for example, is one of the trickier ones. Here golfers aim through four mini-geysers that randomly squirt water into the air.

The Fantasia Gardens snack bar serves light snacks. There is a small video arcade to keep nongolfers occupied. A round on either course costs $9 for adults, $8 for kids ages three through nine. Typical playing time is about an hour. Hours are generally 10 A.M. to midnight, but vary seasonally. For information, call 560-8760.

SPAS AND HEALTH CLUBS: While some of the fitness centers located within WDW hotels are reserved for guests staying at the resort that houses them, several have open-door policies and are accessible to all WDW resort guests. Health clubs include the Contemporary Fitness Center, La Vida Health Club at Coronado Springs, Muscles & Bustles at BoardWalk, and Ship Shape at the Yacht and Beach Club. A single pass includes access to all four; rates are $10 per day, $20 per length of stay, and $35 for a family length of stay (up to five people). The Contemporary Fitness Center features Nautilus equipment, a variety of cardiovascular machines, and massage. The others have more extensive equipment. Ship Shape has a whirlpool and steam room. Muscles & Bustles has a steam room, tanning bed, and massage services. La Vida has a tanning bed and massage services.

Body By Jake at the Dolphin, the fitness center at the Swan, and R.E.S.T. at Old Key West round out the health club options. Body By Jake ($8 per day or $16 for length of stay) is open to guests staying on or off Disney property. The facility at the Swan is free to the hotel's guests. R.E.S.T. is free to all Walt Disney World resort guests.

The spas are located at the Grand Floridian Spa & Health Club and the Sports & Fitness Center at The Villas at the Disney Institute. The huge Sports & Fitness Center at the Disney Institute

(included in Disney Institute program packages; otherwise $15 per day, $35 for a length of stay, $50 for a family of four length of stay) has aerobics, a gymnasium, and a state-of-the-art facility with the best lineup of Cybex machines anywhere. The Grand Floridian Spa & Health Club ($12 per day, $30 for three days, and $31.50 for length of stay) has all that plus a luxurious ambience. There are special spa packages available at each of these resorts.

STOCK CAR RACING: The Richard Petty Driving Experience (RPDE) takes motor-sports fans out of the grandstands and into a scene that most can only dream about: behind the wheel of a speeding stock car. The RPDE, located at the Walt Disney World Speedway, near the Magic Kingdom guest parking lot, is a training ground for racer wannabes. It offers two levels of actual driving experience: "Rookie Experience" and "Experience of a Lifetime." For the less "driven," there is the "Riding Experience," which sends guests zooming around the track at blazing speeds while still maintaining their passenger status. No reservations are required for the Riding Experience. Rides begin at 9 A.M. daily. The cost is about $90.

The Rookie Experience includes instruction, eight high-speed (up to 145 miles per hour) laps around the one-mile oval track, as well as a warm-up and a cool-down lap. The three-hour program costs about $400. Reservations are required.

The Experience of a Lifetime is a 30-lap program completed over three sessions. Participants work on building speed and establishing a comfortable driving line. The cost is about $1,100. Reservations are a must.

The RPDE operates on a daily schedule year-round, with the exception of dates on which actual races are held at the Walt Disney World Speedway. Shuttle transportation is provided from the TTC. Call 800-237-3889 for information or to make reservations. Prices are subject to change.

TRAIL RIDES: Guided horseback rides into pine woods and scrubby palmetto country set off from the front of Fort Wilderness four times daily. This trip is not meant for seasoned gallopers—you can't wander off on your own. The horses have been culled for gentleness, so trips are especially suitable for novices. Cost is $23 per person for a 45-minute tour. Kids under nine are not allowed to ride, and there's a weight limit of 250 pounds. Reservations are necessary, and can be made up to 30 days ahead by calling WDW-PLAY (939-7529).

VOLLEYBALL & BASKETBALL: Except for the volleyball courts at River Country and Typhoon Lagoon, courts are reserved for WDW resort guests. The Grand Floridian, Contemporary, Yacht and Beach Club, Fort Wilderness, Wilderness Lodge, Swan and Dolphin, Coronado Springs, Old Key West, and The Villas at the Disney Institute have volleyball courts. Contemporary, Fort Wilderness, and Old Key West have basketball hoops.

Good Meals, Great Times

Although fast food is in great supply, it is hardly the entire Walt Disney World dining story. Epcot adds international flavors to the WDW menu. Tempting options at the other theme parks, BoardWalk, and Downtown Disney—not to mention new dining frontiers in the ever-growing brood of WDW resorts—make deciding where to eat a mouth-watering dilemma. Disney's ongoing effort to expand its culinary horizons has certainly been successful, producing prominent palate pleasers such as California Grill and Cítricos, plus new family favorites like Crystal Palace.

Because the number and variety of eateries around the World are so large, this chapter presents dining information in three formats. First, to help you find a specific eating spot or watering hole, we've provided an alphabetized directory of all restaurants and lounges on the property with their exact locations. Second, we've included an area-by-area rundown—a comprehensive section whose precise descriptions of food purveyors, including sample menu options, will prove most helpful if you're getting hungry in a particular part of the World. Third, we've set forth a meal-by-meal primer that highlights restaurants by breakfast, lunch, and dinner specialties. We've even indicated entrées for which we think it's worth going a bit out of your way.

Finally, in the chapter's last section, we offer a guide to the varied lounges of Walt Disney World, along with a briefing on special nighttime entertainment options in the World—and assurance that great times are destined to follow.

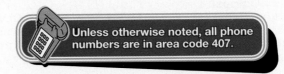

Unless otherwise noted, all phone numbers are in area code 407.

GOOD MEALS, GREAT TIMES

WDW RESTAURANT & LOUNGE INDEX

The list below includes the names and locations of all restaurants and lounges currently operating at Walt Disney World—not only at the theme parks, but at the resorts, Downtown Disney, and other areas of the World. The page numbers provided in parentheses will lead you to the sections following this listing, where restaurants and lounges are described in detail.

Note: The Walt Disney World dining landscape is ever evolving, and while this inventory was correct at press time, changes will inevitably occur. We advise you to call WDW Information (824-4321) or WDW-DINE (939-3463) shortly before your visit to confirm restaurant information.

ABC Commissary: Disney-MGM Studios; near The Great Movie Ride (230)

African Lounge: Animal Kingdom; in Africa, near the bridge to Safari Village (248)

Akershus: Epcot; in the Norway pavilion, in World Showcase (223)

Ale and Compass: Yacht Club resort; in the lobby (250)

Aloha Isle: Magic Kingdom; in Adventureland, near the Swiss Family Treehouse (216)

Artist Point: Wilderness Lodge; in the main lodge building (240)

Atlantic Dance: BoardWalk resort; on the boardwalk's left side (248)

Auntie Gravity's Galactic Goodies: Magic Kingdom; near Merchant of Venus in Tomorrowland (220)

Aunt Polly's Dockside Inn: Magic Kingdom; in Frontierland, on Tom Sawyer Island (217)

Avalunch: Blizzard Beach; near Ski Patrol Training Camp (191)

Aviary Outpost: Discovery Island (197)

Backlot Express: Disney-MGM Studios; near the Epic Stunt Theater (230)

Banana Cabana: Caribbean Beach resort; near the pool (248)

Barefoot Bar: Polynesian resort; near the Swimming Pool Lagoon (250)

Beaches & Cream Soda Shop: Yacht and Beach Club resorts; in the central area between the two resorts (241)

Belle Vue Room: BoardWalk resort; near the lobby (248)

Biergarten: Epcot; to the rear of the St. Georgsplatz area in the Germany pavilion, in World Showcase (223)

Big River Grille & Brewing Works: BoardWalk resort; on the boardwalk's left side, near Jellyrolls (236)

BoardWalk Bakery: BoardWalk resort; on the boardwalk's right side (236)

Boatwright's Dining Hall: Dixie Landings resort; by the Cotton Co-Op lounge (237)

Bonfamille's Cafe: Port Orleans resort; off the main lobby, near the front desk (239)

Bongos Cuban Cafe: Downtown Disney West Side; near the AMC Theatres (233)

Boulangerie Pâtisserie: Epcot; France pavilion, around the corner from Les Chefs de France, in World Showcase (226)

Cabana Bar & Grill: Dolphin resort; by the pool (239)

California Grill: Contemporary resort; on the 15th floor (237)

California Grill Lounge: Contemporary resort; on the 15th floor (248)

Campside Funnel Cakes: Animal Kingdom; in Camp Minnie-Mickey (231)

Cantina de San Angel: Epcot; on the promenade opposite the Mexico pavilion's pyramid in World Showcase (226)

Cape May Cafe: Beach Club resort; adjacent to the lobby (241)

Cap'n Jack's Oyster Bar: Downtown Disney Marketplace; on Lake Buena Vista (233)

Captain Cook's Snack Company: Polynesian resort; on the lobby level of the Great Ceremonial House (239)

Captain's Tavern: Caribbean Beach resort; at Old Port Royale (236)

Casey's Corner: Magic Kingdom; on the west side of Main Street (219)

Catwalk Bar: Disney-MGM Studios; above the Soundstage restaurant (248)

Chef Mickey's: Contemporary resort; on the fourth floor (237)

Chip 'n' Dale's Cookie Cabin: Animal Kingdom; in Camp Minnie-Mickey (231)

Cinderella's Royal Table: Magic Kingdom; in Cinderella Castle (216)

Cítricos: Grand Floridian resort; on the second floor of the main building (238)

Colonel's Cotton Mill: Dixie Landings resort; in the main building (237)

Columbia Harbour House: Magic Kingdom; in Liberty Square, near Fantasyland (218)

Concourse Steakhouse: Contemporary resort; on the fourth floor (237)

Copa Banana: Dolphin resort; lobby level (250)

Copperfield Magic Underground: Disney-MGM Studios; near Tower of Terror (229)

Coral Cafe: Dolphin resort; lower level (239)

Coral Reef: Epcot; in The Living Seas pavilion (221)

Cosmic Ray's Starlight Cafe: Magic Kingdom; in Tomorrowland, across from Tomorrowland Speedway (220)

Cotton Co-Op: Dixie Landings resort; in the main reception area (249)

Crew's Cup: Yacht Club resort; next to the Yachtsman Steakhouse (250)

Crockett's Tavern: Fort Wilderness campground; in Pioneer Hall (249)

Crystal Palace: Magic Kingdom; at the north end of Main Street, near the Adventureland bridge (219)

Diamond Horseshoe Saloon Revue: Magic Kingdom; in Frontierland, at the edge of Liberty Square (217)

Dinosaur Gertie's Ice Cream of Extinction: Disney-MGM Studios; on Echo Lake (230)

Dino Diner: Animal Kingdom; in DinoLand U.S.A., near the bridge to Safari Village (231)

Dolphin Fountain: Dolphin resort; on the lower level (239)

D-Zertz: Pleasure Island; near Pleasure Island Jazz Company (233)

Electric Umbrella: Epcot; in Innoventions Plaza (222)

El Pirata Y el Perico: Magic Kingdom; in Adventureland, opposite Pirates of the Caribbean (216)

Enchanted Grove: Magic Kingdom; on the east side of Fantasyland, opposite Cosmic Ray's Starlight Cafe (217)

End Zone: All-Star Sports resort; in Stadium Hall (236)

ESPN Club: BoardWalk resort; on the right side of the boardwalk, at the end (236)

50's Prime Time Cafe: Disney-MGM Studios; on the south side of Echo Lake (228)

Flame Tree Barbecue: Animal Kingdom; in Safari Village, near the bridge to DinoLand U.S.A. (232)

Flying Fish Cafe: BoardWalk resort; on the boardwalk, near the transportation dock (236)

Food and Fun Center: Contemporary resort; first floor (237)

Forty Thirst Street: Downtown Disney West Side; next to Bongos Cuban Cafe (233)

Fountain View Espresso and Bakery: Epcot; next to Innoventions (222)

Francisco's: Coronado Springs resort; main building (248)

Frostbite Freddie's Frozen Frosty Freshments: Blizzard Beach (191)

Fulton's Crab House: Between Pleasure Island and Downtown Disney Marketplace (233)

Garden Grill: Epcot; on the second floor of The Land pavilion (221)

Garden Grove Cafe: Swan resort; on the first floor (240)

Garden View: Grand Floridian resort; first floor of the main building (249)

Gasparilla Grill & Games: Grand Floridian resort; first floor of the main building (238)

Ghirardelli Soda Fountain and Chocolate Shop: Downtown Disney Marketplace; near World of Disney (234)

Good's Food to Go: Old Key West resort; on the boardwalk (237)

Gourmet Pantry: Downtown Disney Marketplace; near Disney's Days of Christmas (234)

Grand Floridian Cafe: Grand Floridian resort; first floor of the main building (235)

Gurgling Suitcase: Old Key West resort; on the boardwalk (249)

Harambe Fruit Market: Animal Kingdom; Africa's Harambe Village (231)

Harry's Safari Bar & Grille: Dolphin resort; on the third floor (240)

Hollywood & Vine: Disney-MGM Studios; on Hollywood Boulevard (229)

Hollywood Brown Derby: Disney-MGM Studios; on Hollywood Boulevard (228)

Hook's Tavern: Magic Kingdom; in Fantasyland, next to Peter Pan's Flight (217)

House of Blues: Downtown Disney West Side; across from DisneyQuest (234)

Hurricane Hanna's Grill: Yacht and Beach Club resorts; near Stormalong Bay (241)

Intermission: All-Star Music resort; in Melody Hall (236)

Jellyrolls: BoardWalk resort; on the left side of the boardwalk, near Atlantic Dance (248)

Juan & Only's: Dolphin resort; lower level (240)

Kimonos: Swan resort; on the first floor (250)

Kona Cafe: Polynesian resort; on the second floor of the Great Ceremonial House, around the corner from 'Ohana (239)

Kringla Bakeri og Kafe: Epcot; in the Norway pavilion, in World Showcase (226)

Kusafiri Coffee Shop & Bakery: Animal Kingdom; in Africa's Harambe village (232)

Leaning Palms: Typhoon Lagoon; near the main entrance (189)

Leaping Horse Libations: BoardWalk resort; near the Luna Park pool (248)

Le Cellier Steakhouse: Epcot; in the Canada pavilion, in World Showcase (223)

Les Chefs de France: Epcot; in the France pavilion, in World Showcase (223)

Liberty Inn: Epcot; by The American Adventure pavilion, in World Showcase (226)

Liberty Tree Tavern: Magic Kingdom; in Liberty Square (218)

Lobby Court: Swan resort; in the lobby (250)

L'Originale Alfredo di Roma Ristorante: Epcot; on the east side of the piazza in the Italy pavilion, in World Showcase (224)

Lottawatta Lodge: Blizzard Beach; near the main entrance (191)

Lotus Blossom Cafe: Epcot; in the China pavilion in World Showcase (226)

Lumière's Kitchen: Magic Kingdom; in Fantasyland, near Dumbo the Flying Elephant (217)

Lunching Pad at Rockettower Plaza: Magic Kingdom; in Tomorrowland, at the base of Astro Orbiter (220)

Main Street Bake Shop: Magic Kingdom; on the east side of Main Street (220)

Mama Melrose's Ristorante Italiano: Disney-MGM Studios; off New York Street (229)

Mardi Grogs: Port Orleans resort; near the pool (250)

Marrakesh: Epcot; in the Morocco pavilion, in World Showcase (224)

Martha's Vineyard: Beach Club resort; on the first floor (250)

Matsu No Ma: Epcot; in the Mitsukoshi building, in the Japan pavilion, in World Showcase (249)

Maya Grill: Coronado Springs resort; near Pepper Market food court (237)

McDonald's: Downtown Disney Marketplace; near the LEGO Imagination Center (234)

Meadow Trading Post: Fort Wilderness; near the playing fields (196)

Min and Bill's Dockside Diner: Disney-MGM Studios; on Echo Lake (230)

Missing Link Sausage Co.: Pleasure Island; near 8TRAX (234)

Mizner's: Grand Floridian resort; on the second floor of the main building (249)

Mr. Kamal's Burger Grill: Animal Kingdom; in Asia, near Discovery River Boats (231)

Mrs. Potts' Cupboard: Magic Kingdom; in Fantasyland, near Cinderella's Golden Carrousel (217)

Muddy Rivers: Dixie Landings resort; near Ol' Man Island (249)

Munch Wagon: Animal Kingdom; in Conservation Station (231)

Narcoossee's: Grand Floridian resort; at the end of the dock near the marina (238)

Nine Dragons: Epcot; in the China pavilion, in World Showcase (224)

1900 Park Fare: Grand Floridian resort; on the first floor of the main building (238)

Oasis: Magic Kingdom; in Adventureland, near the Jungle Cruise (216)

'Ohana: Polynesian resort; second floor of the Great Ceremonial House (239)

Official All Star Cafe: Disney's Wide World of Sports complex; near main entrance (208)

Old Port Royale: Caribbean Beach resort; on the first floor of the main building (236)

Olivia's Cafe: Old Key West resort; on the boardwalk (237)

Only's Bar & Jail: Dolphin resort; adjacent to Juan & Only's (250)

Outer Rim: Contemporary resort; on the fourth floor (248)

Palio: Swan resort; on the first floor (240)

Pasta Piazza Ristorante: Epcot; in Innoventions Plaza (222)

Pecos Bill Cafe: Magic Kingdom; near the Walt Disney World Railroad depot in Frontierland (217)

Pepper Market: Coronado Springs resort; in the main building (237)

Pinocchio Village Haus: Magic Kingdom; in Fantasyland, next to It's a Small World (217)

Pizzafari: Animal Kingdom; in Safari Village, near bridge to Camp Minnie-Mickey (231)

Planet Hollywood: Downtown Disney West Side; near the AMC Theatres (234)

The Plaza: Magic Kingdom; on Main Street, near the Plaza Ice Cream Parlor (219)

Plaza Ice Cream Parlor: Magic Kingdom; on the east side of Main Street (220)

Plaza Pavilion: Magic Kingdom; by The Plaza restaurant, on Tomorrowland's border (220)

Pop's Place: River Country (193)

Portobello Yacht Club: Pleasure Island; near Fulton's Crab House (234)

Pure and Simple: Epcot; in the Wonders of Life pavilion (222)

Rainforest Cafe: One location is at Downtown Disney Marketplace, near Cap'n Jack's Oyster Bar (235); the other is at Animal Kingdom, near the main entrance (231)

Reflections Gourmet Coffee & Pastries: Disney Institute; near Willow Lake (241)

Refreshment Outpost: Epcot; between the China and Germany pavilions, in World Showcase (227)

Refreshment Port: Epcot; next to the Canada pavilion, in World Showcase (227)

Restaurantosaurus: Animal Kingdom; in DinoLand U.S.A., near Cretaceous Trail (232)

Rip Tide: Beach Club resort; in the lobby (250)

Roaring Fork Snacks: Wilderness Lodge; in the main lodge building (242)

Rose & Crown Pub and Dining Room: Epcot; in the United Kingdom pavilion, in World Showcase (225)

San Angel Inn: Epcot; inside the Mexico pavilion's pyramid, in World Showcase (226)

Sand Bar: Contemporary resort; near the beach (248)

Sand Trap Bar & Grill: Bonnet Creek Golf Club; Osprey Ridge and Eagle Pines (240)

Sassagoula Floatworks & Food Factory: Port Orleans resort; off the main lobby (239)

Scat Cat's Club: Port Orleans resort; next to Bonfamille's Cafe (250)

Sci-Fi Dine-In Theater: Disney-MGM Studios; near Star Tours (229)

Scuttle's Landing: Magic Kingdom; in Fantasyland, near Legend of the Lion King (217)

Seashore Sweets': BoardWalk resort; across from the transportation dock (236)

Seasons Dining Room: The Villas at the Disney Institute; by the Welcome Center (241)

Seasons Lounge: The Villas at the Disney Institute; by Seasons Dining Room (250)

Seasons Terrace: The Villas at the Disney Institute; adjoining Seasons Dining Room (250)

Settlement Trading Post: Fort Wilderness; near the marina (196)

Siesta's: Coronado Springs; by the pool (248)

Silver Screen Spirits: All-Star Movies resort; near the main pool and the World Premiere food court (248)

Singing Spirits: All-Star Music resort; near the pool and Intermission food court (248)

Sleepy Hollow: Magic Kingdom; in Liberty Square, near the Liberty Square bridge (218)

Sommerfest: Epcot; in the Germany pavilion, in World Showcase (227)

Soundstage: Disney-MGM Studios; near the Animation Building (229)

Splash Grill: Swan resort; near the pool (240)

Spoodles: BoardWalk resort; on the right side of the boardwalk, near the bakery (236)

Starring Rolls Bakery: Disney-MGM Studios; on Hollywood Boulevard (230)

Studio Catering Co.: Disney-MGM Studios; near the Backlot Tour (230)

Summerhouse: Grand Floridian resort; near the beach (249)

Sunset Ranch Market: Disney-MGM Studios; on Sunset Boulevard (230)

Sunshine Season Food Fair: Epcot; on the first floor of The Land pavilion (222)

Sunshine Tree Terrace: Magic Kingdom; in Adventureland, near The Enchanted Tiki Room — Under New Management (216)

Tambu: Polynesian resort; on the second floor of the Great Ceremonial House (250)

Tamu Tamu Refreshments: Animal Kingdom; in Harambe village in Africa (232)

Team Spirits: All-Star Music resort; near the pool and End Zone food court (248)

Tempura Kiku: Epcot; on the second floor of the Mitsukoshi building, in the Japan pavilion, in World Showcase (224)

Teppanyaki Dining Rooms: Epcot; on the second floor of the Mitsukoshi building in World Showcase's Japan pavilion (224)

Territory: Wilderness Lodge; in the main lodge building (250)

Thirsty Perch: Discovery Island; near the main entrance (197)

Tony's Town Square: Magic Kingdom; on the east side of Town Square (219)

Toy Story Pizza Planet: Disney-MGM Studios; in the arcade near Muppet*Vision 3-D (230)

Trail's End Buffet: Fort Wilderness resort; in Pioneer Hall (238)

Trout Pass: Wilderness Lodge; near the beach and the pool (250)

Tubbi's: Dolphin resort; on the lower level (240)

Tune-In Lounge: Disney-MGM Studios; adjacent to the 50's Prime Time Cafe (249)

Turtle Shack: Old Key West resort; near Turtle Pond Road (249)

Tusker House: Animal Kingdom; in Africa's Harambe village (232)

Typhoon Tilly's: Typhoon Lagoon; near Shark Reef (189)

Victoria & Albert's: Grand Floridian resort; on the main building's second floor (238)

The Warming Hut: Blizzard Beach; near Summit Plummet (191)

Whispering Canyon Cafe: Wilderness Lodge; in the main lodge building (240)

Wildhorse Saloon: Pleasure Island; near Portobello Yacht Club restaurant (235)

Wolfgang Puck Cafe: Downtown Disney West Side; between House of Blues and Bongos Cuban Cafe (235)

Wolfgang Puck Cafe—The Dining Room: Downtown Disney West Side; between House of Blues and Bongos Cuban Cafe; upstairs above Wolfgang Puck Cafe (235)

Wolfgang Puck Express: Two locations: Downtown Disney Marketplace, near Gourmet Pantry (235); and Downtown Disney West Side, at Wolfgang Puck Cafe (235)

World Premiere: All-Star Movies resort; in Cinema Hall (236)

Yacht Club Galley: Yacht Club resort; off the lobby (241)

Yachtsman Steakhouse: Yacht Club resort; overlooking Stormalong Bay (241)

Yakitori House: Epcot; on the east side of the Japan pavilion, in World Showcase (227)

Special Requests

Full-service eateries can accommodate special dietary needs, providing kosher, low-sodium, lactose-free, and other selections with 24 hours' notice. Make your request when booking your table by calling WDW-DINE (939-3463).

In the Magic Kingdom

The lion's share of eateries here in Walt Disney World's first theme park are fast-food spots. These establishments' colorful facades and costumed servers are natural extensions of the fantasy surrounding the park's seven distinct "lands." The healthy variety of food available on the fly is a testament to Magic Kingdom visitors' typical preference for a quick bite with no need for firm plans. For those who prefer an all-out meal, the park's small handful of table-service restaurants offer fine mealtime escapes in magical settings that only Disney could create. Visitors interested in character meals have breakfast, lunch, and dinner options here (see page 246 for additional details).

First Things First

- As Disney chefs tweak their menus to keep abreast of trends and new concepts are unveiled, the inventory of dining options changes. We advise guests to call WDW-DINE (939-3463) to confirm restaurant information.

- The letters that conclude each entry are a key to meals served there: breakfast (B), lunch (L), dinner (D), or snacks (S).

- As an indication of what you should expect to spend for a meal, we've classified restaurants, based on dinner prices, as very expensive ($35 and up); expensive ($20 to $35); moderate ($10 to $20); or inexpensive (under $10). Prices are based on an average meal for one adult, not including drinks, tax, or tips. Note that lunch generally costs less.

- All Walt Disney World restaurants and fast-food spots (except those with outside seating or at the Swan and Dolphin resorts) are nonsmoking only. Some restaurants at BoardWalk and Downtown Disney have special sections set aside for smokers.

- Priority seating arrangements for most table-service restaurants should be made in advance by calling WDW-DINE (939-3463). For complete details, see page 247 of this chapter.

Adventureland

FAST FOOD & SNACKS

Aloha Isle: This snack stand located near the Swiss Family Treehouse sells pineapple spears and juice, along with other tropical offerings, including pineapple floats and the especially refreshing Dole Whip pineapple soft serve. Inexpensive. S.

El Pirata Y el Perico: The Spanish name of this snack stand, located directly across from Pirates of the Caribbean, means "The Pirate and the Parrot." The offerings include several Mexican items, such as tacos, taco salads, and nachos, as well as hot dogs with chili and cheese. Open seasonally. Inexpensive. L, S.

Oasis: Tucked away near the Jungle Cruise, this is the perfect spot for a soft drink. Inexpensive. S.

Sunshine Tree Terrace: Offerings at this snack spot located near The Enchanted Tiki Room—Under New Management are some of the tastiest in the Magic Kingdom: orange slushes, nonfat frozen yogurt, and the tasty citrus or raspberry swirl—soft-serve nonfat frozen yogurt swirled with frozen juice concentrate. Cappuccino, espresso, and soft drinks are also available. Inexpensive. S.

Fantasyland

TABLE SERVICE

Cinderella's Royal Table: Hostesses at this festive establishment wear French Renaissance–style gowns, while hosts sport medieval tunics with pirate-style blouses, pants, and long vests. The hall itself is high-ceilinged and as majestic as the old mead hall it is designed to represent. Decor tends to royal blues and purples, with tapestry-backed chairs. Cinderella is usually on hand to greet kids and grown-ups alike. As guests of the princess, visitors dine on salads and sandwiches on the midday menu. Dinner includes prime rib (queen and king cuts, of course), spice-crusted salmon, beef tenderloin medaillon and grilled shrimp in cabernet sauce, and herbed chicken.

The Once Upon A Time character breakfast is held every morning. This all-you-can-eat breakfast is $14.95 for adults and $7.95 for children ages 3 through 11. Priority seating suggested (book *early*). Expensive. B, L, D.

FAST FOOD & SNACKS

Enchanted Grove: A small stand that's the perfect spot for a lemonade, lemonade slush, or strawberry soft-serve swirl. Inexpensive. S.

Hook's Tavern: Soft drinks and chips are available at this small refreshment stand just west of Cinderella's Golden Carrousel. Inexpensive. S.

Lumière's Kitchen: Located near Dumbo the Flying Elephant, this spot caters to kids with a variety of selections, including corn dog nuggets and hot dogs, to please even finicky eaters. Adult menus are available. Open seasonally. Inexpensive. L, D, S.

Mrs. Potts' Cupboard: Ice cream gets top billing at this spot near Mr. Toad's Wild Ride. There are soft-serve cones in chocolate, vanilla, and chocolate-vanilla swirl; hot fudge, strawberry shortcake, and brownie sundaes; shakes; and root beer floats. Inexpensive. S.

Pinocchio Village Haus: Located near It's a Small World (some tables offer a peek at the attraction via sizable picture windows), this is another one of those Magic Kingdom restaurants that seem a lot smaller from the outside than they really are, thanks to a labyrinthine arrangement of a half-dozen rooms decorated with antique cuckoo clocks, oak peasant chairs, and murals depicting characters from Pinocchio's story—Figaro the Cat, Cleo the Goldfish, Monstro the Whale, and Geppetto, the puppet's creator. The menu offers hot dogs, burgers, turkey sandwiches, and pasta salad. Inexpensive. L, D, S.

Scuttle's Landing: Soft drinks and shaved ice are the big draw here. Open seasonally. Inexpensive. S.

Frontierland

FAST FOOD & SNACKS

Aunt Polly's Dockside Inn: The much trumpeted sense of getting away from it all that islands always convey can also be found out on Frontierland's Tom Sawyer Island. Though only a couple of minutes' ride across the Rivers of America via the Tom Sawyer Island rafts, this landfall manages to seem remote even when there are dozens of youngsters clambering through its caves, over its hills, and across its rickety barrel bridges. Therein lies the charm of Aunt Polly's. While the adults in a party get some much needed rest and relaxation sipping lemonade in the shade of the old-fashioned porch and watching the riverboats chugging by, the kids can go exploring. And at nearby Fort Langhorn, kids can ping the toy rifles perched on the gun holes.

It doesn't even matter that Aunt Polly's offers a selection barely wider than the fare that the lady might have served young Tom Sawyer himself—peanut-butter-and-jelly and ham-and-cheese sandwiches, chilled

fried chicken, apple pie, soft-serve ice cream, root beer floats, cookies, iced tea, lemonade, and soda. Inexpensive. L, S.

Diamond Horseshoe Saloon Revue: From about 10 A.M. until early evening, a troupe of singers and dancers presents a sometimes corny, occasionally sidesplitting, always entertaining show in this Wild West dancehall saloon. Stop by anytime for sandwiches, salads, hard ice cream, dill pickles, and snacks. Inexpensive. L, S.

Pecos Bill Cafe: This is not one of those Magic Kingdom eateries so tucked away that only those who hunt will find it. Sooner or later, almost every guest passing from Adventureland into Frontierland—ambling by the Frontierland depot of the Walt Disney World Railroad on their way to Splash Mountain—walks by Pecos Bill Cafe. There are tables indoors (in air-conditioned rooms) and outdoors under umbrellas and in an open courtyard. Burgers, sandwiches, salads, and hot dogs are the staples. Inexpensive. L, D, S.

Hot Tip

All WDW table-service restaurants provide a menu geared to kids, and most fast-food spots offer kid-size value meals. Just ask!

Liberty Square

TABLE SERVICE

Liberty Tree Tavern: At this pillared and porticoed eatery opposite the riverboat landing, the floors are wide oak planks, the wallpaper looks as if it might have come from Williamsburg, the curtains hang from cloth loops, and the venetian blinds are made of wood. The rooms are chock-full of mementos that might have been found in the homes of Thomas Jefferson, George Washington, and Ben Franklin, and the window glass was made using 18th-century casting methods. Such charming environs make the food served therein seem almost secondary.

The à la carte lunch includes fresh fish, pot roast, beef stew in a crusty bread bowl, turkey, sandwiches, and hearty soups.

Dinner, an all-you-can-eat feast served family-style, is hosted by Disney characters. Menu items include mixed greens, roast turkey, flank steak, honey mustard ham, mashed potatoes, garden vegetables, and stuffing. The Patriot's Platter character dinner costs $19.95 for adults and $9.95 for children ages 3 through 11. Note that desserts and some beverages cost extra. Priority seating suggested. Expensive. L, D.

FAST FOOD & SNACKS

Columbia Harbour House: A fast-food fish house with some class. Fried fish, fried chicken strips, vegetarian chili or clam chowder in a bread bowl, and assorted sandwiches grace the menu. Even if the food weren't excellent, there are enough antiques and other knickknacks decking the halls to raise this place, located near the Liberty Square entrance to Fantasyland, above the ordinary. Model ships, copper measures, harpoons, nautical instruments, little lace tie-back curtains, and low-beamed ceilings give the restaurant a cozy air. The upstairs dining area is particularly peaceful. Inexpensive. L, D, S.

Sleepy Hollow: Cookie ice cream sandwiches, warm cobblers prepared with seasonal fruits, caramel corn, and other desserts—all made fresh before you—are the sweets for sale at this snack stand located in the The Hall of Presidents neighborhood, near the Liberty Square bridge. It's pleasant to eat on the secluded brick patio outside. Inexpensive. L, D, S.

Healthier Options

Health-conscious folks need not abandon all restraint for want of suitable foodstuffs. Most restaurants offer low-fat, low-cholesterol, low-salt, and vegetarian entrées. Even fast-food stands now feature healthier fare such as fresh salads, grilled chicken sandwiches, fresh fruit, turkey burgers, and nonfat frozen yogurt.

Main Street

TABLE SERVICE

Crystal Palace: One of the Magic Kingdom's landmarks, this restaurant takes its architectural cues from a similar structure that once stood in New York, and from San Francisco's Conservatory of Flowers, which still graces that city's Golden Gate Park. The place is huge but not overwhelming, because the tables are scattered amid a Victorian-style indoor garden, complete with fresh flowers and hanging greenery. Tables in the front look out on flower beds, while those at the east end have views of a secluded courtyard. The restaurant is located on a pathway at the end of Main Street, U.S.A., heading west toward Adventureland.

Three topiaries—Winnie the Pooh, Tigger, and Eeyore—greet guests at the entrance, an indication of the character presence here. None other than Winnie the Pooh himself and his pals circulate throughout meals.

Offerings vary according to season and available produce. The all-you-can-eat buffet features a full variety of traditional breakfast items every morning; a salad bar, deli bar, pasta dishes, chicken, and fish for lunch; and spit-roasted beef, paella, chicken, pastas, fish, carved meats, and inventive sides for dinner. The evening salad bar, with its grilled vegetables, peel-and-eat-shrimp, cold pasta salads, and variety of greens and grains, is first-rate. Kids particularly like the sundae bar offered at lunch and dinner. Cost for breakfast is $13.95 for adults and $7.95 for children ages 3 through 11; lunch is $14.95 for adults and $7.95 for children; dinner is $19.95 for adults and $9.95 for children. Priority seating suggested. Expensive. B, L, D.

The Plaza: This airy, many-windowed establishment, around the corner from the Plaza Ice Cream Parlor, is done up in mirrors with sinuous Art Nouveau frames. The menu offers chef's salads, burgers, and hot and cold sandwiches—plus hard ice cream, milk shakes, floats, and the biggest sundaes in the Magic Kingdom. Café Mocha, which combines chocolate and coffee, is another refreshing specialty. Priority seating suggested. Moderate. L, D, S.

Tony's Town Square: The decor comes straight out of Walt Disney's film *Lady and the Tramp*. The terrazzo-style patio offers a fine view of Town Square. Breakfast options include eggs, *Lady and the Tramp* character waffles, cereals, and freshly baked pull-apart sweet rolls. The lunch menu offers Italian specialties, including chicken Parmesan, T-bone steak, and turkey piccata. Pizzas with selected toppings are good bets. Other staples include Caesar salad, sandwiches, and a variety of pastas. At dinner select from country penne, sautéed shrimp, and chicken Florentine, along with a variety of daily specials. For dessert, Italian pastries and spumoni complement a cup of freshly brewed espresso or cappuccino. Priority seating suggested. Expensive. B, L, D.

FAST FOOD & SNACKS

Casey's Corner: The small round tables at this spacious, old-fashioned red-and-white stop on the west side of Main Street, (located adjacent to Crystal Palace) spill out onto the sidewalk. Except when the weather is terrifically hot, this baseball-themed spot is great for ballpark favorites—hot dogs in jumbo sizes, french fries, brownies, peanuts, soft drinks, and coffee. During daytime hours a pianist plinks away on the restaurant's white upright. Inexpensive. L, D, S.

Main Street Bake Shop: If the sight of this old-fashioned storefront doesn't lure you in, the heavenly aroma most certainly will. A genteel little tearoom, with prim tables and cane chairs, the Main Street Bake Shop is a pleasant place for a light breakfast, midmorning coffee break, or midafternoon rest stop. Assorted pastries, cakes, and pies are the main temptations. Also offered are fresh cookies: chocolate chunk, oatmeal raisin, sugar, and Nestlé's Original Toll House recipe. Ice cream cookie sandwiches are "built to order." Cinnamon rolls are baked on the premises. Inexpensive. B, S.

Plaza Ice Cream Parlor: Ice cream lovers from all over the country converge on this corner of the park, which boasts the Magic Kingdom's largest variety of hard ice cream flavors. Inexpensive. S.

Tomorrowland
FAST FOOD & SNACKS

Auntie Gravity's Galactic Goodies: This small spot located across from the Tomorrowland Speedway (between Merchant of Venus and Mickey's Star Traders) serves strawberry fruit smoothies, soft-serve ice cream, sundaes, floats, fruit cups, juice, and soft drinks. Inexpensive.

Cosmic Ray's Starlight Cafe: The largest fast-food spot in the Magic Kingdom is located directly across from the Tomorrowland Speedway. Three different menus are offered at separate sections along the counter. Cosmic Chicken serves rotisserie chicken; Blast-off Burgers has cheeseburgers, vegetarian burgers, and hot dogs; and Starlight Soup, Salad, Sandwich offers soups, Caesar salads, chef's salads, grilled chicken sandwiches, and cheese steak sandwiches. Inexpensive. L, D, S.

Lunching Pad at Rockettower Plaza: Located at the base of the Astro Orbiter in the center of Tomorrowland's vast concrete plaza, this small spot offers smoked turkey legs, bagel chips, character cookies, and soft drinks. (While you're in the area, take some time to investigate the video phone booths—one is near Buzz Lightyear's Space Ranger Spin, the other is by Astro Orbiter.) Inexpensive. S.

Plaza Pavilion: Just east of The Plaza restaurant on Main Street, this sleek spot on the edge of Tomorrowland serves pan pizzas, fried chicken strips, Italian specialty sandwiches, and salads. Some particularly pleasant tables look past the graceful willow trees nearby, toward the water and an impressive topiary sea serpent. Inexpensive. L, D, S.

GOOD MEALS, GREAT TIMES

Magic Kingdom Mealtime Tips

- The hours from 11 A.M. to 2 P.M., and again from about 5 P.M. to 7 P.M., are the mealtime rush hours in Magic Kingdom restaurants. Try to eat earlier or later whenever possible.
- When a fast-food restaurant has more than one service window, don't just amble into the nearest queue. Instead, inspect them all, because the one farthest from a doorway occasionally will be almost wait-free.
- Table-service restaurants offering full-scale meals are usually less crowded at lunch than they are at dinner.
- To avoid queues, eat lunch or dinner at a restaurant that offers priority seating—Tony's Town Square, Crystal Palace, or The Plaza restaurant on Main Street; Liberty Tree Tavern in Liberty Square; or Cinderella's Royal Table in the castle. Priority seating arrangements can be made in advance by calling WDW-DINE (939-3463). Check for same-day seating at the individual restaurant or City Hall. Refer to page 247 for further details.
- Consider taking the monorail to the Contemporary, Polynesian, or Grand Floridian to have lunch or dinner in a resort restaurant, and then return to the Magic Kingdom later. (Remember to have your hand stamped and keep your ticket for re-entry to the park.)

In Epcot

The various areas that make up Epcot offer a spectrum of eating options that extends from the usual burgers and fries to mouthwatering international specialties. Future World counts a please-all food court among its fast-food spots, plus two table-service restaurants whose menus and atmosphere innovatively reflect the themes of the pavilions they inhabit. World Showcase, on the other hand, is characterized by international flavors. Here, the cuisine of each country is served in settings that strive to transport visitors, if just for the duration of their meal. While the abundance of appealing table-service restaurants makes World Showcase a very popular dining destination, the promenade is also ringed with fast-food spots, most of which feature international fare. Priority seating is an important part of the Epcot dining equation (for complete details, turn to page 247). Character meals are options for breakfast, lunch, and dinner in Future World (for specifics, see page 246).

Future World

TABLE SERVICE

Coral Reef (The Living Seas): Decorated in cool greens and blues to complement its surroundings, this restaurant offers diners a panoramic view of the coral reef through large windows. The windows are eight feet high and more than eight inches thick. The dining room has several tiers, so all guests get a decent view. The menu features a variety of fresh fish and shellfish—including

Hawaiian tuna, Florida snapper, mahimahi, shrimp, swordfish, and salmon—prepared in a number of different ways. Landlubber

selections are also available. The menu may vary seasonally. Priority seating suggested. Expensive. L, D.

Garden Grill (The Land): Sleek upholstered wood-trimmed booths illuminated with handsome brass lamps help to make this an exceptionally attractive eatery. The restaurant itself revolves, past a mural of giant sunflowers and above scenes of the thunderstorm, sandstorm, prairie, and rain forest featured in the Living with the Land boat ride below. The scenes were designed with diners in mind, and provide them with a peek into a farmhouse window that's out of viewing range of the waterborne passengers.

Mickey and Minnie join Chip and Dale to host three character meals here each day.

The all-you-can-eat country breakfast is $14.95 for adults and $8.25 for children ages 3 through 11. Lunch and dinner menus feature rotisserie chicken, hickory-smoked steaks, and fish, with a separate menu for children. The character lunch costs $16.95 for adults and $9.95 for children. Dinner is $17.50 for adults and $9.95 for children. Priority seating suggested. Moderate to expensive. B, L, D.

FAST FOOD & SNACKS

Electric Umbrella (Innoventions): This large fast-food establishment is decorated in shades of blue, mauve, and magenta. It's a particularly good bet when the weather is temperate enough to allow dining at the tables on the terrace outside—or when bound for World Showcase with finicky eaters in tow. Offerings include chicken sandwiches, grilled ham-and-cheese sandwiches, grilled vegetable pita sandwiches, hot dogs, burgers, fruit salad, and chef's salad. Inexpensive. L, D, S.

Fountain View Espresso and Bakery (Innoventions Plaza): Delicious baked goods and desserts—croissants, cheesecake, tiramisu, and éclairs—can be found at this spot across from the Fountain of Nations. Espresso, cappuccino, wine, and beer are among the assorted beverages available here. Inexpensive. B, S.

Pasta Piazza Ristorante (Innoventions): Pizza, pasta, and antipasto salad are among the specialties at this eatery located opposite the Electric Umbrella restaurant. The decor is traditional Italian, accented by some nontraditional neon lights. Inexpensive. B, L, D, S.

Pure and Simple (Wonders of Life): This spot offers a variety of healthy treats, including oat bran waffles with fruit toppings, frozen yogurt, yogurt shakes, muffins, fruit juices, and more. Vegetable pizzas, soups, Caesar salad with diced lemon chicken, and lemon pepper chicken sandwiches are among the lunch options. Inexpensive. B, L, S.

Sunshine Season Food Fair (The Land): One of the most interesting of the Future World eateries, and a wrinkle in the Walt Disney World fast-food scene, this handful of diverse counter-service stands is on the lower level of the pavilion. Each stand in the food court has a farm-style facade done in bright colors, not unlike those that might be found in agricultural exhibit buildings at a midwestern state fair. With bright, umbrella-topped tables nearby, the effect is cheery. Because of the wide variety of foods available here, this is one of the best bets in Epcot for a family that can't agree on what to eat.

Soup & Salad offers Florida seafood chowder, fruit salad, and rotini pasta salad. The Bakery Shop's morning offerings include fresh fruit, bagels with cream

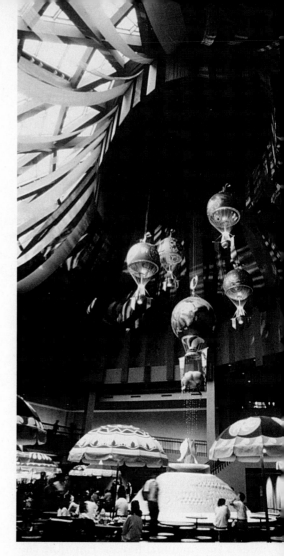

cheese, jumbo cinnamon rolls, Danish pastries, apricot crumb cake, and muffins. After 11 A.M., apple pies appear, along with cheesecake and chocolate cake, strawberry shortcake, rich double-chocolate brownies, hermit cookies with cinnamon—plus absolutely delicious chocolate chip cookies baked on the premises.

The Barbecue stand sells barbecued chicken and ribs smoked on the premises; barbecued beef, pork, or chicken breast sandwiches; and sides of beans, corn-on-the-cob, and corn bread muffins. The Cheese and Pasta stand offers baked macaroni with ham and cheese, tortellini or fettuccine with meat sauce, noodles with Asian-style chicken, and vegetable lasagne. The Sandwich Shop regales the hungry with several hefty combinations, while an ice cream stand tempts guests with cooling cones and cups, frozen yogurt, and sundaes. The Potato Store serves steaming baked potatoes stuffed with Asian-style chicken and vegetables, cheddar cheese and bacon, and other fillings. The Beverage House here proffers an array of soft drinks, beer, wine, and frozen drinks. Inexpensive. B, L, D, S.

World Showcase

TABLE SERVICE

Akershus (Norway): The Norwegian castle of Akershus dominates Oslo's harbor, and is the most impressive of Norway's medieval fortresses. It is actually half fortress and half palace, and many of its grand halls continue to be used for elaborate state banquets. At Epcot's castle-like Akershus, guests are treated to an authentic royal Norwegian buffet called the *koldtbord*, literally "cold table." The diverse mix of offerings includes both hot and cold meats and seafood, and a selection of salads, cheeses, and breads. Traditional Norwegian desserts are also served, as are cocktails and Norwegian beer. Hosts and hostesses are on hand to answer any questions about the menu that guests may have. Priority seating suggested. Moderate to expensive. L, D.

Biergarten (Germany): Located at the rear of the St. Georgsplatz in the Germany pavilion, this huge tiered restaurant is set in a courtyard rimmed with geranium-studded balconies and punctuated by an old mill. It's every bit as jolly as Alfredo's restaurant in the Italy pavilion. This is partly because of the long tables that encourage a certain togetherness among guests—and partly because Beck's beer is served in 33-ounce steins. But equal credit for the gemütlich atmosphere must go to the restaurant's lively entertainment. A German trio performs during lunch. At dinner, yodelers, dancers, and other traditional Bavarian musicians—each clad in lederhosen or dirndl—play accordions, cowbells, a musical saw, and a harplike stringed instrument known as the "wooden laughter." The entertaining dinner shows take place every hour on the half hour. Diners are usually invited to join the fun onstage.

The food is hearty and presented as an all-you-can-eat buffet, featuring assorted sausages (grilled bratwurst, *Debrizinger*, *Bauernwurst*), frankfurters, rotisserie chicken, homemade spaetzle, assorted cold dishes,

potato salad, cucumber salad, and many more German specialties. Because entertainment is intermittent, there's plenty of time to enjoy the pleasant setting, with the big mill waterwheel slowly turning and the sound of water splashing into the millstream blending with the rousing oompah music. Priority seating suggested, particularly during peak seasons (book *early*). Moderate to expensive. L, D.

Le Cellier Steakhouse (Canada): Tucked away on the lowest level of the pavilion near Victoria Gardens, this low-ceilinged, lantern-lighted, stone-walled establishment looks a little like the ancient wine cellars for which it is named. It offers a full menu of Canadian foods, with hearty open-face steak sandwiches and steak salads also available for lunch, and roast prime rib and steaks added to the offerings at dinner. Tangy Canadian cheddar cheese serves as the base of a rich soup. Excellent maple-glazed salmon, and penne and wild mushrooms in pesto cream sauce (also with chicken or shrimp) round out the selection of entrées. For dessert, try the apple bread pudding with maple cinnamon ice cream or chocolate "moose" with raspberry sauce. Canada's own Molson and Labatt's beers and Inniskillin wine are served. This tempting combination makes Le Cellier Steakhouse a prime destination. Priority seating suggested. Moderate. L, D, S.

Les Chefs de France (France): This recently expanded restaurant (which took over the space formerly occupied by Bistro de Paris and Au Petit Cafe), has a bright, airy feel, with yellow and creme-colored walls drenched in natural light. It boasts a glass-enclosed "outside" dining area with a conservatory motif, as well as a more intimate second-floor dining room.

Having undergone extensive refurbishment and expansion in late 1997, this popular eatery reopened with a new look and a new menu, while retaining its old-world charm and team of internationally acclaimed chefs. Paul Bocuse operates a restaurant outside Lyons, France, and Roger Vergé runs one just north of the French Riviera. Together with Gaston Lenôtre (widely recognized as France's premier preparer of pastries and other delicious dessert delicacies), they form a most unusual, and absolutely formidable, gastronomic trio. Bocuse, Vergé, and Lenôtre have designed a menu that features fresh ingredients readily available from Florida purveyors. In addition, the restaurant imports as many key ingredients from France as possible. The French chefs make regular visits to Walt Disney World to supervise the restaurant and to adjust certain items on the menu.

As you might expect, the fare here is fiercely French, but the foundation of the menu is nouvelle cuisine, which involves lighter sauces using much less cream and butter than in classic French cooking. The lunch and dinner menus vary, with lunch being slightly more limited and featuring such lighter items as quiche lorraine and niçoise salad. Menu items served at both meals include sautéed chicken breast with wild mushrooms, grilled salmon on polenta, and braised beef in red Burgundy wine beside spinach ravioli. Soups and appetizers, such as onion soup and escargot, are all-day staples. Apple tart, chocolate crêpes, peach melba, and chocolate mousse cake are the dessert specialties of note.

Be aware that this can be one of the most expensive of all World Showcase restaurants. Priority seating suggested (book *early*). Expensive. L, D.

L'Originale Alfredo di Roma Ristorante (Italy): This restaurant's trompe l'oeil perspective paintings make diners believe they're seeing real scenes rather than mere murals, and lend character to the decor of this popular establishment. As in the famous Roman restaurant of the same name, the house specialty is fettuccine Alfredo—wide, flat noodles tossed in a sauce made of butter and imported Parmesan cheese. But many other sizes and shapes of pasta, all of it made right on the premises, are also available; they are significantly enhanced by tomato, meat, pesto (basil, garlic, and Parmesan), or carbonara (egg, bacon, cream, and pecorino cheese) sauces. There are also a number of less familiar Italian preparations involving chicken, eggplant, seafood, sausage, and veal, all of which are very good. For dessert, choose from specialties such as ricotta cheesecake, spumoni, tortoni, or gelato. Even if you don't eat here, it's fun to stop and just peer through the glass kitchen windows to watch the cooks cranking out the rigatoni, ziti, linguine, lasagne, fettuccine, and spaghetti (which, the eminently readable menu reminds guests, were brought from Europe to America by Thomas Jefferson in 1786). Priority seating suggested. Expensive. L, D.

Marrakesh (Morocco): The most savory part of the Morocco pavilion features a variety of examples of traditional and modern Moroccan cuisine. Waiters are dressed in traditional Moroccan costumes. Menu specialties include roast lamb, chicken brochette, and couscous (steamed semolina served with your choice of lamb, chicken, or vegetables). Sampler platters are also available. The beautiful tilework was done by Moroccan craftsmen. Belly dancers and musicians entertain diners at both lunch and dinner. Priority seating suggested. Expensive. L, D.

Mitsukoshi (Japan): This complex of dining and drinking spots, all operated by the Japanese firm for which it is named, occupies the second level of the large structure on the west side of the Japan pavilion. There are two options. *Tempura Kiku* occupies a small corner of the Mitsukoshi building that's

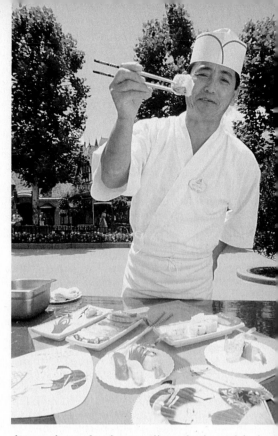

devoted to the batter-dipped, deep-fried chicken, beef, seafood, and fresh vegetables that are collectively known as tempura. The individual tidbits are crisp and delicious. Priority seating not available. Expensive. L, D. *Teppanyaki Dining Rooms* is composed of five rooms not unlike those popularized by the Benihana chain all around America. Guests sit counter-style around large flat grills while white-hatted chefs chop vegetables, meat, and fish at lightning speed and then stir-fry it all just as quickly. Whether the chopping and cooking accompany a mildly comic routine depends on the chef, but in any case the establishment is quite convivial. The seating arrangements make it natural to strike up a conversation with fellow diners; in fact, it's almost impossible to keep to yourself. Priority seating suggested. Expensive. L, D.

Nine Dragons (China): This stop on Epcot's varied international restaurant tour offers meals prepared in provincial Chinese cooking styles, including Mandarin, Cantonese, Hunan, Szechuan, and Kiangche. Entrées include braised duck (served Cantonese style), Kang Bao chicken (stir-fried chicken, peanuts, and dried hot peppers), and beef and jade tree (Chinese broccoli and sliced steak). Appetizers range from Chinese pickled cabbage to pan-fried dumplings and hot-and-sour soup. A selection of Chinese teas, beers, and wines is available. The varied dessert menu features red-bean ice cream, toffee apples, and assorted Chinese pastries. Priority seating suggested. Moderate to expensive. L, D.

Rose & Crown Pub and Dining Room (United Kingdom): The fare here tends toward pub grub—that is, fish-and-chips and traditional meat pies. For lunch, however, it's also possible to order an open-face roast beef sandwich or the Ploughmans Lunch (sliced turkey and ham, English cheeses, and fresh bread). At dinner the standard offerings are supplemented by roast prime rib with horseradish sauce, cornish game hen, and grilled lamb steak. For an appetizer, we recommend the sautéed mushrooms in cream sauce on puff pastry. For dessert there's traditional sherry trifle, a confection of layered whipped cream, custard, strawberries, and sherry-flavored sponge cake; apple-blackberry crumble; and chocolate cake. Bass ale from England, Tennent's lager from Scotland, and Harp lager and Guinness stout, both from Ireland, are on tap. (They're served cold, in the American fashion, not at room temperature, as the British prefer.)

The decor is beautiful, mainly polished woods, etched glass, and brass accents. In fine weather it's pleasant to lunch under the sunny yellow umbrellas on the terrace outside and watch the *FriendShip* water taxis cruising across World Showcase Lagoon; a late dinner on the water has an added perk—front-row seating for the nightly fireworks show. On the little island just to the east, the wind ruffles the leaves of the Lombardy poplars, a species of tree that is found along roadsides all over Europe.

As for the pub's architecture, it incorporates three distinct styles. The wall facing the World Showcase Promenade is reminiscent of urban establishments popular in Britain since the 1890s, while that on the south side evokes London's 17th-century Cheshire Cheese pub, with its brick-walled flagstone terrace, slate roof, and half-timbered exterior. The canal facade, with its stone wall and clay-tile roof, reminds visitors of the charming pubs so common in the English countryside.

The pub section of the Rose & Crown serves such snacks as Stilton cheese and fresh fruit platters, sausage rolls, and mini meat pies—along with all the brews noted above and traditional British mixed drinks, such as shandies (Bass ale and ginger ale), lager with lime juice, black velvets (Guinness stout and champagne), and black and tans (Bass ale and Guinness stout). This drinking and snacking spot is quite popular, so it's often necessary to queue up at the door. But the wait is seldom very long, since few guests linger over their drinks. Priority seating is not available in the pub area, but suggested for the adjacent dining room. Moderate to expensive. L, D, S.

San Angel Inn (Mexico): The food at this establishment located to the rear of the plaza inside the Mexico pyramid (a corporate cousin of the famous Mexico City restaurant of the same name) may come as a surprise to most visitors. Although the tacos and tortillas and other specialties that usually fall under the broad umbrella of Mexican food are available, the menu also offers a wide variety of more subtly flavored fish, poultry, and meat dishes.

To start, there's *queso fundido* for two (melted cheese and Mexican pork sausage with corn or flour tortillas). As entrées, the menu offers *sopes de pollo* (fried corn dough shells topped with refried beans, chicken with green tomatillo sauce, and cheese); grilled tenderloin of beef served with a chicken enchilada, guacamole, and refried beans; *mole poblano* (chicken simmered with spices and a small amount of chocolate); *huachinango a la veracruzana* (fresh fillet of red snapper poached in wine with onions, tomatoes, and peppers); and much more that is good and tasty. Mexican desserts are largely unfamiliar to North Americans, with the possible exceptions of the custard known as flan, and *arroz con leche*, best known in the United States as rice pudding. Still, such desserts as chocolate Kahlúa mousse pie and *helado con cajeta* (vanilla ice cream with milk-caramel topping) are well worth trying. Dos Equis beer, tart lemon-flavored water, and delicious margaritas make good accompaniments. Priority seating suggested. Expensive. L, D.

FAST FOOD & SNACKS

Boulangerie Pâtisserie (France): This bakery and pastry shop in the France pavilion is not hard to find: Just follow the wonderful aroma, then watch the crowds line up to consume the establishment's flaky croissants, éclairs, fruit tarts, and chocolate mousse. The treats are served under the management of the stellar trio of chefs who operate the popular Les Chefs de France restaurant not far away—Paul Bocuse, Roger Vergé, and Gaston Lenôtre. Hint for those who hate to wait: This has become a favorite snacking stop among Epcot veterans; your best bet is to stop here as soon as World Showcase opens at 11 A.M. or half an hour before park closing. Inexpensive. S.

Cantina de San Angel (Mexico): Located along the World Showcase Promenade, just outside the entrance to Mexico's pyramid, this fast-food stand serves beef-filled soft tortillas; *tacos al carbón*, flour tortillas filled with grilled chicken breast strips, onions, and peppers, served with refried beans and salsa; and *churros*, a sort of fried dough rolled in cinnamon and sugar. The Cantina is first-rate for a tasty rest stop, and even more so for its outdoor lagoonside seating. Dos Equis beer, margaritas, and watermelon juice are available, and the establishment's plant-edged terrace makes a fine grandstand for people-watching. Inexpensive. L, D, S.

Kringla Bakeri og Kafe (Norway): Tucked between the Norway pavilion's wooden church and a cluster of shops, this eating spot serves *kringles*, sweet candied pretzels eaten on special occasions in Norway; *vaflers*, heart-shaped waffles topped with powdered sugar and jam; *kransekake*, almond-pastry rings; and *smørbrøds*, open-face sandwiches of smoked salmon, roast beef, or turkey. Ringnes beer, brewed in Norway, is also available. There is also a pleasant, shaded outdoor eating area. Inexpensive. L, D, S.

Liberty Inn (The American Adventure): To many foreigners, American food means burgers, hot dogs, and french fries, and these are the staples at the Liberty Inn, located alongside the entrance to The American Adventure show on the far end of the World Showcase Lagoon. Salads, grilled chicken sandwiches, ice cream, apple pastries, and chocolate chip cookies round out the selections. As a result, the place is a delight for small children, and also quite a pleasant spot for their parents. There is veranda seating, a fountain, and an impressive array of antique-looking decoys and chests. Inexpensive. L, D, S.

Lotus Blossom Cafe (China): Adjacent to Yong Feng Shangdian shopping gallery in the China pavilion, this fast-food counter offers sweet-and-sour pork, egg rolls, and soup. There is a covered outdoor seating area nearby. Inexpensive. L, D.

Refreshment Outpost (between Germany and China): This is a perfect spot for a refreshing cold drink. Frozen yogurt and ice cream are also served. Inexpensive. S.

Refreshment Port (Canada): Another good spot for a quick thirst quencher. Canadian beer, wine coolers, iced tea, and lemonade are served, plus hot dogs, nachos, fresh fruit, and frozen yogurt. Inexpensive. S.

Sommerfest (Germany): Bratwurst sandwiches, soft pretzels, Black Forest cake, apple strudel, Beck's beer, and wine are offered at this outdoor establishment, located at the rear of the Germany pavilion; seating is nearby. Inexpensive. L, D, S.

Yakitori House (Japan): Located in the gardens to the left of the plaza, the restaurant occupies a scaled-down version of the 16th-century Katsura Imperial Summer Palace in Kyoto; sliding screens, lanterns, and kimono-clad servers add to the atmosphere. *Guydon* is a stewlike concoction flavored with soy sauce, spices, and the Japanese rice wine known as sake, served over rice. That staple, along with skewered chicken known as *yakitori* (it's basted with soy sauce and sesame oil as it broils), teriyaki chicken sandwiches, and Japanese sweets and beverages, typifies the offerings here. Inexpensive. L, D, S.

Epcot Mealtime Tips

• The international restaurants of World Showcase offer some of the best dining on the property. Since many of them are very popular, it's a good idea to arrange advance priority seating for any table-service restaurants by calling WDW-DINE (939-3463) long before arriving. However, it's important to note that many tables are left available for same-day seating. To make arrangements, head straight for a WorldKey Information Service terminal or Guest Relations first thing in the morning. Lunch can also be booked at the individual restaurants. Refer to page 247 for more details.

• If you aren't able to secure priority seating for dinner, don't despair. There are tasty alternatives to a table-service meal. Japan has Tempura Kiku, a full-service spot with batter-dipped, deep-fried meats and vegetables (and no priority seating available), and Yakitori House, good for skewered bits of barbecued beef and chicken. Sample Mexican specialties at Cantina de San Angel (whose lagoonside tables provide a fine view of the sun setting behind Epcot). Also try the open-face sandwiches at Kringla Bakeri og Kafe in Norway, or the sweet-and-sour pork at China's Lotus Blossom Cafe.

• Cravings for more conventional fast foods will be satisfied at the Electric Umbrella in Innoventions and at the Liberty Inn in The American Adventure. The Pasta Piazza Ristorante in Innoventions serves Italian fare. The Sunshine Season Food Fair in The Land pavilion offers a little bit of everything.

• There's always a good menu selection even for unadventurous eaters—even in the more exotic restaurants of World Showcase. If you're undecided, ask at Guest Relations to see a book of menus.

• Don't dismiss the idea of an early seating if you can get it: If you have lunch at 11 A.M., a 5 P.M. dinner will not only be welcome, but more important, it will provide the opportunity to spend the most pleasant and uncrowded evening hours enjoying the Epcot attractions.

• Lunch provides guests with another chance to enjoy the most popular Epcot restaurants. It also has an additional appeal: With priority seating for 1 P.M., it's possible to spend some of the most crowded hours in the park consuming a pleasant meal while less fortunate visitors are waiting in some of the longest lines of the day.

In the Disney-MGM Studios

The eateries at the Disney-MGM Studios are a breed apart. Some feature decor that returns guests to a bygone era; others recapture memorable moments from the big or small screen. All reprise a beloved part of Hollywood's star-studded heritage. The Studios has five full-service restaurants, whose atmospheres and menus are so distinct they sate altogether different moods and whims. Priority seating is available for these dining rooms (for details, turn to page 247). Soundstage restaurant offers character meals (see page 246 for specifics). A solid—and fairly diverse—ensemble of fast-food places hits the spot for eaters on the move.

TABLE SERVICE

50's Prime Time Cafe: The setting is straight out of your favorite sitcoms of the 1950s. Each of the plastic-laminate kitchen tables is set under a pull-down lamp, evoking a suburban kitchenette. Video screens around the room broadcast black-and-white clips from favorite fifties comedies (all related to food). Meals are served on either Fiesta Ware plates or TV dinner–style compartment trays. The waitresses play "Mom" with considerable enthusiasm, making recommendations and encouraging guests to clean their plates (*or no dessert!*).

The menu is packed with "comfort foods." For openers there's a choice of chicken noodle soup, chili, or the French Fry Feast, served either plain or with chili and cheese. Specialties of the house include Magnificent Meat Loaf, served with mashed potatoes and mushroom gravy; fried chicken; and Granny's Pot Roast. There are also Caesar salads, club sandwiches, and Aunt Selma's Chicken Salad. Milk shakes, ice cream sodas, and root beer floats are filling accompaniments. And when you've finished everything on your plate, "Mom" will ask if you'd like dessert. Standouts include

s'mores, a graham cracker topped with chocolate and toasted marshmallows (you'll feel like you're back at summer camp); sundaes; banana splits; and apple pie à la mode. A full bar is available. Kids love this place. Priority seating suggested. Moderate. L, D, S.

Hollywood Brown Derby: The home of the famous Cobb salad is alive and well. This re-creation of the former Vine Street mainstay is quite faithful, right down to the caricatures (reproduced from the original Derby collection) that cover the walls. Arch gossip queen rivals Louella Parsons and Hedda Hopper (portrayed by convincing actresses) still reign over the restaurant from reserved tables, just as they did in the heyday of the real Brown Derby. The restaurant is decorated predominantly in teak and mahogany, and the elegant chandeliers and perimeter lamps (shaped like miniature derbies) are reminiscent of those in the original eatery.

The menu features the famed Cobb salad, created by owner Bob Cobb in the 1930s. It's a mixture of ever-so-finely chopped fresh salad greens, tomato, bacon, turkey, egg, blue cheese, and avocado, served with french dressing. A modern incarnation of the salad is available with shrimp or chicken. Other menu selections of note include sushi and crab-and-roast-corn quesadilla "previews" and New York Strip Steak, shrimp tortelloni, and sautéed grouper "feature attractions." The dessert tray is tempting—particularly the grapefruit cake, a Brown Derby institution. The slightly formal atmosphere is not likely to enchant most kids. Priority seating suggested. Expensive. L, D.

Mama Melrose's Ristorante Italiano: This quirky Italian restaurant (with a California twist) is located in a warehouse that has been converted into a dining room. Appetizer pizzas are prepared in a wood-burning oven. The menu also features lasagne, chicken, veal, pasta (including a popular all-you-can-eat pasta special), and vegetarian options. More creative dishes include sautéed crusted veal scallopini topped with lemon vinaigrette, and seared ahi tuna in raspberry glaze. Note that the dinner hour ends a bit early here. Priority seating suggested. Moderate to expensive. L, D.

Sci-Fi Dine-In Theater: This 250-seat eatery re-creates a 1950s drive-in theater. The tables are actually flashy, 1950s-era cars, complete with fins and whitewalls. Fiber-optic stars twinkle overhead in the "night sky," and real drive-in theater speakers are mounted beside each car. All the tables face a large screen, where a 45-minute compilation of the best (and worst) of science fiction trailers and cartoons play in a continuous loop.

The restaurant is also notable for its huge hot and cold sandwiches. Meals include Attack of the Killer Stacked Sandwich (turkey, roast beef, ham, and swiss cheese)

Coming Attraction

Opening in late 1999, **Copperfield Magic Underground** offers a truly magical dining experience. As guests chow down on American and international dishes, grand illusions are performed in a setting reflecting the history and mystery of magic. Part of a new chain of eateries to which master illusionist David Copperfield has given his name, this spot is accessible from both inside and outside the park. Admission to the Disney-MGM Studios is not necessary to enter the restaurant. Expensive. L, D.

---

and Monster from the Inferno (a flame-broiled hamburger). Tossed in Space is an oriental salad, and Creature from the Pasta Lagoon is linguine in cream sauce. There's also a slate of tempting desserts, including The Cheesecake That Ate New York, Milky-Way-Out Milk Shakes, and The Big Bang (a colossal sundae made with vanilla ice cream and many toppings). Priority seating suggested. Moderate to expensive. L, D.

Soundstage: This cavernous restaurant in the Animation Courtyard has been transformed into a character buffet, featuring stars from animated classics. Characters from such films as *Aladdin*, *Disney's The Hunchback of Notre Dame*, and *Mulan* gather at this restaurant all day long. Music from the films plays in the background. The buffet offers a salad bar, pasta, herb-baked chicken, lasagne, baked fish, roast pork, and various accompaniments. Priority seating suggested. Moderate to expensive. B, L.

CAFETERIA SERVICE

Hollywood & Vine: The distinctive Art Deco facade ushers guests into a contemporary version of a 1950s diner—all stainless steel with pink accents. An elaborate 42- by 8-foot wall mural depicts notable Hollywood landmarks, including the Disney Studios, Columbia Ranch, and Warner Brothers (back when they were the only studios in the San Fernando Valley). At the center of the mural is the Carthay Circle Theatre, where *Snow White* premiered in 1937.

The 368-seat cafeteria presents a varied menu. At breakfast, there's the Hollywood Scramble, two eggs served with bacon or sausage and a choice of potatoes or grits and a breakfast biscuit; french toast; pancakes; omelettes; assorted hot and cold cereals; and

fresh fruit. Muffins, pastries, and croissants are also served. Lunch features a variety of salads. Baby-back ribs, roast chicken, and spaghetti and meatballs are offered. Pies head the dessert list. Beer and wine are available, and a children's menu is posted. Inexpensive to moderate. B, L, D, S.

FAST FOOD & SNACKS

ABC Commissary: This restaurant located near the Chinese Theater features chicken breast sandwiches, chicken nuggets, burgers, deli subs, and milk shakes. Inexpensive. L, D.

Backlot Express: This fast-food spot looks like the old crafts shops on a studio backlot. There's a paint shop, stunt hall, sculpture shop, and model shop. The paint shop has paint-speckled floors, chairs, and tables; the prop shop is decked out in car engines, bumpers, and fan belts. There is outdoor seating amid stored streetlights, plants, and trees. Menu offerings include burgers, hot dogs, chicken Caesar salad, grilled chicken sandwiches, tuna subs, and chili. For dessert, there's chocolate-chip cheesecake, brownies, apple pie, and fresh fruit. Beer is available. Inexpensive. L, D, S.

Dinosaur Gertie's: "Ice Cream of Extinction" claims the sign at this giant dinosaur set on Echo Lake. And indeed, a selection of ice cream bars and frozen slush drinks disappear rather quickly. Inexpensive. S.

Min & Bill's Dockside Diner: "There's good eats in our galley" proclaims the welcoming sign posted on the *S.S. Down the Hatch*, a bit of "California crazy" 1950s architecture. The little tramp steamer, complete with a cartoonlike smokestack, mast, and booms, never sets sail. Min & Bill's offerings include taco salads, nachos, and soft-shell tacos, all available with beef or chicken. Soft-serve ice cream is available in cups or cones with a variety of toppings. Inexpensive. L, D, S.

Starring Rolls Bakery: Freshly baked rolls, pastries, muffins, croissants, and sugar-free desserts are sold at this sweet-smelling shop. Coffee, tea, and soft drinks are also served,

making this a good place for an eat-and-run breakfast. For lunch, ready-made sandwiches with ham and cheese, chicken salad, or tuna salad are available. Inexpensive. B, L, S.

Studio Catering Co.: Guests on the Backlot Tour come across this spot at the end of the tram ride. Situated next to the Honey, I Shrunk the Kids Movie Set Adventure playground, the eatery offers barbecued pork, beef, and chicken sandwiches; turkey and cheese sandwiches; and snacks. There is a separate line for cones, sundaes, and shakes made with chocolate and vanilla soft-serve ice cream. Beer is available at a nearby stand. Inexpensive. S.

Sunset Ranch Market: Several food stands on Sunset Boulevard offer good snacking opportunities and quick bites. Yellow and white umbrellas dot the outdoor seating area. Rosie's Red Hot Dogs specializes in the obvious, serving a curious assortment of hot dogs, including foot-long options, plus barbecued beef sandwiches. Catalina Eddie's offers frozen yogurt and fruit drinks, plus tuna and chicken salad sandwiches. The turkey leg cart also offers baked potatoes with toppings. Fresh fruit and vegetables, fruit juices, and soft drinks are available at Anaheim Produce. Inexpensive. L, D, S.

Toy Story Pizza Planet: This arcade looks as if it were plucked out of the film *Toy Story*. The centerpiece is a Space Crane, complete with aliens and mechanical grabber. A limited menu includes individual pizzas, salads, desserts, and juice. Cappuccino and espresso are available. Inexpensive. L, D, S.

In Animal Kingdom

Whether you eat like a bird or more like a horse, you'll have no trouble finding something to sink your teeth into at one of Animal Kingdom's many eateries. The emphasis at Disney's newest theme park is on fast food, with Rainforest Cafe as the only table-service establishment. The menagerie of quick-service options cater to carnivores and herbivores alike, featuring everything from freshly tossed Caesar salad to chicken roasted in a 16-foot "wall of flames." Beer, including Safari Amber specialty brew, and wine are served at most restaurants.

TABLE SERVICE

Rainforest Cafe: Like The Oasis, the region of Animal Kingdom that it borders, this cafe is a lush, soothing tropical jungle. Unlike The Oasis, any quiet moment here is merely a calm before the storm—as brief, dramatic thunderstorms occur throughout the day *inside* the restaurant. Gushing waterfalls, twisting tree trunks, and colorful fish add to the ambience. The environmentally conscious cuisine includes items like Planet Earth Pasta and the Plant Sandwich. (The Calypso Dip—fresh salmon, artichoke hearts, onions, spices, and cheese served with warm pita—is an especially tantalizing appetizer.) There's no net-caught fish on the menu, nor beef from countries that destroy rain forest land to raise cattle. An equally elaborate shop proffers logo merchandise, animal puppets and prints, and glow-in-the-dark toys.

Note: The restaurant and shop are accessible from both inside and outside Animal Kingdom, so admission to the park is not necessary to enter. It is located at the park

entrance. Priority seating suggested for breakfast (available 30 days ahead) and lunch and dinner (just 7 days prior). Moderate. B, L, D, S.

FAST FOOD & SNACKS

Campside Funnel Cakes: This Camp Minnie-Mickey spot stands by with corn dogs and funnel cakes. Inexpensive. L, D, S.

Chip 'n' Dale's Cookie Cabin: For a sweet treat, head to Camp Minnie-Mickey for delicious, freshly baked cookies (chocolate chip, macadamia nut, and sugar) and ice cream sandwiches. Inexpensive. S.

Dino Diner: In DinoLand U.S.A., near the entrance, is a small wagon with pastries and muffins at breakfast and smoked turkey legs throughout the day. Inexpensive. S.

Flame Tree Barbecue: You will probably start licking your chops before you even arrive here, as the aroma of barbecue wafts not-so-subtly by. This fast-food establishment serves up a savory selection of barbecued sandwiches and platters, all wood-roasted and fresh from the smoker. Try the tomato-based barbecue sauce or the mustard-based Carolina-style sauce with your smoked beef brisket, St. Louis ribs, and pulled pork. Smoked turkey, a vegetarian wrap, and apple pie round out the options. There's endless outdoor seating along Discovery River. Located in Safari Village, near the bridge to DinoLand U.S.A. Inexpensive. L, D, S.

Harambe Fruit Market: The healthy choice for snacking at Animal Kingdom is this fruit stand near the entrance to Kilimanjaro Safaris. Inexpensive. S.

Kusafiri Coffee Shop & Bakery: The bakery inside Tusker House provides a steady stream of fresh-from-the-oven breakfast treats and assorted desserts, plus cappuccino and espresso. Inexpensive. B, S.

Mr. Kamal's Burger Grill: Located next to the Discovery River Boats, at Upcountry Landing between Africa and Asia, this spot has juicy broiled burgers served with chips. The seating area nearby is small, but has an excellent view of The Tree of Life. Inexpensive. L, D, S.

Munch Wagon: Head to this stand at Conservation Station for hot dogs and snacks. Inexpensive. L, D, S.

Pizzafari: Individual pizzas are available plain, with pepperoni, and deluxe (with a variety of meats and vegetables). In addition to the cheese-laden bill of fare, the specialties here include an excellent Caesar salad with mesquite-grilled chicken and a roast vegetable calzone. If you'd like, dessert can be chocolate cake. Brightly colored animal murals decorate this counter-service restaurant, located in Safari Village, near the bridge to Camp-Minnie Mickey. Inexpensive. L, D, S.

Restaurantosaurus: Located in the heart of DinoLand U.S.A., this spot is themed as a campsite for student paleontologists. It's filled with fossils, bones, and such; class notes line the walls. This eatery specializes in "dino-mite" fast food at lunch and dinner: burgers, chicken salad, hot dogs, and salads—plus McDonald's french fries, chicken nuggets, and Happy Meals. Breakfast is an all-you-can-eat character buffet, called Donald's Prehistoric Breakfastosaurus. It's an entertaining meal,

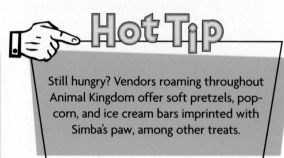

Still hungry? Vendors roaming throughout Animal Kingdom offer soft pretzels, popcorn, and ice cream bars imprinted with Simba's paw, among other treats.

powered by the amusing antics of resident students, who wait tables between classes and banter about who left dirty laundry in their dorm lofts. Cost is $13.95 for adults; $7.95 for kids ages 3 through 11. Priority seating suggested for breakfast. Inexpensive. B, L, D, S.

Tamu Tamu Refreshments: Got a hankering for something cool and creamy? Stop by this snack spot in Africa's Harambe (across from Tusker House). Here you can indulge a sweet tooth with soft-serve frozen yogurt and ice cream cones, floats, and sundaes. There's a small outdoor seating nook next door. Inexpensive. S.

Tusker House: Harambe village sets the stage for an exceptional dining adventure at this top-notch fast-food restaurant, themed as

DID YOU KNOW...

There are no plastic cup lids, coffee stirrers, or straws used in Animal Kingdom, since they could be harmful to the animals.

a safari orientation center. Seating inside is quite civilized, with cherry-wood-colored tables and carved chair backs; there's also outdoor seating under the thatched roof. The far-reaching menu—which happens to be one of the best in the park—features rotisserie chicken cooked in a 16-foot "wall of flames." Other highlights include the grilled chicken salad served in a bread bowl, roast vegetable sandwiches served with tabbouleh, and grilled chicken with portobello mushrooms. Fried chicken, spit-roasted prime rib, and side dishes such as fresh vegetables and garlic-mashed potatoes round out the creative options. Inexpensive. L, D, S.

Animal Kingdom Mealtime Tips

- Restaurantosaurus and Rainforest Cafe are the only restaurants to offer full breakfasts; a handful of stands, including Dino Diner, supply light options.
- The only restaurant that offers priority seating for all meals is Rainforest Cafe. To arrange for priority seating in advance, available 30 days ahead for breakfast and 7 days prior for other meals, call WDW-DINE (939-3463). Refer to page 247 for details. To obtain same-day seating, go straight to the restaurant. Without priority seating, expect to wait a bit, since this is the only table-service restaurant in the park.
- The many seating pavilions along Discovery River near Flame Tree Barbecue provide waterside dining that's nicely removed from the hubbub of Safari Village; it may be relatively calm here even during prime mealtimes.
- A great place to meet Donald, Mickey, Minnie, and Goofy is at Restaurantosaurus during the daily character breakfast. Don't forget to make priority seating arrangements.

In Downtown Disney

The vast region known as Downtown Disney encompasses the Marketplace, Pleasure Island, and the West Side. While an admission fee applies after 7 P.M. for Pleasure Island club-goers, there is no charge simply to dine at any of Pleasure Island's full-service restaurants. (There is never a fee to roam the West Side or Marketplace.) On average, Downtown Disney restaurants operate from 11 A.M. to midnight; most of the snack spots are open from 11 A.M. to 2 A.M. For up-to-the-minute details on hours call 824-4321. It's worth noting that while the restaurants really hop at dinnertime, none are terribly crowded at lunch, with the exception of weekends.

Bongos Cuban Cafe (West Side): This sizzling creation of Gloria Estefan and her husband spices up the Downtown Disney dining repertoire with a menu driven by Cuban and Latin American flavors. Its slate of traditional and nouvelle Cuban dishes, such as black bean soup, steak topped with onions, and flan, tantalize taste buds. Indoors, the elaborate mosaic mural and palm-leaf railings set the scene; the balcony for outdoor seating wraps around a three-story pineapple. A take-out window provides snacks on the go. Priority seating not available. Moderate to expensive. L, D, S.

Cap'n Jack's Oyster Bar (Marketplace): This pier house juts right out over Lake Buena Vista, providing water views. The appetizer menu is so full of good things—peel-and-eat shrimp, garlic oysters, and clam chowder—that it's as good for a light lunch or dinner as it is for a snack. Entrées extend to crab cakes, lobster, mahimahi, and "land lubber" specials. There is a tempting variety of wines, microbrew beers, and other cocktails—and the house's special frozen margaritas are as tasty as they are beautiful. Cap'n Jack's is a terrific place to be, especially late afternoon, as the sun streams through the narrow-slatted blinds and glints on the polished tables and the copper above the bar. Moderate. L, D, S.

D-Zertz (Pleasure Island): Pastries, chocolates, candy, frozen yogurt, and other such confections are the desserts available here. Coffee and cappuccino are also served, making it a pleasant spot for a quick snack. Inexpensive. S.

Forty Thirst Street (West Side): For a refreshing treat, this place is a fine choice. Pastries, smoothies, frozen yogurt, coffee coolers, and other sweet solutions are the bill of fare. There's also a wide selection of coffee and cappuccino. Inexpensive. S.

Fulton's Crab House (Between Pleasure Island and Marketplace; 934-2628): This traditional seafood house, operated by Levy Restaurants, occupies the three-deck riverboat formerly known as the *Empress Lilly*. Permanently docked on the western edge of Lake Buena Vista, it is a tribute to Robert Fulton, who invented the steamboat. The place is so serious about seafood that it has hooked up with fishermen worldwide to ensure that the truckloads of fish and shellfish arriving daily at Fulton's back door are at their freshest.

The menu changes each day to reflect new arrivals, but is always brimming with several types of crabs, oysters, and fish, plus lobster, steaks, grilled chicken, grilled vegetables, and combination platters. Signature dishes include cioppino, a savory San Francisco–style seafood stew with a tomato broth base. Accompaniments extend to corn-whipped potatoes and grilled asparagus. Desserts, coffee, and specialty drinks are also served.

Fulton's handsome polished-wood interior is awash in nautical knickknacks and nostalgia. Seating on the deck is sometimes available. The adjoining Stone Crab lounge has a mouthwatering raw bar—excellent for a snack and the site of a reasonably priced lunch. A grand character breakfast with Captain Mickey and friends is held twice daily (seatings are at 8:30 A.M. and

10 A.M.). The meal features scrambled eggs, chicken-apple sausage, hash browns, apple pastry, fruit, and mini muffins. Priority seating suggested for breakfast and dinner. Expensive. B, L, D, S.

Ghirardelli Soda Fountain and Chocolate Shop (Marketplace): San Francisco's famous sweetmaker finally comes east with a soda fountain extraordinaire. Stop in for a chocolaty treat, root beer float, or refreshing malt. Antique chocolate-making equipment demonstrates how the famous Ghirardelli chocolate got its start. There's no better place to please a sweet tooth. Inexpensive. S.

Gourmet Pantry (Marketplace): Though it's technically a shop, this food-oriented establishment is positively brimming with sweet and savory possibilities. Among the delectables standing by for snackers and impromptu picnickers are specialty salads and sandwiches, tasty heros sold by the inch, fresh-baked cookies and desserts, Godiva chocolates, nuts, beer, wine, spirits, and gourmet coffees. Seating is available right outside and also along the waterfront on Lake Buena Vista. Inexpensive. B, L, D, S.

House of Blues (West Side): The nightclub that Blues Brother Dan Aykroyd helped launch doubles as a Mississippi Delta–inspired dining spot. House of Blues gives Downtown Disney a culinary boost from the Bayou—namely home-style Cajun and Creole cooking. Finally, Walt Disney World has a haven for diners desperately seeking to have their fill of such savory things as jambalaya, étouffée, and home-made bread pudding. A gospel brunch is presented on Sundays. Priority seating not available. Moderate. L, D, S.

McDonald's (Marketplace): The Golden Arches and all of its Mc-specialties (plus pizza) are on hand until the wee hours in this installation of the familiar fast-food establishment, located on the western edge of the Marketplace. Inexpensive. B, L, D, S.

Missing Link Sausage Co. (Pleasure Island): Hot dogs, bratwurst, kielbasa, and sausages (including a chicken-apple variety, and both mild and hot Italian links) dominate the menu of this snack spot across from 8TRAX. Cheese steaks are also available. Inexpensive. L, D, S.

The lines for Planet Hollywood are usually shortest between 1 P.M. and 5 P.M.

Planet Hollywood (West Side): This branch of the international restaurant chain is a standout for its spherical silhouette. Co-owned by Arnold Schwarzenegger, Sylvester Stallone, Bruce Willis, and Demi Moore, this globe is built on three levels. Classic movie and television memorabilia abound.

The creative, wide-ranging menu features first-rate salads, sandwiches, pasta dishes, burgers, appetizer pizzas, fajitas, and dessert specialties. Be sure to consider sampling the blackened shrimp, Far East chicken salad, vegetable burger, or pasta

primavera. Cap off the meal with a piece of butter rum cake or a generous helping of Arnold Schwarzenegger's mother's apple strudel. Priority seating not available. Smoking is permitted. Moderate. L, D, S.

Portobello Yacht Club (Pleasure Island; 934-8888): The elegant Bermuda-style house combines high gables and beamed ceilings, bright Mediterranean colors and earthy tones. This was the first dining spot opened by the Levy Restaurants of Chicago, and is one of our favorites on WDW property. The establishment is divided into several informal dining rooms, each of which displays a collection of maritime memorabilia.

But food is definitely the highlight of the Portobello Yacht Club experience. The bustling open kitchen turns out grilled meat and fish and absolutely delicious small gourmet pizzas baked in the wood-burning oven. Try the *quattro formaggi*, a four-cheese pie that's a true taste treat and a

great appetizer or snack. Pasta offerings include *spaghettini alla Portobello* (pasta with shrimp, scallops, clams, mussels, crab legs, tomatoes, garlic, olive oil, wine, and herbs) and *penne all'arrabiata* (long pasta tubes with plum tomatoes, mushrooms, pancetta, garlic, onions, and fresh herbs). Be sure to save room for desserts such as *crema brucciata*, white chocolate custard with a caramelized sugar glaze; or *cioccolato paradiso*, a layer cake with chocolate ganache frosting, chocolate toffee crunch filling, and warm caramel sauce. Portobello also offers a selection of specialty coffees and an impressive wine list. Priority seating suggested. Expensive. L, D, S.

Rainforest Cafe (Downtown Disney Marketplace): There's no mistaking the environmental orientation of this Amazon-emulating eatery near Cap'n Jack's Oyster Bar. The incredible dining environs transport guests to a makeshift rain forest, complete with banyan trees, tropical fish, gushing waterfalls, and a friendly population of hand-raised parrots. A talking tree offers a constant stream of ecological insights, and animal experts are on hand to field questions. Sophisticated special effects envelop guests in tropical storms, complete with lightning and thunder. Menu items include Planet Earth Pasta, Island Hopper Chicken, and the Plant Sandwich (portobello mushrooms, zucchini, roasted red peppers, and fresh spinach). A merchandise shop stocks logo clothing. Priority seating not available. Moderate to expensive. L, D, S.

Wildhorse Saloon (Pleasure Island): The restaurant in this new club serves up good old-fashioned country cooking. There's smoked pulled pork sandwiches, chicken fried steak, fried catfish, barbecued baby-back ribs, and, of course, grits to accompany the live country bands and line dance lessons. There may be an entertainment charge in the evening. Priority seating not available. Moderate. L, D, S.

Wolfgang Puck Cafe (West Side): Wolfgang Puck's choice of Walt Disney World for his Florida debut is sure to spur a surge in cravings for his trademark California cuisine. Among his specialties are gourmet pizzas, Thai chicken *satay*, pastas with fresh vegetables, Chinois Chicken Salad, and rotisserie chicken. The menu is equal parts sophisticated and straightforward—and ever so fresh. There's also an attractive sushi bar. Colorful mosaics decorate his resaurants. Priority seating not available. Moderate to expensive. L, D, S.

Wolfgang Puck Cafe—The Dining Room (West Side): The formal upstairs area in the cafe is devoted to the more elaborate of Wolfgang Puck's cuisine. Consider baby vegetable risotto and grilled chicken with squash ravioli in a sage brown butter sauce. Priority seating suggested. Expensive. D.

Wolfgang Puck Express (Marketplace and West Side): Renowned chef Wolfgang Puck turns his talents to fast service and signature treats, including gourmet wood-fired pizzas, rotisserie chicken, seasonal soups, focaccia sandwiches, and fresh salads—including his famous Chinois Chicken Salad. Inexpensive. L, D, S.

Crossroads of Lake Buena Vista

WDW visitors can get everything from soup to McNuggets at the Crossroads of Lake Buena Vista shopping center, near the resorts on Hotel Plaza Boulevard. Choices include Pebbles (the best bet for adults), Perkins (popular with families), T.G.I. Friday's, Red Lobster, McDonald's, Taco Bell, Jungle Jim's, Pacino's, Chevy's Mexican Restaurant, and Pizzeria Uno.

In the WDW Resorts

Among the more pleasant surprises at Walt Disney World is the delightful theming of the Disney hotels. Each resort sports a fanciful setting quite foreign to Central Florida, reminiscent of such places as the Pacific Northwest; the more regional-minded offer a tasty sampling of the native cuisine to complete the picture. Whereas the deluxe properties provide a variety of dining options, including at least one full-service restaurant, moderate resorts feature a sprawling food court plus an informal dining room, and the value-oriented All-Star resorts keep guests' appetites in check with huge food courts.

Suffice it to say that the possibilities range from hearty dinners served family-style on lazy susans to innovative cuisine you might not expect from Disney, presented in settings worthy of special occasions. Priority seating is an important part of the resorts' full-service dining circuit (for complete details turn to page 247). Character meals are an option for breakfast, Sunday brunch, and dinner (for specifics see page 246).

All-Star Resorts

Each of these resorts features a themed central food court. The **End Zone** food court in Stadium Hall at the All-Star Sports resort, the **Intermission** food court in Melody Hall at the All-Star Music resort, and the **World Premiere** food court in Cinema Hall at the All-Star Movies resort have similar food stands. The selections include pasta, pizza, chicken, ribs, burgers, hot dogs, sandwiches, salads, frozen yogurt, and a wide variety of baked goods. Inexpensive. B, L, D, S.

BoardWalk

Big River Grille & Brewing Works: Guests observe (and later sample) as the brewmaster creates three flagship ales and two seasonal brews at this working brewpub. The menu features a selection of sandwiches and salads, plus creative variations on pub favorites, such as veal meatloaf with Tilt Pale Ale sauce and lobster pot pie. Moderate. L, D, S.

BoardWalk Bakery: The aromas wafting from Spoodles' next-door neighbor on the boardwalk reveal the fresh-baked goods therein. Display windows allow guests to watch bakers at work. Inexpensive. B, S.

ESPN Club: A sports bar–family restaurant one-two punch, ESPN Club surrounds guests with no fewer than 80 TV monitors, so no one misses a play. The fare includes burgers, sandwiches, and a variety of salads and entrées. Moderate. L, D, S.

Flying Fish Cafe: This upbeat eatery delivers creative seasonal menus with an emphasis on seafood and healthy options. As an example of the entrées created in the open "on-stage" kitchen, consider the potato-wrapped yellowtail snapper. Steaks are also served. Save room for the chocolate lava cake. Priority seating is suggested. Seating is available at the chef's counter. Expensive. D.

Seashore Sweets': Located next to the Flying Fish Cafe, this old-fashioned spot sates sweet tooths with candies, saltwater taffy, and ice cream and frozen yogurt. Specialty coffees are also offered. Inexpensive. S.

Spoodles: This family-oriented restaurant with butcher-block tables and Mediterranean tastes is on the boardwalk between Seashore Sweets' and the BoardWalk Bakery. The lunch and dinner menus highlight specialties from Greece, Spain, Northern Africa, and Italy, and

encourage diners to share dishes and try new foods. Offerings range from pizzas baked in wood-burning ovens to such creations as yogurt-marinated chicken kebabs served with corn risotto. The breakfast buffet features eggs, meats, fish, cereal, and french toast. A take-out window allows passersby to buy pizza by the slice. Priority seating suggested. Moderate to expensive. B, L, D.

Caribbean Beach

Captain's Tavern: Prime rib, chicken, and pork loin are on the menu at this cozy 200-seat restaurant located within Old Port Royale. Tropical drinks, beer, wine, and cocktails are also served. Priority seating suggested. Moderate. D, S.

Old Port Royale: The food court in Old Port Royale features a large dining area and the following fast-food eateries. *Bridgetown Broiler* offers spit-roasted chicken and home-style meals. *Cinnamon Bay Bakery* serves croissants, freshly baked rolls, pastries, ice cream, and other high-calorie treats.

Italian specialties are the order at the *Kingston Pasta Shop*. Soups, salads, and hot and cold sandwiches make up the selections at *Montego's Deli*. Burgers and grilled chicken sandwiches are among the offerings at *Port Royale Hamburger Shop*. And pizza is available by the slice or the pie at *Royale Pizza Shop*. Inexpensive. B, L, D, S.

Contemporary

California Grill: Perched on the hotel's 15th floor, with terrific views of sunsets and Magic Kingdom fireworks, this acclaimed restaurant offers the best in West Coast cuisine in a stylish, relaxing atmosphere. (It has been named "restaurant of choice" by *Orlando Magazine*.) The ever-changing menu is defined by sophisticated use of fresh produce. Wood-fired California pizzas, alderwood-smoked salmon, sushi, spit-roasted chicken, and jumbo soufflés are made to order in an open kitchen. Grilled pork tenderloin with polenta and balsamic-vinegar smothered cremini mushrooms suggest the chef's culinary prowess. There's even a vegetarian zone on the menu. The excellent wine list is updated daily. Priority seating suggested (book *early*). Expensive. D.

Chef Mickey's: As Chef Mickey and pals cook up a buffet-style feast, a glass window affords views of the passing monorail. Colorful life-size illustrations of Disney characters decorate the room. The changing menu takes advantage of seasonal offerings; a sundae bar provides a sweet finish. Priority seating suggested. Moderate to expensive. B, D.

Concourse Steakhouse: This spot offers omelettes, pancakes, and fresh fruit for breakfast. At lunch there are salads, soups, burgers, pizzas, and sandwiches. Dinner adds steaks, seafood, and oak-roasted prime rib to the menu. The wine list is updated daily. Priority seating suggested. Moderate to expensive. B, L, D.

Food and Fun Center: On the first floor adjacent to the arcade, this casual spot serves light fare 24 hours a day. Inexpensive. B, L, D, S.

Coronado Springs

Maya Grill: The only full-service restaurant at this resort, it features Latin American dishes. Signature items include grilled chicken breast with black beans and Mayan salsa, pumpkin-seed-encrusted snapper filet, and broiled beef tenderloin with *chimichurri* sauce. Many items are cooked over an open-pit wood-fired grill. Maya Grill is located next to the Pepper Market food court. Priority seating suggested. Expensive. B, D.

Pepper Market: This food court, modeled after an open-air market, has a large seating area and lots of stands where vendors sell pizza, sandwiches, salads, burgers, stir fry, Mexican specialties, baked goods, margaritas, and more. Inexpensive to moderate. B, L, D, S.

Disney's Old Key West

Good's Food to Go: Hamburgers, cheeseburgers, grilled chicken sandwiches, salads, ice cream, and frozen yogurt are among the offerings. Inexpensive. L, D, S.

Olivia's Cafe: An assortment of Key West favorites, including Key lime pie and conch fritters, are featured alongside contemporary southern fare. The menu changes seasonally. A Winnie the Pooh character breakfast is held Sunday, Monday, and Wednesday. Priority seating suggested. Moderate. B, L, D.

Dixie Landings

Boatwright's Dining Hall: Be sure to notice the boat that's being built in this table-service eatery. The specialties of the house include Cajun dishes as well as American home-style favorites. Priority seating suggested. Moderate. B, D.

Colonel's Cotton Mill: This high-ceilinged food court styled in the image of a working cotton mill offers half a dozen food counters and a sprawling seating area. Collectively, the stands offer pizza; pasta; calzones; fried, grilled, and spit-roasted chicken; burgers; barbecued ribs; salads; sandwiches; and fresh baked goods. There's also an all-you-can-eat breakfast deal. For guests on the go, the food court's deli doubles as a convenience store, stocking sandwiches, beer, wine, snack items, and prepared salads. Inexpensive. B, L, D, S.

Fort Wilderness

Most people cook their own meals here; ample supplies are available at both the Meadow Trading Post and the Settlement Trading Post (open from 8 A.M. to 10 P.M. in winter, to 11 P.M. in summer).

Trail's End Buffet: This informal log-walled restaurant offers an inexpensive, all-you-can-eat breakfast, including grits, biscuits, gravy, and a "breakfast pizza" that vaguely resembles an omelette. Hearty lunches and dinners feature barbecued chicken, fish, chicken pot pie, and spare ribs. There are sandwiches and a taco bar at lunch. Pizza is served every night from 9:30 P.M. until 11 P.M. (until midnight on weekends). Beer and wine are served by the glass or by the pitcher. Inexpensive to moderate. B, L, D, S.

Grand Floridian

Cítricos: The newest addition to the Grand Floridian's impressive restaurant lineup specializes in market-fresh Floridian-Mediterranean cooking. The fare varies seasonally but may include grilled tiger shrimp with sweet potato puree, fig compote, and ten-spice sauce; or braised veal shank with orzo pasta and a soy sauce glaze, presented with stylish simplicity. The menu suggests a wine from the extensive international list for each appetizer, entrée, and dessert; for $20 the waiter will bring one for each of three courses. The stunning view of the Seven Seas Lagoon is a year-round staple. A private dining room is available for up to 14 people. Priority seating suggested. Expensive. D.

Gasparilla Grill & Games: Grilled chicken, hamburgers, pizza, hot dogs, and soft-serve ice cream are the mainstays at this 24-hour take-out, self-service restaurant near the pool. Continental breakfast is also available. Inexpensive. B, L, D, S.

Grand Floridian Cafe: Southern cooking is the specialty at this picturesque spot. Although the menu varies, selections may include fried chicken and Atlantic swordfish. There are also salads and an assortment of more traditional entrées. Priority seating available. Moderate to expensive. B, L, D.

Narcoossee's: The partially open kitchen is the focal point at this casual, airy octagonal dining spot on the shores of the Grand Floridian beach. Specialties of the house, which vary seasonally, may include turkey-portobello meat loaf with red-skin mashed potatoes and porcini cream sauce, or seared tuna with chilled vegetable couscous. Staples include charbroiled meats, Florida seafood, and vegetarian options. Priority seating suggested. Expensive. L, D.

1900 Park Fare: The all-American menu takes a backseat to the decor in this buffet restaurant. Big Bertha, a band organ built in Paris nearly a century ago, sits 15 feet above the floor in a proscenium. The instrument simultaneously plays pipes, drums, bells, cymbals, and xylophone. Mary Poppins, Alice in Wonderland, and other characters mingle with guests during breakfast. The dinner buffet features seafood, salads, vegetables, breads, and prime rib. Mickey and Minnie entertain at dinner. The offerings change weekly. Priority seating suggested. Expensive. B, D.

Victoria & Albert's: The premier restaurant of not only the Grand Floridian, but probably the entire Walt Disney World complex. The intimate dining room seats only 60, and elegant touches include Royal Doulton china, Sambonet silver, and Schott-Zweisel crystal. The menu is customized daily. Each night there are fish, fowl, red meat, veal, and lamb selections, which depend on the best ingredients in the market and are described in detail by your waiter. The chef may even make a personal appearance to accommodate special requests from patrons, or guests may choose to dine at the chef's table in the kitchen (for an additional charge). There are also choices of two soups, two salads, and desserts, including specialty soufflés of fresh berries, chocolate, or Grand Marnier. There is an extensive wine list, and wine pairings are available with each course.

Once guests have made their selections, they are presented a personalized souvenir menu. At the completion of the meal, women receive a long-stemmed rose. Jackets are required. One oddity of note: Every host and hostess at the restaurant is named Victoria or Albert. Priority seating necessary. Very expensive. D.

Polynesian

Captain Cook's Snack Company: A good spot for continental breakfast, hamburgers, hot dogs, fruit salad, and snacks; cans of beer are also available. Open 24 hours. Inexpensive. B, L, D, S.

Kona Cafe: Located on the second floor of the Great Ceremonial House, just around the corner from 'Ohana, this casual restaurant (formerly named the Coral Isle Cafe) was recently refurbished. There's an enhanced South Seas decor and menu, as well as a new coffee bar. While it serves the usual assortment of traditional breakfast items, lunch and dinner menus feature Asian-influenced entrées. A variety of tempting desserts are among the offerings. All things considered, it's a good choice when you want a no-fuss meal. Priority seating available. Moderate. B, L, D, S.

'Ohana: On the second floor of the Great Ceremonial House, this restaurant features a 16-foot-long open fire pit. Dinner choices in the all-you-can-eat family-style feast include shrimp, poultry, pork, and beef, all roasted on skewers up to three feet long. Meats are marinated in original combinations of soy, ginger, lemongrass, or garlic, and are served family-style with an assortment of fresh vegetables, salads, and homemade bread. The meal ends with fresh pineapple with caramel dipping sauce, or additional dessert offerings (for an extra charge) such as passion fruit crème brûlée. The room itself is large and open and offers fine views across the Seven Seas Lagoon all the way to Cinderella Castle. Minnie's Menehune character breakfast is held daily. Polynesian singers entertain at dinner, while periodic hula hoop and coconut rolling contests amuse children. Priority seating suggested. Expensive. B, D.

Port Orleans

Bonfamille's Cafe: The name of this full-service restaurant derives from the Disney movie *The Aristocats*. Steaks, seafood, and Creole cooking highlight the menu. Breakfast is also served. Priority seating suggested. Moderate. B, D.

Sassagoula Floatworks & Food Factory: The stands at this festive food court feature pizza, pasta, gumbo, burgers, sandwiches, soups, salads, spit-roasted chicken, barbecued ribs, ice cream, and a full selection of fresh bakery products, including beignets. Inexpensive. B, L, D, S.

Swan & Dolphin

Cabana Bar & Grill: Burgers, grilled chicken sandwiches, fresh fruit, and yogurt are offered at this full-service poolside eatery. Inexpensive. L, S.

Coral Cafe: Buffets are offered for breakfast and dinner in this bright and casual restaurant. An à la carte menu is also available, offering turkey burgers, chicken, club sandwiches, pasta, and cheese steaks. Located at the Dolphin. Moderate. B, L, D, S.

Dolphin Fountain: Homemade ice cream is the highlight here. Flavors include dark chocolate, cappuccino, and mint chocolate chip. Oreo and Heath Bar mixes are available in waffle cones, cups, or as part of super sundaes. Burgers, shakes, and malts are also available. The old-time 1950s atmosphere is enhanced by an energetic staff that breaks into song and dance several times a day. Inexpensive to moderate. L, D, S.

Garden Grove Cafe (934-1609): Situated in a five-story greenhouse, this Swan dining spot offers a full breakfast menu, and fresh fish and shellfish at lunch. At dinner, the restaurant is transformed into Gulliver's Grill, where you can order Blushklooshen (red snapper) and drink Caff Dupooshpoosh (double espresso) from oversize cups. Desserts are baked fresh daily in an open pastry kitchen. As you approach the restaurant, take a look through the glass windows to see the chefs at work. Character breakfasts and dinners are held here on certain days. Reservations suggested for dinner. Expensive. B, L, D, S.

Harry's Safari Bar & Grille (934-4889): Grilled steaks, seafood, and chicken seasoned with herbs bought by "Harry" during his world travels mark the adventurous menu. On Sunday there is a character brunch. Reservations suggested for dinner, necessary for brunch. Located at the Dolphin resort. Expensive. D, Sunday brunch.

Juan & Only's (934-4889): This festive Dolphin restaurant features authentic Mexican food. Specialties include fresh *pico de gallo* served with blue corn and spicy red chips; grilled beef, chicken, shrimp, and meatless fajitas from the fajita bar; chimichangas; burritos; taco salads; and other Mexican fare. Reservations suggested. Moderate to expensive. D.

Par for the Course

The pleasant **Sand Trap Bar & Grill** in the Bonnet Creek Golf Club is a convenient dining option for golfers playing the adjacent Eagle Pines and Osprey Ridge courses. It's also close to the Magic Kingdom resorts. In addition to a variety of appetizers, burgers, Reuben sandwiches, barbecued pork, and grilled chicken sandwiches are served. There is a full bar; ice cream and milk shakes are also available. Moderate. L, D, S.

Palio (934-1609): This Italian bistro gets high marks for its bruschetta, focaccia, pasta, and pizza. Other specialties include veal and fish dishes. A strolling musician adds to the ambience. Reservations suggested. Located at the Swan. Expensive. D.

Splash Grill: Burgers and other grilled fare join ice cream and frozen yogurt on the menu at this Swan poolside spot. Beer and frozen drinks are served. Prepackaged snacks are also on hand. Inexpensive. B, L, S.

Tubbi's: Checkerboard decor and a jukebox raise this cafeteria above the norm. The food, including meatball subs and pizza, is fresh, and the lines are seldom long. The adjoining convenience store (open 24 hours) at the Dolphin resort stocks snacks, sundries, and lots of baby items. Inexpensive. B, L, D, S.

Wilderness Lodge

Artist Point: Decorated with artwork representing the painters who first chronicled the Northwest landscape, this fine dining spot offers a creative menu that incorporates wild game as well as more traditional items such as steaks, salmon, and other Pacific seafood. The solid wine list spotlights wines from the Pacific Northwest. A character

breakfast hosted by Winnie the Pooh and friends is served every morning. Priority seating suggested. Expensive. B, D.

Roaring Fork Snacks: Salads, burgers, sandwiches, yogurt, and snacks are available at this simple nook adjacent to the hotel's arcade. Inexpensive. B, L, D, S.

Whispering Canyon Cafe: This traditional family-style restaurant is open for all-day dining. Hearty all-you-can-eat fare includes wood-smoked barbecued meats with a variety of sides and salads, plus homemade desserts (for an additional charge). Assorted sandwiches and salads are available during lunch. Priority seating suggested. Moderate. B, L, D.

The Villas at the Disney Institute

Reflections Gourmet Coffee & Pastries: Located next to Willow Lake, this is a good spot for coffee and pastries. Assorted sandwiches and salads are available during lunch. Inexpensive. B, L.

Seasons Dining Room: Even the setup of this restaurant is seasonally driven. Four dining rooms are decorated to reflect the distinct seasons. The menu takes on a Floridian twist, featuring the freshest items the state has to offer, changing seasonally, of course. The lunch menu has many lighter salads, sandwiches, seafood, and pasta—perhaps yucca-wrapped chicken breast, cornflake-crusted catfish, and vegetable lasagne. Dinner offerings might include orangewood smoked beef tenderloin, mustard-crusted rack of lamb, citrus cilantro pasta in cream, roasted pork tenderloin, pan-fried striped bass, and portobello mushroom and vegetable strudel. Priority seating suggested. Expensive. B, L, D.

Yacht & Beach Club

Beaches & Cream Soda Shop: This restaurant straddles the Yacht and Beach Club. Patterned after a turn-of-the-century ice cream parlor, it features oversize sundaes, cones, floats, shakes, and sodas, as well as the Fenway Park Burger—which can be ordered as a single, double, triple, or home run. Breakfast items are available as well. Inexpensive to moderate. B, L, D, S.

Cape May Cafe: An all-you-can-eat New England clambake is held each evening at the Beach Club. A cooking pit used for steaming is in full view of diners, and menu items include clams, mussels, chicken, shrimp, red-skin potatoes, and chowder. Lobster is available for an extra charge. There is a character breakfast buffet each morning. Priority seating suggested. Moderate to expensive. B, D.

Hurricane Hanna's Grill: Located in the Stormalong Bay area. Hot dogs, burgers, sandwiches, french fries, and ice cream are on the menu. There is also a full bar. Inexpensive. L, S.

Yacht Club Galley: Vivid ceramic-tile tabletops help emphasize the yachting theme here at the Yacht Club. Breakfast features a buffet and a full menu; lunch and dinner are à la carte only. Priority seating suggested. Moderate. B, L, D.

Yachtsman Steakhouse: As its name implies, beef is the specialty of the house. Guests can see the butcher choosing cuts of meat in the glassed-in shop, and watch meals being prepared in the display kitchen. Fresh seafood and chicken are available. Located at the Yacht Club. Priority seating suggested. Expensive. D.

In the Resorts on Hotel Plaza Boulevard

Dining options in the resorts that line Hotel Plaza Boulevard include casual cafes, themed restaurants, and upscale dining rooms. The larger properties offer more choices, of course, but even the smaller hotels each have a family-style eatery on the premises. If you go to a movie or dance way past midnight at Downtown Disney, you can still count on a late-night bite at the Buena Vista Palace or the Grosvenor.

BUENA VISTA PALACE: Arthur's 27 has an international menu and boasts a dramatic view over Downtown Disney. Very expensive. D. The lively **Outback** restaurant (not part of the similarly named chain), with Australia-inspired decor and a multilevel waterfall, serves dinner with an accent on steaks and fish. Moderate. D. The gardenlike **Watercress Cafe** offers full meals and snacks, as well as a Sunday character breakfast. Moderate to expensive. B, L, D, S. The adjoining **Watercress Pastry Shop** serves baked goods, sandwiches, and fruit, and is open 24 hours a day. Inexpensive. B, L, D, S. **Recreation Island Pool Snack Bar** serves specialty sandwiches, salads, and burgers, plus frozen drinks and cocktails. Inexpensive to moderate. B, L, S. **Courtyard Mini-Market** has outdoor seating and window service for spa smoothies and prepackaged deli sandwiches and subs. Inexpensive. B, L, D, S.

COURTYARD BY MARRIOTT: Courtyard Cafe & Grille offers a salad bar, as well as an eclectic menu ranging from salads and sandwiches to seafood. There is a breakfast buffet, but guests may also order from an à la carte menu. Moderate. B, L, D. **Village Deli** features muffins, sandwiches, Pizza Hut pizza, and TCBY yogurt. Inexpensive. B, L, D, S. The **2 Go** breakfast bar is adjacent to an open seating area in the atrium lobby. Inexpensive. B.

DOUBLETREE GUEST SUITES: Streamers offers classic American dishes as well as shrimp tortellini and filet mignon. The breakfast buffet is outstanding. Moderate. B, L, D, S. **Streamers Market** provides snack items and groceries. Inexpensive. S.

GROSVENOR: Casual **Baskervilles** restaurant has a Sherlock Holmes theme, complete with two Mystery Shows every Saturday night. The menu features steaks, seafood, soups, salads, sandwiches, and burgers. A Wednesday character dinner complements the hotel's character breakfasts, held on Tuesday, Thursday, and Saturday. Moderate. B, L (weekdays only), D. **Crumpet's Cafe**, open 24 hours, serves continental breakfast and lighter fare. Inexpensive. B, L, S.

HILTON: Festive **Finn's Grill** specializes in fresh seafood, steaks, and pasta served in an old Key West atmosphere. Moderate to expensive. D. At classy **Benihana** Japanese steak house, chefs put on a tableside show; there's also a sushi bar. Moderate. D. **Chatham House** serves a hearty breakfast (characters put in appearances on Sunday); soups, salads, sandwiches, pizza, pasta, and fish and meat dishes are options for lunch or dinner. Inexpensive to moderate. B, L, D. **The Terrace** offers outdoor seating and items from the Chatham House menu. Inexpensive to moderate. B, L. The **Old-Fashioned Soda Shoppe** features snacks and fast food, including ice cream and pizza. Inexpensive. L, D, S. **John T's Sports Bar** serves light fare and cocktails. Inexpensive to moderate. L, S. **Rum Largo Poolside Bar & Cafe** supplies salads, sandwiches, and burgers alfresco. Inexpensive. L, D, S. **Mainstreet Market** is a gourmet deli and country store rolled into one. Inexpensive. B, L, D, S.

ROYAL PLAZA: Verandah Cafe serves full-service, buffet, and family-style meals. Inexpensive to moderate. B, L, D, S. The hotel deli has yogurt, espresso, and take-out items. Inexpensive. B, L, S.

TRAVELODGE: Traders offers buffet and à la carte breakfast as well as à la carte dinner featuring fresh seafood and steaks. Moderate. B, D. **Parakeet Cafe** provides pizza, salads, sandwiches, and snacks. Inexpensive. B, L, S.

GOOD MEALS, GREAT TIMES

MEAL BY MEAL

When you're looking for something special in the way of a meal, and you're willing to go a bit out of your way to find it, the descriptions below should provide suggestions to sate your appetite. What follows are the highlights of WDW breakfasts, lunches, and dinners. This is a selective list; for complete information see the preceding listings under "Restaurants of WDW."

Breakfast

Most people opt for an early-morning meal at their own hotel. At many of the WDW resorts, it's also possible to order breakfast from room service the night before. But those who decide to venture farther afield will be amazed at the choices available.

In the Magic Kingdom, consider stopping by the Main Street Bake Shop or a fast-food spot—since many serve coffee and pastries in the morning. For a hearty breakfast, try the Crystal Palace or Cinderella's Royal Table. In Epcot, the Sunshine Season Food Fair in The Land offers bagels and delicious pastries. Fountain View Espresso and Bakery next to Innoventions has a great selection of pastries and specialty coffees. At the Disney-MGM Studios, try a home-cooked breakfast at the Hollywood & Vine cafeteria or coffee and a croissant at the Starring Rolls Bakery. If you are looking for breakfast at Animal Kingdom, consider Kusafiri Coffee Shop & Bakery for a quick bite, Rainforest Cafe for a more substantial meal, or Donald's Prehistoric Breakfastosaurus at Restaurantosaurus for an entertaining character meal.

Lunch

Breaking up a day in the theme parks with lunch at a WDW resort can provide the energy needed to keep you going until closing time. Choice lunch spots in the Downtown Disney Marketplace are Wolfgang Puck Express and Cap'n Jack's Oyster Bar. At Pleasure Island, the Portobello Yacht Club's terrific individual pizzas hit the spot; ditto the seafood chowder and raw bar in the Stone Crab lounge at Fulton's Crab House. Burgers, salads, pastas, and desserts are good at Planet Hollywood.

If you can't tear yourself away from the Magic Kingdom to go elsewhere for lunch, there's still no lack of selection. Burgers and fries are for sale at practically every turn, but better yet are the fried fish and chicken served at Columbia Harbour House in Liberty Square, the turkey dinners and salads served at the Liberty Tree Tavern, also in Liberty Square, and the pizza at the Plaza Pavilion in Tomorrowland.

In Epcot, lunch is a prime opportunity to sample the World Showcase table-service restaurants offering ethnic specialties. Meat pies and fish-and-chips may be found at the Rose & Crown Pub and Dining Room. Stir-fried meats and vegetables are the prime fare at the Teppanyaki Dining Rooms. Try not to miss the *queso fundido* at Mexico's San Angel Inn restaurant. Germany's Biergarten has lively entertainment and a hearty buffet throughout the day. The most elaborate cooking is done at Italy's Alfredo's and at France's Les Chefs de France. Among full-service eateries in Future World, the Garden Grill is special for its family-style rotisserie chicken and hickory-smoked steaks.

Notable ethnic fast food is available at Japan's Yakitori House, Norway's Kringla Bakeri og Kafe, and Mexico's Cantina de San Angel. For burgers and other standard fast-food fare, try the Liberty Inn at The American Adventure. The Sunshine Season Food Fair in The Land offers a cornucopia of choices, from baked potatoes, soups, and salads to barbecue and more—and is therefore an ideal place for a family that can't arrive at a consensus.

At the Disney-MGM Studios, consider the famous Cobb salad at the Hollywood Brown Derby; a good home-cooked meal at the 50's Prime Time Cafe; the character buffet at the Soundstage; or huge sandwiches, salads, and pastas at the Sci-Fi Dine-In Theater. The fast-food restaurant of choice is Backlot Express for chili, charbroiled chicken, and burgers. When the lunchtime hunger pangs strike at Animal Kingdom, head straight to Tusker House, the most creative fast-food option.

Dinner

There's a boundless selection, from the humblest snack center to Victoria & Albert's. New restaurants popping up all over the World are continually changing the face of the dining scene, and the best of Walt Disney World's dinners are sure to impress. The fact that the famed L.A. chef Wolfgang Puck opened a restaurant here is testament to the World's upwardly mobile culinary consciousness. Factor this kitchen can-do into the unique only-at-WDW atmosphere, and it's obvious why good choices abound for a night on the World.

WDW resorts are prime territory to find an exceptional meal. At the top of the special occasion list is Victoria & Albert's at the Grand Floridian, for one of the more extravagant meals money can buy. Try the wine pairings with each course for an extra treat. Don't overlook Cítricos, also at the Grand Floridian, for a first-rate meal. 'Ohana at the Polynesian delivers a South Sea feast. Yachtsman Steakhouse at the Yacht Club is good for a hearty meal. Artist Point at the Wilderness Lodge keeps us coming back for more tastes of the Pacific Northwest (and that heavenly berry cobbler). California Grill at the Contemporary is another find, where the panorama of the Magic Kingdom would warrant a visit even if the cuisine (paired with a wide selection of California wines) weren't excellent.

Elsewhere in the World, the Hollywood Brown Derby at the Disney-MGM Studios is the most elegant theme park meal around. Cinderella's Royal Table, inside the castle at the Magic Kingdom, also offers a premier dining experience. At Epcot, head directly to one of the international restaurants in World Showcase. Animal Kingdom's Rainforest Cafe serves up tasty meals in a tropical paradise.

Some of our old-time favorites are at Downtown Disney. Fulton's Crab House is the best bet on-property for fresh seafood that seems to arrive hourly, served in a knockout setting. For a culinary treat, consider the California specialties at Wolfgang Puck Cafe and the more formal dining room upstairs. Portobello Yacht Club is a standby; we could recommend any number of the Italian specialties on the menu (and we've tried quite a few, including all of the desserts).

Of course, some of the aforementioned suggestions require a baby-sitter, since not a kid in the world (especially not *this* World) would sit still through such a meal. On the other hand, there are plenty of great meals to be had with kids in tow. Refer to the box below for our recommendations, many of which are suitable dinner options for kids and adults alike. Note that nearly all of the restaurants listed have been tested by the kids who help create *Birnbaum's Walt Disney World For Kids, By Kids*.

Best Bets for Family Fare

Children are welcome at every Walt Disney World restaurant, but the leisurely pace of service at some places can make kids fidget. Still, there are plenty of choices that are well suited to dining *en famille*. Resort restaurants that are especially good for families include Chef Mickey's at the Contemporary resort and Whispering Canyon Cafe at the Wilderness Lodge. The buffet-style clambake held at Cape May Cafe in the Beach Club resort is a hit with kids, as is any other buffet-style meal where they can serve themselves. The food courts at the Caribbean Beach, Coronado Springs, Port Orleans, Dixie Landings, and the All-Star resorts are other options for finicky eaters.

Most of the restaurants at the Magic Kingdom cater to kids, but Pecos Bill Cafe (for burgers and fries) and Tony's Town Square (for pizza) get particularly high marks. The character meals at the Crystal Palace offer a welcome compromise for kids and parents alike (the meals suit both tastes, and characters keep kids entertained).

At Epcot, Pasta Piazza Ristorante and Liberty Inn are top picks for kids who love fast food. Garden Grill in The Land pavilion provides a family-style character meal that kids and adults appreciate (served all day). Sunshine Season Food Fair, also in The Land, is a huge food court with myriad choices—a good option for family members with differing tastes.

At the Disney-MGM Studios, kids enjoy the Sci-Fi Dine-In Theater and 50's Prime Time Cafe. The character buffet at Soundstage is also a top choice for breakfast or lunch. Other options include a quicker meal at Hollywood & Vine, ABC Commissary, or Backlot Express.

One of the best places to dine out with kids is Planet Hollywood at Pleasure Island. The movie memorabilia hanging from the ceiling and the great food are always a hit. Also try the Rainforest Cafe at either the Downtown Disney Marketplace or Animal Kingdom. Each is a themed restaurant with environmental (and kid) appeal.

Dinner Shows

The fact that Disney is the expert in family entertainment is nowhere more strongly apparent than amid the whooping and hollering troupe of singers and dancers who race toward the stage at Fort Wilderness resort's Pioneer Hall. As guests plow through barbecued ribs, fried chicken, and strawberry shortcake, these enthusiastic performers sing, dance, and joke up a storm. It's all in the course of an evening at the Hoop-Dee-Doo Musical Revue, presented nightly at 5 P.M., 7:15 P.M., and 9:30 P.M. Cost is $38 per adult and $19.50 for children (ages 3 through 11).

Also presented at Fort Wilderness is the All-American Backyard Barbecue. A country band gets guests out on the floor to kick up their heels (the line dance lessons help, too), and Disney characters join in the fun. Dinner consists of plenty of picnic favorites: barbecued ribs and chicken, corn-on-the-cob, and baked beans. The seasonal dinner show costs $37 per adult and $25 for children (including tax and tip).

Mickey's Tropical Luau, presented daily at 4:30 P.M. at the Polynesian resort, is a Polynesian show geared toward the younger set. Disney characters, dressed in traditional costumes, dance alongside the Polynesian performers. A full dinner complete with dessert is served. Cost is $33 for adults and $16 for children.

The Polynesian Luau at the Polynesian resort also has its moments. The show is presented nightly at 6:45 P.M. and 9:30 P.M. The performers' dancing is some of the most authentic this side of Hawaii. Many of the WDW dancers have studied at the well-respected Polynesian Cultural Center in Hawaii. A full Polynesian-style meal, including roasted chicken, spareribs, and a fruity dessert is served. Cost is $38 for adults and $19.50 for children.

While not offering a full dinner show, the Biergarten at Epcot's Germany pavilion entertains diners with a musical trio during lunch and throughout the evening with intermittent shows featuring traditional German musicians, yodelers, and dancers. A hefty buffet is served. Lunch is $10.95 for adults, $5.50 for children; dinner is $15.75 for adults, $6.99 for children.

Plan to arrive at least 15 minutes before showtime, and allow time for transportation and parking. (Note that prices, which with the exception of the Backyard Barbecue do not include tax or gratuity, are subject to change.)

Reservations: Arrangements for dinner shows can be made up to two years in advance by calling WDW-DINE (939-3463). Groups of eight or more should call 939-7707. Make reservations for the Hoop-Dee-Doo Musical Revue well in advance, since tickets for this show are generally harder to come by. *Also, it's very important to note that cancellations for any dinner shows must be made at least 48 hours before showtime to avoid paying full price.*

Dining with Disney Characters

At some sites, food takes second place to Mickey Mouse, Donald Duck, Minnie Mouse, Goofy, and the rest of the Disney gang, who take turns making special appearances at these especially delightful affairs. Options abound, as the characters host meals throughout the day all over the World. Unless otherwise noted, character meals below are offered daily, and priority seating arrangements can generally be made up to 60 days in advance by calling WDW-DINE (939-3463). We strongly suggest making these arrangements prior to your visit, especially during busy seasons. Also, be sure to arrive at least 15 minutes before your seating time. Walk-ins are possible, but highly unlikely for any except the Swan's first-come, first-served character breakfast (held Saturday at the hotel's Garden Grove Cafe). Bottomless buffets and all-you-can-eat family-style dining are the rule, particularly for breakfast, but specific offerings vary from place to place. Finally, as you make note of the following menu of character affairs—organized by meal—keep in mind that the lineup is subject to change.

Character Restaurants: Meals with the Disney characters have become so popular that there are now several restaurants dedicated to providing them all day long. Winnie the Pooh entertains during the buffet-style meals at Crystal Palace in the Magic Kingdom. Epcot has its family-style Garden Grill restaurant, with homey fare and Chip and Dale appearances. In the Disney-MGM Studios, characters from the most recent animated films preside over buffet-style breakfast and lunch at the Soundstage restaurant. At the Contemporary resort, Chef Mickey and friends cook up a buffet-style breakfast and dinner (at Chef Mickey's restaurant, of course). Breakfast costs $13.95 to $14.95 for adults and $7.95 to $8.25 for children 3 through 11. For other meals, cost ranges from $14.95 to $19.95 for adults, and from $7.95 to $9.95 for children.

Breakfast: Fulton's Crab House (between Pleasure Island and the Downtown Disney Marketplace) is the site of the biggest character shindig around, hosted by Captain Mickey and crew. There are two seatings every morning. Guests may also have breakfast with characters at 1900 Park Fare in the Grand Floridian resort (Mary Poppins drops in); at Artist Point in the Wilderness Lodge (Winnie the Pooh and friends host a rustic affair); at Cape May Cafe in the Beach Club resort (Goofy runs the show); at Olivia's Cafe at Old Key West (Pals of Pooh are here on Sunday, Monday, and Wednesday); and at 'Ohana in the Polynesian resort (where Minnie's Menehune breakfast carries the South Seas theme). Character breakfasts are also served in the theme parks. Among the more popular is the Once Upon A Time breakfast at Cinderella's Royal Table in the Magic Kingdom. The newest addition is Donald's Prehistoric Breakfastosaurus at Restaurantosaurus in Animal Kingdom. Prices range from $12.95 to $15.95 for adults, and from $7.95 to $9.95 for children.

Sunday Brunch: Disney favorites host brunch at Harry's Safari Bar & Grille in the Dolphin resort (call 934-4889 in advance for reservations). Prices are $16.95 for adults and $10.50 for children 3 through 11.

Dinners: The Liberty Tree Tavern in the Magic Kingdom hosts a character supper. Character dinners are also held at 1900 Park Fare in the Grand Floridian resort. Gulliver's Grill at Garden Grove in the Swan holds a character dinner each Monday, Thursday, and Friday (on certain nights *The Lion King* characters pay a visit); call 934-1609 to make reservations. Prices are about $19.95 to $21.95 for adults, $9.95 to $12.95 for children 3 through 11; the à la carte meal at the Swan may run higher.

All About Priority Seating

Priority seating has replaced reservations at almost all WDW full-service restaurants. Disney initiated the policy to provide the assurance of a reservation without the delays caused by no-shows and late-comers. Ideally, the system ensures that guests are not left waiting if a table is available. Here's how it works: You call ahead to request a priority seating time; then you arrive at the assigned time and check in, and then receive the next available table that can accommodate your party. The priority seating system works very much like reservations, so you will always be seated before any walk-ins.

We strongly recommend making advance arrangements and arriving about 15 minutes early. Priority seating times can generally be secured up to 60 days ahead by calling WDW-DINE (939-3463). Hours are Monday through Friday from 7 A.M. to 10 P.M.; Saturday, Sunday, and holidays from 7 A.M. to 8 P.M. The number of tables available in advance varies. If you are unable to book a table ahead of time, try to make same-day arrangements (for details about how to do this in the theme parks, see the listings below).

While priority seating is the prevalent policy at WDW restaurants, there are several exceptions in which tables may be booked solely via traditional reservations. Most notably, reservations are necessary for certain dinner shows—the Hoop-Dee-Doo Musical Revue, All-American Backyard Barbecue, Mickey's Tropical Luau, and the Polynesian Luau; they can be made up to two years ahead through WDW-DINE (939-3463). If you can't get a table for an early performance, try for a later one (usually less heavily booked). Also falling outside the priority seating domain are Harry's Safari Bar & Grille and Juan & Only's at the Dolphin resort (934-4889), Palio and Garden Grove Cafe at the Swan resort (934-1609), Fulton's Crab House (934-2628), and Portobello Yacht Club (934-8888).

A concise guide to WDW restaurants that offer priority seating is provided below. For at-a-glance advice about the necessity of priority seating arrangements (or reservations) at specific restaurants, consult the chart on pages 20 and 21 of *Getting Ready to Go*.

Note: Because the dining scene at Walt Disney World is tremendously dynamic and procedures have changed more than a few times over the years, we advise calling WDW-DINE (939-3463) to confirm current policies.

MAGIC KINGDOM: Priority seating is suggested at Tony's Town Square, The Plaza, Crystal Palace, and Liberty Tree Tavern; necessary at Cinderella's Royal Table. For same-day seating, go to the restaurant or City Hall.

EPCOT: Advance priority seating arrangements are strongly recommended for nearly all full-service restaurants at Epcot, particularly for dinner. However, on the day of your visit, it is possible to book lunch or dinner tables via WorldKey Information System screens. Look for the screens at Guest Relations on the east side of the pathway between Future World and World Showcase, and in Germany. Same-day lunch tables can also be booked in person at the chosen restaurant. Never bypass an eatery for which you have a sudden appetite; occasionally, you can walk right in. Note that priority seating is not available for Tempura Kiku.

DISNEY-MGM STUDIOS: Priority seating is suggested for 50's Prime Time Cafe, Hollywood Brown Derby, Mama Melrose's Ristorante Italiano, Sci-Fi Dine-In Theater, and Soundstage. Go to Hollywood Junction or the chosen restaurant for same-day seating.

DOWNTOWN DISNEY: Priority seating is suggested at Wolfgang Puck Cafe—The Dining Room.

WDW RESORTS: Priority seating is suggested for full-service resort restaurants, with a few exceptions (where it's necessary or offered only for dinner); a complete lineup follows. *Beach Club:* Cape May Cafe. *BoardWalk:* Flying Fish Cafe, Spoodles. *Dixie Landings:* Boatwright's Dining Hall. *Caribbean Beach:* Captain's Tavern. *Contemporary:* California Grill, Chef Mickey's, Concourse Steakhouse. *Coronado Springs:* Maya Grill. *Disney Institute:* Seasons Dining Room. *Dixie Landings:* Boatwright's Dining Hall. *Grand Floridian:* Cítricos, Grand Floridian Cafe, Narcoossee's, 1900 Park Fare, Victoria & Albert's. *Old Key West:* Olivia's Cafe. *Polynesian:* Kona Cafe, 'Ohana. *Port Orleans:* Bonfamille's Cafe. *Wilderness Lodge:* Artist Point, Whispering Canyon Cafe. *Yacht Club:* Yacht Club Galley, Yachtsman Steakhouse.

LOUNGES OF WDW

No one ever said the Magic Kingdom's no-liquor policy means that everyone in the World is a teetotaler. Actually, some of WDW's tastiest offerings are liquid (and decidedly alcoholic), and some of its most entertaining places are its bars and lounges.

Hours vary depending on the locale, but generally watering holes at Epcot, Disney-MGM Studios, and Animal Kingdom shut their doors at park closing. Pool bars at the resorts generally keep daytime pool hours. Last call at lounges in the resorts is anywhere from 10 P.M. to midnight. Downtown Disney Marketplace spots stay open until the shops close, usually 11 P.M. The clubs at Pleasure Island and the West Side keep things going until 2 A.M. Note that specialty drinks sans alcohol are available at all establishments.

ALL-STAR MOVIES, ALL-STAR MUSIC, & ALL-STAR SPORTS

Silver Screen Spirits at All-Star Movies, **Singing Spirits** at All-Star Music, and **Team Spirits** at All-Star Sports serve beer, wine, and specialty drinks by the pool.

ANIMAL KINGDOM

African Lounge: Enjoy Safari Amber beer and African music out under the thatched roof.

Rainforest Cafe: The Magic Mushroom bar serves fruit blends and specialty drinks.

BOARDWALK

Atlantic Dance: This dance hall showcases hors d'oeuvres, desserts, a full bar, 25 specialty drinks, and premium cigars.

Big River Grille & Brewing Works: A working brewpub where patrons can order appetizers at the bar and sample the brewmaster's flagship ales and specialty beers.

Belle Vue Room: Snacks and a full bar accompany old-time tunes from antique radios in this lobby cocktail lounge.

ESPN Club: The ultimate sports bar provides live radio and television broadcasts along with a menu of ballpark favorites.

Jellyrolls: Dueling pianos and lively sing-alongs are the draw at this unique club, serving beer and other drinks.

Leaping Horse Libations: The pool bar offers cocktails, tuna sandwiches, fruit salad, and garden salads in a carnival setting.

BONNET CREEK GOLF CLUB

Sand Trap Bar & Grill: Appetizers and sandwiches supplement the array of libations offered at this fully stocked bar.

CARIBBEAN BEACH

Banana Cabana: All types of drinks and fast-food items are served at this poolside bar.

Captain's Tavern: Tropical drinks, beer, wine, and cocktails are served at this restaurant lounge in Old Port Royale. Items from the restaurant are available during dinner hours.

CONTEMPORARY

California Grill Lounge: Prime 15th-story digs eye-level to the Magic Kingdom fireworks. A large selection of California wine (all available by the glass), all manner of other drinks, and items from the restaurant menu are offered in this atmospheric spot adjoining the California Grill.

Outer Rim: This lounge overlooking Bay Lake serves beer, wine, cocktails, appetizers, and desserts.

Sand Bar: A full bar and fast-food items are offered poolside, weather permitting.

CORONADO SPRINGS

Francisco's: Located in the main building, this lounge serves specialty drinks, beer, wine, and light Mexican snacks.

Siesta's: Swimmers can take time out for burgers, sandwiches, tacos, and cocktails at this convenient spot near the pool in the Dig Site area.

DISNEY-MGM STUDIOS

Catwalk Bar: Above the Soundstage restaurant sits this cocktail lounge resembling a movie prop storage area. Appetizers, specialty drinks, beer, and wine are served.

Tune-In Lounge: A sitcom living room setting, with couches, chairs, and TV dinner–tray tables, characterizes this lounge next to the 50's Prime Time Cafe. Waiters in V-neck sweaters play the roles of sitcom "Dads," and old TV sets play scenes from beloved sitcoms. Appetizers, mixed drinks, beer, and wine are served.

DISNEY'S OLD KEY WEST

Gurgling Suitcase: This pocket-size lounge on the Turtle Krawl boardwalk serves an assortment of Key West specialties along with traditional cocktails, beer, and wine.

Turtle Shack: Refreshments at this poolside spot include beer, specialty drinks, and fast-food items.

DIXIE LANDINGS

Cotton Co-Op: Situated in a room designed as a cotton exchange, this lounge features specialty drinks as well as some light hors d'oeuvres. There is entertainment here five nights a week.

Muddy Rivers: The poolside bar serves beer, specialty concoctions, and selected fast-food items.

DOWNTOWN DISNEY

All clubs have bars serving specialty drinks (with and without alcohol), beer, wine, and cocktails. The **Stone Crab** lounge inside **Fulton's Crab House** (between Pleasure Island and Marketplace) and **Bongos Cuban Cafe** (Downtown Disney West Side) are notable for exotic cocktails and outdoor seating. Pleasure Island's **Portobello Yacht Club** also has

a pleasant lounge. The **Rainforest Cafe** is the site of the whimsical Magic Mushroom bar.

Cap'n Jack's Oyster Bar (Downtown Disney Marketplace): Agleam with copper and right on the water, this bar's specialty is its delicious strawberry margaritas. The nibbles of garlic oysters, clam chowder, and shrimp on the appetizer menu are great for a snack, but substantial enough for a meal.

EPCOT

All restaurants, including some of the fast-food spots, serve alcoholic beverages. Restaurants such as the San Angel Inn have a small lounge at which patrons may wait for tables. Then there are a few other places that specialize in spirituous liquid refreshments:

Matsu No Ma: In addition to exotic sake-based specialty drinks, this Japan pavilion establishment offers a fine panoramic view over the whole of Epcot—including the World Showcase Lagoon, with Spaceship Earth as a backdrop—one of the best vistas of the property available. Japanese beer, green tea, and sushi are also served.

Rose & Crown Pub: This watering hole— a veritable symphony of polished woods, brass, and etched glass—adjoins the Rose & Crown Dining Room in the United Kingdom pavilion. British, Irish, and Scottish beers are available, along with a score of specialty drinks and appetizing snacks imported from the other side of the Atlantic. An entertaining pianist plays and sings just about any request well into the evening.

Sommerfest: Just outside the Biergarten restaurant in Germany, there's a small shaded terrace where soft pretzels, bratwurst, Black Forest cake, steins of Beck's beer, and German wine are available.

FORT WILDERNESS

Crockett's Tavern: Cocktails, beer, wine, appetizers, and light sandwiches are served.

GRAND FLORIDIAN

Garden View: A view of the lushly landscaped pool and garden area makes this lounge a pleasant place to meet for a drink or dessert. Afternoon tea is also served here.

Mizner's: Named after the eccentric architect who defined much of the flavor of southeastern Florida's Gold Coast, this handsome retreat is on the second floor of the main building. Ports, brandies, and appetizers are featured.

Narcoossee's: This lagoonside bar-within-a-restaurant offers a variety of international wines, also available on the outside terrace.

Summerhouse: This bar between the pool and the beach stands by with beer, frozen drinks, and fast-food items.

At many Walt Disney World lounges, you can order food from a neighboring or nearby restaurant's menu.

POLYNESIAN

Barefoot Bar: This oasis next to the swimming pool lagoon serves beer, frozen tropical drinks, and fast food. Seasonal.

Tambu: Adjoining 'Ohana restaurant, this bar offers Polynesian-style appetizers and specialty drinks in a tropical setting.

PORT ORLEANS

Mardi Grogs: Beer, specialty drinks, popcorn, hot dogs, and hot pretzels are among the offerings at this poolside spot.

Scat Cat's Club: Traditional offerings from the bar join New Orleans specialties and hors d'oeuvres at this comfy little lounge. There is musical entertainment here five nights a week.

SWAN & DOLPHIN

Cabana Bar & Grill: Beer, frozen drinks, and fast-food selections are the main offerings at this Dolphin poolside spot.

Copa Banana: Tabletops in this Dolphin bar resemble slices of fruit, and giant pineapples and palm trees offer a fitting backdrop for tropical libations, deejay music, and karaoke. There is also a large-screen TV.

Harry's Safari Bar: Join the peripatetic "Harry" for a drink and maybe a story or two in this Dolphin restaurant bar. Appetizers, a house microbrew, and unique specialty drinks are featured.

Kimonos: This Swan spot, attractively decorated in Japanese style, has a full bar, as well as sushi and a variety of oriental specialties.

Lobby Court: The winding corridors of the Swan lobby have comfortable couches and chairs, punctuated by pianos where able musicians often perform. Specialty coffees, desserts, and wines by the glass are featured. A special menu with ports, cognacs, and cigars is offered seasonally.

Only's Bar & Jail: Rare tequilas, an array of margaritas, sangria, and beers from every region of Mexico join Mexican-style appetizers on the menu here at the Dolphin. The small, atmospheric lounge, adjacent to Juan & Only's restaurant, resembles a jail.

Splash Grill: Beer, frozen drinks, and fast food are served at this Swan poolside cafe.

THE VILLAS AT THE DISNEY INSTITUTE

Seasons Lounge: A comfortable and inviting setting adjoining the Seasons Dining Room, this lounge serves specialty drinks, cocktails, beer, and wine.

Seasons Terrace: The covered outdoor seating area of Seasons Dining Room, overlooking the golf course and waterways, is a pleasant spot for drinks and a light bite.

WILDERNESS LODGE

Territory: Located between Artist Point and Whispering Canyon Cafe, this homage to the Old West is a nice spot for a light lunch or predinner treat. Appetizers, microbrew beer, wine, and specialty drinks are served.

Trout Pass: This poolside bar serves beer, frozen drinks, and snacks.

YACHT AND BEACH CLUB

Ale and Compass: The lobby watering hole proffers a specialty drink menu complete with coffee and ale.

Crew's Cup: Styled after a New England waterfront pub, this lounge has a masculine feel to it. It's right next door to the Yachtsman Steakhouse, has almost 40 beers on hand, and is a choice spot for a drink before dinner.

Hurricane Hanna's Grill: This poolside refreshment spot, located near Stormalong Bay between the Yacht and the Beach Club, offers specialty drinks, frozen drinks, and beer as well as a selection of fast-food items.

Martha's Vineyard: A light and airy atmosphere prevails at this cozy retreat. Wines from a real Martha's Vineyard winery, as well as selections from California, Long Island, and European vineyards, are on the extensive list. While wine is the house specialty, this is a full bar. Hors d'oeuvres and desserts are served.

Rip Tide: This lobby bar features California wines, wine coolers, and frosty drinks that are consistent with the hotel's beachside theme.

More Special Nighttime Fun

GOOD MEALS, GREAT TIMES

The Magic Kingdom takes on additional dazzle after dark. SpectroMagic is a procession so amazing that it alone is worth the trip to Walt Disney World. Epcot is particularly lovely at night, when the lights sparkle on the lagoon, Spaceship Earth is aglow, and fireworks light up the sky. And the Disney-MGM Studios is home to the terrific Fantasmic! show. But there are always a handful of other special happenings and events going on after dark throughout the World. Call 824-4321 to find out what's in store for your next visit.

CAMPFIRE PROGRAM: This event at Fort Wilderness, held nightly near Meadow Trading Post at the center of the campground, features a sing-along, Disney movies, and cartoons. Open only to WDW resort guests.

ELECTRICAL WATER PAGEANT: Best seen from a beach on Bay Lake, this show is a 1,000-foot-long string of illuminated floating creatures. Guest Services or City Hall can tell you when and where it can be seen—usually it's visible at 9 P.M. from the Polynesian, 9:20 P.M. from the Grand Floridian, 9:35 P.M. from the Wilderness Lodge, 9:45 P.M. from Fort Wilderness, and 10:05 P.M. from the Contemporary.

FANTASMIC!: This extravaganza, which premiered in late 1998, takes guests inside the dreams of Mickey Mouse, where he creates dancing waters, animated fountains, and balls of fire. The Disney characters, including those nightmare-inducing villains, also appear in the show. The action occurs at park closing in an amphitheater behind Tower of Terror.

FANTASY IN THE SKY: When the Magic Kingdom is open late, it features nightly fireworks. The show lasts six minutes, and outshines displays many times its length.

ILLUMINATIONS: This nightly show is an absolutely spectacular display of music, laser lights, fireworks, and fountains that can be seen from any point on the World Showcase Promenade at Epcot, usually at park closing. Check at Guest Relations for the exact time.

Note: The show will change to mark the millennium starting in October 1999, probably under a new name.

SPECTROMAGIC: The Magic Kingdom's biggest extravaganza, this parade makes its way down Main Street on select nights throughout the year, twice a night during busy seasons. The advanced technology incorporates holograms, special lighting techniques, and a state-of-the-art sound system.

TENNIS: Courts at the Contemporary, Grand Floridian, Fort Wilderness, Yacht and Beach Club, Old Key West, BoardWalk, and The Villas at the Disney Institute are usually open until 7 P.M. Those at the Swan and Dolphin are open 24 hours a day.

INDEX

COUPONS

DISNEY'S VERO BEACH RESORT

Up to 25% off Accommodations

- Receive 10% off when arriving 2/19/99–3/18/99.
- Receive 25% off when arriving 1/1/99–2/11/99, 4/11/99–5/27/99, 5/31/99–7/1/99, 7/4/99–9/2/99, 9/6/99–11/23/99, and 11/27/99–12/23/99.

Subject to terms and conditions on reverse side.

DISNEY'S HILTON HEAD ISLAND RESORT

Up to 25% off Accommodations

- Receive 10% off when arriving 3/12/99–3/25/99.
- Receive 25% off when arriving 1/1/99–3/11/99, 4/11/99–5/27/99, 5/31/99–6/3/99, 8/29/99–9/2/99, 9/6/99–11/23/99, and 11/27/99–12/24/99.

Subject to terms and conditions on reverse side.

ONE CAR CLASS UPGRADE

Present this certificate at a participating National® rental counter in the U.S. or National Tilden® rental counter in Canada for a one-car class upgrade on a Compact through Full-size 2-door up to a Full-size 4-door car. Valid at participating National locations in the U.S. and National Tilden locations in Canada.

RESERVATIONS RECOMMENDED. CONTACT YOUR TRAVEL AGENT OR NATIONAL TODAY AT 1-800-CAR-RENT®.

Subject to terms and conditions on reverse side.

PC# 016254-0
Valid through December 31, 1999

"did somebody say McDonald's?"™

Receive a FREE

Big Mac® Sandwich, Quarter Pounder®* with Cheese Sandwich *or* 6pc. Chicken McNuggets® *when you purchase a large French fry and medium soft drink.* *(See back for details)*

© 1998 McDonald's Corporation

10% discount off any meal at

at the Disney Institute

Featuring Classic Floridian cuisine with a new twist.

1999 AAA VACATIONS® Exclusive Offer

Carry the Magic Around with a AAA Tote Bag!

When you purchase a AAA Vacations® package to the Walt Disney World® Resort at your AAA travel office, you can redeem this coupon for a canvas AAA tote bag.

Ask your AAA travel agent for details.

™

*Weight before cooking 4 ounces (113.4 grams)

Specialties include Orangewood Beef Tenderloin,
Striped Bass with Key Lime Butter Sauce, Orange
Chili Pepper Shrimp, and more.

Terms and Conditions